A Trilogy of Freud's Major Fallacies

ARMANDO FERRARO, M.D.

VANTAGE PRESS
New York   Washington   Atlanta   Hollywood

Published by Vantage Press, Inc.
516 West 34th Street, New York, New York 10001

Manufactured in the United States of America
Standard Book Number 533-03584-8

Library of Congress Catalog Card No.: 77-94260

DEDICATED TO THE MEMORY OF MY VERY LOVING AND
VERY MUCH LOVED WIFE NORMA, MY CONSTANT AND
GENTLE COMPANION OF MY LIFE FOR FORTY-SEVEN YEARS

Contents

Introduction

by
Dr. Nolan D. C. Lewis
Former Chairman of the Department of Psychiatry
Columbia University—New York
and
Former Director of the New York State Institute and Hospital—N.Y.

From time to time, through the years, criticisms have been made of various parts of Freud's theoretical construction, but few of the critics have substituted corrections that have been accepted by other students of psychoanalysis or psychodynamics. Freud's theories of meanings as distinct from his studies of the neuroses, seem to have been the area of objections. However in the present book, the author, a neuropsychiatrist of many years of clinical and research experience, had not only given in details his reason for his critical comments, but also has pointed out the credit which should be given Freud, for certain basic psychological processes that are valuable in practice, and have stood the test of time. While there are indeed contradictions and paradoxes in Freud's concepts, it is clear that he, more than any other psychologist of his day, strove for formulations of what was taking place in the tremendous complexity of the mind which in its developmental processes seems actually to present many paradoxes. Therefore a critical summary and evaluation of the psychoanalytic hypotheses and theories, with which this book is concerned, is a timely effort to point out the many obscurities, ambiguities and contradictions in Freud's "Metapsychological construction."

A most important contribution proposed by the author is that of substituting Freud's concept of the libido in terms of *a displaceable energy* possessing a sexual quality, and capable of mobility of its own, with that which he calls an *"Affective formation, a psychic structure,"* made of an *inseparable combination of an "idea" with its related affective quality*. It is the "affective formation" which is capable in its entirety of idea and affective quality, to undergo displacement and replacement by some other "affective formation" in its entirety of "idea and quality." The author's thesis contrasts evidently with Freud's concept of the "displacement" of only the libido in terms of a *detachable and movable "psychic energy."*

The energy activating the various "Affective formations," is not in the author's view a "psychic energy" possessing an affective quality, the sexual quality in the case of the libido as originally conceived by Freud, but a physico-biological energy which the author calls "Organismic energy" which is the same energy which activates all the somatic functions operating at a certain moment of our intrauterine organization, and the integration and synthesis of which, results at a certain point in the *automatic development* of an entirely new function *"The Psychic Function"* to which now becomes entrusted the translation of all those various somatic stimuli, into ideational representations, the earliest "psychic structures."

On the basis of the "displacement" and replacement of "Affective formations," the author approaches the problem of "Repression," "Regression," and of the development of the Ego in its normal and pathological aspects. He thus avoids Freud's pitfall of a Libido construed in terms of a sexual energy undergoing separation from its attached idea, and which so liberated is capable to attach itself to some other idea as in the case of Repression, or to regress into the Ego itself where it may result into either the Ego's normal character formation, or into some of the Ego's pathological conditions.

In this text Dr. Ferraro has presented a wealth of clearly written information in a complex field. The number of references and liberal quotations from Freud's publications as a background for his critical evaluation gives us some idea of the vast amount of research devoted to this preparation, and the serious thoughts that have gone into this scholarly presentation. And as such I may say that it is worthy of being read by all interested in the origin of behavior, as it offers a stimulating informative exploration of the complex concepts and problems, as they evolved in the historical development of psychoanalysis.

Nolan D. C. Lewis, M.D.

NOTE: This introduction was written by Dr. Lewis in 1972 at the time when this book in more general terms was entitled: *Freud Revisited—A Critique of His Assumptions.* Since then I have revised the book and directed my criticism to (A) Freud's

Libido Theory, (B) to his distinguishing "sexuality" from "genitality," and (C) to his view of the origin and structure of the "Unconscious." Consequently I have changed the title of my book into the present one of *A Trilogy of Freud's Major Fallacies*.

Armando Ferraro, M.D.

Preface

This book is not directed at the criticism of Freud's new method of treatment of the neuroses by his psychoanalytic technique of free associations and *regression of the patient's ego* to his very early memories. That method employed by Freud, while the patient *is awake* is a derivation from the "cathartic" method which J. Breuer and Freud himself had at first used in questioning their neurotic patients while under "hypnosis." Viewed in the broad terms of a therapeutic method, Freud's new psychoanalytic technique has proven a very useful weapon in the psychiatrist's hands.

But when Freud attempted to create out of that technique the basis for his new brand of psychology which he called *"metapsychology,"* he found himself enmeshed in a series of assumptions, conjectures, hypotheses, and suppositions, which eventually lead him to formulate ever more compound assumptions, all of which lacked the possibility of verification.

It is against this mass of unsubstantiated hypotheses that in this book I have directed my criticism. Though in the course of my presentation, I have mentioned here and there, the occurrence of various lesser contradictions, in Freud's elaboration of his "metapsychology," I have concentrated my attention particularly upon three major areas which constitute what I have called his "Three Major Fallacies" under the heading of: *A Trilogy of Freud's Major Fallacies* which refers particularly to his "fallacy of his libido theory," his fallacy of differentiating between "Sexuality" and "Genitality," and his "fallacy of his concept of the origin, nature, and characteristics of his Unconscious."

I know of no other attempt at formulating and integrating a critical detailed approach to Freud's entire "Metapsychological construction." I also know of no other critical approach to Freud's major fallacies that has been accompanied by an integrated alternative approach, in each of the three fields of his major fallacies.

Recently I have heard from an authoritative source that: "Freud is passé," and that other scholastic approaches have replaced his pathogenic theories of the neuroses. Unsatisfied by this simplistic explanation, I felt therefore that there should be a need for some detailed discussion of why Freud's approach to both the pathological, as well as to the normal development of the Ego should be considered as "passé," which could bring into the open and into detail, the reason for such a statement.

I consider therefore my contribution to this subject as a very needed one which should be welcomed by all psychiatrists, psychologists, psychoanalysts, and by all students of human behavior.

"La critique est aisé, mais l'art est difficile" says an old French adage (Criticism is easy, but the art is difficult). It is therefore in the spirit of avoiding the pitfalls of a criticism lacking a thorough discussion, and with the objective in mind of offering some plausible alternative to what I have criticized, that I present this book: *A Trilogy of Freud's Major Fallacies*. In it, it is true that my own alternatives are the product of assumptions, but so were the *numerous assumptions* of Freud, including *the obscure "leap from the soma to the psyche,"* when he introduced his concept of the "Instinct of life." My alternatives have, however, the advantage of allowing to any student the privilege of making his own choice, a choice that he could not have exercised, had he been limited to subscribe to Freud's only available metapsychological construction.

I am referring particularly to Freud's concept of the existence of a special mobile and displaceable "Psychic energy" endowed with a sexual quality, as Freud originally conceived it, and capable to detach itself from any idea or group of ideas to which it was attached and attach itself to some other idea or constellation of ideas.

That concept of Freud upon which he had based his "Libido theory," and the important mechanisms of *Repression and Regression*, I refute repeatedly in this book. I instead have repeatedly replaced it with the concept of *mobile and displaceable "psychic structures"* made of "an idea or of ideas" which have acquired their proper affective quality. Once the idea acquires its affective quality, it constitutes a single unit from which its quality, sexual or not, cannot become separated, as maintained by Freud in reference to the energic sexual quality. This inseparable combination of an idea and of its attached affective quality, I have called an "affective formation" and in that sense a "psychic structure." It is this psychic structure which is mobile and displaceable. The energy responsible for the displacement of ideas or of "Affective formation" is not a psychic energy as conceived by Freud, but I call it a somatic "organismic energy." Without entering into the details which I will discuss and clarify in the three separate portions of this Trilogy, I may anticipate my conclusions in the following few words which epitomize the entire concept of this book: my views differ fundamentally from those of Freud who believes in the existence and operation of a mobile and displaceable special energy, the psychic energy, a concept to which I do not subscribe. I believe instead in the existence and operation in our psychic apparatus, of mobile and displaceable and replaceable *psychic structures* made of ideas and of ideas attached to their affective qualities with which they constitute an inseparable unit. These units I have called "Affective formations." These psychic structures constitute the very fabric of our psychic apparatus.

The energy which activates these ideas and attached affective qualities is not a psychic energy, but the same somatic chemico-biological energy which activates the various somatic functions already operating in the course of our somatic intrauterine organization. *Out of the integration and synthesis* of these various somatic functions, there automatically develops an entire new function, *"The Psychic Function"* entrusted with the first translation of the various somatic stimuli, into some sort of ideational representation which gradually acquires its own affective quality. These ideational representations and acquired affective qualities, constitute precisely our first "psychic structures" which are the only ones endowed with mobility and capability of displacement and replacement.

It follows that such ideas (psychic structures) born of the activity of the newly developed "Psychic Function," which itself was activated at its onset by the somatic energy of the various somatic functions already operating in the course of our intrauterine somatic existence, need not require from their very onset, neither the existence nor the cooperation of an additional and elusive specific "psychic energy."

Armando Ferraro, M.D.

PART ONE

The Fallacy of Freud's Libido Theory

Contents

CHAPTER I

Psychic Energy

Freud's erroneous assumption of the existence and operation
of a "psychic energy" in terms of a "libido" conceived as a displaceable quantitative and qualitative sexual energy.

Presumably the "libido theory" began to germinate in Freud's mind
soon after he had become interested in the pathogenesis and
psychodynamics of the neuroses, mainly hysteria and obsessive
neurosis. He first established to his own satisfaction the sexual origin of these neuroses which, in 1894, he had referred to under the
heading of "defence neuropsychoses."

In Freud's view the major mental mechanism for their development consisted in a voluntary inhibition (repression) on the part of
the patients, of objectionable thoughts which at a certain moment
presented themselves to their mind. Because such thoughts were
made mostly of reprehensible sexual ideas and related activating
psychic energy, Freud endeavored to investigate the source and nature of that energy. In a first attempt, he presented us with his far
reaching assumption of the existence and operation in our mind of a
special psychic sexual energy, later called libido, capable of detachment from one idea to which it was attached and attachment to
some other idea as in the case of obsessive neurosis, or capable of
discharging itself into some other sort of motor or sensory innervation, as in the case of hysteria.

Referring to that displaceable energy, Freud expressed himself
in the following manner:

> Among the psychic functions there is something which should
> be differentiated (*A sum of excitation—an amount of affect*)
> something having the attribute of a quantity although we

5

possess no means of measuring it, a something which is capable of increase, decrease, displacement and discharge, and
which extends over the memory-traces of an idea, like an electric charge over the surface of the body.[1]

With that assumption in mind of an energy possessing an affective quality, Freud undertook the analysis of his cases of hysteria
and obsessive neurosis. In his words:

The patients whom I have analysed had enjoyed good mental
health up to the time at which an intolerable idea presented
itself within the content of their ideational life—that is to say
until their Ego was confronted, by an experience, an idea, *a
feeling arousing an affect so painful*, that the person resolved
to forget it, since he had no confidence in his power to resolve
the incompatibility between the unbearable idea and his Ego,
by the process of thoughts. *Such unbearable ideas develop in
women, chiefly in connection with sexual experiences and sensations*, and the patients can recollect with the most satisfaction and minuteness *their efforts at defence, their resolution to
"push the thing out, not to think of it, to suppress it"*....I
know that this kind of forgetting did not succeed with the patients whom I have analysed, but led to various pathological
reactions, giving rise to either Hysteria, Obsession, or to an
Hallucinatory psychosis.[2] [italics mine]

It is at this point that Freud for the first time advanced his concept of the mechanism of that defense, a concept that presented itself
to his mind in the form of what in his own words, he called simply
"a customary psychological abstraction" and which he introduced in
the following manner:

The task which the Ego undertakes of treating the unbearable
idea as non-arrivée—is absolutely unsolvable; *both the
memory-trace and the affect attached to the idea are there once
and for all, and it is no longer possible to extirpate them*. But
it amounts to an approximate fulfillment of this task, if the
Ego succeeds in transforming a strong idea into a weak one,
in depriving it of its affect—the quantity of excitation with
which the idea is charged. The weak idea will then make
practically no demands on the work of association; the quantity of excitation however, *which is then detached from the
idea*, must be utilized in another direction.[3] [italics mine]

It would seem from these two above quotes that the suppression
of the reprehensible idea and attached affect which the patient
wished deliberately and resolutely to put out of his mind, must not
have succeeded at first, so that the patient must have continued to

be haunted by the memory of that reprehensible idea and attached affect, time and time again, until something happened. That something occurred when according to Freud, *the patient's Ego succeeded finally in depriving the reprehensible sexual idea from its affective quality*, which as we have seen Freud had endowed with an energic attribute which at first he called "affect" and later on "charge of affect" which in the case of the libido, represented the sexual energy of the idea.

Without entering for the moment, into the discussion of Freud's *"customary psychological abstraction,"* I will simply recall his statement that: "In Hysteria, the unbearable idea is rendered innocuous by the quantity of excitation attached to it, being transmuted into some bodily form of expression."[4] This process Freud called "conversion." In the case of "obsessions and phobias," where the capacity to conversion is absent, the affect, evidently always in terms of an *energic quality*, could instead detach itself from the reprehensible idea and attach itself to some other idea which is not unbearable, but which through this false connection grows to obsession. In Freud's view that was, shortly speaking, the psychological theory of obsessions and phobias.[5]

At this point Freud tried to clarify his "psychological abstraction" of the separation of the idea from its energic quality, the libido, by stating that,

> The detachment of the sexual idea from its affect and the connection of the latter with another idea, suited to it, but not intolerable, are processes which occur outside consciousness— they may be presumed but cannot be proved by any clinical psychological analysis. These processes are not of a psychological nature at all, *but are physical processes*, the psychic consequences of which are so represented, as if what is expressed by the words "detachment of the idea from its affect and false connection of the latter," had really happened.[6] [italics mine]

Apart from the obscurity of that reference to physical processes underlying psychic processes, and for which Freud at that time had not prepared the ground for our acceptance, all that he had succeeded in doing with that statement was to say that the detachment of the affect from a given idea, took place outside our awareness, that is in what he called the Unconscious. But in 1894, Freud had not as yet provided us with any clue of how he had concluded that *a sum of "somatic excitation"* could at a certain moment become transformed *into a psychic excitation* i.e. into "psychic energy." Neither had Freud explained how in hysteria, a *psychic sexual energy*, the libido, could be converted into an energy capable of activating a somatic innervation. Nor had Freud explained how in obsessive neurosis, a "psychic energy" the libido, possessing a definite sexual quality, could, after it had become detached from a reprehensible idea, cathect some other idea without imparting to the resulting obsessive idea, the same sexual quality.

It was the subsequent year, 1895, that Freud returned to the question of the transformation of somatic excitations into "psychic energy" in his paper on "Anxiety Neurosis." In that paper referring precisely to that special sexual energy, the libido, he expressed himself as follows:

> In the sexually mature organism, somatic sexual excitation is produced probably continuously, *and periodically acts as a psychical stimulus.* In order to define this idea more clearly, let us interpolate that this somatic sexual excitation takes the form of pressure on the wall of the "vesiculae seminales" which are linked with nerve-endings; this visceral excitation will then actually develop continuously, *but only when it reaches a certain height,* will it be sufficient to overcome the resistance in the path to the cerebral cortex, and express itself as a psychic stimulus. *Thereupon the constellation of sexual ideas existing in the mind* becomes charged with energy, and a psychical state of libidinous tension comes into existence, bringing with it the impulse to relieve tension.[7]

One would assume that in Freud's views the transformation of the somatic sexual excitations from the genital organs into a psychic stimulus, must have implied also the imparting of the same sexual quality, to that resulting psychic stimulus, that is to that resulting "psychic energy," inasmuch as the sexual somatic excitations could not have lost their sexual quality in the course of their traveling to the brain. This constitutes an important point, considering also that Freud had not clarified the meaning of the sexual ideas which were already operating in the mind. Was he referring simply to the masculine or feminine gender that those ideas represented, or was he referring to ideas already cathected by an operating sexual psychic energy? And if so why were the ideas so sexually charged, inoperative in the mind, and waiting so to speak, for additional sexual energy in order to elicit that impulse towards discharge? Was it necessary therefore for the psychic energy to reach a certain quantity in the brain, before becoming operationally effective, just as it had seem necessary for Freud that the somatic sexual excitations reach a certain intensity, in order to reach the brain and become sexual excitations?

In the statement in question, what Freud had succeeded in conveying to us was simply that the somatic excitations, originating in the sexual organs, once they had reached a certain intensity and once they had succeeded in overcoming resistances in their path and reached the cerebral cortex, they automatically become transformed into "psychic energy" possessing the same quality of the original somatic genital excitations.

Presented in those terms, it would seem that at this point the sexual energy, i.e., the libido in this case, must have been considered by Freud as being *ontogenetically developed* in the course of our somatic and functional organization. There was no reference as yet, on Freud's part, to the instinctual nature of the sexual energy inherited at birth, in terms of the energy of the inherited sexual instinct, which energy he later equated with the energy of the *"Instinct of Life."*

At any rate, irrespective of its ontogenetic or instinctual origin, it was that "psychic sexual energy," the libido, that became now attached to a given idea and that imparted to it, its sexual affective quality. Being endowed with an energic attribute, that libido according to Freud, could now become detached from that idea and displaced upon some other idea, or utilized in activating some motor or sensory innervation. By considering the libido as a "psychic energy" endowed with that special sexual quality, Freud had therefore assigned to the libido two distinct attributes, the quantitative energic attribute, and the qualitative sexual attribute.

On this subject several questions come to my mind: Was it necessary for the libido to be considered as a psychic energy possessing a special sexual quality which it imparts to a given idea? Once an idea has acquired, let us say, its sexual quality, can that idea become separated from that quality? Why did Freud assign the attribute of displacement only to the psychic energy, the libido, which allegedly imparts to the idea that sexual quality, and ignore the possibility that there is some other energy which is responsible for the displacement *of the idea itself*, which idea is therefore independent from that alleged quantitative and qualitative psychic sexual energy?

The answers to these questions will become clear in the course of this chapter. For the moment I will simply anticipate the following assumptions which I will submit in this chapter for critical considerations: The sexual quality, i.e. the libidinal quality which a given idea may acquire at a certain moment, does not depend upon any psychic sexual energy *which, in my view, does not exist as such.* It depends upon other factors. Once an idea has acquired its sexual or otherwise affective quality, *it constitutes with that quality, sexual or otherwise, a single unit, a combination that cannot undergo separation.* The mobility of that unit made of an idea and of its inseparable affective quality, is dependent upon the energy that propels *the idea itself*, and not upon its sexual quality which possesses no energic attribute.

If one were to subscribe to these assumptions of mine, and particularly to the one that once an idea has acquired its affective quality, it constitutes with it, an indivisible unit, and that such a unit could displace itself in its entirety, in virtue of the energy proper to the idea, and therefore not of a psychic energy, but of the original somatic energy of the idea, there would be no longer question of a sexual psychic energy, capable of detaching itself from a given idea, displace itself, and attach itself to some other idea.

In Freud's view the new idea would still be cathected by the same sexual energy withdrawn and displaced from the previous idea. In that case that simple transfer of the sexual energy from one idea to another, would nullify evidently the purpose of repression in Freud's terms. Indeed it was only in 1923 that Freud, in connection with the process of identification of the ego with some abandoned sexual object, resorted to the new assumption that a desexualization of the sexual energy takes place in the course of its displacement from a given sexual object to the ego itself.

Returning to my assumption of the indivisible unit made of the combination of its two components: idea and related affective quality, I propose to call that unit an "affective formation." *It is that "affective formation"* in its entirety of idea and quality that can undergo, (by virtue of the energy of the idea itself and not of its quality) displacement and replacement by some other *"affective formation."*

It is the displacement of ideas and of "affective formations" and their replacement by other ideas or "affective formations" that in my views constitute the fabric of the functional operation of our "psychic apparatus." Such an assumption seems to me a more viable one than that of a detachable and movable "psychic energy" possessing a sexual quality, that displaces itself from one idea to another, and which should impart to the latter that same sexual quality. In that context, Freud's purpose of repression in the development of a *nonsexual* obsessive idea would be defeated.

It goes without saying that in my views, not all ideas possess an affective quality, in which case they may be considered as "neutral ideas" so to speak, though they are also capable of displacement and replacement by some other ideas. As for the energy that activates the various ideas separately, or in combination with their quality as "affective formations," I consider that energy as an attribute of the ideas themselves individually or as a component of the "affective formation," and not the attribute of the affective quality, the libidinal quality of those formations. I will develop further this point in the body of this chapter.

My assumptions constitute evidently quite a contrast with those of Freud, who considered as viable his own proposition that under repression (inhibition), a separation occurs between an idea and its libidinal quality (in the case of a sexual idea), a quality to which he had assigned an energic attribute and which separately could undergo displacement of its own upon some other idea. In my assumption there would be no room for a separation between an idea and its affective quality, the latter erroneously conceived by Freud as a displaceable "psychic energy," possessing a sexual quality (in the case of the libido).

It is interesting to note that in connection with what I have called an "affective formation," which constitutes an inseparable unit made of an idea and its affective quality, Freud himself seems to have been pretty close to that same concept when in his paper of 1894, *The Defence Neuro-psychoses,* he had stated as I have reported on page 6 of the subject of defense, that the task which the ego undertakes in defense, of treating the unbearable idea as non-arrivée, was absolutely unsolvable because both the memory-traces and the affect attached to it, are there once and for all.[8] Unfortunately Freud failed to develop his own view of a repressed idea remaining there once and for all, attached to its own affective quality, and developed instead the different approach which he so expressed:

> But it amounts to an approximate fulfillment of that task of the Ego, if it succeeds in transforming a strong idea into a weak one, in depriving it of its affect—the quantity of excitations with which the idea is charged. The weak idea will then make practically no demands on the work of association; the quantity of excitation however which is then detached from the idea must be utilized in another direction.[9]

Unfortunately Freud used this erroneous assumption for the theoretical construction of his entire "libido theory" and applied it particularly to the development of the ego, in both its normal and pathological aspects. That assumption which Freud had originally advanced on the simple ground of what he had called *a "customary psychological abstraction"* became in my opinion Freud's greatest conceptual error, responsible for what I have called "The Fallacy of Freud's Libido Theory."

Let me now return to the origin of Freud's alleged "Psychic energy." Was it an *ontogenetically* developed energy, or was the libido *the inherited sexual energy of the sexual instincts* which Freud subsequently equated with the energy of the elusive "Instinct of Life?" The question arises from the fact that in his paper on "Anxiety Neurosis" of 1895, Freud, as I have already mentioned, seemed to have opted for an ontogenetically created psychic energy, when he had stated that the somatic sexual excitations originating in the genital organs, become transformed directly into psychic sexual excitations, *the moment they reach a certain intensity* which allows them to win resistances and reach the cerebral cortex. It was only later that Freud referring to the "psychic energy" spoke more explicitly of an inherited sexual instinct, and of an activating instinctual sexual energy.

That Freud in his writings subsequent to 1895 had considered "psychic energy" (in terms of libido) as only an inherited instinctual energy attached to the sexual instincts, is in fact documented by his paper *Repression*[10] dated 1915, where he spoke of *an instinct-presentation* by which he understood an idea or a group of ideas cathected by a definite psychic energy, the libido in the case of a *"sexual instinct-presentation."* In that paper referring to the repression of a sexual instinct-presentation, he expressed his view that besides the idea to be repressed, there is something else, another presentation of the instinct to be considered. This other element undergoes, in his view, a repression which may be quite different from that of the idea. In Freud's words,

> We have adopted the term "charge of affect" for this other element in the mental presentation. *It represents that part of the instinct which has become detached from the idea* .... From this point on, in describing a case of repression, we must follow the fate of the idea which undergoes repression *separately from that of the instinctual energy attached to the idea.*[11] [italics mine]

There seems to be no doubt that in this passage, contrary to his statement of 1895, Freud now considered "psychic energy" and its representative, the libido, in terms of an instinctual energy attached to the ideational representation of the sexual instincts, and no longer in terms of a direct transformation of the somatic sexual excitations originating in the genitals, into a sexual psychic energy, once they succeeded in reaching the cerebral cortex.

Freud's change of position from the ontogenetic development of the "sexual psychic energy," to that of its inherited instinctual origin, seems to me as having been introduced in somewhat contradictory terms. If indeed one considers Freud's latest views expressed in his posthumously published *An Outline of Psychoanalysis* (1940), where he had stated that *the somatic processes constitute the true essence of what is mental.* Freud in that statement had implied that the mental processes were activated *not by a "psychic energy"* but by the same somatic energy which had activated these somatic processes and which in themselves, constituted *the true essence of what is mental.*

That view was expressed by Freud in connection with his other statement in the same "outline" that the conscious mental processes do not form unbroken series which are complete in themselves, inasmuch as they are present at a certain moment and disappear at another. As a result he had concluded that:

> There is no alternative to the assumption that there are physical or somatic processes which accompany the mental ones, and which must admittedly be more complete than the mental series, since some of them have conscious processes parallel to them but others have not. It thus becomes natural *to lay stress in psychology upon these somatic processes, and to see in them the essence of what is mental,* and to try to arrive at some other assessment of the conscious processes. . . . It is this precisely that psychoanalysis is obliged to assert.[12]

There seems to be no question that in that statement Freud had considered the somatic processes—an uninterrupted line of activity—as constituting the essence of mental processes which now and then could become conscious. There was however no mention in that statement of any operating mental energy outside that which activated the somatic processes, *which in themselves constituted what is essentially mental.* In that statement Freud had also implied very clearly that what was essentially mental was at first the expression of an uninterrupted unconscious activity. Thus, Freud remained faithful to Th. Lipps whose contention was that mental processes were unconscious in their first developmental stage, and became conscious in a subsequent stage.

Unfortunately, Freud failed to consider the alternate assumption that in their first stage mental processes could represent the expression of *conscious* instead of *unconscious* activities, a gap which I have tried to fill by assuming the original conscious nature of our mental processes, at the hands of a newly developed "psychic function," a point which I will develop in this chapter.

Parenthetically, I must note that though Freud at some point spoke of the somatic processes *as accompanying the mental ones* and at another point *as accessory processes*, he ultimately ended by considering the somatic processes as representing in themselves *what is essentially mental*. In other words those somatic processes, at a certain point, *with no explanation at all, became eo-ipso (by their own nature), mental processes.*

It is at this point that there occurs the contradiction to which I have referred, concerning the nature of the energy that activates those mental processes, allegedly unconscious at their very onset. *If the uninterrupted line of the somatic processes represents what is essentially mental*, then what is mental does not need for its expression the intervention of an additional superfluous psychic energy. The somatic energy which presided over those somatic processes in which Freud saw the essence of what is mental, should have been the same energy that had presided over all that was mental.

The assumption of a separate "psychic energy" would thus become a superfluous construct. Furthermore if the somatic processes represented what was essentially mental at its onset, it would be consistent to assume that *the further development of what is mental* should continue to be governed by the same somatic energy which had presided over the original somatic processes.

Is there some other alternative to that of Freud who viewed the "psychic energy" as being different from the somatic energy, and who conceived it in terms of a mental energy possessing a special affective quality (the sexual quality in the case of the libido), and capable of attachment to a given idea, detachment from that idea and capable to attach itself to some other idea, or discharge itself through some other modality?

Is there a special function which develops at a certain moment of our somatic organization, and which could account for the development of our mental life, independently from the existence and operation of an alleged "psychic energy"?

I have answered affirmatively the first question in the preceding pages where I have advanced the assumption that an affective quality, a mental quality, the libidinal quality for instance, possesses no energic attribute, and that once an idea had acquired its proper affective quality, it constitutes with it an inseparable unit, and that such a combination which I have called an "affective formation" can only displace itself in its entirety of idea and quality, and can be replaced by some other "affective formation" in its entirety of idea and related affective quality. I have also assumed *that it is the idea which possesses the energic attribute*, that permits the "Affective formation" to undergo displacement, combination and replacement, and that such an energic attribute does not belong to the affective quality, the libidinal quality for instance, viewed in terms of a "psychic energy."

In order to answer the second question, if there exists an intermediary function which could account for the development of mental processes out of somatic processes, independently from the operation of a "psychic energy," I will have to go further back than Freud did when he first introduced his assumption of a "psychic energy." I therefore will have to take into consideration the origin of those ideas that Freud in 1894 had assumed to be cathected by the sexual psychic energy. How did such ideas come into existence?

To answer that question, I will assume that those ideas represent the product of a newly developed *"Psychic function" which makes its first automatic appearance, at a certain moment of our intrauterine somatic and biological organization in the form, so to speak, of a super-function, born of the integration and synthesis of the various somatic functions which already were operating in that organization.*

Among those incipient somatic functions, I include also that of the incipient nervous system which ultimately will constitute the structural organ of that constantly developing new "psychic function." I furthermore assume that once that new "psychic function" has made its appearance, *its first main task would be that of translating, so to speak, the various somatic stimuli related to the activities of the already operating somatic functions, into some sort of ideational representations.* These are the ideas to which Freud had referred in 1894, when he considered them as the recipients of the psychic libidinal energy. But at that time Freud failed to discuss the origin of those ideas. My assumption of the development and intervention of a newly developed "psychic function" responsible for the development of those ideas, fills that important gap.

The question now arises as to the nature of the energy involved in the development of this new "Psychic function." To Freud's assumption that it is a "psychic energy" that governs our mental processes, I submit the alternative assumption that there should be no reason to consider the energy that governs the onset and development of that new "psychic function" any different from the somatic energy, which had governed the activities of the various somatic functions, out of the synthesis and integration of which, the new "psychic function" first developed. That somatic energy I presume to be a physico-biological energy, and for it I am proposing the designation of *organismic energy.*

I therefore find it difficult to subscribe for instance, to the remarks by M. Ostow, a staunch defender of Freud's concept of "psychic energy" when at the meeting of the New York Academy of Sciences in 1959, he stated that:

> It is irrelevant when we talk about instinctual energy to bring about the question of metabolic energy. In the first place Freud never had in mind this when he wrote about instinctual energy, and I do not believe that any serious thinker in the field of psychoanalysis considers that instinctual energy is a function of metabolic energy available in the brain. Instinctual energy is conceived at an entirely different level of conceptualization; it is a completely different thing. Instinctual energy refers only to the fact that the animal or man in question *seems to be striving to achieve some particular goal. The energy is a hypothetical quantity.* The relation of this psychic energy to any metabolic energy, if such a relation exists, is certainly one that nobody has explored or stated specifically.[13] [italics mine]

Concerning those remarks, I must first recall the fact that in 1895, in his paper on "Anxiety Neurosis," Freud had dealt precisely with *a biological energy* that is the one represented by the somatic excitations originating in the sexual organs, and which only subsequently became *transmuted* into psychic excitations, that is into psychic energy, once those somatic excitations, which had attained a certain height, had reached the cerebral cortex. In that concept there was no question in Freud's mind of instinctual energy in terms of a hypothetical quantity, as Ostow maintained. In addition, the latter should have referred himself to Freud's ultimate views published in his posthumous *Outline of Psychoanalysis*[14] (1940) that the somatic processes *constituted the essence of what is mental*, thus indicating clearly that mental processes originated in his views from the activity of the same biological energy that had presided over the activities of those somatic processes.

Furthermore, when M. Ostow attributes to Freud the concept of an instinctual energy *in term of a drive, that is of a striving to achieve some particular goal, he equates that instinctual energy* with some "psychic function" capable of directing a drive, a function to which he had made no mention, and which Freud himself had not as yet contemplated in those terms. Freud's *original assumption of a "psychic energy"* was neither that of a "Psychic function" nor that of a drive, but that of a definite quantitative and qualitative energy (a sum of excitation—an amount of affect) capable of displacement like an electric current capable of detaching itself from some idea and move on to some other idea. As for the libido, the psychic sexual energy, Freud in his early writings considered it not only as representing the transformation of a genital somatic energy into a psychic one, but also as the product of *a special chemistry*, different from that which generated the energy governing the ego-instincts of self-preservation. And even when Freud in 1920 introduced his new assumption of the instinct of life and of the instinct of death, he referred to their respective energies as comparable to the two different energies that govern the corresponding anabolic and catabolic processes operating within a single animal cells. In light of these considerations, to think of a "psychic energy" as a hypothetical quantity or as a drive to achieve a particular mental goal, would be altering what Freud himself had wished to convey to us in his original writings.

In addition, Ostow's interpretation did not take into consideration the origin of the ideas which enter into the formulation of the striving to achieve some particular goal, and which ideas are in my views the product of a "psychic function" born of the integration and synthesis of various somatic functions. It follows that the energy which presided over the first formulation and subsequent activities of those ideas, must have been the same biological energy that had activated the somatic functions, out of which the new "psychic function" had developed. In that light to qualify as "psychic energy" an energy, only because it activates the newly developed "psychic function" and its related product the ideas, would constitute an untenable conclusion.

A pertinent question could now be raised: At what stage of man's structural and biological intrauterine organization, does the new "psychic function" develop and become operative? In the case of the unicellular animal, one could assume that a psychic function presumably develops automatically in it, the moment the animal enters into the world by conjugation or parthenogenesis, inasmuch as from its very inception, the animal constitutes a well-integrated functional unit, and inasmuch as there seems to be no possibility in it to undergo further development beyond the somato-psychic confines of its own species. The answer is far from being so simple, when it comes to humans. At what point of *the human ontogenetic development* the "psychic function" makes its appearance, we cannot even hypothetically assume, because of our ignorance of the time at which the fertilized egg may be considered structurally and biologically a complete functional unit. Yet there must be a time when the human embryo or fetus develops ontogenetically its new "psychic function." That moment I assume to be, the one when some sort of synthesis and integration of various somatic functions take place in our intrauterine somatic and biological organization.

Evidently my assumption of the development of a "psychic function" out of the integration of the various somatic and biological activities, *an assumption which entails a leap from the soma to the psyche*, is a conjectural one, which is beyond any means of verification. But so were the many assumptions introduced by Freud *and accepted by his followers*. I am referring particularly to Freud's basic assumption of the development of the "instinct of life" which transforms the inanimate matter into a living organic matter. In his words:

> At one time or another *by some operation of forces which baffles conjectures*, the properties of Life awakened in the lifeless matter. Perhaps the process was a prototype *resembling that other one which later in a certain stratum of living matter, gave rise to consciousness.*[15] [italics mine]

By the same token, we may assume that by some operation which also baffles conjectures, a new "psychic function" develops out of the integration and synthesis of the various somatic functions already operating in our intrauterine organization.

By the same token, I may now add to my assumption of a newly developed "Psychic function," the other assumption that *consciousness* is inherent to mental life at its very onset, that is at the time of the first formulation of the ideas, at the hands of the newly developed "Psychic function," an assumption that contrasts with Freud's views that our mental life in its first stage is an unconscious one, becoming conscious only at a second stage. Surprisingly enough, however, is the fact that Freud in his correspondence with Fliess had also expressed an opinion which contradicts his own assumption of a first unconscious stage for our mental life, when in connection with *the perception* of the somatic stimuli originating from our various functioning organs he had stated that *"perceptions by their very nature, eo-ipso involve consciousness."*[16] That would mean that they are automatically conscious.

Evidently that statement would seem to indicate that consciousness is the first expression of mental life and that it is born out of the perception of the somatic stimuli. The only ingredient missing in Freud's approach would be the operation of a new "Psychic function" responsible for the translation of those perceptions in terms of ideational constructs. My own assumption fills that gap inasmuch as it relates consciousness to the development of a new "psychic function" born of the integration and synthesis of various somatic functions. It is that "psychic function" that presides over the translation of the various somatic stimuli into perceptions, in terms of ideational representations.

I assume furthermore that out of the accumulation, associations, and interplay of various ideational representations and related affective qualities, there develops in the course of our somatic intrauterine organization, an elementary mental structure, that of *a "protopathic ego" as a result of which our somatic organization achieves the first conscious realization of its own existence.* In that respect my views differ also from Freud's original views that at birth the ego was not as yet functioning.

Assuming that we now possess the knowledge of the development of the various ideas at the hands of the newly developed "Psychic function," how do these ideas acquire their respective affective qualities so as to constitute what I have called *an "affective formation?"* Do these ideas need the intervention of a "special psychic energy" to impart to them such qualities? I feel that we can dispense with the concept of "psychic energy" possessing a given affective quality which it imparts to the ideas, inasmuch as I assume that the ideational representations of the various somatic stimuli born of their translation at the hands of the "Psychic function," *carry with them automatically the quality of the specific stimuli from which they have originated,* though we do not know in what form such a primordial quality is expressed. Once these ideational representations have acquired their first affective quality, thus resulting in the creation of various different "affective formations," these formations undergo subsequently *a series of associative processes* with other "Affective formations" already operating in the mind. Through such associative processes and their combinations, newer and more numerous "affective formations" that is ideas and related new qualities come into existence.

Under that assumption, there would be no need to resort to the operation of a "psychic energy" to which to assign the task of imparting to those ideas an energic affective quality. In my view, as I have already stated, the energic attribute belongs properly to the ideas and not to their qualities. In fact, as I have already said, the ideas being the product of the "psychic function" ontogenetically developed, the energy which continues to activate them, once they have come into existence, can be no other than that same somatic "Organismic energy" which presided over the development of the "psychic function," the generator of those ideas. That should dispose also of the need of relying upon a "psychic energy" in terms of inherited qualitative instinctual energy.

At this point, it may seem that in his investigation of the origin of the "psychic energy," Freud had completely neglected to look into the development of a "psychic function." This is however not entirely true because in part III of his *Project for a Scientific Psychology* (1895) published after his death, there is a mention of *a special psychic function of attention*, though Freud did not delve into that function with his usual eagerness. As a result, after a brief but unsatisfactory return on this subject in his *Interpretation of Dreams* he dropped entirely the mention of that function, never referring to it in his subsequent writings. However in his early remarks on this special function of attention, Freud had never dealt specifically with it, and never referred to its being responsible, as I have assumed, for the first translation of the stimuli originating from the various somatic functions, into ideas, nor did he ever deal with the subsequent acquisition by these ideas of their affective qualities, along the lines which I have assumed.

In his early remarks of 1895 on this "function of attention," Freud after having stated that a perception excites the perceptual system, and that such a perception *eo-ipso* (by its own nature) involves consciousness of quality, he added the following:

I therefore suggest that it is such an indication of quality which interests the *"psychic system"* in the perception. *Here we seem to have the mechanism of psychical Attention....* I find it hard to give any mechanical (automatic) explanation of its origin. I believe therefore that it is *biologically determined*, that is that it has been left in the course of our psychic evolution.[17] [italics mine]

The reference to an operating psychic function of attention, was again made by Freud in his letter to W. Fliess of January 1, 1896, and subsequently in his *Interpretation of Dreams* (1900), where he spoke of that special function in the following terms: Becoming conscious is connected with the "application of a *particular psychic function of Attention*, a function which as it seems is only available in a specific quantity, and it may have been diverted from a train of thought, on to some other purpose."[18] [italics mine] And again in that same publication, Freud had stated that in order for excitatory processes occurring in the preconscious, to enter consciousness, they need the fulfillment of certain conditions such as for instance: "That they reach a certain degree of intensity, and that the function which can be described as attention, be distributed in a particular way."[19]

No further mention of that particular function of attention is found in Freud's subsequent writings, as if he wished to avoid being involved in any discussion of how that "psychic function" develops. The fact remains however that Freud's reference to the origin of that function which he had assumed to be biologically determined seems to have implied *its ontogenetic origin* and not instinctual, and that his qualification of "special" for that function, seems also to have implied its derivation from a more *"general psychic function"* which Freud however never mentioned nor discussed.

One may therefore justly inquire why Freud introduced his assumption of a "special function" of attention without first introducing the concept of a "general Psychic function" of which "attention" could have represented a special facet of its development. One may also inquire why Freud did not involve himself, even if only in speculative terms, which he so frequently did in other instances, on the origin and on the first task of that "general Psychic function" in the creation of ideas. It sound strange indeed that Freud, so involved in our instinctual life, never dealt except casually and indirectly in his posthumous publication *An Outline of Psychoanalysis,* with the problem of the nature and origin of our mental processes, in the form of ideas, which after all constitute the fabric of our psychic apparatus. It is true that Freud from the very beginning, in his correspondence with Fliess, had stated that perceptions by our sense-organs *involved eo-ipso consciousness*, but he never dealt with the role that the psychic function of attention played in the development of that consciousness.

That special function of attention was unfortunately introduced by Freud in a passing fashion and in vague and inadequate terms. Indeed if we consider that according to Freud that specific function of attention was *biologically determined*, its activating energy must have been of the same nature of that which had activated our entire biological organization. It follows that when Freud spoke of the function of attention as the cathecting energy of the neurones bearers of the perceptual cathexes, that cathecting energy of attention being of a biological nature and ontogenetically developed, could not represent a "psychic energy" in the terms, later advanced by Freud, of a quantitative and qualitative inherited instinctual mental force.

One last remark may be in order at this point, and concerns the possible reason why Freud may have desisted from referring to that "special psychic function of attention." I am referring to his introduction in his *Interpretation of Dreams*[20] of a new *"special psychic organ"* which he called *"the special organ of consciousness for the perception of psychic qualities."* With the operation of that special organ which I will discuss in part three of this trilogy, where I will deal with the problem of consciousness, Freud seemed to have superseded the need for a psychic function, let alone for that special psychic function of attention, which from then on, he soft-pedaled and abandoned, by default so to speak, without any further explanation.

Even among the die-hard orthodox analysts, some of them questioned the validity of Freud's concept of "psychic energy," though they unfortunately offered no alternative to it. That attitude was particularly reflected in some psychoanalytic meetings among which I will single out that of the American Psychoanalytic Association in December 1962, and that of the New York Academy of Sciences held in 1959. Evidently I will not be able to report all of the discussions which took place at those meetings, but I will mention some of the statements that better reflect the obscurities surrounding Freud's concept of "psychic energy."

At the first meeting above mentioned, A. H. Modell[21] underlined the fact that Freud used the words "psychic energy" in three different senses: as a metaphorical description of observable phenomena, as a part of a hypothetical construction of the model of the mind, and as an energic concept embodied in the activity of the pleasure-principle. Modell warned therefore that, if when speaking in the sense of psychic energy, we lose our own awareness of that distinction and if: "We permit ourselves to become unaware of this distinction between what is observed and what is constructed, we will become lost in the maze of our own theories."[22] He however offered no theoretical alternative as to how we should conceptualize a psychic energy, so often clearly expressed by Freud in terms of a movable energy, a physical concept, possessing an affective quality, a mental concept.

To state that Freud used the words "psychic energy" as a metaphorical description of observable phenomena cannot be reconciled with the fact that Freud: a) considered psychic energy as a concrete form of energy born of the *transformation* of somatic excitations into psychic excitations, b) that he had assigned to that energy a mobility comparable to that of an electric current, c) that he had considered that energy capable to be subjected to a withdrawal from an object and reinstated into the ego in terms of ego-libido or ego-narcissism, as it occurs in "Schizophrenia" (1915),[23] or leading to the identification of the ego with an abandoned object, as it occurs in Melancholia (1917),[24] d) that in 1905 in his "Three Essays on the Theory of Sexuality" he distinguished between the psychic energy, the libido, possessing a sexual quality, and the psychic energy underlying mental processes in general: "We distinguish thus libido in respect of its special origin from the energy which must be supposed to underlie mental processes in general, and we thus also attribute a qualitative character to it,"[25] and e) that he even assigned to the libido, a sexual psychic energy, a special chemistry related to the activities of the sexual functions, and contrasting with the energy underlying the nutritive processes.

To force the meaning of a "metaphor" to Freud's concept of a sexual psychic energy, though it would represent a convenient way to avoid any deeper insight in the nature of that energy, would be to infirm all the important functions which Freud had intended to assign to the libido, the movable psychic sexual energy born of a special chemistry. Considerations of the same nature would apply to the statement made by Karush, Kardiner, and Ovesey in their "Methodological Review of Freud's Concepts" that:

> The metaphoric significance of psychic energy has been lost
> and the theoretical construction has taken all the force of an

established fact. In actuality energic explanations are no explanation at all. They are merely tautological restatements of the dynamics in different terms.[26]

In my opinion, it was not so much the fault of the readers for having lost the alleged metaphoric concept of "psychic energy" as it was that of Freud himself who certainly went beyond the metaphoric meaning of "psychic energy" when: 1) In 1894 he had assigned to the "psychic energy" the value of an actual quantitative and qualitative force (a sum of excitations—an amount of affect), 2) When in 1895 in his paper on "Anxiety" he had considered "psychic energy" as deriving directly from the transformation of the somatic excitations originating in the sexual organs (somatic energy) into psychic excitations (psychic energy), 3) When in 1905 in his "Three Essays on Sexuality," he referred to the libido, in terms of an elusive floating sexual energy in his statement that: "When it is withdrawn from the object, *it is held in suspense in peculiar conditions of tension*, and is finally drawn back into the Ego so that it becomes Ego-libido once again."[27] [italics mine] A floating energy kept in suspense can hardly be conceived in a metaphorical light, and 4) When as I have already stated, Freud had assigned to the "psychic sexual energy" a definite origin from a special somatic chemistry.

That Freud intended to deal with the libido in terms of an actual psychic energy possessing a special sexual quality, and not with a metaphorical concept is supported also by his subsequent introduction of the process of *"desexualization"* of that energy in the process of identification as it occurs, according to him, in the course of both the normal and pathological development of the ego. In the course of those developments, Freud had clearly stated that "the regression of the Libido into the Ego implied a process of desexualization." One could hardly desexualize an energy metaphorically conceived and allow that energy to continue to operate as a neutral psychic energy.

I will now continue with my comments on the "Proceedings of the American Psychoanalytic Association" on this subject of "psychic energy." At that meeting R. W. Waelder felt that we never can do without quantitative concepts, though he was negatively impressed by the vagueness of the energic concept of psychic energy, of its use both as a drive and as a physical concept, and by the concept of the transformation of psychic energy from one type to another, and stressed the difficulties of *measuring* psychic energy, inasmuch as we are uncertain of what is being measured. He suggested that we free ourselves from the concept of measurement derived from physical science and that: "Measurements of psychic energy could be undertaken on the basis of the evaluation which people put on things, just as it is done in economics whose prices are held as a kind of measurement."[28]

M. Ostow[29] defended the concept of psychic energy because it has pedagogic, heuristic, and explanatory values. In his view it is the only quantitative factor in psychoanalysis which allows a distinction between psychic energy as *the impetus of an impulse*, and psychic energy as *a kind of ego-fuel supply*. He assigned to psychic energy the dual function of activating both the impulse or any condensation of them, and that of activating a whole host of secondary clinical symptoms resulting from the deviations of the ego's libido content, the ego-fuel, from its normal range, that is either in excess or in deficiency of that energy. The tranquilizing drugs reduce the energy available to the ego, whereas the anti-depressants, the energizers, result in manifestations of energy plethora, by increasing the libido available to the ego. In his estimation: "The realm of physiological observation does not render the concept of psychic energy obsolete, this concept being useful because there are certain clinical phenomena which cannot be understood without it."[30]

In my opinion, such an increase or decrease of an alleged ego-fuel supply in terms of a psychic energy through the action of energizers or tranquilizing drugs, is an erroneous assumption inasmuch as that increase or decrease of energy should be related *to an excessive or deficient production* of biological energy, and not of psychic energy, under the influence of the pharmaco-dynamic drugs. These drugs *induce an increase or decrease of excitations which they exercise upon the nervous system*. These increased or decreased *somatic excitations* continue to feed the "psychic function" which is entrusted with their translation into ideational representations. When now the ego is faced with an increased or diminished activity of the "Psychic function" in terms of an increased or decreased amount of ideational representations and related affective qualities, i.e. of "Affective formations" *the ego reacts accordingly* to these formations with manifestations of either increased somatic activity and euphoria, or with diminished somatic activity and depression, both observable clinically. But the energy which is originally induced by the drugs, and the resulting stimuli which are subsequently translated into ideas and "affective formations" by the "psychic function," and the resulting *reactions of the ego* to those increased or decreased amount of ideas or of "Affective formations" are not dependent upon the activity of a *"psychic-ego-fuel,"* but upon the activity of the neurobiological fuel which induced the increase or decrease of stimulation in the nervous system.

At the same meeting, R. Holt[31] felt that although the concept of psychic energy is highly useful, *it is long overdue for a complete overhaul*, considering that it is at present built into the basic model, the very fabric of the analytical theory. In his estimation the development of cybernetics provides a more useful model for psychoanalysis. There, the energy is considered primarily *as a signal* and the quantitative aspects are less significant.

L. Kubie also opposed the energic concept of psychic energy remarking that: Our modern conception of a communication machine

> *is one* which receives and transmits signals, scans, paces, orders, codifies them and solves problems like a computer. This model makes possible a wholly different approach as a result of which, *we can and must dispense with the wholly misleading concept of psychic energy.*[32] [italics mine]

Kubie's approach harmonizes well with that expressed by W. S. McCullough at another meeting where he had stated that

> Biologists following the lead of physicists, used to think that energy was the most significant variable in living systems. But within the last few years, as the result of the development of thermodynamics and information theory, particularly of systems as it is applied to servo-mechanisms, they have come to realize that the crucial thing is not energy but order, that is the degree of the system that we may call "negative entropy."[33]

The inconclusiveness of the whole discussion on "psychic energy," may be summarized by the words of R. Holt that: "We obviously do best to keep *patching* the old theory and get what mileage we can do out of it, until we can trade it for a new model."[34] Also by the words of D. Beres that:

> Though the tools of psychoanalysis do not permit an examination of the biological sources of psychic energy, I consider the instinctual drive theory as a working hypothesis, and the concept of psychic energy a postulate which has not yet reached the status of a scientific law, but that until we have a better theory we should not discard.[35]

At the New York Academy of Sciences, a special meeting was devoted in 1959 to the "*Systematic restatement of the Libido Theory.*" Limiting myself only to some of the statements made at that meeting, I will recall Pumpian-Mindlin reference to the following statement made by Kubie:

> It is my thesis that the easy assumption of quantitative vari-
> ables, as the only ultimate explanation of every variation in
> behavior is one of the seductive fallacies to which all
> psychological theorizing is prone

to which statement Pumpian-Mindlin added:

> At the present time the energic economic aspects of the libido
> theory cannot be reduced to an operational level in their pres-
> ent form. . . . In my opinion this can be done only with the
> further clarification and reformulation in the form of a con-
> stant field theory that would focus our attention on problems
> arising in the field of object-relations.[36]

The point that Pumpian-Mindlin wished to make was that as a close system of operation, psychoanalysis was unable to furnish us with an efficient system of operational theory applicable to clinical problems. In his views in the close system model, from which the main dynamic concepts were derived, the activity of our psychic apparatus is determined in such a way that, if any one of the initial conditions or any part of the process are altered, the end result will also be altered. In contrast, open systems operate on the principle of *equifinality*, that is that the same final state may be reached from different initial conditions and in different ways. In his opinion, it is because of this shift from the close to the open-system model, that psychoanalysis in recent years became concerned with problems of counter-transference, and that it became necessary to consider more actively the interaction, that is the field between the analyst and the patient.

In more precise terms, Von Bertanlaffy expressed the same concept when he compared the scientific world picture of the past with that of recent decades:

> In the world view called mechanistic, born of classical physics
> of the 19th century, the aimless play of the atoms governed by
> the inexorable laws of mechanical causality, produced all
> phenomena in the world, inanimate, living or mental. No
> room was left for any directiveness, order or telos. The world
> of the organism appeared a mere product of chance, accumu-
> lated by the senseless play of mutation at random, and selec-
> tion; the mental world as a curious and rather inconsequen-
> tial epiphenomenon of material events. . . . Now we may state
> as characteristic of modern science that this scheme of isola-
> ble units acting in one way causality, has proven to be insuf-
> ficient.[37]

In Sanford's views,[38] another participant to that meeting, the dynamics of mental processes vary in the course of growth and in mental illness, so that instead of having the idea that all psychoanalysis must be a closed system model, or that we must have an open system, we had better orient ourselves into thinking that sometimes we may invoke one model for some processes, and another for other processes. The concept of a psychic energy as a fluid current moving through towards discharge, a closed system concept, may be used in the case of id psychology, such as in the interpretation of dreams and of unconscious conflicts, whereas one needs an open model concept, such as the tripartite one of the id, the ego, and the super ego, to take care of problems that stress the relationship between the psychic apparatus and the environment.

In my opinion, that discussion of the usefulness of a given system, which was meant to emphasize the advantages or disadvantages of either the closed or the open system operating in our psychic apparatus, did not bring out the fact that in his writings, Freud had made use of both systems, though he never seemed to attach importance to their designation. Thus while in many of *his theoretical assumptions*, he seemed to have made use of what we may consider as a closed system, in dealing with *clinical problems*, he certainly made use of what we may consider as an open system model. We therefore are too eager to read in Freud's writings his reference or preference for this or that particular model. Freud built up his own psychology as he went along, and did not seem to mind what designation was to be subsequently attached to his eclectic mode of investigation. Any attempt to force Freud's intention within a certain operational framework, seems to me a futile one. In this respect I am inclined to agree with Beres[38] that he doubted very much if Freud ever used models in the sense we attribute to them now a day, inasmuch as he never committed himself to what has been called 'the fluid hydraulic model' or for that matter to any other model. He never changed models because he never created permanent models.

Indeed, when Freud first dealt with the conflictual theory of the neuroses (1894), he must have been operating on the basis of an open system model, when he pitted one against the other, the sexual impulses and the ego's demand for morality, a conflict which evidently implied the operation of environmental factors. On the other hand in his *Project for a Scientific Psychology* (1895),[39] when dealing with neuronal activities and related neural inhibitions, Freud seemed to have made use of what appears to be a closed model system, when he referred *to the ego as "an organized group of neurones."*

In spite of all of the earnest discussions in which the participants in the meeting of the psychoanalytic association on the subject of "psychic energy" engaged themselves, they seemed to have reached only the conclusion that the concept of psychic energy should be either discarded or modified, but that in the meantime we should make the best use of it, as it stands.

Nor did the participants in the meeting of the New York Academy of Sciences reach any agreement on the libido theory as formulated by Freud. Nor did any of the participants in the two meetings propose any possible replacement of the concept of "Psychic energy" with that of a newly developed *"Psychic function"* activated by the same biological energy which activates the various somatic functions, out of the integration of which the new "psychic function" was born. Furthermore none of the participants in both meetings discussed the libido theory in the erroneous terms formulated by Freud, that under repression a separation occurred between the idea to be repressed and its alleged charge of affect, the libido, made of a quantitative and qualitative sexual energy, which once freed from the idea underwent displacement and attachment to some other idea. They all therefore missed the opportunity to advance the possibility that a given idea and its related and attached affective quality form an indivisible unit *"the Affective formation,"* which under the energic power of the idea and not of its energic quality, is capable of displacement in its entirety and replacement by some other unit also in its entirety.

They consequently missed the opportunity to envisage the possibility that there might have been an energy responsible directly for the activation of the ideas before and after they had acquired their affective qualities, and independently from an alleged "psychic energy." They therefore failed to assign to the ideas and not to their quality, the energic attribute which permits to the ideas or to the "affective formations" made of ideas and attached affective qualities, their mobility and displacement.

Any idea born of the activities of the newly developed "psychic function" which latter is governed by an "organismic energy" must evidently depend for its mobility and displacement from that same biological energy. Had such an assumption been presented and discussed as a viable one at the various scientific meetings, it might have disposed once and for all of Freud's erroneous assumption that it was the affective quality of an idea, the libido, which possessing an energic attribute, was capable to attach or detach itself at will from an idea, or become disposed of, in some other convenient form.

To sum it up briefly, I have proposed to substitute the untenable assumption advanced by Freud of the existence and operation of a libido in terms of a "mobile psychic energy" possessing a sexual quality and that of its instinctual origin. That sexual energy in Freud's contention is thus capable of detachment from a given idea, attachment to some other idea or capable of finding discharge in some other expedient way. In that light the "psychic energy" would constitute the dominant factor in the activities of our psychic apparatus.

The substitutive assumption which I offer is that there is no "psychic energy" be it sexual or otherwise capable of governing the functioning of our psychic apparatus. Instead I assume that it is the idea possessing no affective quality, or the idea which has acquired an affective quality (the latter constituting an inseparable unit which I have called an "Affective formation"), that can undergo displacement and replacement by some other idea or by some other "affective formation." I also assume that all ideas are the product of a new "psychic function" ontogenetically developed from the integration and synthesis of the somatic functions already operating in a developing organism. Ideas and "affective formations" are activated by the same somatic energy which presides over the development of the new "psychic function."

These assumptions of mine which I consider more tenable and viable than those of Freud, fall much better in line within the framework of an academic psychology which deals with the displacement and replacement of ideas and attached affective qualities, and the mobility and interplay of which, constitute the fabric of our operating "psychic apparatus," free from the vagaries of an elusive "psychic energy."

Freud definitely opposed this approach of the mobility of the ideas themselves when he summarized his views on this subject in the last edition (1932) of his *Interpretation of Dreams,* where in reference to the replacement of ideas or group of ideas from one locality to another, he felt that it would be much better to say that some particular mental grouping has had a cathexis of energy attached to it, or withdrawn from it. In those terms, those psychic structures may have come under the sway of a particular agency or been withdrawn from that agency. Freud thus felt that which is mobile is *not the psychical structure* itself, but its innervation.[40]

The importance of my assumption that it is precisely not the mobility of the "psychic energy" but of the psychic structure, of what I have called an "affective formation" made of the combination of an idea and of its affective quality, constituting an inseparable unit, *the mobility of which depends on the energy of the idea* and not the energy of its alleged quality, will be reflected in the next chapter, "Repression." It is because I do not subscribe to the separation of an "affective formation" into its component parts of "idea" and "affective quality" that I will disagree in that next chapter with Freud's original "customary psychological abstraction"[41] that under the impact of repression, the idea becomes separated from its affective quality, which, according to him, possesses an energic attribute that allows to displace itself upon some other idea.

Why did Freud deny a mobility to the psychic structures when he himself seems to have admitted that mobility in the unconscious, of memory traces, which are, in fact, psychical structures, and when in his discussion of why the reactivation of the memory traces of a pleasurable sexual experience, which represents a psychic structure, should result in the case of obsessive neurosis, in a painful affect that necessitates repression? An affect cannot be separated from an accompanying ideational representation which is a psychic structure.

In his draft K to Fliess, Freud in fact seems to have admitted *the mobility of psychic structures* in the form of memory-traces when he stated the following:

> We can suppose that it is the later convergence of the passive [painful] experience with the pleasurable one, that adds the unpleasure to the pleasurable memory, and makes Repression possible.

In this instance, experiences referred to by Freud are evidently made of displaceable ideas and related affective qualities.

Furthermore, in his paper "Repression" (1915), Freud, speaking of the fate of the repressed instinctual impulse, stated as follows:

> Its activity will not result in the abrogation of the repression, but it will certainly set in motion all the processes *which terminate in a breaking through into consciousness by circuitous routes.*

By such circuitous routes, Freud meant the transformation of the repressed offensive idea, into substitute nonoffensive ideas. In that statement, Freud, though referring to the mobility of the cathexis passing from the repressed idea upon the substitute idea, had no means to exclude the alternate assumption that it may have been the mobility of the repressed idea and its association with neighborhood ideas, and not the mobility of the alleged psychic energy, that resulted into the transformation of the repressed idea into an acceptable substitute idea.

Later, in his paper "The Unconscious," Freud spoke, in fact, of substitute ideas which had replaced the repressed idea, and which through associative circuitous routes, had reentered consciousness in some nonobjectionable form. It is such substitute ideational formations and related affective qualities, that are in fact "psychic structures" which have now taken over the representation of what had been repressed. How do such substitute formations develop? In my estimation, it is only by the mobility of the repressed psychic structures and of their association with mobile neighborhood ideas. However, the energy which presides over such mobility is the somatic "organismic energy" that activates the ideas themselves, and not the alleged "psychic energy" of Freud which possesses a special mental quality.

If now I assume that in the unconscious, mobility of individual ideas or group of ideas and related affective qualities, does actually take place, there is no reason to deny the same mobility to psychical structures operating in the conscious and activated by the same somatic "organismic energy," thus avoiding Freud's concept of the immobility of the psychic structures, and the mobility only of the "psychic energy."

Furthermore, when Freud spoke of the two main characteristics of the unconscious processes, he referred to the character of 1) displacement, and 2) condensation. Now both these characteristics need not be linked to the activity only of the "psychic energy" and to the immobility of the psychical structures. The word "condensation" does also imply the mobility of the ideas themselves which succeed to fuse together and need not be necessarily bound as Freud advocates, to the mobility only of the psychic energy which affects the immovable ideational representations.

The question of the mobility of the psychic structures, made of ideas or group of ideas and related affective qualities, has an important bearing on Freud's fallacy that in repression a separation occurs between a repressed idea and its activating "psychic energy." While the activating psychic energy proceeds to activate other psychic structures, the fate of the ideas deprived of their activating energy, remains obscure.

After the manuscript of this book had been edited by its publishers, Vantage Press, I had the delayed opportunity to read the content of the third quarterly issue of the 1977 *Journal of the American Psychoanalytic Association*[42] devoted mainly to a renewed discussion of the problem of "psychic energy," a discussion already undertaken by the association in 1963.

Having read the very interesting papers and discussions by R. Wallenstein, Allan D. Rosenblath and James T. Thichstrum, Milton Horowitz, Merton M. Gill, Adrienne Aplegarth, Don R. Swanson, Robert Dickes and Daniel S. Papernick, Jerome L. Weinberger, and Jules Glenn, presented at that special symposium, I found them to be excellent presentations and discussions of various frames of references to the application of Freud's concept of "psychic energy." There was an excellent discussion of the problems of "quantity" in psychoanalytic theory, and an excellent presentation of the problems of "Energy, Information, and Motivation."

However, not all those excellent papers did reject *categorically* Freud's concept of the existence and operation of a movable psychic energy that can be attached or withdrawn from a mental group of ideas, as Freud still maintained as recently as 1933, the date of the last English edition of his *Interpretation of Dreams*, long after he had developed his concept of the drives. In that edition, he still maintained that what he regarded as mobile was not the psychical structure itself, but its *innervation*, a term often used by Freud to mean the transmission of energy.

In all those papers and discussions I did not find, however, any attempt at presenting some substitute assumption to Freud's concept of "psychic energy" in harmony and along the lines which I have presented in this first chapter of my book, that is, of the development and activity of a "new psychic function," not to be confused with "psychic energy," born automatically at a certain moment of our *somatic intrauterine organization*, out of the integration and synthesis of the somatic functions operating at that moment in that organization. In my assumption the "new psychic function" has the task of *translating the various stimuli* generated by the various somatic functions already operating in that organization *into their first ideational representations*, thus constituting the very first foundations in the ontogenetic development of our psychic apparatus.

These original "ideational representations," by the very nature of the special somatic stimuli which they represent, and also as a result of their association or combination with other ideational representations already operating functionally, may acquire different affective qualities, thus resulting in the creation of what I have called "affective formation" that is, of an idea with its attached affective quality, a unit which I consider indivisible. It is those simple "ideational representations," or the resulting "affective formations," that constitute *the psychic structures*, the very fabric of our developing psychic apparatus.

Nowhere in those elaborated papers did I find a statement assigning explicitly the attribute of mobility and displacement to those "psychic structures," contrary to the views of Freud, who in 1933 still assigned such an attribute exclusively to the "psychic energy." Nowhere in those papers and related discussions did I find any substantial reference to the operation of the "psychic structures" at the hands of some other qualified energy apt to replace Freud's "psychic energy," nor any clear reference to the fact that such "psychic structures" were activated by some somatic biological and chemo-physical energy, an energy which in this book I have specifically called *"organismic energy"*: the same energy which, in my assumption, was responsible for the development of the "new psychic function," which, in turn, was directly responsible for the development of the first ideational representations" of the various somatic stimuli.

It follows that the "psychic function" must have utilized the same somatic energy in order to fulfill its creative task of translating somatic stimuli into "ideational representations." These ideas must have been, therefore, endowed automatically with the same type of somatic energy possessed by their own creator, an energy which rendered them capable, from then on, of mobility and displacement necessary for their further development into more complex psychic structures.

I may add that though the papers and discussions presented at the above meeting may have implied tacitly, the mobility, displacement and interaction of various "psychic structures," none of those papers *reflected in no uncertain terms* Freud's axiomatic denial of the mobility of psychic structures *while admitting only* the mobility of the "psychic energy".

From all of the above comments, it follows that even though, for the special circumstances of my living, since last year, in a small city of Florida where I have had a difficult access to that very recent number of the *Journal of the American Psychoanalytic Association*, my belated reading of its content has not affected the priority of my original assumption, on the basis of which I have written the first chapter of this book, an assumption which runs all through my book and which is based upon my central concept that it is the mobility, displacement, and association and combinations of the various mobile psychic structures activated by an "organismic energy," and not by a "psychic energy" that could explain to us the complexities of our mental processes and their related affective changes, that lead to our ultimate feelings and behavioral activities.

Nor has such a delay in any way affected the priority of the new principle, which I have introduced under the name of "The Principle of Intussusception," from the Latin *intra*, inside, and *suscipere*, to take in, a functional principle which, in my views, governs the fact that older psychic structures may be absorbed by the new developing structures. I have developed in some detail the functioning of that principle in Chapter 4 of Part III of this book.

I may add that in my book I have made no attempt at scrutinizing the various theories of learning, information, motivation, and personality development, and, therefore, I have not undertaken the discussion of the numerous and excellent publications that deal with such important subjects, many of which I have in my library.

My object in this book, outside the important discussion of Freud's three major fallacies, was also to introduce and discuss my concept of the ontogenetic development of our psychic apparatus, based on the assumption of an automatic development of a new "psychic function" at a certain moment of our somatic intrauterine organization, and also on the assumption that there is no mobile psychic energy as predicated by Freud, and *that which is mobile and displaceable are, in my views, the psychic structures* to which Freud had denied any mobility, structures in which I have assumed to be activated by what I have called "the organismic energy."

The application of my new basic assumption of the mobility of the "psychic structures" made of simple ideas, or of affective ideas, and which I have used in my criticism of Freud's libido theory, of his views on sexuality, and of his views of the normal and pathological development of the ego, *rests now in the hands of present and future students* who may wish or may not wish to utilize my assumptions in their possible application to the problems of information, learning, motivation, and personality development, and in their role in shaping our behavioral activities.

Chapter II

Repression

I. Freud's error that in repression a separation occurs between the idea to be repressed and its libido, the latter in terms of a movable qualitative sexual energy.
II. A critique of Freud's views on the developmental stages of the process of repression.
III. Contrasting interpretation by Freud's followers of his original views of the conscious nature of repression.

I

The clinical concept of repression constitutes in my estimation Freud's major contribution to the value of psychoanalysis. It was repression that later on opened the door to Freud's interpretation of dreams.

As far back as 1894, in his first paper *The Defence Neuropsychoses,* Freud had equated defense with inhibition, later on called repression, and had made of that mechanism of defense the basis for his psychological assumption that in the course of defense, a separation occurred between the idea to be repressed and its activating energy, the libido conceived in terms of a movable and displaceable psychic energy possessing a specific sexual quality.

In his letter of October 20, 1895, to his friend W. Fliess, Freud referred to the importance of repression. In his words: "Today I gave my second lecture on Hysteria, making repression the central point; they liked it but I shall not publish it."[1] Subsequently in his paper of 1896: Further remarks on the Defence Neuro-psychoses[2] Freud wrote again as follows: "My experience in the last two years of work has strengthened in me my surmise that defence is the nucleus of the psychic mechanism of the neuroses, and have made possible to

36

me to give their psychological theory a clinical basis."[3]

Later, in 1907, in his comments on Jensens' novel *Gradiva*, Freud described repression as a: "Purely dynamic expression which takes account of the interplay of the mental forces, and which implies that there is a force present, which is seeking to bring about all kinds of psychic effects, including that of becoming conscious."[4] In 1924, in *The History of the Psychoanalytic Movement*,[5] Freud was again very explicit over the importance of repression, so much so that in his estimation:

> *The doctrine of repression is the foundation stone upon which the whole structure of psychoanalysis rests, the most essential part of it.* Yet it is nothing but a theoretical formulation of a phenomenon which may be observed to recur as often as one undertakes an analysis of a neurotic, without resorting to hypnosis.[6] [italics mine]

In his very late paper of 1936 *A Disturbance Memory on the Acropolis*, Freud referring to the various methods of defence of the ego, which his daughter Anna had prepared for publication, stated that: "The most primitive and thorough going of these methods, *Repression was the starting point of the whole of our deeper understanding of psychopathology*."[7] [italics mine]

It would seem however, that repression was not an original idea of Freud, but as he himself recounted in his History of the Psychoanalytic movement (1914):

> The doctrine of repression quite certainly came to me independently of any other sources . . . and for a long time I imagined it to be entirely my own, until Otto Rank showed me the passage in Schopenhauer's "Word as Will and Idea" . . . What he says there about the struggle against acceptance of a painful part of reality, fits my conception of repression so completely, that I am again indebted for having made a discovery, to not being a wide reader.[8]

Walter Riese in his paper *The pre-Freudian Origin of Psychoanalysis*, published in 1958, confirmed the priority of Schopenhauer in having introduced the concept of repression, and then added the following:

> We are able to expand Rank's historical discovery and to include the use of the very term Repression appearing for the first time in one of Schopenhauer's minor writings i.e. "Essays on the Philosophy and Science of nature." Significantly he used it also in connection with sexual impulses.[9]

In a footnote to that page, Walther Riese added that: M. Dorer in his *Historische Grundlage der Psychoanalyse* (1932) quoted a passage from Freud's writings which showed that Freud was familiar with Schopenhauer's views on sexuality and repression. Furthermore on page 84 of Dorer's opus, Riese remarked that the author had stated that the philosopher Herbert had also anticipated the concept and term of repression. Be that as it may, Freud seems however to have been the first one to apply repression to the clinical approach to the neuroses, and in that sense deserves the credit for having introduced it as an instrument of "psychoanalysis."

Freud's relentless efforts at understanding the mechanics of repression had already been expressed in 1895 in his posthumously published correspondence with his friend W. Fliess. Reading through that correspondence, and through the content of his "Project for a Scientific Psychology" also posthumously published, one can better appreciate Freud's efforts in that direction. In a letter to Fliess dated August 6, 1895, Freud wrote as follows: "I believe I found my way to the understanding of pathological defence, and with it to the understanding of many pathological processes. . . . The psychological theory I needed yielded only to laborious assaults. I hope it is not dream-gold."[10] Ten days later he again wrote:

> All I was trying to do was to explain *defence*, but I found myself explaining something from the very heart of nature. I found myself wrestling with the problem of quality, of sleep and memory, in short with the whole psychology. I want to hear no more of it.[11]

On October 8, 1895 Freud returned again on this important subject which he had apparently condensed in a notebook, which unfortunately was never found, but concerning which Freud felt that it only took the subject to a certain point, from which he had to start from scratch again. What did not as yet hang together was not the mechanism, but the explanation of repression.[12]

Twelve days later, October 20, 1895, Freud was all enthusiastic and elated at having all of a sudden, realized all that he needed in connection with repression and neuroses;

> One strenuous night last week, when I was in a stage of painful discomfort, in which my brain works best, the barrier suddenly lifted, the veils dropped, and it was possible to see from the details of neurosis, all the way to the very conditioning of consciousness . . . to the two biological rules of attention *and defence*, . . . the state of the sexual group, *the sexual determi-*

nation of repression. . . . The whole thing held together, and
still does. I can naturally hardly contain myself with de-
light.[13] [italics mine]

But eleven days later, Freud still felt that he had not yet put the
pieces of the puzzle in the right place, though all of his theories converged, where he had opportunities of clearing things up.[14]

A very first *published mention* of defense (repression), prior to
its being mentioned in Fliess' correspondence, is found in Breuer's
and Freud's collaborative paper on *Hysteria*[15] (1893), where the authors considered for the first time the point that certain unpleasant
memories could be subjected to condemnation by means of relegating
them to the unconscious. It is on that basis that they ultimately concluded that hysterical patients suffered essentially from the con-
sequences of reminiscences of unpleasant memories, which they had
repressed, but which under hypnosis could be reactivated with un-
diminished vividness and affect.

The relegation to the unconscious of such memories, was explained in one group of patients by the fact that, at the time of the
occurrence of the given unpleasant experience, the patients had not
undergone a proper affective reaction i.e. the patients ˙had not
reacted properly to that experience. These patients constituted the
group of hysterics, whom the following year Freud designated as the
group of *"retention hysteria."* In a second group Breuer and Freud
felt that at the time of the unpleasant experience, the patients' mental condition was in a particular state, that Breuer had designated
as "hypnoid state," and in the course of which the ideas emerging in
it, were cut off from associative connections with the rest of the content of consciousness. This group Breuer designated as *"hypnoid hysteria."* The subsequent year (1894), Freud added a third group, that
of *"defence hysteria,"* based on the operation of repression, and from
then on he involved himself in the study of that particular group.

At that time, Freud believed not only that hysteria and obsessive neurosis were related to sexuality in general, but that in both
neuroses the patients had experienced in early childhood, an early
sexual shock in the course of unpleasurable passive seduction, followed later, in the cases of obsessive neuroses, by some pleasurable
sexual experience. That belief he communicated to W. Fliess in his
letter of October 15, 1895:

> Have I revealed to you the great clinical secret? Hysteria is
> the consequence of a *pre-sexual sexual shock*. Obsessional
> neurosis is the consequence of a *pre-sexual sexual pleasure*,
> later transformed into guilt. Pre-sexual means before puberty,
> before the production of the sexual substance; the relevant
> events become effective only as memories.[16]

In a further elaboration of "that clinical secret," Freud felt that
in hysteria it was the reactivation of the memory of the painful sexual experience of seduction in early childhood, that subsequently in
later life, prompted repression of any sexual thought or impulse. In
obsessive neurosis it was the recollection of the memory of some active pleasurable sexual experience, which strangely enough, elicited
an ultimate painful affect, which consequently had to be repressed.

Why should the reactivation of the memory *of a pleasurable*
sexual experience, result in the case of obsessive neurosis, *in a painful affect that* necessitates repression? This was conveniently explained by Freud by stating that in his obsessive patients, prior to
the pleasurable active sexual experience, there had taken place at
an earlier age, an unpleasurable passive sexual experience. As a result he assumed that *a psychic relationship of convergence* had been
established between the two groups of memory-traces, and that in
such convergence, the memory trace of the first painful sexual experience, dominated the recollection of the subsequent pleasurable
one and thus was the cause of the subsequent repression. That view
he elaborated in his draft K, forwarded to Fliess and dated January
1, 1896.[17] Consequently in his view, repression of sexual thoughts or
impulses in later years, was possible only for those people in whom a
sexual experience could reactivate the painful memory-trace of an
earlier infantile sexual trauma.[18]

In his first published paper *The Defence Neuro-psychoses*, Freud
was of the opinion that repression of sexuality was the initial and
common defense operating in both hysteria and obsessive neurosis,
though the two neuroses subsequently differed in their development.
In both neuroses, he had assumed that *repression* resulted at first in
a separation between the idea representing the sexual reprehensible
impulse, from its libido, that is from its energic and qualitative
charge of affect. It was following that separation that the development of the two neuroses varied. In hysteria *the detached affect* possessing an energic attribute *became directly transmuted into some*

somatic sensory or motor innervation, whereas in obsessive neurosis, the detached affect did not undergo such a transmutation, *but instead became attached to some new idea*, which through that false connection, entered consciousness in the form of a repetitive idea.

Parenthetically, I should point here to an evident contradiction in Freud's views of 1894 and those of 1915, concerning the fate of the repressed idea and of its charge of affect in "conversion hysteria." While in 1894 Freud had stated that it was *"the charge of affect"* which had undergone a direct transmutation in some motor or sensory innervation, in 1915 in his paper *Repression*[19] he stated that the "charge of affect" had been mastered by the repression, and that it was because of the complete success of repression that in hysteria no anxiety appeared as a replacement of that repressed affect. As for the fate of the repressed idea, while in 1894 Freud had stated that once the idea had been deprived by repression, from its charge of affect, *it became a weak idea*, which from then on, *formed the nucleus of a secondary psychical group*,[20] in 1915 he stated that the repressed idea had completely been withdrawn from consciousness, and that *as a substitute formation*, and concurrently as a symptom there appeared *"an excessive innervation* (in typical case, a somatic innervation) sometime of motor character, either as an excitation or as an inhibition."[21] Therefore it was no longer the *affect* which became transmuted in somatic innervation, but the repressed idea.

Another contradiction concerns also the fate of the repressed idea in obsessive neurosis. In 1894 Freud had assumed that following repression, *the original idea remained in consciousness in a peculiar state of isolation, detached from all associations*, while the "charge of affect" as such attached itself to some other idea. In 1915 Freud maintained instead that the repressed sexual idea, no longer remained in consciousness, but was relegated to the unconscious, where it became replaced by some other trivial or indifferent idea. In that same paper, he also stated that the "charge of affect" of the repressed idea became transformed in the unconscious into some other affect, such as dread, pangs of conscience, and self-reproaches, prior to its becoming attached to some other idea.

While Freud's assumption that under repression a separation occurred between the ideational portion of an instinctual presentation and its charge of affect, *"remained from then on the pillar of Freud's subsequent development of his Libido theory,"* the flimsy and poorly documented assumption which he advanced in 1895 of a first passive painful sexual experience in childhood, as the etiological factor in the development of hysteria, and of a pleasurable sexual experience preceded by an earlier painful sexual experience in childhood as the etiological factor in obsessive neurosis, *lived a very short life*.

Indeed, less than two years later, Freud presumably on the basis of more accurate history-taking in his patients, rejected the above hurriedly formulated etiological theory, admitted his error, and confessed his disarray in a letter to his friend Fliess dated September 21, 1897, where he expresses the feeling that he no longer believed in his neurotica and that he had failed to reach the theoretical understanding of repression and its play of forces.[22] Subsequently in 1914 in his *History of the Psychoanalytic Movement*, Freud returned on that error in the following terms:

> When this etiology broke under its own Improbability, and under contradictions in definitely ascertainable circumstances, the result was at first *helpless bewilderment*. Analysis had led me the right paths to these sexual traumas, and yet there were not true. *Reality was lost from under* one's own feet. *At that time I would have gladly given up the whole thing.* Perhaps I persevered only because I had no choice and could not then begin at anything else. At last came the reflection that after all, one has no right to despair because one has been deceived "in one's expectation: one must revise them."[23] [italics mine]

Animated by that resolve, Freud returned to his investigation of the phenomenon of repression, and searched for a substitute factor to take place of the actuality of the childhood's sexual experiences and thus fell upon the existence in childhood of sexual fantasies, the memory-traces of which would be reactivated and thus replace the actuality of a sexual experience. It is interesting to note that it was in a first draft to Fliess dated May 25, 1897, *four months before his repudiation* of the etiological value of the childhood's sexual experiences, that Freud's attention had already been attracted by this subject of fantasies. According to that draft, Freud believed that fantasies arose from an unconscious combination of things experienced and heard, constructed for the particular purpose to make inaccessible the memory from which symptoms generate, and that the fantasies were constructed by a process of fusion and distortion. Thus a fragment of a visual scene, could be joined to a fragment of an auditory one, and made into a fantasy. This was why it makes it im-

possible to trace their original connection. However, if the intensity
of such a fantasy increases to a point at which it would have to force
its way into consciousness, Freud believed that it would be repressed
and that as a result, a symptom would develop by means of a backward drive from the fantasy to its constituent memories.[24] Parenthetically this seems to be the first reference to the harking back of
a mental representation to its underlying memory-traces, a process
which three years later (1900) in *The Interpretation of Dreams* Freud
designated for the first time as *Regression*."

It was evidently a very convenient opening for Freud to fall
back upon those sexual fantasies as a substitute for the reality of
childhood's sexual experience which in the past he had taken for
granted. However Freud's acceptance of the sexual fantasies as a
substitute for an actual sexual experience, must have taken some
time and must have met with some struggle in his own mind, considering that in the letter of September 21, 1897, that same letter in
which he had repudiated the reality of childhood's sexual experiences, *Freud had not* asserted that childhood's fantasies could replace
the actuality of sexual experiences. *On the contrary* in discussing
fantasies in general, in that same letter he had remarked that in the
unconscious there being no indication of reality, it was impossible to
distinguish between truth and emotionally charged fiction, *and what
is more important, is that he doubted that fantasies could actually become activated by later sexual experiences*. That is my interpretation
of the word "arguable" used by Freud in the following statement: "It
again seems arguable that it is later experiences which give rise to
phantasies, which throw back to childhood."[25] It would therefore
seem that it must have taken some self-persuasion on Freud's part
to convince himself subsequently that all sexual fantasies of childhood could be reactivated by later sexual experiences. It would also
seem that Freud's final acceptance in his favor of the argued subject,
could sound as a convenient acceptance on his part, meant to soft-
pedal his initial error of early sexual experience in childhood.

What strikes me as a relevant observation in connection with
Freud's rejection of the actuality of those childhood's sexual experiences, is that while he made that rejection in his private letter to
Fliess dated September 1897, he still upheld that view in his published paper of 1898 *Sexuality in the Etiology of the Neuroses*.[26] In
that paper, though he did not qualify those sexual experiences as
passive and painful, or active and pleasurable, Freud nevertheless,
referring to the consideration that *the evolution of the species man*,
strives to prevent extensive sexual activity during childhood, reiterated his point of view that:

It is perhaps possible to understand through considerations of this kind, why sexual experiences in childhood *are bound to have a pathogenic effect.* ... This subsequent effect can only originate in the mental traces which have been left behind by the infantile sexual experience.[27]

No rejection of this view nor any reference to its substitution with that of sexual fantasies is to be found in this paper.

Freud apparently acknowledged *in print his error only eight years later* in 1905 in his paper *My Views on the Part Played by Sexuality in the Etiology of the Neuroses*, where he emphasized *the importance of sexual fantasies* for the first time, and on the basis of which he could then state that by introducing this element of fantasies: *"I was able to correct the most momentous of my early errors."*[28] That Freud *must not have been in a hurry to acknowledge publicly that error*, is evidenced by his comments to Fliess, in that letter of September 1897 in which he had first acknowledged his error:

> Certainly *I shall not tell it to Gath*, or publish it in the street of Askalon in the land of the philistines, but between ourselves, I have a feeling more of a triumph than of defeat, (which cannot be right).[29]

Let me return again to the kernel of Freud's libido theory, that is, to his assumption that under repression a separation occurs between a reprehensible idea and its libido that is its sexual "charge of affect." That assumption was first developed by Freud in 1894 in his paper *The Defence Neuro-psychoses* when referring to the time elapsed between the wish of a patient to forget, to push out of his mind an objectionable thought, and the appearance of neurotic symptoms he had stated that on this subject he had formed an opinion based on what he had called *"a customary psychological abstraction."* In his words which I have already recalled in chapter I:

> The task which the Ego undertakes in defence, of treating the unbearable idea as *non arrivée* is absolutely unsolvable; *both the memory-traces and the affect attached to the idea, are there once and for all, and it is no longer possible to extirpate them.* But it amounts to an approximate fulfillment of that task if the Ego succeeds in transforming a strong idea into a weak one, in depriving it of its affect—the quantity of excitation— with which the idea is charged. The weak idea will then make

practically no demands on the work of association; the quantity of excitation however, which is then detached from the idea, must be utilized in another direction. . . . In Hysteria the unbearable idea is rendered innocuous *by the quantity of excitation attached to it, being transmuted in some bodily form of expression*, a process for which I would like to propose the name of *conversion*.[30]

If the capacity for "conversion" does not exist as it is the case in the obsessive neurotic patient, *and yet the separation of the affect from an unbearable idea, is nevertheless undertaken* as a defense against the latter, then according to Freud:

> *This affect must persist in the psychical sphere. Thus weakened, the idea remains present in consciousness, detached from all associations; but its affect now freed from it, attaches itself to other ideas which are not in themselves unbearable,* but which through this false connection grow to be obsessions. This is shortly the psychological theory of obsessions and phobias which I mentioned to start with. . . . It is possible to demonstrate *the ultimate source of the affect which is now falsely attached to some other idea.* In all cases that I have analysed it was *in the sexual life* that a painful affect—of precisely the same quality of that attaching to the obsession, had originated.[31] [italics mine]

On the basis of such statements, Freud had clearly maintained that it was the libido in terms of the specific sexual "charge of affect" *made of an energic quantity and related sexual quality*, that becomes separated from a reprehensible idea, and that subsequently it either becomes attached to some other idea, or becomes discharged in some transmuted form.

It is that erroneous assumption which I presume, had not been carefully weighed by Freud, that led him into the fallacious theoretical path of what he later called the "libido theory." In introducing the assumption of the existence of an energic quantity to which he had assigned an affective sexual quality, Freud fell into three major misconceptions: 1) That an energy, a physical concept, could be endowed *with an affective quality*, a mental concept. That misconception resulted from his original assumption that a sum of somatic excitations originating from the sexual organs, after having reached a certain height could automatically become transformed into psychic excitations (psychic energy) which must have implied the retention of the sexual quality of the somatic excitations from which they originated; 2) That a sexual psychic energy, the libido, if prevented from operating in the proper direction, could perform the function of a somatic neural energy, and as such be able to put in motion some somatic motor or sensory innervation, as in the case of "conversion Hysteria"; 3) That having centered his attention upon the origin of the "psychic energy," he failed to inquire at the same time, about *the origin of the ideas which constitute the fabric of our psychic apparatus*, and about the nature of the energy that activates such ideas.

Had Freud paid heed to the origin of those ideas, he may have assumed that they could have been the product of a new operating function, the "Psychic function" to which could have been entrusted the task of translating the stimuli originating from the various somatic functions into their corresponding "ideational representations." He could also have assumed that such a new "Psychic function" was born of the integration and synthesis of the various somatic functions already in operation in the course of our intrauterine organization, and that consequently that "Psychic function" must have been activated and governed by the same physico-biological energy that was responsible for the activation of those somatic functions. He could then have assumed that the *ideas* which were the product of that "Psychic function" must have been activated at their onset as well as subsequently by the same biological energy that governed that function. Freud would have had no need therefore to resort to an additional superfluous energy, his alleged "Psychic energy."

Freud could also have assumed that once the ideas born from the newly developed Psychic function, had subsequently somehow acquired an affective quality, it would have been those ideas and not their affective qualities i.e. their charge of affect that would have been responsible for their mobility and displacement. Freud could also have assumed that once an idea had acquired its affective quality, it would have constituted with that quality, an inseparable combination, a unit which I have called an "affective formation" capable of undergoing displacement in its entirety of idea and quality, and replacement by some other "Affective formation" in its entirety of idea and quality.

And to think that Freud had come very near to my assumption of an inseparable formation between an idea and its affective quality, when he had stated, as I have already mentioned, that an "unbearable idea and *the affect attached to it*, cannot be considered as 'non-arrivée' inasmuch as both the memory-traces *and the affect attached to the idea are there once and for all.*"[32]

Had Freud considered the various alternative assumptions which I have offered, he could have concluded, as I have concluded, that the displacement of an idea or of an *"Affective formation"* takes place under the power of the idea, and not under the power of the affective quality, which possesses no energic attribute. As a result, Freud's own assumption of a psychic energy possessing a sexual quality, and capable of attaching itself to a given idea, or of detaching itself from that idea and of attaching itself to some other idea, would have had to be considered as a no longer viable and acceptable assumption.

It was unfortunate therefore that Freud rejected the assumption of an intrinsic mobility of the idea to which belonged the energic attribute, and supported instead that of a mobile and displaceable psychic energy, an erroneous assumption, which he applied to his own formulation of the normal and pathological development of the ego. It is that erroneous assumption on Freud's part that I am discussing in Part One of this trilogy under the heading of "The Fallacy of Freud's Libido Theory."

What do I propose to substitute for Freud's libido theory? I propose the introduction of the following assumptions: a) That in addition to the various somatic and biological functions already operating *in the course of our intrauterine organization,* there develops at a certain moment a new *"Psychic function" which is born automatically out of the integration and synthesis of those somatic functions.* b) That the first task of that new psychic function is *to translate* the various somatic stimuli generated by the various somatic functions, *into ideas, that is into ideational representations,* no matter how primordial these may be. c) That the various ideas acquire subsequently an "affective quality" in relation to the sensory quality of the somatic stimuli from which they derive, and in relation to the association of those ideas with other ideas already possessing an affective quality, and already operating in our mind. d) That once the idea has acquired its affective quality, it constitutes with it an inseparable unit, *an inseparable combination,* which I have called an *"Affective formation"* and which is capable of displacement in its entirety. So constituted, an "Affective formation" can be replaced by some other "Affective formation." e) That the energic attribute responsible for the displacement of an "Affective formation" belongs to the ideational component of that formation. f) That the energy with which that idea is endowed is the same chemico-physico-biological energy which had presided over the development of the new "psychic function" born of the integration and synthesis of the various somatic functions, including that of the incipient nervous system already operating in our intrauterine organization. g) That the energy which activates a sexual "Affective formation" cannot be that of its sexual quality, which quality does not possess an energic attribute. It follows that a quality, lacking an energic attribute cannot become separated from the idea that it qualifies, and therefore cannot become directed upon some other idea. h) That the assumption of a replacement of let us say, a sexual "Affective formation" by some other non-sexual "Affective formation," while freeing us from the erroneous concept of a detachable sexual energy, the libido, from its attached idea, would conform much better with a type of psychology that considers the operation of mobile, displaceable, and replaceable ideas or of ideas possessing already an affective quality, and the activities of which constitutes the fabric and function of our "psychic apparatus." That "psychic apparatus" need not be envisaged as Freud did as an organization operating by means *of a mobile psychic energy* and of a separation of an affective quality from its attached idea, the former being erroneously conceived in terms of a displaceable energy possessing a given affective quality.

We all are familiar indeed with what we experience in the course of our daily mental life, that is the frequent and abrupt replacement of a given idea with some other one, none of the two possessing any affective quality, or of the abrupt displacement of a given "Affective formation" by some other "Affective formation," that is of an idea and its attached different affective quality. We are also familiar with the fact we so often allow ourselves to daydream or fantasize even though for brief moments, by means of displacement and replacement of ideas or of "Affective formations" by some other ideas or "Affective formations." In that situation we hardly felt the need to explain our fantasies beyond that of a simple displacement of given ideational formations and attached affective qualities and their replacement by other ideational formations and related quality. Nor have we ever contemplated the need of a separation of our ideational contents from their attached affective qualities, the latter in terms of a released, *qualitative psychic energy*. Even in pathological conditions, the replacement of a thought-process related to reality, by some other thought-process belonging to some distorted psychological reality, could be reduced to a matter of displacements and substitutions of real ideas or "Affective formations" for unreal ideas or unreal Affective formations. It follows that there would be no need also in those conditions to resort to an alleged separation of an idea from its affective quality, the latter erroneously endowed with an energic attribute, and the attachment of the latter to some other fantasized idea.

It seems unfortunate that Freud's followers, who assigned to psychic energy the meaning of a simple metaphorical value on Freud's part, had forgotten that in his early writings Freud had supported not only a specific chemical origin to the sexual energy, but had also considered that "psychic energy" not as a hypothetical quantity, but as an actual force which developed *out of a direct transformation of somatic excitations into psychic excitations*. The mechanics of that transformation were unfortunately not explained by him who thus left to us that explanation. However to state simply as Freud did in his paper *Anxiety Neurosis* that a somatic excitation (a somatic energy) originating in the sexual organs, once it had attained a certain height and had reached the brain, automatically becomes transformed into a psychic energy possessing the same sexual quality of the genital somatic excitations, seems to me a very convenient way out of a difficult situation. I would assume that it would have made Freud's task less difficult had he interposed between the somatic excitations and their translation into psychic excitations the activity *of a newly developed "Psychic function"* along the lines which I have discussed in chapter I, and briefly restated in the preceding pages.

It seems obvious also that when Freud failed to interpose between these two somatic and psychic excitations, the operation of a newly developed "Psychic function" entrusted with the task of translating the various somatic excitations into ideational representations, he naturally failed at the same time to take into consideration the possible fact that the resulting ideas born of that new "Psychic function" must have been activated from then on by the same somatic energy that had presided over the development of that new "Psychic function" and which in turn had presided over the generation of those ideas. Had Freud resorted to the assumption of the existence and operation of a newly developed" Psychic function," he would have had no reason then to resort to a psychic energy being born of an alleged transformation of a somatic energy into a psychic energy intended to activate those ideas, nor to resort to the operation of an alleged instinctual psychic energy.

That such a "psychic energy" could not have been conceived by Freud in hypothetical or metaphorical terms, as maintained by his followers, seems also supported by his own conclusions in his posthumously published *An Outline of Psychoanalysis* (1940)[33] where he assumed *that the uninterrupted somatic processes constitute the essence of what is mental.* By so stating Freud supported not only the somatic nature of the energy that activated those somatic processes, but by implication supported also the somatic nature of the energy that activated *"whatever in the somatic processes constituted the essence of what is mental."* In this last publication, what was essentially mental, seemed to have been reduced by Freud to a special expression of *the somatic processes and related somatic energy* with no mention at all of an operating "psychic energy."

Freud however never retreated from his earliest *"customary psychological abstraction"* that under repression, a separation occurred between a given reprehensible idea, and its energic affective quality, its libido, and proceeded with the development of that psychological abstraction in his paper *Repression* published twenty years later in 1915. By that time Freud had somewhat modified his views of 1895 concerning the *ontogenetic* development of the libido from a direct transformation of the somatic genital excitations into sexual psychic energy, and dealt instead with that sexual energy in terms of the *instinctual energy of the sexual instincts inherited at birth.* It was in reference to that instinctual sexual energy that Freud in that paper referring to the repression *of an instinct-presentation,* by which he understood an idea or group of ideas which is cathected with a definite amount of the mental energy (libido, interest) pertaining to an instinct, stated the following:

> *Now clinical observations forced us to dissect something that hitherto we have conceived as a single unity,* for it shows that besides the idea, there is something else, another presentation of the instinct to be considered, *that this other element undergoes a repression, which may be quite different from that of the idea.*[34] [italics mine]

I consider that statement by Freud that the distinction between the fate of the idea and of its cathecting energy *was forced upon him by clinical observation*, a rather loose way of expression, which incidentally was not uncommon in Freud's writings. Indeed that distinction had already been introduced by Freud in his early writings as a simple conjecture which in 1894 he had designated as a "customary psychological abstraction." Nothing could have prevented Freud from resorting to some other "psychological abstraction" such as for instance the replacement under repression, *of a forbidden instinctual presentation in its entirety by some other instinctual or non-instinctual and not forbidden presentation in its entirety* of idea and quality. No psychological abstraction involving a separation between the idea and its affect need have been considered by Freud *as having been forced upon him by the clinical observation of his patients*. That particular psychological abstraction which he presented and developed from then on, *was the choice* of Freud's own selective thinking.

Evidently unconcerned by those considerations, Freud continued as follows:

> We have adopted the term *"charge of affect"* for this other element in the mental presentation; *it represents the part of the instinct which has become detached from the idea*, and finds proportionate expression according to its quantity in processes which become observable to perception as affect. From this point on, in describing a case of repression we must follow up the fate of the idea which undergoes repression, *from that of the instinctual energy attached to the idea*.[35] [italics mine]

In the first part of that entire statement, Freud having mentioned mental energy not only in terms of interests but also in terms of libido, that is of the sexual mental energy cathecting a given idea, it would seem to me that *by instinct-presentation*, he was actually referring *to the combination of an idea with its energic sexual and mental quality*. In that context, it seems to me that Freud was again quite close to my concept of an "Affective formation" made of an idea and of its related affective quality, the difference being however that I consider that combination *an inseparable one*, and that furthermore I assign the energic attribute not to the "charge of affect" (the affective quality of the idea), but to the idea itself.

Evidently, had Freud assigned the energic attribute to the idea and not to its affective quality, he would have had to revise his basic assumption that an energy possessing a mental affective quality, could detach itself from a given idea and dispose of itself in various other ways. Such a revision which would have destroyed his Libido theory, Freud naturally did not wish to undertake.

Thus, securely entrenched in his belief of the viability of his Libido theory, Freud in 1915 and in 1917, extended the application of that theory of the neuroses to two other pathological conditions, that of "schizophrenia" and that of "Melancholia," and in 1923, to the normal development of the Ego. I will discuss that extension in the two following chapters. For the present I will limit my discussion to Freud's chronological development of repression.

II

A Critique of Freud's Views
on the Developmental Stages of
the Process of Repression

In his paper of 1905, entitled *My Views on the Part Played by Sexuality in the Etiology of the Neuroses*, Freud elaborated upon his concept of repression first introduced in 1894 in terms of a "defense mechanism." Now he referred to that mechanism *as already operating in childhood*. Thus is connection with the sexual excitations of early life, he felt that the important thing was evidently not the stimulation that the person had experienced during childhood but how he reacted to these experiences, with repression or not. Consequently in his view, the sexually mature neurotic regularly carried with him *a fragment of sexual repression from his childhood days*, a fragment which came to expression under the stress imposed upon him by real life.[36] That reference to "fragments of childhood's repression" was Freud's first step in establishing a chronological development of repression, a task which he pursued in his paper of 1911, *A Case of Paranoia*, where he distinguished three developmental stages of repression, that of "fixation," that of "repression proper," and that of "the return of the repressed."

The first stage of "fixation" was, in Freud's opinion of that time, the necessary condition for all repressions. He described "fixation" in the following terms:

> One instinct or instinctual component *fails to accompany the rest* along the anticipated path of development, and in consequence of its inhibition in development, it is left behind at a more infantile stage. The libidinal current in question, then behaves in regard to late psychological structures, as though it belonged to the system of the Unconscious, *as though it was repressed*.[37] [italics mine]

One may already question Freud's attempt at forcing a similarity between "Fixation" in terms of an arrest on the path of development, and inhibition in terms of Repression, a true defense mechanism. An arrest of development may be accounted for by some genetic factor, and if so, need not imply a similarity to Repression. Furthermore the fact that the genetic forces operate outside our awareness, in a descriptive Unconscious so to speak, does not justify their being equated with, or similar to Repression, the mechanism of which operates in the Unconscious as a system.

That Freud may have had second thoughts on this subject seems indicated by the fact that four years later in his paper *Repression* (1915), he returned to that first stage of development of Repression, and laid stress upon what he then called *"Primal Repression,"* but no longer upon "Fixation," which he once had considered as a primary and necessary condition for Repression. In his words:

> Now we have reason for assuming a *"Primal Repression,"* a first phase of Repression, which consists in a denial entry into consciousness to the mental (ideational presentation) of the instinct. This is *accompanied by Fixation*: the ideational presentation in question persists unaltered from then onward, *and the instinct remains attached* to it.[38] [italics mine]

In this statement Freud considered therefore "Fixation" no longer in terms of an original arrest of development, nor of a "primary inhibition," but as what seems to be the corollary of an already operating "Primal Repression" which in turn he considered as being followed by a second developmental stage, that of "Repression proper."

Though clarifying the subject of Fixation, Freud's above statement involved some new ambiguities. First was the fact that in his views in "Primal repression," the ideational representation to be denied entry into Consciousness remained in the Unconscious attached to its "charge of energy" i.e. to its affect, which he now loosely called "instinct." Thus no mention was made in "Primal repression" of a different fate to be assigned to the two portions constituting the "instinct-presentation," once it had been denied entry into Consciousness. This point which does not seem to have been properly considered by Freud seems to me, on the contrary, of great importance in view of his admission that in spite of "Primary repression" the instinct i.e. the charge of affect, remained attached to the idea. By so doing Freud was admitting that following "Primal repression," the combination of an idea and of its attached charge of affect persisted in the Unconscious. Such an intact combination of an idea and related affective quality operating in the Unconscious, a combination which I have called an "Affective formation" could in that light undergo displacement and replacement by some other intact combination without the necessity for that combination to undergo a separation of the idea from its affective quality. Freud's acceptance of the persistence in the Unconscious of the intact combination of an idea and of its attached affect, should have raised in his mind the possibility that by such a statement he was jeopardizing the basis of his own "Libido theory."

Secondly was the fact that Freud having considered "Primal repression" as a denial of entry into consciousness to the ideational representation and attached "charge of affect" of a given "instinctual presentation," he must have implied that at that time, there already was a conflict going on between that instinctual presentation and *some opposing mental agency*. But Freud never discussed the nature of that agency. In fact in Freud's views, "Primal repression" was operating at a time when no differentiation had as yet occurred between the Unconscious and the Preconscious-Conscious system. And yet there must have been some agency operating at the time of the "Primal repression" to prevent the entry into consciousness of that instinctual presentation. And from where could that agency operate if not from the Preconscious-Conscious system itself? But Freud did not say.

Nor did Freud clarify the nature of that agency in his subsequent paper *The Unconscious* (1915) where having returned to this same subject, he simply reiterated that "Primal repression" became operative at a time prior to the development of the Ego inasmuch as at that time the Ego, made of the Cs. and Pcs. systems, had not as yet become differentiated from the Unconscious. In his words: "The withdrawal of preconscious cathexes (from the idea to be repressed) would fail to explain the process of 'Primal repression' for here we have to consider an unconscious idea which as yet, had received no cathexis from the Pcs. and therefore cannot be deprived from it."[39] Unable to make use of ego-cathexes and yet needing a mental agency that presided over the operation of "Primal repression," Freud then devised the convenient but untenable operation of a so-called "Anti-cathexis," *operating at the time of the "Primal repression*," a time at which *no* preconscious or conscious cathexes were as yet operating. Freud resorting to this devise of "Anti-cathexis" did not help clarifying the nature of the mental agency involved in the repressing conflict at the time of the "Primal repression."

The whole concept of Anti-cathexes in their relationship to the Conscious, the Preconscious, and Unconscious systems, is indeed complex and not always clear in Freud's presentation. On the basis of his untenable assumption that under repression a given idea becomes separated from its alleged "charge of affect" because of the withdrawal from the idea of all Pcs.-Cs. cathexes, Freud had also stated that:

> The repressed idea (which has been relegated to the unconscious) remains there without cathexis, or receives cathexis from the Unconscious, or retains in the Unconscious the cathexis which it previously had.[40]

Leaving aside the ambiguity which I have already discussed, of Freud's last portion of that statement that a repressed idea could retain in the Unconscious its own cathexis, an assumption which clashes with his basic one, that following repression a separation occurs between the idea and its alleged charge of affect, and that each separated portion would be subjected to a different fate, Freud stipulated furthermore *that the repressed idea which had retained its own cathexis* or received cathexis from the Unconscious, could renew its attempts at re-entering consciousness. To avoid such continuous attempts of the return of the repressed in consciousness, or to avoid the entry into consciousness of an idea barred from that entry by the "Primal repression," Freud assumed the intervention of some counterforce that could maintain in operation any stage of the repression. That contributory force to the maintenance of repression in all its stages, was assumed by him to be a force which he designated "Anti-cathexis" by means of which the repressed presentation is prevented from freeing itself from Repression.

In the discussion of what constituted Anti-cathexis in the three major neuroses, Freud in his paper *The Unconscious* (1915) stated that in the case of *Anxiety-Hysteria*, the Anti-cathexis was represented by the non-objectionable substitute idea which following Repression had replaced by means of associations in the Unconscious, the objectionable idea and which as substitute was allowed to enter consciousness, where acting as a counterforce secured the maintenance in the Unconscious of the original repressed idea. In this case, Repression *preceded* the development of the "Anti-cathexis."

In *conversion-hysteria*, the repression *preceded* also the development of the "Anti-cathexis," the latter proceeding from the system Cs. and expressing itself in the converted symptoms of motor or sensory innervation, which in that form discharged in the Conscious system the pressure of the repressed idea. It is with the help of those symptoms acting as "Anti-cathexes" that the repressed idea could be retained in the Unconscious.

With reference to the obsessional neurosis, Freud always in his paper *The Unconscious* had stated that: "Here the Anti-cathexis of the system Cs. comes most noticeable in the fore-ground. *It is this that brings about the first repression in the shape of a reaction-formation*, and later it is at this point at which the repressed idea breaks through."[41] In this neurosis, it would seem therefore that the Anti-cathexis precedes evidently the development of Repression.

But Freud in his paper *Repression* published in that same year (1915) seems to have held a different opinion concerning Obsessive neurosis, when having stated that *repression becomes first operative* against the Libido, he subsequently added:

> At first repression is completely successful, the ideational content is rejected and the affect made to disappear. As a substitute formation there arises an alteration of the Ego, an increased sensitiveness of conscience.[42]

Evidently it is that increased sensitiveness of conscience *which having followed the intervention of repression acted now as anti-cathexis.* Hence because it was repression that induced that anti-cathexis, repression preceded the latter's development.

There seems therefore to be a contradiction as far as Obsessive neurosis is concerned, between Freud's views in his paper *The Unconscious* that it was the anti-cathexis of the system Cs. that brought about the first repression, and the view expressed in his paper *Repression* published that same year, that it was repression that brought about the substitute formation of an increased sensitiveness of conscience, which then acted as Anti-cathexis. As a matter of fact, the latter view concerning Obsessive neurosis, was the very original view advanced by Freud on January 1, 1896, in his draft K to his friend Fliess in which he had stated that *it was after Repression* of the recollected memory of an active pleasurable sexual experience of childhood, and its accompanied feeling of self-reproach, that there appeared in consciousness an antithetic symptom i.e. some nuance of conscientiousness, which operated as Anti-cathexis.

But in his paper *Repression*, Freud, after having restated that it was Repression which induced the development of the antithetic formation i.e. of an "increased sensitivity of conscience" along the same line of 1896, now created some confusion when he added: "Repression as it invariably does, has brought about a withdrawal of the libido, but for this purpose made use of a "reaction-formation" by intensifying an antithesis."[43] Thus it would seem that an antithetic process was already operating in the Ego prior to the intervention of Repression, considering that in order for the Ego to withdraw its libido, that is to repress it, *it had to intensify an already existing antithesis*, by making use of a reaction-formation, that is of an already operating Anti-cathexis.

It would seem, therefore, that it was following the establishment and use of *a reaction-formation*, that the Ego could perform its task of Repression which consists in the actual withdrawal by the Ego of its Cs.-Pcs. cathexes from the idea to be repressed. Evidently that view contrasts with Freud's views expressed in the early part of the same paper that it was the Repression that induced the first appearance of an antithesis in terms of "a *nuance of conscientiousness*."

To render matters more confusing, Freud in discussing the same subject in his publication of the same year, 1915, *The Unconscious*, after having stated that the mechanism of Repression is based upon the operation of two processes: 1) Withdrawal of Cs.-Pcs. cathexes, and 2) the operation of Anti-cathexes, he made the following observation: "*It is quite possible that the cathexis withdrawn from the idea is the very one used for anti-cathexis*."[44] [italics mine]. We thus find ourselves plunged again in the difficult evaluation of Freud's contradictory views as to the precedence of Repression over Anti-cathexis or vice versa. It would seem indeed that if the withdrawal of Cs.-Pcs. cathexes which constitutes the essence of Repression, precedes the development of Anti-cathexes, that statement contradicts again the one that Repression in order to operate makes use of a reaction-formation which intensifies an already existing Anti-cathexis.

Before I advance some personal thoughts on this subject of the chronological relationship to one another of the two processes of Repression and Anti-cathexes, I would like to return for a moment to Freud's assumption that in "Primal repression," only the Anti-cathexes were at work, when he stated that: "In Primal repression the anti-cathexis is the sole mechanism operating in it."[45] If this were the case, and if as Freud maintained, at the time of "primal repression," there was not as yet a differentiation between the Cs.—Pcs. systems and the Ucs., from where did the anti-cathexes originate that incited "primal repression"? Evidently not from the Cs.—Pcs. systems.

On this subject also Freud seemed quite contradictory in his presentation. I am referring particularly to his statement that in order to maintain *Repression* proper which he assumed to consist in the withdrawal from a given presentation, of all Cs. and Pcs. cathexes, he felt that we need an additional operating process and that such a process could be found only in the assumption of an anti-cathexis. By that means, the system Pcs. guarded itself against the intrusion of an unconscious idea.[46] By so assuming, Freud felt that in "repression proper," there occurred not only a withdrawal of the Cs.—Pcs. cathexes but also the intervention of anti-cathexes, and that more importantly, such anti-cathexes had become established in the system Pcs.

But, while in that passage Freud was evidently referring only to "repression proper," he strangely enough seemed to have had extended to "Primal repression" the concept of *anti-cathexes established also in the Pcs. system*, when without any explanation he immediately stated the following: "This is which represents the continuous effort demanded by a "Primal repression." The anti-cathexis is the sole mechanism of 'Primal repression.' "[47]

It would seem that at this point Freud must have lost track of his previous statement that "Primal repression" occurred at a time when no differentiation had as yet become established between the Ucs. and the Pcs.-Cs. systems, so that no Cs.-Pcs. cathexes could have become established in the latter systems. How could we now explain such discrepancies in Freud's writings? Could it be that Freud had begun to have some second thoughts over his original assumption of the existence and operation of a "Primal repression" in the terms originally formulated by him?

And now for my own thoughts on this subject of anti-cathexes, thoughts intended to clarify possibly the confusing chronological relationship between them and Repression. In my view all "Anti-cathexes develop only after a differentiation had occurred between the Ucs. and the Cs.-Pcs. systems, so that their first appearance is closely related to the development of a primordial conscious system, a system which contrary to Lipps's and Freud's assumption does not develop from the unconscious system, but constitutes instead, in my view the source from which Freud's Unconscious subsequently developed.

Assuming, therefore, the existence at birth, if not sooner in the course of our intrauterine life, of an already operating conscious system, we can speculate that from very early childhood our elementary Ego is taught to accept whatever guidelines are imparted to it, first by our parents in terms of obedience, and subsequently by teachers, all of whom instill in us moral and religious behavioral precepts.

That code of behavior and thinking which we are taught and which we accept, constitutes in my opinion the first defensive armor bestowed upon us and intended to protect us from any opposing influence to its effectiveness. The elements of that first code I consider as constituting the first and "primal" Anti-cathexes, which become operative as soon as conflictual situations develop between us and our own impulses and our environment. It is because of the existence of such "Primal anti-cathexes" that Repression is subsequently allowed to operate in terms of a voluntary rejection of thoughts or impulses which clash with our first learned and accepted code of beliefs and behavior.

Following repeated experiences of voluntary repressions, there presumably develops in us what Freud considered "an Alteration of the Ego" in terms of *an increased sensitivity of conscience*, and which from then on, constitutes a source of additional Anti-cathexes which reinforce the earlier group of the learned behavioral Anti-cathexes. To these two groups, the first imparted to us in the course of our early upbringing, and the second derived from the operation of repeated Repressions, other Anti-cathexes are subsequently added in the form of the various substitute formations which operate as symptoms in the course of a neurosis, and as such contribute to the maintenance of Repression. In that context some Anti-cathexes precede, while some others follow the intervention of Repression. Such a chronological approach to the development of Anti-cathexes would accommodate both the concept of Anti-cathexes preceding Repression, and that of Repression leading to the development of new Anti-cathexes. My assumptions on this subject would have no relation to the assumption of "Primal repression" in the terms formulated originally by Freud, that is operating at a time when no differentiation had as yet occurred between the Ucs. and the Cs.-Pcs. systems, and which assumption I consider to be an erroneous one.

One wonders why Freud in 1915 had introduced his new assumption of the operation of a "Primal repression" as the first developmental stage of "Repression proper?" Was it because he wished now to establish the importance of a previous "Primal repression" as a force which in the Unconscious exercises the important task of attracting whatever material has to undergo a subsequent "Repression

59

proper?" This may have been his intention in the light of his subsequent statement that:

> It is a mistake to emphasize only the rejection which operates from the side of consciousness, upon what is to be repressed. We have to consider just as such the *attraction exercised by what was originally repressed*, upon everything with which it can establish connection. Probably the tendency to repression would fail of its purpose, if there were not something previously repressed, if these forces did not cooperate, ready to assimilate that which is rejected from consciousness.[48]

If this were the case, why couldn't Freud have assigned that power of attraction to all sorts of actually early *Repressions proper* which occurred in early childhood at the earlier levels of the Ego's development, not differently from what occurred subsequently in later life? Had he done that, he would have had no need to resort to the obscure assumption of "Primal repressions" operating allegedly at a time prior to the differentiation of the Cs.-Pcs. systems from the Ucs, an assumption which he subsequently compromised when he referred to the Anti-cathexes of "Primal repression" as having been established in the Pcs. system.

My having returned to the discussion of Freud's earlier assumption of a "Primal repression" seems justified by the fact that following his two papers on *Repression* and *The Unconscious*, Freud seemed to have lost track of his earlier views on "Primal repression" which *he unconspicuously let fade away* by actually replacing them as he should have done earlier, with the simpler and more logical concept of *"earlier repressions of childhood,"* the dynamic of which does not differ from that of "Repression proper."

Strangely, however, that important change was never openly heralded by Freud, and was instead introduced by him, in a so to speak surreptitious manner, which avoided him the necessity to openly reject his earlier views of "Primal repression" introduced in 1915. A first inkling of Freud's views came eleven years later in his publication *Inhibitions Symptoms and Anxiety* (1926) where he stated that:

> Far too little is known as yet about the background and preliminary stages of Repression. There is a danger of overestimating the part played in repression by the Superego. We cannot at the present say whether it is the emergence of the Superego which provides the line of demarcation between *Primal repression* and after-expulsion (Repression proper). At any rate the earliest outbreaks of Anxiety which are of a very

intense kind, occur before the Superego had been differentiated.[49]

In this statement, Freud indicated his hesitancy in establishing
a line of demarcation between the "Primal repression" and Repression proper, based upon the development of the Superego. But that
question had never been raised before by him, inasmuch as he had
related "Primal repression" to a period of life, when not only the
Superego, but also the Cs.-Pcs. Ego had not as yet become differentiated. Of course if an Ego had not as yet become operative at the
time of "Primal repression," anxiety could not have developed and
Repression could not have taken place at all. If then anxiety was
necessary for the development of the earlier repressions of childhood,
which Freud *still continued ambiguously* to call "Primal repression,"
those earlier repressions of childhood could not be differentiated in
their mechanism of production from the later Repressions of life,
both being triggered by Anxiety.

It was still without any reference to his rejection of his early assumption of a "Primal repression" construed in the obscure terms of
1915, that Freud returned on this subject of the early repressions of
childhood in 1932 in his *New Introductory Lectures* where he concluded that:

> It is only the later repressions that exhibit the mechanism we
> have described, in which anxiety is awakened as a signal of
> an earlier situation of danger. *The first and original repres-
> sions arise directly from traumatic moments* when the Ego
> meets with an excessively great libidinal demand. They con-
> struct their anxiety afresh, although it is true on the model of
> the birth.[50] [italics mine]

At this point, Freud was no longer referring to "Primal repression" in his original concept, but only to *the earlier repressions of
childhood*," at which time the Ego already differentiated was faced
with an excessive amount of instinctual demands which it could not
negotiate, thus constituting a "traumatic situation" which automatically triggered off Anxiety and its subsequent Repression. Yet it is
only by inference that one could have seized Freud's rejection of his
earlier assumption of a "Primal repression" and its being replaced
by the new concept of the first and original repressions of childhood,
which differed from the repressions of later life, only on the ground
that in the latter, Anxiety was not automatically generated by the
presence of danger, but released so to speak voluntarily by the Ego

who remembered previous analogous situations and from which danger could now be anticipated.

Freud's tacit abandonment of his earlier assumption of a "Primal repression" was picked up by Ch. Brenner in his paper *Repression in Freud's writings* (1957) where he concluded that at a certain point *Freud must have abandoned his original position on "Primal repression"* and that:

> His eventual view about infantile or primal repression and its causes and mechanisms, were not essentially different from those of repression in later life. However Anxiety was typically produced on an economic or quantitative basis, while in later life Anxiety was typically of the signal variety.[51]

Brenner, however, could only assume that Freud had actually abandoned his original position on "Primal repression," but did not refer to any particular passage where Freud had openly acknowledged his rejection of "Primal repression."

In the meantime the entire question of the developmental stages of Repression had become again confused by Freud's other statement that:

> Before the mental organization reaches the stage of sharp distinction between what is conscious and what is unconscious the other vicissitudes which may befall instincts e.g. reversal into the opposite, or turning round upon the subject, deal with the task of mastering impulses.

These various vicissitudes of the instincts including Regression, were later accepted to be genuine instinctual processes and labeled "defence mechanisms" by Anna Freud in her book *The Ego and the Mechanisms of Defence*[52] (1936).

Considering that "Primary repression" took also place, in Freud's view, at a time when no differentiation had as yet occurred between the Unconscious and the Conscious, could it be that Freud had originally considered "Primal repression" also as a genuine instinctual process, though he never referred to it as "a vicissitude of the instincts." I found no elaboration of this particular point in Freud's subsequent writings, before or after he had abandoned his views on the existence and operation of a "Primal Repression." In the next chapter, I will discuss the controversial relationship of "Regression," one of the alleged instinctual processes of Defense, to Repression itself.

III

CONTRASTING INTERPRETATION BY FREUD'S FOLLOWERS
OF HIS ORIGINAL VIEWS OF THE CONSCIOUS NATURE
OF REPRESSION

Let me go back to Freud's original views on the development of repression presented in his first paper *The Defence Neuro-psychoses* (1894). In that paper Freud considered inhibition, which he later called repression, *as being voluntarily induced by his patients* and therefore operating at a conscious level. Referring to the group of hysterics cataloged under the heading of "Defence-hysteria," Freud remarked that these patients enjoyed mental health up to the time at which an intolerable idea presented itself, or an intolerable experience occurred, the corresponding affect of which was so unpleasant that the patient resolved for forget it. In that paper he did not state that repression was induced unconsciously, but on the contrary he underscored in no uncertain terms the voluntary motivation of the repression when he emphasized the fact that these patients had enjoyed good mental health up to that time at which an intolerable idea presented itself, an idea, a feeling arousing an affect so painful that the person resolved to forget, considering that such unbearable ideas developed in women chiefly in connection with sexual experiences and sensations. In this connection Freud added:

> *The patients can recollect with the most satisfactory minuteness their efforts at defence, their resolution to push the thing out, not to think of it. . . .* In at least a number of cases the patient themselves will inform us of the fact that the phobia or obsession made its appearance, *after this effort of will had apparently succeeded in its aim.*[53] [italics mine]

I must also recall Freud's statement of 1915 in his paper *Repression* which I have already quoted, that in considering repression, "It would be a mistake *to emphasize only the rejection which operates from the side of Consciousness upon what is to be repressed.*[54] (italics mine) It was thus evident that in 1915 the rejection in question, i.e., the repression, was in Freud's view initiated by the conscious system.

But in his earlier second paper of 1896, *Further Remarks on the Defence Neuro-psychoses*, Freud had used for the first time in parenthesis the word "Unconscious," in connection with repression in hysteria, obsessive neurosis, and paranoia:

> One point of view showed itself as applying in common to all
> these affections: their symptoms arise through the
> mechanism of (*Unconscious*) defence that is through an at-
> tempt to repress an intolerable idea, which was in painful op-
> position to the patient's Ego.[55] [italics mine]

The inclusion of the word "Unconscious" in parenthesis was interpreted by many of Freud's followers as meaning that Repression
was an entirely unconscious process *in its motivation, initiation, and
execution.* In my view, the execution of Repression may well take
place ultimately by means of psychological or otherwise processes
which operate outside our awareness, *but its motivation and initiation* are always in my estimation conscious voluntary processes, at
the time of the first repression.

That Freud in the above quotation must have referred only to
"Unconscious" in terms of *mechanisms of execution of the Repression,
and not to its motivation and initiation*, is supported by his reference
to the initial voluntary phase of Repression, when he stated:

> Between the patient's efforts of will, which successfully rep-
> resses the intolerable sexual idea, and the appearance of the
> obsessional idea, there is a gap which the theory here de-
> veloped, aims at filling in. The detachment of the sexual idea
> from its affect, and the connection of the latter with another
> idea . . . are processes which occur outside consciousness.[56]

Furthermore, in his subsequent paper *Repression* (1915), Freud
returned to the subject of the voluntary initiation of Repression,
when in connection with the product of free associations he stated
that:

> We then observe that the patient can go on spinning a whole
> chain of such associations, till he is brought up in the midst of
> them, against some thought-formation, the relation of which
> to what is repressed acts so intensely, *that he is compelled to
> repeat his attempt at Repression.*[57] [italics mine]

And again in discussing the formation of an unrepressed derivative
out of the repressed material he added:

> It is an every day occurrence that such a derivative can re-
> main unrepressed so long as it represents only a small
> amount of energy, although its content is of such nature as to
> give rise to a conflict *with conscious control.* . . . As soon as an

idea which is fundamentally offensive exceeds a certain degree of strength, the conflict takes on actuality, and it is precisely the activation of the idea that leads to its repression.[58]

And in his *New Introductory Lectures* (1933), Freud returning to the subject of repression, spoke of the function of the Ego in that process. We have said what the Ego does: "it makes use of experimental cathexes the process of thinking) and starts up the pleasure-unpleasure automatism by means of a signal of anxiety.[59] Finally I must recall Freud's statement in his paper *Repression* (1915), where he spoke of Repression as "an operation of rejection on the part of consciousness."[60] In all these statements it seems clear that Freud considered *motivation and initiation* of Repression as the expression and function of a voluntary process.

Yet, in spite of those statements, Freud followers seem to have interpreted his views in the sense that Repression was not only executed, *but also motivated and initiated* in the Unconscious. Thus for instance, Otto Fenichel in *The Psychoanalytic Theory of the Neuroses*, described Repression as: *"An unconsciously purposeful forgetting or not becoming aware* of internal or external events which as a rule represent possible temptations or punishments for, or mere allusions to objectionable instinctual demands."[61] And Ernest Glover who in his *Psychoanalysis* (1939), speaking of Repression as a withdrawal of energy stated that: "The withdrawal is effected by the deeper Unconscious part of the Ego."[62] Less dogmatic on this subject is Charles Brenner who accepts the fact that Repression may be also voluntarily initiated by the Ego though that instance is according to him referred to as *"Suppression."* In his estimation:

> It is more than likely that there are intermediates between suppression and repression, and that it may even be that there is no truly sharp line between suppression and repression, and it may even be that there are intermediates between suppression and repression. However when we use the word Repression we mean that the barring from consciousness, and the erection of a durable anti-cathexis have taken place unconsciously.[63]

The fact remains however that because of Brenner's reference to the absence of that line of demarcation, the *motivation and initiation*, not only of Repression, but also of Suppression could also take place in the Unconscious. In that case Suppression would lose its main differential characteristic.

In my opinion, *all repressions* at their first formulation are motivated and initiate voluntarily by a conscious Ego operating at various stages of its development from childhood to adulthood. It is only following that initial voluntary phase which represents the repeated voluntary efforts and the duration of which varies greatly, that Repression becomes stabilized, at first through *repetitive* and ultimately through the unconscious mechanism of *conditioning.*

Before closing this chapter on Repression, it might be interesting to recall some pertinent remarks by Freud, which seem to indicate that in his writings, he became quite vacillating at times on the subject of his own very important assumption that in Repression, a separation of an idea, or ideational representation of an impulse, from its activating sexual energy does take place.

Let me begin with what Freud, later on in his paper of 1915, considered to be the function of Repression upon what he had called "an instinct-presentation." In Freud's words by that term *"instinct-presentation,"* he understood an idea or group of ideas, which is cathected "by a definite amount of the mental energy (Libido-Interest) pertaining to an instinct."[64] To this passage I would offer the following comments: Because Freud referred to mental energy also in terms of Libido as the cathecting energy of an idea or group of ideas, in other words of a sexual energy attached to those ideas, it had seemed to me that by "instinct-presentation," Freud was referring also to an idea attached *to its instinctual energic sexual quality.* In that light it seemed to me that Freud in spite of his support that: "in describing a case of Repression, we must follow up the fate of the idea which undergoes repression, *from that of the instinctual energy attached to the idea,"* he had come pretty near to *my concept of an "affective formation"* which I had conceived as the combination of an idea and of its attached affective sexual quality, irrespective of the origin of the latter, ontogenetic or instinctual. My views differed also from those of Freud in that I considered that the combination of an idea attached to its affective sexual quality constitutes *an inseparable unit,* whereas in Freud's original views (1894), the sexual affective quality of an idea possessed itself *an energic attribute* which allowed it to become detached from the idea. Also in my view, that instinct-presentation is activated by *the energy of the idea itself* and not by that of its quality.

Unfortunately, my impression that at a certain moment Freud may have envisaged also the possibility that an idea attached to its related affective quality constituted also an indivisible unit along the lines of my "affective formation" was short-lived, because in his subsequent writings, Freud never altered his original basic assumption that under repression a separation of an idea from its energic qualifying quality actually occurred. Instead he pursued his own assumption, applied it to the development not only of the neuroses, but to the development of other important pathological conditions such as Schizophrenia and Melancholia, and subsequently extended it to the development of the normal Ego by means of Identification.

However, having put my mind at rest on this subject of how I differed from Freud's point of view, I later found reasons for revamping my earlier impression that Freud in 1915 had possibly with his term "Instinct presentation" come near to my concept of an "affective formation" made of the indivisible combination of an idea and of its attached affective quality. That revamping of the above earlier impression was prompted by the reading of Freud's *Autobiography* copyrighted in 1935 and again copyrighted in 1952 by W. W. Norton under the title: *An Autobiographical Study*. In Section III dealing in part with the problem of Repression, a section published forty-one years after he had introduced his "psychological abstraction" that under repression, there occurs a separation between the idea to be repressed and its attached cathecting Libido, an abstraction upon which he had subsequently founded his "Libido theory." *Freud seemed to have all of a sudden soft-pedaled that abstraction.* Indeed in his *Autobiography*, he seemed to have referred to Repression *as a mechanism which affected an impulse and its activating sexual energy, the Libido, as a unit*, with no particular mention of the separation of the idea from its attached sexual energy.

I have received that renewed impression from a long passage which I consider important to quote, inasmuch as in it, Freud was dealing with the conflict existing between two dynamic quantities; the instinct and the Ego's resistances. According to him:

> In normal cases, these two quantities, let us call them the instincts and the resistances, would struggle with each other for some time, in the fullest light of consciousness, until the instinct was repudiated and the charge of energy withdrawn from it. This would have been the normal solution.[65]

But in pathological cases, things according to Freud are quite different. In his words:

> In a neurosis however (for reasons still unknown) the conflict

found a different outcome. The Ego drew back, as it were, after the first shock of its conflict with the objectionable impulse; it debarred the impulse from access to consciousness and to direct motor discharge.

At this point it again occurred to me that by the word *impulse*, Freud must have meant what in 1915 he had called an "instinct presentation" made up of an "idea cathected with a definite amount of the mental energy, the Libido pertaining to it. Now Freud continued: *"But at the same time the impulse retained its full charge of energy."*[66] Freud furthermore added: "I named that process Repression."[67]

It would seem to me that if the ideational portion of the instinctual presentation, and which now Freud called "the impulse" retained after Repression, its own charge of affect as a unit, that view amounts in my estimation to my own concept of an "affective formation" made up of an idea and of its inseparable affective quality.

Then Freud continued:

> It was obviously a primary mechanism of defence, comparable to an attempt at flight, and was only a forerunner of the later developed normal condemning judgement. The first act of repression involved further consequences. In the first place the Ego was obliged to protect itself against the constant threat of a renewed advance on the part of the repressed impulse, by making a permanent expenditure of energy, a counter-charge, an anti-cathexis, and it thus impoverished itself. On the other hand the repressed impulse [idea and energy] which now was unconscious was able to find means of discharge and of substitute gratification by circuitous routes which were nevertheless distorted and deflected from their aim owing to the resistance of the Ego.

Here seems the appropriate point to remark that notwithstanding Repression, "the instinct-presentation" as intended by Freud, as made up of an idea and of its cathecting sexual energy, constituted still a unit in the Unconscious. No reason was given as to why that unit should become separated so as to liberate the sexual cathecting energy. It is at this point, therefore, that a substitute concept to the mobility of an alleged sexual quality endowed with its special energy, should have been entertained and replaced by that of the mobility of an "affective formation" in its entirety of idea and affective quality, under the energic power of the idea itself and not of its quality.

And yet in his *Autobiography*, Freud seemed to state now that the Ego having disbarred from consciousness the objectionable impulse and related attached "charge of affect," that impulse (Freud's instinct-presentation) retained in the unconscious its full charge of quantitative and qualitative energy, and constantly threatened to reenter consciousness. There was no mention in that passage of the separation of the "charge of affect" from the reprehensible idea of the impulse or "instinct-presentation," but on the contrary a reference to the renewed effort of the repressed impulse *in its entirety of idea and qualitative energy* (Freud's instinct-presentation) to reenter consciousness. Furthermore Freud referred to Conversion hysteria as the result of the instinctual presentation in its entirety, having found through a circuitous route, its discharge along the nerve-supply of the body. No special mention was reiterated of a separation of the instinct-presentation of the impulse, the ideational representation, from its related attached sexual energy.

In those terms, it may seem that Freud in his *Autobiography* may have come very close to consider his "instinct-presentation" in terms of what I have considered an "affective formation," made up of an inseparable combination of an idea and of its affective quality. So that when he spoke of a breakthrough of the objectionable instinct-presentation and related full charge of affect, which both had been retained in the Unconscious, he must not have been far away from contemplating a "displacement" of the instinct-presentation in its entirety of ideas or group of ideas and related attached cathecting sexual energy, in terms of my "affective formation" and of its replacement by some other non-objectionable "Affective formation," which as such could break through in Consciousness.

What should we conclude from all these considerations? Could it be that Freud in his *Autobiographical Study*, first published in 1935 may have realized, three years prior to his death, the enormity of his erroneous original assumption that under Repression a separation occurred between the ideational portion of an "instinct-presentation" made of idea and attached cathecting "charge of affect," and of his erroneous assumption of a different fate destined to each one of those components? And could it be possible that in a subtle way, Freud was advancing a substitute assumption, that of the displacement of an instinct-presentation in its entirety of an idea and related full affective quality and the replacement of that combination by some other combination made of a new ideational presentation and related full affective quality? And if that had been the case, could it be that Freud may not have at that time weighed properly the destructive blow which, by that presumed substitutive assumption, he himself would be inflicting to his own "Libido theory?"

Chapter III

Regression

I. Freud's unsubstantiated assumption of two different types of Regression: "the Regression of the Ego" and "The Regression of the Libido."
II. Freud's unsubstantiated assumption that "Identification" results from the regression into the Ego of the Libido alone, in terms of a qualitative sexual energy.

I

Regression, a most important psychodynamic mechanism which Freud utilized ultimately in dealing with the normal and pathological development of the Ego, was first introduced by him in 1900 in his publication *The Interpretation of Dreams* in a subdivision of chapter VII. In it Freud presented us with a schematic linear diagram of our Psychic apparatus. In which the sensory perception system was placed on the left side of the line, and the motor system, controlled by the Ego, on its right, the two extreme systems being separated by the system Unconscious.

He also assumed that the perceptual excitations that were received during the waking state, proceeded from the left (Perceptual system) and were directed towards the right, where they could result in some motor action, thanks to the flow of the directional current from the perceptual end of the Psychic apparatus towards its motor end. At night, the flow of that current according to Freud's diagram, ceased to operate in that established direction, and thus left unopposed the flow of excitations which were directed in the opposite direction, that is from the motor to the perceptual end. On that basis, Freud explained the formation of hallucinatory dreams.

70

The only way in which we can describe what happens in hallucinatory dreams, is by saying that the excitation moves in a backward direction. Instead of being transmitted to the motor end of the apparatus, it moves towards the sensory end, and finally reaches the perceptual system. If we describe as progressive the direction taken by the psychical process arising from the Unconscious during waking life, then we may speak of dreams as having *a regressive character*.[1]

In another passage, Freud stated that this psychological process of regression occurred, not only in dreams, but also in the course of normal mental activities in our daily life, in terms of recollections:

Intentional recollection and other constituent processes of our normal thinking, *involve a retrogressive movement in the psychical apparatus, from a complex ideational act to the raw material of the memory-traces underlying it....I believe the name Regression* is of help to us, insofar as it connects a fact that was already known to us, with our schematic picture, in which the mental apparatus was given a sense of direction.[2]

In a subsequent passage, Freud extended the application of the word regression *to what occurs in the waking state of some pathological cases*, where regression occurs in spite of a sensory current flowing without interruption in a forward direction. In explaining the hallucinations in hysteria and paranoia and of visions in normally mental subjects, Freud felt that they are in fact regressions, that is, thoughts transformed into images. He indicated, however, that the only thoughts that undergo this transformation are those which are intimately linked with memories that have been suppressed or have remained unconscious.[3]

In a further reference to suppression in the psychoneuroses, Freud confirmed that view when he stated that:

For evidence in such instances of the regressive transformation of thoughts, we must not overlook the influence of memories mostly from childhood which have been suppressed, or have remained unconscious. The thoughts which are connected with memory of this kind, and which *are forbidden expression by the censorship*, are as it were attracted by the memory into regression, as being the form of representation in which the memory itself is couched.[4] [italics mine]

It would seem that in that passage, Freud had used as interchangeable the meaning of the words "suppression" and "repression."

Thus, in 1900, Freud having considered that *intentional recollec-*

tion in the course of our normal thinking processes, that is in the course of our normal health, involved *a regression* in the sense of a harking back of a thought-process to its underlying memory-traces, he did not at that time relate however that regression to any prior suppression or repression. On the other hand in pathological conditions such as that of neuroses, regression was linked by him, with earlier memories that had been suppressed or repressed. In the latter cases, Freud had therefore assumed that regression would occur only if repression or suppression had been exercised sometime in the patient's past. In that context, in pathological conditions, which are the ones in which we are interested, Freud meant to emphasize the point that *Repression does precede chronologically the intervention of Regression.*

That Regression in the case of pathological conditions was considered by Freud as following the operation in the past of some repression, that is of some opposing force, was expressed by him in this other passage:

> We have put forward the view that in all probability this regression whenever it may occur, *is an effort of the resistance opposing the progress in consciousness*, of a thought along the normal path *and of a simultaneous attraction* upon the thought by the presence of memory-traces.[5]

Freud did not elaborate at that time on the nature of the mental structure which offered that resistance. It was only in his subsequent writings that he spoke of resistances emanating from the Ego, a great portion of which in his views operated in the Unconscious.

Up to this point, it would seem therefore that in Regression as a whole and especially in that of "intentional recollection," Freud was dealing only with what he subsequently called *"The Regression of the Ego,"* meaning the harking back of thought processes to the raw material of memory-traces underlying them, an operation intentionally undertaken by the Ego itself.

But in 1905 when Freud introduced his *Three Theories on Sexuality*, he approached the subject of Regression from an entirely new angle, that of "The Regression of the Libido," a new process which he added to that of "The Regression of the Ego." By *"Regression of the Libido,"* he now meant two different processes: I) *The harking back of the sexual organization to any one of its formative stages.* That Regression of the Libido differed vastly from the Regression of the Ego inasmuch as it involved the Regression of the sexual organization, which was not controlled by the Ego, but was constitutionally determined, each stage of it following the other, as the permanent tooth follows the milk-tooth. It is in those terms that Freud introduced for the first time his assumption of "The Regression of the Libido" an assumption which I consider erroneous, as I will discuss later on.

II) The other process involved in Freud's assumption of a "Regression of the Libido" was that of the regression into the Ego *of only the Libido in terms of a sexual energy* i.e. of a sexual charge of affect, once that Libido following Repression had become separated from a given person which it had abandoned. Of course that process was a corollary of Freud's previous erroneous assumption that because of Repression, a separation occurs between the idea to be repressed, and its charge of sexual energy (Libido) which was then free to attach itself to some other idea or discharge itself in some other independent fashion.

I have discussed at length in chapters I and II the untenability of that assumption of a separation of an idea from its alleged affective energy considering that in my view, once an idea has acquired its related affective quality, sexual or not, it constitutes with it, a combination which cannot undergo separation, but can be replaced in its entirety by some other combination of idea and quality. That indivisible combination I have called an *"Affective formation."* On that basis, I could not subscribe to that other concept of Freud of a "Regression of the libido" as meaning the regression alone of the Libido alone in terms of an affective quality possessing an alleged energic attribute. In other words I could not subscribe to his assumption of a separation of a quality in terms of a "sexual charge" from its related idea.

That Freud referred to the "Regression of the Libido" in the actual terms of a Regression *of the sexual energy alone*, was evidenced by the following passage in his *Three Essays on the Theory of Sexuality* (1905). When speaking of the Libido withdrawn from a sexual object and on its regressive course into the Ego, he added that: "When it is withdrawn from the object, *it is held in suspension in peculiar conditions of tension, and is finally drawn into the Ego* so that it becomes Ego-libido again."[6]

Assuming that my objections to Freud's meaning of the *"Regression of the Libido" in both the terms of a Regression of the sexual or-*

ganization, or of that of the Regression of the sexual energy alone into the Ego, are accepted as valid, I would propose that these two meanings of the "Regression of the Libido" be replaced by the same single designation of "Regression of the Ego," in the terms of what Freud himself had construed in 1900, that is of the harking back of the Ego's thought-processes to their underlying memory-traces i.e. of "the Regression of the Ego," the only understandable mechanism of Regression.

My proposition is based upon the point that instead of referring to the assumption of a Regression of a sexual organization *constitutionally determined and therefore outside the governing control of the Ego,* we should refer to the more plausible assumption that, whenever faced with an objectionable or dangerous sexual idea, independently of the time at which the idea presents itself, the Ego need only *to resort to an intentional recollection of some underlying memory-trace of some analogous dangerous situation which had occurred at any previous period of the past, and independently from any alleged constitutional stage of development of the sexual organization.* That recollection can evidently be governed by the Ego. But the Ego has no controlling power over the Regression of its sexual organization at any one of its constitutionally determined stages.

Once that intentional recollection on the part of the Ego has taken place, the Ego can now resort to *Repression* as a defense against any similar objectionable situation of the past, and which now presents itself again. In that context, the Ego's intentional harking back to underlying memory-traces should be justifiably called "Regression of the *Ego*" and not "Regression of the Libido."

If now one subscribes also to my view that an ideational presentation, once it had acquired a sexual quality, constitutes with it a single unit an "affective formation" which cannot undergo separation, but is capable of displacement and replacement in its entirety, by some other "Affective formation," one could find another reason for *not accepting* Freud's assumption of the separation of the Libido in terms of a "sexual energy" from its attached idea, and its Regression into the Ego. Consequently the meaning of "Regression of the Libido" in terms of the Regression of the sexual energy *alone into the Ego,* would have to be also rejected.

But Freud did not seem inclined to resort to any other alternative than that of establishing two different types of Regression, that of the Ego and that of the Libido. He consequently continued to apply his concept of the "Regression of the Libido" in its special meaning and which he distinguished from the "Regression of the

Ego." In a subsequent paper *"Predisposition to Obsessive Neurosis"* (1913), Freud in fact returned to the concept of the "Regression of the Libido" in the terms again of the regression of the sexual organization to some of its prior formative stages. In that same paper, he considered not only the development of the Obsessive neurosis, but also the normal development of *the ego's character formation*, particularly in the female, in terms of the "regression of the libido" in its meaning of a regression of the "sexual organization" to *its earlier formative anal sadistic stage.*

Referring to the ego's character formation of the female, Freud wrote in fact that:

> It is well known and has been a matter for much complaint that women often alter strangely in character after they have abandoned their genital functions. They become quarrelsome, peevish and argumentative, petty and miserly; in fact they display sadistic and anal-erotic traits which were not theirs in the era of their womanliness. Writers and satirists have in all ages launched their invectives against the old termagant into which the sweeten maiden, the loving woman, the tender mother has deteriorated. This metamorphosis corresponds, as can be seen, *with a regression of sexual life to the pre-genital anal-sadistic level*, the one in which we have found the predisposition to Obsessional neurosis."[7]

In his subsequent paper, *Repression* (1915), Freud referring again to Obsessive neurosis, reiterated his views of 1913 in the new statement that this neurosis was based upon the *"Regression of the Libido"* in terms of the Regression *of the sexual organization to its prior anal-sadistic stage of development.* He then amplified his views by adding that in this neurosis:

> We are first in doubt as to what it is that we have to regard as the repressed instinctual presentation, a libidinal or a hostile trend. This uncertainty arises because the Obsessive neurosis *rests on the premise of a regression by means of which a sadistic trend has been substituted for a tender one. It is this hostile impulse against a loved person, which has undergone repression.*[8] [italics mine]

In other words Repression operated only after the sexual organization of the Libido had regressed to its earlier anal-sadistic stage of development.

In that context, it would seem that Freud had overlooked his statement of 1900 in his *Interpretation of Dreams* that *in pathologi-*

cal conditions, Regression takes effect *only* if a previous Repression had occurred, so that at that time the chronology for the development of Regression was Repression first and Regression next. But now in 1915 having made no mention of previous Repression, he considered Regression first and then Repression. Nor had Freud at this point altered his designation of the Regression occurring in Obsessive neurosis by naming it "Regression of the Ego" which on the basis of my previous considerations on this subject should have been more appropriately designated than that of "Regression of the Libido."

In the meantime, in 1914, in a paragraph added to page 548 of *The Interpretation of Dreams*, Freud amplified his views of "Regression" in general, be it in the course of dreams, or in the course of a psychoneurosis. Without any specific reference to the "Regression of the Ego" or of "the Libido," Freud in that paragraph distinguished three kinds of Regression: *the Topographical Regression, the Temporal Regression, and the Formal Regression*, the latter referring to the primitive methods of expression and representation.[9] In his subsequent paper *A Metapsychological Supplement to the Theory of Dreams* (1916), Freud then stated that in the Psychoneuroses, it was the *Temporal type of Regression* which was operative:

> When we investigate psychoneurotic conditions we find in each of them, occasion to comment upon a so-called *"Temporal Regression"* i.e. the particular extent to which each of them retraces the stages of its evolution. We distinguish two such regressions—*one in the development of the Ego, and the other in that of the Libido*.[10] [italics mine]

In the absence of any specification on Freud's part, it would seem that in the Psychoneuroses, "Temporal Regression" could refer to either a "Regression of the Ego" or to the "Regression of the Libido." Considering however that both types of Temporal Regression could in my opinion involve the simple process of a harking back of the Ego to underlying memory-traces, *that is to a recollection*, be it intentional or not, of past experiences and feelings, be they sexual or not, I fail to see why *both types of Temporal Regression*, could not have been designated by Freud as simply "Regression of the Ego."

What is retrievable are the underlying memory-traces and feelings related to some past experience at whatever temporal period of life it had occurred. That temporal recollection of underlying memory-traces *need not be arbitrarily identified* with any of the alleged stages of the sexual development, which stages are according to Freud constitutionally determined and are therefore independent from any participation of the Ego to that determination. These constitutionally determined stages cannot therefore be reformulated at will, but events occurring at any period of past life, but not related to genetically constituted stages, can be recollected and relived by means of memory-traces. Hence it would be erroneous to designate as "Regression of the Libido" that process of *the harking back of thought-processes, to their underlying memory-traces*, a harking back which should be more appropriately called "Regression of the Ego."

That Freud himself, at a certain point of his investigation of the neuroses, seems to have dealt with Regression in general, without any distinction between the "Regression of the Ego" and the "Regression of the Libido" seems supported by the following passage in his *History of the Psychoanalytic Movement* (1914):

> We let the patient's attention to the traumatic scene in which the symptoms had arisen, endeavored to find the mental conflict inherent in it, and to release the suppressed affect. In the course of this we discovered the mental process so characteristic of the neuroses which I later named *Regression*. The patient's associations led back from the scene which one was trying to elucidate, *to earlier experiences* and compel the analysis which had to correct the present to occupy itself with the past. The regression led constantly further backwards; at first it seemed to bring us regularly to puberty; later on, failures and points which still awaited explanation, beckoned the analytic work still further back into years of childhood which had hitherto been inaccessible to any kind of exploration. *This regressing trend became an important character of analysis.* It appeared that psychoanalysis could explain nothing without referring back to something past; more, that every pathogenic experience implied a previous one, which though in itself not pathogenic, had yet endowed the latter with its pathogenic quality.[11] [italics mine]

Having made no distinction between the "Regression of the Ego" and that of the "Libido" in that passage, it would seem that such a matter was of little concern to Freud, as long as the principle involved was that of the harking back of a given thought-process to its underlying memory-traces. But this is what constitutes precisely a "Regression of the Ego," be it spontaneously induced or by questioning in the course of a psychoanalytic session. Its designation as "Regression of the Libido" referable to the Regression of the sexual organization constitutionally determined, to any one of its formative stages, an entirely different frame of reference, would have been in my opinion entirely unjustified. It follows that Freud in that *History of the Psychoanalytic Movement* when he discussed the important regressive character of analysis, he was referring only to the "Regression of the ego." The "Regression of the Libido" in the two meanings assigned to it by Freud, did not seem to deserve any special mention in that history.

In reference to his subsequent assumption of the "Regression of the Libido" in terms of the Regression of the sexual organization to one of its formative stages of development, Freud, as I have already stated, had already implied in 1905 "Regression of the Libido" in terms of a movable sexual energy alone, when referring to it he wrote that such a Libido: "When withdrawn from an object, it is held in suspension in peculiar conditions of tension, and finally withdrawn into the Ego."[12] It was on that basis that Freud in 1915 revamped his assumption of 1905 concerning the Regression of the sexual energy *alone* into the Ego and applied it to the pathological condition of Schizophrenia. Two years later (1917), he extended the application of that same concept of the Regression of the Libido in terms of the sexual energy alone to another important pathological condition, that of "Melancholia."

Concerning schizophrenia, a narcissistic condition, Freud differentiated it from the transference neuroses by pointing out that in the latter following the abandonment of the real object due to Repression: "The Libido withdrawn from the real object reverted first to "an object in phantasy, and then to one that had been repressed (introversion). But object-cathexis in general is, in such cases retained with great energy."[13]

However, according to Freud, in Schizophrenia, he had been obliged to assume that:

> After the process of Repression, the withdrawn Libido does not seek a new object, *but retreats into the Ego, that is to say that here the object-cathexes are given up, and a primitive objectless condition of narcissism is established.* The incapacity of these patients to transference . . . their subsequent inaccessibility to therapeutic efforts . . . the repudiation of the outer world characteristics of them . . . all these clinical features, seem to accord excellently with the assumption that object-cathexes are relinquished.

Presumably the regressed Libido into the Ego must increase also the normal narcissistic condition of the Ego.

II

It was, however, in 1917 in his paper *Mourning and Melancholia* that Freud had the greatest opportunity to further develop his new meaning of the *"Regression of the Libido"* in terms *only* of the regression of the sexual energy alone into the Ego. In this type of Regression, the Libido having abandoned its object, instead of remaining objectless in the Ego as it is the case in Schizophrenia, establishes in it what Freud called an *"Identification of the Ego" with the abandoned sexual object*. According to Freud in fact, if one listens patiently to the many and various self-accusations of those suffering from Melancholia, one cannot in the end avoid the impression that the most violent of them are hardly at all applicable to the patient himself, but that with some insignificant modifications they do fit someone else, some persons whom the patient loves, has loved or ought to love. In Freud's words: "So we get the key to the clinical picture, by perceiving that the self reproaches *are reproaches against a loved object which have been shifted on to the patient's own Ego*."[14]

Once this is recognized, there is no difficulty according to Freud, in reconstructing the process:

> First there existed an object-choice, the Libido had attached itself to a certain person; then owing to a real injury or disappointment concerned with the loved person, the object-relationship was undermined. The result was not the normal one of the withdrawal of the Libido from the object and transference of it to a new one, but something different. . . . The object-cathexis proved to have little power of resistance and was abandoned; but the free Libido was withdrawn into the Ego and not directed to another object. It did not find application there however, in any one of several possible ways, *but served simply to establish an identification of the Ego with the abandoned object*. Thus the shadow of the object fell upon the Ego, so that the latter could henceforth be criticized by a special mental faculty, like an object, like the forsaken object.[15] [italics mine]

Apart from the difficulty of conceptualizing Identification with Freud's loose term of *"the shadow of the object simply falling upon the Ego, after the object had been abandoned,"* it seems evident that

79

in his discussion of "Melancholia," Freud had returned to his original *"psychological abstraction"* of 1894 when he first assumed that as a result of Repression, the energic libido, the charge of sexual affect, becomes detached from the repressed idea, attaches itself to some other idea or becomes utilized along some other channel of discharge. The only difference between 1894 and 1917, is that now Freud adds the assumption that the liberated energy regresses into the Ego, where it leads to Identification of the Ego with the abandoned object, a new form of discharge for that energy.

Up to this point, Freud by the word "Libido," intended to designate no more and no less than the energy of the sexual instincts, thus making of the Libido a clear-cut sexual energy. It was only in 1920 in his publication *Beyond the Pleasure Principle* that Freud very conveniently extended the meaning of the Libido to the energy of an alleged "Instinct of Life" which he conveniently also equated henceforth with the sexual instincts. I will return later on this particular point.

That basic assumption of a displaceable sexual energy susceptible to withdrawal from a given object and regression into the Ego as in the particular case of "melancholia," so as to establish identification of the Ego with the lost object, fits very well within the framework of Freud's Libido theory, of which it represents a simple variant. It is that same Libido theory expanded now as to include the special outcome of Identification in a pathological case, that was subsequently applied by Freud in the discussion of the normal development of the Ego.

That last application was undertaken by Freud only six years later in his publication *The Ego and the Id* (1923) where having first recalled that in "Melancholia," an object which was lost had been re-established within the ego by means of identification, he then added:

> When this explanation was first proposed however, we did not appreciate the full significance of the process and did not know how common and how typical it is. Since then we have come to understand that this kind of substitution has a great share in determining *the form taken by the Ego*, and that it contributes materially towards building up what is called his character."[16]

In another passage, Freud reiterated that view:

> At any rate that process especially in the early phases of development, is a very frequent one and it points to the conclu-

sion that the character of the Ego is a precipitate of abandoned object-cathexes, and that it contains a record of past
object-cathexes.[17]

And it was in that spirit that he concluded that in women who had
many love affairs, he had no difficulty in finding vestiges of their
object-cathexes, in the traits of their character. In the light of this
new approach to the development of the ego's character, it would
seem to me that for a moment Freud must have lost track of what
he had assumed the case to be, in the development of the "anal
character," especially in women which in 1913 he had attributed to
the *"regression of the libido" in terms of the regression of the sexual
organization to its anal-sadistic formative stage*, and not to the "regression of the libido" as he now interpreted it, that is in terms of
the regression of the sexual energy (libido) alone withdrawn from an
object or person, into the ego, where it leads to the identification of
the ego with the abandoned object.[18]

Considering that at this point Freud had no longer made mention of the woman's character development in terms of the regression of the *"libido's organization"* to its anal formative stage, we are
at a loss in evaluating Freud's oscillations in attributing different
mechanisms to the character-formation in women. Could it be that
Freud played his various assumptions by ear as he went along, according to the convenient needs of his theoretical construction at
each particular period of his writings?

I will return to this subject of identification in the next chapter.
For the moment I will only proceed with a further discussion of the
"regression of the libido," as opposed to that of the ego in the ambiguous terms conceived by Freud.

In 1926, in his book *Inhibitions, Symptoms and Anxiety*,[19] Freud
referring to the "Regression of the Libido" which occurs in obsessive
neurosis where according to his assumption, the genital organization
turns out to be weak and insufficiently resistant, he clearly stated
that: *"When the Ego begins its defensive actions, the first thing it
succeeds in doing*, is to throw back in part or altogether the genital
organization on to its earlier sadistic level. This phenomenon of Regression is decisive for all that follows."[20] That point Freud later
restated by saying that: *"In bringing regression about, the Ego scores
the first point* in its defence against the demands of the libido."[21]

How can we conceptualize an Ego as being capable of throwing
back a genital organization *constitutionally determined*? A genital
organization so constituted would seem to me, hardly susceptible of
reverting to one of its formative stages (Regression of the Libido)

under the simple prompting of the Ego, which has no jurisdiction over that constitutionally determined organization. But what the Ego can do is to resort to *the recollection of experiences and feelings* related to some earlier period of life, be these experiences of a sexual or non-sexual nature. The Ego can do no more. This harking back by the Ego to the underlying memory-traces even if related to a given sexual thought-process, should therefore be considered as a "Regression of the ego" and not as a "Regression of the Libido."

Freud's erroneous assumption that the Ego is the governing power in inducing the "Regression of the Libido" in terms of the Regression of the sexual organization from its constitutional genital stage to its constitutional anal-sadistic level, in Obsessive neurosis as well as in the women's character-formation as he first had postulated becomes further complicated by his views that in Melancholia, two different types of *Regression of the Libido* are at work, the one dealing with the regression of the sexual energy alone into the Ego where it leads to the Identification of the Ego with the abandoned object, and the other with *the Regression of the sexual organization*, to its constitutional anal-sadistic formative stage. In Freud's words:

> The self-torments of the Melancholiacs signify . . . a gratification of the sadistic tendencies and of hate, both of which relate to an object, and in this way have both turned around upon the self. . . . *The Melancholiac's erotic cathexis of his object thus undergoes a twofold fate*: part of it regresses to identification, but the other part, under the influence of the conflict of ambivalence, is reduced to the stage of sadism which is nearer to his conflict. It is this sadism and only this that solves the riddle of the tendency to suicide which makes Melancholia so interesting and so dangerous.[22]

How could the Ego on one hand govern the Regression of the sexual energy *alone* by separating it from its object and directing it *entirely* upon itself so as to induce an identification between itself and the abandoned object, *and at the same time preside over* the Regression of its constitutionally determined sexual organization and stop that regression at its Anal-sadistic formative stage, and still retain at that stage a portion of its libidinal charge? Of course there is no limit to speculative and obscure conjectures, but how many of these should we accept blindly, especially if they are made of contrasting elements? Conjectures should not be construed as articles of faith, no matter who is the authority from whom they emanate.

In that same book, *Anxiety*, Freud expressed also some views regarding a "metapsychological explanation of Regression": "I am inclined to find it in a 'defusion of instinct,' in a detachment of the erotic components, which *at the beginning of the genital stage*, have become joined to the destructive cathexes belonging to the sadistic phase."[23] It is in this connection that Freud assumed that: "In bringing regression about, the Ego scores the first point in its defensive struggle against the demands of the Libido."[24]

It is strange that Freud had stated that the erotic components become joined to the destructive cathexes only at the beginning of the genital stage, which must have meant at the "phallic stage" that Freud had designated also as the "infantile stage of the genital organization." But that infantile genital stage follows the anal-sadistic stage of the sexual development. And yet at that anal stage, both the erotic instinctual sexual constructive component and the destructive one *had already become joined and operative*. In the child, Freud had indeed referred to that operative combination when he spoke of the sexual pleasure attached to his anal function of evacuation of feces, alternating at will with the sexual pleasure related to *his retention* of the feces, the latter being the expression of the destructive sadistic-hostile instinctual component of the sexual organization directed against the parents at the time of his toilet-training. Thus the joining of both the erotic and sadistic-destructive components occurs at the anal stage of the child's sexual development, an earlier stage than that of the infantile genital organization.

At any rate, in the absence of any clarification, one wonders how the Ego at the infantile genital stage, or at a later genital stage, can preside over the degradation of the Libido by means of *defusing* the combination of the constructive and destructive instinct components and allow the regression *only of the erotic energy into the Ego*, or allow the regression of the Ego's constitutionally determined sexual organization to its earlier anal stage of development. I am sure that one would be curious to hear more on the mechanism of that *obscure defusion* of the instincts and of its ambiguous application by Freud to the child's sexual development.

And yet, ambiguous as they were, Freud's views on "The Regression of the Ego" and of that of the Libido, were blindly accepted by the growing number of his followers. And to think that Freud himself was not so very sure of his own conjectures on this subject of "The Regression of the libido" in *Melancholia*, when in his conclusion he stated that:

In the opening remarks of this paper I admitted that the empirical material upon which this study is founded, does not supply all the fact that we could wish. *On the assumption that the result of observation would accord with our inferences,* we should not hesitate to include among the special characteristics of Melancholia, a regression from object-cathexis to the still narcissistic oral phase of the Libido.[25]

Nor may I add to the objectless Ego's narcissistic stage that Freud had assumed to take place in Schizophrenia.

That Freud had put inferences and conjectures ahead of observation, represented also quite a departure from his own tenet that observation alone constituted the basis upon which psychoanalysis had developed. In Melancholia, it would seem that Freud expected observation to fit eventually into what he had assumed theoretically.

I would like now to face right away the objection that somebody may raise that after all, Freud's views of the "Regression of the Ego" did not differ from those of his "Regression of the Libido" inasmuch they both were based upon the same retracing by the ego of the evolutive steps of its own development and the retracing by the Ego also of the various evolutive steps of the organization of its Libido.

To this I would answer that in the "Regression of the Ego," the patient's Ego by reactivating the underlying memory-traces of his present thought-processes, may be actually retracing their evolutive steps, a task feasible. But in the "Regression of the Libido," Freud had assigned to the Ego the impossible task of retracing the various steps of its constitutionally determined sexual organization, an organization of which the Ego had no knowledge in those specific terms.

All that the Ego can do is to reactivate memory-traces of events and feelings which it had actually experienced at some given time in the past. But it could not induce the Regression of its constitutionally determined sexual organization to some of its formative stages an organization upon which steps and characteristics it had no power.

It goes without saying that if the memory-traces of previous experiences or feelings to which the Ego harks back are vivid enough and have made a strong impression upon an individual, that recollection, be it automatic or voluntary, can strongly influence him and result in his modeling his present behavior to his past reactions to those past experiences or feelings, and thus urge him to display manifest behavioral patterns which are considered neurotic.

Returning to the discussion of the "Regression of the Libido," it follows that its concept based upon the retracing and re-establishing in their properly intended constitutional terms the various evolutionary stages of its sexual organization, having no ground upon which to stand, the only form of Regression that can be accepted would be, in my opinion, that of "The Regression of the Ego" in terms of a harking back by the Ego, of its present thought-processes and attached affective qualities, to their underlying memory-traces related to past experiences and related feelings. This is why I have suggested that if we wish to assign to the Ego the task of initiating defense by means of Regression, we should consider only the operation of a "Regression of the ego" and eliminate that of the Regression of the Libido in the terms advocated by Freud, of a regression of the sexual organization at any one of its alleged constitutionally determined formative stages of which the Ego has no knowledge and upon which it had no power in those specific terms.

Different considerations should apply to Freud's additional meaning assigned to the "Regression of the Libido" in terms of the regression into the Ego *of the sexual energy alone*, once it had become detached from an abandoned love-object. That new meaning Freud had already applied in the discussion of the pathological condition of *Schizophrenia* (1915) and of that of *Melancholia* (1917), and subsequently applied in 1923 to the formation of the Ego's character by means of Identification. Evidently that new meaning of the "Regression of the Libido" in terms *of the regression of the sexual energy alone into the Ego* could not be reduced to the mass meaning of the "Regression of the Ego." Indeed that new meaning of the "Regression of the Libido," introduced by Freud, *did not rest* upon the harking back to memory-traces, a characteristic of the "Regression of the Ego," but upon Freud's original "psychological abstraction of 1894 of the separation of the Libido from the idea to which it was attached. That separation of the Libido as a quantitative and qualitative sexual energy from an idea to be repressed had already been applied by Freud in explaining the symptoms of Hysteria and Obsessive neurosis.

I have already objected to that assumption of the separation of an idea from its affective quality when at various points of this trilogy, I have assumed that once an idea has acquired its affective quality, it constitutes with that quality an inseparable unit which I have called an "affective formation," which itself is capable *in its entirety* of displacement. The energic attribute for that displacement belongs to the idea itself and not to its affective quality.

And yet all of Freud's assumptions have been accepted by his followers as articles of faith, and they as a whole, never questioned their validity and never thought of offering some more plausible alternative to them.

This seems to me the most opportune point to discuss Freud's assumption that the Identification of the Ego with an abandoned love-object, resulted from the Regression into the Ego of the Libido alone in terms of the sexual energy, once it had become separated from that object. Freud never discussed that point. He limited himself to the statement that once the Libido in terms of the free sexual energy had become separated from the abandoned object, and had regressed into the Ego, *it served simply to establish an identification of the Ego with the abandoned object.*[26] That Freud was actually in the dark as to the mechanism of Identification was restated by him six years later in his publication of 1923 *'The Ego and the ID'* when referring to the same process of identification which he then had assumed to occur also in the course of the normal development of the Ego, he had stated that:

> When it happens that a person has to give up a sexual object, there quite often ensues a modification which can only be described as a reinstatement of the object within the Ego, as it occurs in Melancholia; *the exact nature of that substitution is as yet unknown to us.* It may be that by undertaking this *introjection*, which is a kind of regression to the mechanism of the oral phase the Ego makes it easier for an object to be given up, or renders that process possible. It may even be that this *Identification* is the sole condition under which the Id can give up its object.[27] [italics mine]

Freud, in this passage, used interchangeably the words identification, introjection, and substitution, though in my opinion substitution expresses quite a different meaning than Introjection or Identification. Introjection would seem closer to Identification, whereas Substitution could indicate a replacement of an object by another, but not Identification, or for that matter not even introjection. The fact remains however that Freud had no knowledge of the exact mechanism of Identification. And that seems to me, to be as it should be, considering that Freud related Identification to that *elusive and obscure operation of the sexual energy alone*, withdrawn into the Ego after it had abandoned its object.

How could an energy alone induce by itself an Identification of the Ego with an object that having been abandoned, did not participate in the withdrawal of the libido into the Ego? By the same token, Introjection of an abandoned object into the Ego would also be out of the question, inasmuch as the regressed sexual energy into the Ego did not carry with it the abandoned object. The only acceptable mechanism for Identification would be that of assuming a *substitution of the Ego for a given object*, provided however that in the process of Regression into the Ego, we were to include *not only the free sexual energy, but also the ideational representation of the abandoned object*.

In other words, Freud should have included in the process of Regression of the Libido into the Ego, not only of the sexual energy but also of *the ideational representation* of the allegedly abandoned object, to which the sexual energy, *its affective quality, should have remained attached*. By so doing Freud would have found himself on sounder grounds because a regression or a withdrawal into the Ego of the ideational representation of an object in combination with its affective quality, would have rendered possible the understanding of *the partial or total substitution of the Ego* for the ideational representation of the regressed object and attached affective quality.

Of course a consideration of this nature would bring us back again to the contention which I have developed in Chapter I, that once an ideational representation has acquired its own affective quality, libidinal or otherwise, it constitutes with it an indivisible unit which I have called an "Affective formation" which cannot undergo separation, but can undergo *displacement in its entirety, and replacement by some other "Affective formation" in its entirety*. We would be dealing therefore not with an Identification or Introjection, but with a *Substitution* of one or more "Affective formations" representing the Ego, for one or more "Affective formations" that represent the object which had regressed into the Ego with its attached affective quality.

That replacement of the Ego for the regressed object and attached affective quality, sexual or not, should not be however designated Identification, inasmuch as it does not involve *absorption* by the Ego of the withdrawn object and related attached quality, but simply *a replacement, a substitution of some of the "Affective formations" of pertinence of the Ego*, for some or all the "Affective formations" of pertinence of the object.

In *normal* conditions, that substitution of *some* of the "Affective formations" of the regressed object, does not lead to a loss of identity on the part of the Ego. The Ego is indeed constituted by a great number of "Affective formations," and its disposing of *some* of them for their replacement by *some* of the "Affective formations" of pertinence of the object, would preserve most of its integrity. In *pathological* conditions, as I will explain further in the next chapter, *the substitution i.e. the replacement* of the Ego's "Affective formations" for those of the object may become a total one, and only in such event that complete substitution of the Ego for the object could be labeled Identification, provided that we understand by that term a pathological condition.

With the assumption of the displacement of ideas or of "Affective formations," the latter made of ideas and attached affective qualities, there would be no reason to resort to the assumption of a psychic energy possessing a sexual quality, the Libido, which having regressed *alone* into the Ego, once it had become detached from the object which it had abandoned, is then capable on its own, of leading in some mysterious way, to the Identification of the Ego with the abandoned object.

Nor would there be the need to resort to the assumption that once that detached alleged sexual energy regresses into the Ego, *it may lose its sexual quality*. Having to deal only with displacements and replacements of "Affective formations," it becomes understandable that an "Affective formation" possessing a sexual affective quality, can be replaced by some other "Affective formations" possessing some affective quality *other than the sexual one*, thus avoiding the necessity for the former to lose its sexual quality.

These assumptions of mine, which I present for consideration could represent the appropriate step necessary to put to rest the *untenable* "customary psychological abstraction" advanced by Freud, of a separation, under repression, of a given idea from its affective quality, the latter having been endowed by Freud with an energic attribute. As I have assumed in Chapter One, the energic attribute belongs to the idea and not to its affective quality. In the next chapter I will discuss the subject of "Desexualization" and "Sublimation" of the alleged sexual energy in the terms advanced by Freud.

In reference to the concept of the "Regression of the Libido," Freud had been quite oscillating in applying it and of withdrawing it at his own convenience, to the clinical problem of the Phobias in children and in adults. In his early writings of 1894 and 1896 on the subject of Phobias and Obsessive neuroses, Freud never mentioned Regression for the very good reason that it was only in 1900 that he first introduced the concept of Regression. But in 1905, five years later, in dealing with the "Phobias" in terms of "Anxiety Hysteria," he still did not refer to *Regression* as one of the pathogenic mechanisms of that neurosis.

It was only in 1918 in his paper *From the History of an Infantile Neurosis*, that Freud applied the concept of Regression to the phobias of that particular case. That case referred to a patient whose phobia as a child consisted in his fears of being devoured by a wolf. That phobia of childhood had preceded the development in the same patient, later in life, of an "Obsessive neurosis." In discussing that early phobia of childhood, Freud considered it as the expression of the *"Regression of the libido"* in that child, in terms of a regression *of his sexual organization to its earliest oral stage of development*, which Freud had associated also with the nutritional instincts. Freud spoke therefore of the child's fear of being devoured by a wolf as the result of the "Regression of his Libido" to its oral stage of development, which as I have said was associated at that stage with the nutritional needs of the child: In this phase, the sexual aim could only *be cannibalism—eating*; it makes its appearance with our present patient, by means of Regression from a higher stage to the form of being eaten by the wolf.[28] Regression of the Libido in terms of the regression of the sexual organization, was mentioned again by Freud *in 1926 in his book on "Anxiety"* when referring to the phobia of the same patient of 1918, he stated that: "Such a phobia contained no suggestion of castration, *because the oral regression it had undergone*, had removed it from the phallic stage.[29]

Contradicting however the occurrence in that child of a "Regression of the Libido" as first assumed, Freud in that same book tried at a certain point to differentiate all Phobias of childhood from those of grown-up persons. In children Freud no longer referred now to the *"Regression of the Libido"* in terms of a Regression of the sexual organization to which he had resorted in 1918, but considered all Phobias of childhood as the expression of *"Anxiety"* in general, which developed automatically as a simple affective reaction to the traumatic presence of danger. On the other hand in the Phobias of the grown-up persons, he now *for the first time* resorted for their explanation to a process of Regression. But he did not refer to that regression as the *"Regression of the Libido,"* but to that other type of regression, *the "Regression of the Ego"* that is of the temporal hark-

89

ing back by the ego, of a thought-process of his, to its underlying memory-traces, a process which he had introduced in 1900.

Thus, in the case of "Agoraphobia of grown-ups," Freud stated that:

> The symptomatology of Agoraphobia is complicated by the fact that the Ego does not confine itself to making a renunciation. In order to rob the situation of danger, it usually *effects a temporal regression in infancy, or in extreme cases to pre-natal days*, that is at a time when the individual was in his mother's womb and protected against the danger which beset him in the present. A regression of this kind now becomes a condition whose fulfilment exempts the Ego from making its renunciation. For instance an Agoraphopic patient may be able to walk in the street, provided he is accompanied, like a small child by some one he knows and trusts.[30] [italics mine]

Apart from the fact that Freud having considered that in the grown-up the "Regression of the Ego" could go back to its intrauterine period of life, that view would contrast with Freud's other view that the Ego is not as yet operating at birth, and therefore could not be active during intrauterine life in terms of memory-traces. But Freud in 1923 excluded now in the phobias of children the intervention of the "Regression of the Libido," a view which he had supported in 1918. Furthermore in 1923 he supported the view that the Regression operating in the Phobias of the *grown-up* was not the one which he once had assumed to be operating in children, that is "The Regression of the Libido," but that of "The Regression of the Ego."

Faced with so many changes in Freud's views, one may justly question how many of these changes may have been dictated by *actual clinical observation, and how many represented pure theoretical speculations* which in this case as in others, were formulated by Freud as he went along, under the prompting of his prolific and imaginative mind.

I will now discuss briefly the chronological relationship of Regression to Repression as it unfolds in Freud's writings.

To do this, I should go back to Freud's draft K, of January first 1896, where he had stated that in obsessive neurosis the first thing to present itself to the patient's mind is the *recollection* of a pleasurable sexual experience of childhood. In his words:

When this experience is recollected later, it gives rise to a release of unpleasure; and in particular what first emerges is a
self-reproach which is conscious. Indeed it appears as though
the whole psychical complex *"recollection and self-reproach"* is
conscious at first.[31]

In that recollection Freud evidently did not refer to any form of Regression for the obvious reason that at that time he had not as yet
introduced that concept of Regression. But in that draft K, Freud did
not mention any Repression having preceded that recollection of a
past pleasurable active sexual experience.

In that draft, therefore, when did defense of the Ego in terms of
Repression enter into action? It was only following that recollection
which Freud later in 1900 considered as a "Regression of the Ego" to
its underlying memory-traces. Thus in 1896 it was following that
recollection and related affective self-reproach. In other words following the "Regression of the Ego," that Repression intervened. In
Freud's words: "Later without anything fresh happening, *both recollection and self-reproach are repressed*, and in their place an antithetic symptom is formed *some nuance of conscientiousness.*"[32] It is that
conscientiousness that may have become obsessive subsequently. In
that context it would seem clearly that the "Regression of the Ego"
in terms of harking back to the recollected underlying memory-
traces *has preceded* the intervention of Repression.

Later, in 1896, Freud in his paper *Further Remarks on the Defence Neuro-psychoses*, discussing again the mechanism of production
of the Obsessive neurosis, assigned to it the same formula: "Obsessions are always *reproaches re-emerging in a transmuted form under
repression*—reproaches which invariably relate to a sexual deed performed with pleasure in childhood."[33] Limiting my remarks to the
first part of this statement, it would appear again that recollection
of the memory-traces of some past sexual experience and related
self-reproaches constituted exactly what Freud later on called the
"Regression of the Ego" and which he now conceived to be the first
stage of development of an Obsessive neurosis. It was only later that
Repression intervened and transmuted the entire recollection into a
"nuance of conscientiousness" i.e. a "sensitivity of conscience" which
could become an obsessive phenomenon. No direct mention was included by Freud of the operation of a previous Repression having
preceded the "Regression of the Ego," so that the chronological formula for the development of an obsessive neurosis still remained
that of regression—repression-Obsession.

But in 1900, Freud, in his *Interpretation of Dreams*, stated that in pathological cases which evidently included Obsessive neurosis, Regression occurred only if a Repression had been previously exercized by the patient. In those terms the chronological formula for the development of the obsessive neurosis was evidently changed into that of repression-regression—obsession.

It is interesting to note that in the body of that paper of 1896 on *Further Remarks on the Defence-Neuro-psychoses* Freud seemed to have anticipated the views which he expressed in 1900 in his *Interpretation of Dreams* where he stated that: "In all my cases of Obsessive neuroses I have found moreover *a substratum of hysterical symptoms* which can be traced to a scene of sexual passivity of earlier date than the pleasurable activity."[34] In that light if one considers that according to Freud, it was the Repression of the memory of some previous passive unpleasant sexual experience of seduction, or as he put it later of some repressed fantasy, that resulted in the development of the symptoms of Hysteria, it would seem that for Freud it must have been Repression that constituted the substratum upon which later on, the Regression of the Ego in terms of recollection became operative. It was the subsequent Repression of that recollection that resulted in its transmutation of sensitivity of conscience which could become an obsession.

It is that new formula which Freud had anticipated in 1896 and which read as follows: Repression—Regression—Repression that Freud ultimately adopted in 1900 in his *Interpretation of Dreams* and which he reiterated in 1926 in his publication: *Inhibitions, Symptoms and Anxiety* where he stated again that:

> Obsessive neurosis originates no doubts in the same situation of the warding-off of the libidinal demands of the Oedipus complex. Indeed every Obsessional neurosis seems to have *a substratum of hysterical symptoms*, that have been formed at a very early age. But it is subsequently shaped along quite different lines owing to a constitutional factor.[35]

Apart from that flimsy *constitutional factor* which in Obsessive neurosis Freud had assumed to consist *in both an alleged weakness of the genital organization*, as a result of which it becomes easy for that organization to regress to some of its earlier formative stages, and in an alleged major disposition to an ambivalence towards love and hate, Freud in 1926 seems to have maintained the view which he had anticipated in 1896 and which he had clearly expressed in 1900, of the precedence of *a previous hysterical Repression* as a preparatory stage for the Regression of the sexual organization in Obsessive neurosis.

One cannot help note, however, the difficulty of following Freud's views on this subject of the chronological steps of development of an Obsessive neurosis. In fact in his original draft K of 1896 to his friend Fliess,[36] he assumed that it was the recollection of a past pleasurable sexual experience and its related feeling of reproach, a situation which later Freud called Regression of the Ego, that first appeared on the scene. It was only subsequently that Repression intervened as a result of which the recollected self-reproaches reappeared in the transmuted form of extreme sensitivity of conscience, which latter could become obsessive. The chronological formula for the development of an obsessive neurosis was therefore at that time: Regression—Repression—Obsession.

Later, in 1900, Freud explicitly referred to the view that a hysterical Repression constituted the substratum upon which an Obsessive neurosis developed, a view which he had mentioned in passing in his second paper of 1896 on the defence neuro-psychoses.[37] In this light, the chronological formula for the development of an Obsessive neurosis was changed into the following: Repression—Regression—Repression.

But in his paper of 1915, *Repression*, Freud made no further reference to the hysterical substratum and related repression as the first step of development of an obsessive neurosis and simply reiterated his views that *obsessive neurosis rests on the premise of a prior regression*, and that at first one may be in doubt as to what it is that we have to regard as the repressed instinct-presentation, a libidinal or a hostile trend. This is because in his view, obsessional neurosis rests precisely on the premise of that regression by the means of which a sadistic trend has been substituted for a tender one. It is this hostile impulse against a loved person which, according to Freud, undergoes repression.[38] It would seem therefore that in this view, Freud having omitted any mention of a substratum of hysteriac repression, he had returned again to his original chronological formula for the development of obsessive neurosis that of regression—repression—obsession, which he had advanced in his Draft K of 1896.

It would seem, however, that in the above passage, Freud was referring to regression not in terms of the "regression of the ego" as he did in 1896, but in terms of the "regression of the Libido." I feel justified in so assuming by the fact that in 1917 in his subsequent paper *Melancholia*,[39] Freud, in speaking of the feeling of hostility of the melancholiac against a person that he once had loved, *attributed that change* of love into hostility, to a regression of the libido to its earlier hostile-sadistic formative stage. Ambiguities of this sort do not evidently help to clarify Freud's ultimate position on this issue of chronological relationship of regression to repression.

But no sooner one tried to clarify that relationship, that another ambiguity seemed to surface in a new statement by Freud in his new publication of 1926 on the subject of anxiety, where he considered no longer the chronological relationship of regression to repression, and asserted that regression and repression were two distinct and independent mechanisms of defense: "In this connection," Freud asserted,

> we shall find advantageous to distinguish the more general notion of "defence" from repression. Repression is only one of the mechanisms which defence makes use of[40] . . . In obsessive neurosis we can take the *regression of the Libido*, as the fundamental characteristic of the affection.[41]

In this statement Freud confirms therefore the impression which I have expressed in my previous paragraph that the regression in question was no longer the "regression of the ego" as implied in his draft K of 1896, but a "regression of the libido."

Having now taken note of Freud's most recent views of 1926 that regression was a separate mechanism of defense, independent of repression, I was then surprised to read in his *New Introductory Lectures* published in 1932, six years later, the following ambiguous passage related to repression:

> In many cases the repressed impulse may retain its libidinal cathexis, and continues to exist unaltered in the Id. In other instances it seems to undergo complete destruction, in which case its libido is finally diverted to other channels. . . . Clinical experience has further taught us that in great many cases *instead of the usual result of repression, a degradation of the libido takes place, a regression of the libidinal organization to an earlier stage of development.* . . . This of course can only occur in the Id. . . .[42] [italics mine]

In that statement it would seem that though Repression and Regression had been previously (1926) considered as two independent mechanisms of defense, Freud now (1932) establishes a genetic dependence of Regression upon Repression. The latter instead of resorting *to its usual withdrawal of the Cs.-Pcs. cathexes from the idea to be repressed*, proceeds to the Regression (Degradation) of the sexual organization. Hence Regression became a modality of Repression and no longer a separate mechanism of defense.

Freud's ambiguous statement of 1932, was picked up by Charles

Brenner who commenting on the point that in that statement, Freud
had depicted Regression as a result of Repression, he expressed the
opinion that:

> It is clear that Freud did not bother to distinguish clearly be-
> tween the concept of defence in general and that of Repression
> in particular, *since he referred to Regression as a consequence
> of Repression*, rather than one of the mechanisms which
> might operate in addition to the mechanism of Repression.[43]
> [italics mine]

In my estimation what Brenner attributed simply to a lack of clarity
on Freud's part, could be attributed instead to the fact that Freud in
1932 may have again undergone a change of mind concerning the
fluid state of the chronological relation of Regression to Repression,
a change which he did not care to further discuss.

Libido and Ego Development

I. Freud's ambiguous concept of "Identification" in the course
of the ego's normal and pathological development
II. Freud's ambiguous concept of desexualized and sublimated
libido

I

In his early writings, Freud had assumed the operation of two types
of "psychic energies," the one activating the sexual instincts which
he designated "libido" and the other activating the ego-instincts of
self-preservation which remained elusive for many years. In 1905,
Freud reiterated that view in his *Three Essays on the Theory of Sexuality*, where he expressed his view that by distinguishing between
libidinal and other forms of psychic energy, he presumed that the
sexual processes occurring in the organism could be distinguished
from the nutritive processes by a special chemistry.[1]

At first, Freud had assumed that such a libidinal energy was all
stored in the ego where it constituted what he called ego-libido or
narcissistic libido. In Freud's view such an ego-libido was however
conveniently accessible to analytic study only when it had become
object-libido. That ego-libido or narcissistic libido constituted for
Freud the great reservoir from which the object-cathexes were sent
out and subsequently withdrawn once more. In Freud's words:

> The narcissistic libidinal cathexis of the Ego is the original
> state of things realized in earliest childhood, and is merely
> screened by the later extrusion of the libido, but in essentials
> persists behind them.[2]

In 1920, in *Beyond the Pleasure Principle*, Freud again reiterated that same view that through the study of the libido develop-

ment of the child in its earliest phases, it became clear that *the ego was the true and original reservoir of the libido* which is extended to the object from this.[3] However, in 1923, in *The Ego and the Id*, Freud expressed a different view on this reservoir of the libido when he assumed that at the very beginning, all the libido was accumulated in the id, and that part of it was sent out by the id into erotic object-cathexes. It is then that the ego attempts to attain possession of this object-libido and to force itself upon the id as a love-object. It followed that the narcissism of the ego was thus a secondary one, acquired by the withdrawal of the libido from the objects.[4] This was a far cry from what Freud before had considered the "ego-narcissism" to be, that is a primary condition.

One is therefore justly surprised to read *again* in Freud's posthumous publication, *An Outline of Psychoanalysis*, (1940) that everything we know about the libido relates to the ego in which the whole available amount of libido,

> is at first stored up. We call this state of things, absolute, *"Primary narcissism."* It continues until the ego begins to cathect the presentation of objects with libido. *Throughout life the ego remains the great reservoir from which libidinal cathexes are sent out on to objects and into which they are once more* withdrawn, like the pseudopodia of a body of protoplasma.[5] [italics mine]

This was another far cry from Freud's view of 1923 and a return to his views of 1905, 1914, and 1920.

One cannot help remark that Freud's oscillations also on that particular subject could not have been dictated by clinical observations, but that must have been the expression of his imaginative mind at work, and which at times was in contradiction with itself.

At any rate, it was on the basis of *the mobility of that libido in terms of a sexual energy*, be it primarily stored in the ego or in the id, and subsequently transferred upon objects or persons from which subsequently the ego attempted to take possession, that Freud rested the development of his libido theory. It was indeed on the basis of that theory that Freud approached the psychodynamics of the psychoneuroses which in 1905 he introduced in the following terms:

> We thus reach the idea of a quantity of libido, to the mental representation of which we give the name of "ego-libido," *and whose production, increase or diminution, distribution or displacement should affords us possibilities for explaining the psycho-sexual phenomena* observed.[6]

It was in accordance with his "Libido theory" that Freud subsequently approached the psychodynamics of two other important pathological conditions, *Schizophrenia* in 1915 and *Melancholia* in 1917. In *Schizophrenia*, as I have already mentioned in the previous chapter, Freud assumed that the Libido attached to a certain person or object, could, under the influence of Repression, become separated from that object or person *which it abandons*, and become withdrawn from it. That withdrawn Libido would not however seek a new person or object to which to attach itself, *but would instead regress into the Ego, where the objectless condition of narcissism already operating in that Ego, would be either reinforced or reestablished.* That reinforcement in the patient of his "Ego-narcissistic Libido" would explain the shut-in character and aloofness of the schizophrenic patient, his repudiation of the outer world, and his withdrawn personality.

In *Melancholia* on the other hand, the patient who is the prey of a deep depression, underrates himself, belittles himself, and accuses himself of all sorts of wrongdoings and degrading feelings. All these symptoms Freud attributed to a mechanism by which the Libido *in terms of sexual energy*, previously attached to a person, becomes under the influence of Repression, separated from that person *which it abandons*, and regresses into the patient's Ego where it results in an *Identification* of that Ego with that particular person whom the patient had previously loved, but has now either lost or abandoned. It follows that the self-reproaches and self-accusations which constitute the major symptoms of Melancholia, are in reality reproaches and accusations which are not directed at the patient itself, but at the person with whom the patient's Ego had identified itself.

It is, however, interesting to note that even though in Schizophrenia, Freud had not specifically referred to *Identification* as the result of the withdrawal into the Ego of the object-cathexis i.e. in terms of the sexual energy withdrawn from the abandoned object, that process of Identification of the Ego with the abandoned object, seems to have been accepted by him in the case of a young schizophrenic woman that a colleague of Freud, Dr. Tausk of Vienna, had called to his attention by means of notes. These notes came to Freud at a time when he was searching for confirmation for his assumption that, in some stages of Schizophrenia, a patient could express himself by means of what he called "Organ-speech."

The above case was that of a young schizophrenic girl who in her speech complained on one occasion, that "her eyes were not right and that they had been twisted." On another occasion, referring to one of her visits to church, "she felt compelled to change the position of her feet while standing up," as if somebody had placed her feet in that certain position. Dr. Tausk who had analyzed the patient had interpreted those statements as follows: The utterances that her eyes were twisted, meant that they were not her eyes any more, that her lover had twisted her eyes, that he was a shammer, an eye-twister, and that now she saw the world with different eyes. The reference of having been forced while standing in church, to assume a certain position, was also interpreted by Dr. Tausk as meaning that she had become like her lover, as common as him, though she actually was a refined girl; that he had made her like himself by leading her to think that he was superior to her, and that now she had become like him, because she thought that she would be better off, if she were like him. Ultimately Dr. Tausk concluded that the various verbal remarks of his patient stood *as an indication of her having identified herself with her lover*.[7] It seems strange therefore that in referring to that case, Freud did not express some objection to Dr. Tausk's interpretation, which evidently seemed to infirm his own views that in Schizophrenia, contrary to Melancholia, the Libido withdrawn from the abandoned object, and which regressed into the ego, ended only in reestablishing or in increasing the Ego-narcissism, but not in the Identification of the Ego with the abandoned object.

On this subject of Identification taking place in Melancholia, I have already expressed my views in the preceding chapter. Very briefly I will repeat that in Freud's assumption *what is withdrawn into the Ego in that pathological condition*, is only the free Libido in terms of *free sexual energy*, after it had detached itself from the object. This abandoned object to which that energy was attached did not follow the Libido into the Ego, inasmuch as in Freud's words:

> The object-cathexis proved to have little power of resistance
> *and was abandoned; but the free libido was withdrawn into
> the Ego, and not directed to another object.*[8] [italics mine]

At that time (1917), Libido referred only to the energy of the sexual instincts.

That process of the withdrawal of the "free libido" alone into the Ego, was interpreted by a follower of Freud, Otto Rank, as meaning a "Regression of the Libido" in terms of Freud's own meaning of a Regression of the sexual organization to its very early stage of

"Ego-narcissism." That interpretation seems to have been supported by Freud who included among the characteristics of Melancholia "a regression from object-cathexis to the still narcissistic oral phase of the Libido."[9] That oral phase was also referred by Freud as a preliminary stage of the process of Identification, at which phase the Ego first adopts an object: "The Ego wishes to incorporate this object into itself, and the method by which it would do so at this oral or cannibalistic stage, is by devouring it."[10]

Freud's consideration of the "Regression of the Libido" in Melancholia, in terms of the Regression of the sexual organization at its oral stage of development, meets with the same objections which I have already raised, when in a previous chapter I stated that the Ego could have no influence in reversing the course of an organization which follows constitutional lines for its development. On the other hand, Freud consideration of the withdrawal of the Libido alone in terms of a sexual energy once separated from its object to which it imparts its sexual quality, and the Regression of that energy alone into the Ego is also open to the same criticism which I have already raised on this subject.

It is on this particular point that Freud, in my opinion, erred because he had failed to take into consideration the fact that although the concrete object itself may have been abandoned, its ideational representation in fantasy must have been retained, and that it was that ideational representation of the object abandoned, in combination with its attached and inseparable affective quality, sexual or not, that had regressed into the Ego. In other words Freud should have dealt with displacement into the Ego, in terms of substitution of "Affective formations" of the Ego, made of given ideas and attached affective quality, for "Affective formations" of pertinence of the abandoned object. There would have been no need for Freud to resort to the separation of the Libido in terms of an affective energic quality, from the ideational representation of the abandoned object of which the Libido represented that energic quality.

Had Freud taken into account such mechanism of Identification, by referring it, not to his obscure assumption of an "absorption or introjection" of the object into the ego, considering that the ego had been abandoned, but to the replacement of all or parts of the components, "Affective formations" representing the Ego, by all or parts of the "Affective formations" representing the abandoned object. In the case of a total replacement of the Ego by the abandoned object, we would have been dealing evidently with a total identification of the Ego with the abandoned object. There would have been no room in that context for Freud's ambiguous terms of a "Regression into the ego" of the Libidinal qualitative energy alone, separated from its object.

Of course these considerations rest upon the basic assumption which I have introduced and developed in chapter I, that an ideational representation of an object or person, once it had acquired its affective quality, sexual or otherwise, it constitutes with it *an indivisible unit* that cannot undergo separation. That indivisible combination I have designated "Affective formation," so that instead of speaking of a separate displacement into the Ego of the Libido alone, in terms of a sexual energy, we should be speaking of displacements of "Affective formations" of pertinence of the ego, and their replacement by "Affective formations" of pertinence of the object.

Such an assumption of mine rests furthermore upon the other assumption which I have also introduced and developed in chapter I of part one of the trilogy, that an affective quality, the sexual quality in the case of the libido, does not possess an energic attribute, inasmuch as that attribute belongs to the related idea. It follows that the Libido in terms only of a sexual quality, has no power to displace itself from the idea to which it is attached. That power belongs to the idea which is therefore responsible for the displacement of all "Affective formations" in their entirety, made each one by an ideational representation and related affective quality. I have also assumed and discussed in the same chapter I, the point that any idea, that is any ideational representation of a given somatic stimulus, is activated by the same biological energy which had presided over the development of the *new "Psychic function"* born of the integration and synthesis of the various somatic functions which were already operating at a certain moment of our intrauterine somatic organization. It is that new "Psychic function" that translates into ideational representations the various somatic stimuli which it perceives, and which are generated by the various somatic functions. All initial ideas, i.e. ideational representations, being the product of this new "Psychic function" must of necessity be governed by the same biological energy which had governed the various somatic functions, from which the new "Psychic function" had originated, an energy which I have designated "Organismic energy."

Though Freud spoke of the Identification of the Ego with the abandoned object, he knew nothing of this process of reinstatement of the object into the Ego, so much so that in 1923 in *The Ego and the Id*, six years later, he still felt that: The nature of this substitution is as yet unknown to us.[11] I will not return over the point that Freud in that quote had used the word *"substitution,"* instead of Identification, or absorption, or introjection. I would like to offer instead, even though it may appear repetitious, an explanation for that obscure process that Freud called simply Identification.

That explanation is based upon my assumption that the fabric of our Ego is made of a large number of ideas and of "Affective formations" in a state of continuous flux. Both the ideas and the "Affective formations" possess an energic attribute which allows them to undergo displacement within the confines of our Psychic apparatus. I have also assumed that such an energic attribute belongs only to the components ideas of those formations and not to their affective qualities, i.e. to the Libido for instance in the case of the sexual quality. I have also assumed than when an object has to be abandoned for whatever reason it may be, its ideational representation and attached affective quality, that is the resulting combination which I have considered to be indivisible and which I have called *"Affective formation,"* does not cease to linger and operate in our mind, up to the time when either automatically or under the prompting of the Ego, it undergoes displacement and replacement by some other "Affective formation" of the pertinence of the Ego.

In the event of a *partial* replacement, i.e. substitution of its "Affective formation" by the Ego, the latter continues to retain most of its mental fabric, with the exception of that portion which had been substituted by those other "Affective formations." In that event, one should not designate as Identification such a partial substitution on the part of the Ego. At the most one could speak of some *"alteration of the Ego,"* not different from that alteration which in 1896 in his draft K to W. Fliess, he had assumed to occur in Obsessive neurosis, following repression of the recollection of an active and pleasant sexual experience of childhood and related self-reproach. That Repression was followed by a simple alteration of the Ego in terms of "an increased sensitivity of conscience."

We must also remember that under normal conditions, some alteration of a loving Ego takes place under the influence of the loved person, without resulting for its explanation to a total Identification of the loving ego with that loved person. However in certain pathological conditions, a large number or even the total sum of the "Affective formations" which constitute the fabric of the operating Ego, could be replaced by "Affective formations" of pertinence of some other person or of a certain abandoned one, and as a result of which a total pathological substitution of the Ego for that of some other person or for that of the lost person, could occur. In that case one could justifiably speak of "Identification" provided it be qualified as pathological. This would be the type of pathological Identification that underlies the Melancholiac, or the Megalomaniac paranoid who believes that he is God, Croesus, or Napoleon, and whose Ego had undergone a complete substitution.

In 1923, in *The Ego and the Id*, Freud extended the application of the concept of Identification which he had first introduced in Melancholia in 1917, to the normal development of the Ego. Recalling the point that in *Melancholia,* he had assumed that the regressed Libido into the Ego had resulted in its Identification with an abandoned object he then added:

> When this explanation was first proposed we however did not appreciate the full significance of the process, and did not know how common and typical it is. Since then we have come to understand that *this kind of substitution* has a great share in determining the form taken by the Ego and that it contributes materially towards building up its character.[12] [italics-mine]

It is interesting to note that in this passage, Freud used again the word *"substitution"* and not "Identification," a designation which in my opinion renders more accurately the mechanism of that phenomenon, the mechanics of which Freud had admitted to be unknown to him.

It is also interesting to note at this point, that Freud did not refer to the fact that in this substitution (Identification), it was the Libido in terms only of a sexual energy that was involved in it. That left open the question if he possibly was dealing with a displacement of the combination of some of the ideational representations of the object and of their attached "Affective qualities," that is of some of its "Affective formations," which replaced some of the "Affective formations" of the Ego. Such an approach which would have entailed a substitution of "Affective formations" by other "Affective formations" would have consequently excluded the explanation that the sexual energy *alone* first attached to an object and subsequently withdrawn into the Ego, could have resulted in the Identification of the Ego with a given object.

In the normal development of the Ego by means of Identification, Freud had distinguished two separate periods. The first period he considered to be a most important, profound and lasting, and he designated it as the "Primary Identification with the parents." That Identification was not considered by him as being the consequence or outcome of an object-cathexis, but a first direct and immediate Identification that takes place earlier that any object-cathexis. Having so assumed, Freud failed however to clarify two important points: 1) The mechanism of that direct "primary Identification", and 2) the nature of the energy presiding over that "primary Identification."

Concerning the mechanism of formation of that "primary Identification," Freud failed to mention any participation in it of the *specific ideational representation of the "parental figure,"* which he should have done, inasmuch as in the absence of that participation, no identification, introjection, or substitution of the ego with the "parental figure" could have taken place. All this without mentioning the need for the affective qualities attached to that ideational representation of the parents, to participate also in that "primary Identification."

Furthermore, some sort of energy must have been involved in that process of "primary Identification." If it were not an object-cathexis, as understood by him, why didn't Freud specify the origin and nature of the energy involved in that process? An elaboration of these points would have helped greatly the understanding of what Freud had meant by immediate and direct Identification of the child with his parents. Evidently if by identification, Freud had explained to us that he had meant the replacement of only some of the ideational representations and related affective qualities which constitute the fabric of the child's Ego, for some of the ideational representations of the parent's figure, things might have been better understood. In that case however, Freud would have come very close to what I have assumed to be i.e. an "alteration of the Ego" but not an Identification with the parents, which latter would have entailed a complete surrender of the child's own Ego.

This might be the place to mention the important process of *"imitation"* which characterizes the child's early developmental activities from his first smile and his first vocal sounds considered as imitations of the smile and of the endearing sounds of the parents, to the later imitation of gestures and mannerisms of this parents. As a whole this process of imitation on the part of the child could indeed be reduced also to a partial replacement of the "Affective formations" of the child's Ego, for those of the parental "Affective formation."

Having failed to refer to the involvement of the ideational representation and related affective qualities of the object itself, in the process of Identification, or to the important process of imitation, Freud left also unexplained why he had considered "Primary identification" of the child in the same light as the Identification taking place in Melancholia, when in that "Primary identification," no libido in terms of a sexual cathexis was involved, inasmuch as it took place earlier than any object-cathexis. Of course by that time (1923), Freud in his previous publication *Beyond the Pleasure Principle* (1920) in order to escape the criticism of a pan-sexual approach in his special brand of psychology, had very conveniently identified the libido as the energy activating not only the sexual instincts, but also the elusive "Instict of life" as well as the Ego-instincts of self-preservation. Thus contrary to his original position, he now identified with the sexual instincts those Ego instincts of self-preservation which he once had considered as the antagonists to the sexual instincts.

Concerning now the second point, that is that of the nature of the energy at work in "Primary Identification," Freud had intimated that it was not the sexual cathexis already attached to some object that was responsible for that process. In this connection I repeat, we must admit that some sort of energy must have been at work at the time of that Identification and thus responsible for the cathecting of the parental figures. It would therefore seem that, strictly speaking, Freud's statement that no object cathexis was as yet at work in "Primary Identification," must have fallen short of his intention. It would have been more appropriate indeed, if at this point in connection with the energy governing "Primary Identification" Freud instead of no-object cathexis, had referred to what in his subsequent elaboration of the Libido in his publication *The Ego and the Id*, he had considered the operation of an energy which was not sexual, but *neutral* and functioning in that capacity prior or in conjunction with the development of a specific sexual object-cathexis. That neutral energy could have well represented the energy operating at the time of "Primal repression."

Following that stage of "Primary identification" in which no sexual object-libido is involved, a new phase of Identification takes place according to Freud, that which is related to the child investing his sexual Libido onto his parents, at the time of the Oedipal stage of his sexual organization. In Freud's views, subsequent to that investment, under the threat of punishment (castration) the child is forced to repress the impulses of that stage and to resolve them. For that purpose the Ego withdraws in itself the Libido invested in his parents, and as a result identifies himself with them, a process which leads ultimately to the development of the Super-ego. Hence Freud's conclusion that the Super-ego is the heir to the Oedipus complex.

But Freud did not enter further into the dynamics of that Identification, implying simply that it followed the same line as that taking place in Melancholia. But in that pathological condition, Freud had referred distinctly to the abandonment of the object by its cathecting Libido energy, which all alone regressed into the Ego, and made no mention of the regression into the Ego of an ideational representation of the abandoned object. In that light the Identification of the Ego with the abandoned object, had remained beyond understanding. The same applies now to the resolution of the Oedipal situation where Freud, having referred to the withdrawal of Libido into the Ego, failed to mention the Regression also into the child's ego of the ideational representation of the parental figure, to which the Libido was attached and which in my views cannot become separated from that representation. This leaves us again in the dark as to the dynamics through which the identification of the child's Ego with the parents actually takes place in Freud's terms at this *particular Oedipal stage*. I feel therefore justified in raising against Freud's assumption of the identification of the child's Ego with his parents at the Oedipal stage, the same objections which I have raised in Melancholia, against the Identification of the Ego with an object that had been abandoned and the sexual energy of which had *alone* regressed into the ego.

In addition to my disagreement with Freud's assumption of Identification by means of the simple withdrawal into the Ego of the *Libido alone* in terms of a sexual energy, unaccompanied by the ideational representation of the object which has been abandoned, there also remains the criticism raised against Freud, that no matter if it concerns the pathological condition of Melancholia, or the resolution of the Oedipal situation necessary for the subsequent normal development of the Ego, the energy involved in the development of these two processes seemed always to be the Libido *in terms of the energy of the sexual instincts*, from which Identification depended. It is true, as I have already stated that Freud in 1920 *conveniently identified* the sexual instincts with the "Instinct of Life" *and with the Ego-instincts of self-preservation*, and that he had considered their activating energy as a binding energy for which he had retained the designation of Libido which he originally had assigned only to the energy of the sexual instincts. The ego-instincts of self-preservation had been considered originally as the antagonists of the sexual instincts. But Freud's personal philosophical beliefs on those subjects, particularly in connection with the newly introduced "Instinct of Death," are not convincing and remain therefore a matter of high speculation.

II

FREUD'S AMBIGUOUS CONCEPT OF
DESEXUALIZED AND SUBLIMATED LIBIDO

Desiring now to extricate himself further from that growing criticism of pan-sexualism attached to his own brand of psychology, Freud, in apparent desperation, resorted to another assumption, that of the "Desexualization" of the Libido involved in the development of Identification in the various instances envisaged by him. Thus referring to that Libido, Freud at one point assumed that: "The transformation of object-libido into narcissistic libido, which thus takes place, implies a process of desexualization; it is consequently a kind of sublimation."[13] And at another point he stated that: "The transformation of erotic libido into the ego-libido "of course involves an abandonment of sexual aims, a de-sexualization."[14]

Freud reached his assumption of the de-sexualization of the libido, step by step. He first discussed various possibilities concerning the interpretation of the symptoms of "paranoia." Without engaging myself too deeply into that discussion, I will emphasize one point which was presented by Freud in discussing that mental condition. In it, he felt that another possible mechanism could be operating, and consisting in some ambivalent attitude being present from the onset, so that the transformation is effected by means of a reactive shifting of cathexes from the erotic impulses and used to supplement the hostile energy. He felt, however, that not quite the same thing happens when a hostile attitude of rivalry is overcome and leads to homosexuality. In that case the hostile attitude having no prospect of gratification, becomes replaced by a loving attitude for which there is more hope of satisfaction. So there was no need, in both instances, to assume a direct transformation of hate into love, or vice-versa, a transformation which he considered incompatible

107

with a qualitative distinction between the two classes of instincts.[15]

A second step was then taken by Freud when he assumed that by including in our calculations the mechanism by means of which love can be changed into hate, he had tacitly made another assumption, that of admitting that there existed in the mind—whether in the ego or in the id—*a displaceable energy which is in itself neutral*, but capable of joining forces either with an erotic or with a destructive impulse, and thus augment their respective cathexes. *Without assuming the existence of a displaceable energy of that kind, Freud felt that he could make no headway.*[16]

It sounds strange, however, that it took Freud almost thirty years (1894–1923) to assume the existence of an alleged psychic energy which possessed *no affective quality*, and which contrasted with his earlier view of a dominant libido construed as a mobile psychic energy possessing a sexual affective quality. Had Freud assumed from the very beginning the existence and operation of a neutral energy, he might have come closer to assuming that the energy activating both somatic and nutritive functions, *as well as the mental functions*, may have been a single energy and one of a biological nature.

Having now assumed the existence of a neutral psychic energy, Freud now introduced another assumption for which he admitted however to have no proof to offer:

> It seems a plausible view that this neutral displaceable energy which is probably active alike in the Ego and in the Id, proceeds from *the narcissistic reservoir* of the Libido i.e. that it is *desexualized Eros*. The erotic instincts appear altogether more plastic, more readily diverted and displaced than the destructive instincts.[17] [italics mine]

It must be pointed however that in the above statement Freud no longer referred to the reservoir of the Libido as being in the Id, as he had assumed in 1920.[18] *but in the Ego* in terms of a narcissistic Ego. He however did not comment on this change of mind on his part and a return to a former assumption on this subject.

From there on, the final assumption was easy to formulate, i.e. that the transformation of the erotic libido into Ego-libido "involves an abandonment of sexual aim, a Desexualization."[19] Thus in the development of the process of Desexualization, we were presented with a series of steps which unfortunately were based simply on *"further psychological abstractions"* on the part of Freud. Even accepting the existence and operation of a "neutral psychic energy,"

Freud did not grapple with the mechanics of how Desexualization actually takes place. Let us take for instance the question of Identification of the child with the parents at the time of the resolution of his Oedipal complex, that is at the time of the withdrawal of his sexual libido from the parents and its regression into the Ego. Now admitting the point that what has been withdrawn into the child's Ego is the same Libido which he had invested in his parents, in what manner has that sexual libido, that sexual energy, become desexualized? There seems to be no answer except that of a speculative assumption. How indeed could a sexual energy lose its sexual attribute by the mere fact of its having become detached from an object and withdrawn into the Ego?

One could speculate that through the Regression of the Libido into the Ego, the Ego could increase the amount of Libido which it already possesses in its connotation of narcissistic libido, but one can hardly conceptualize the loss of the sexual quality on the part of that regressed Libido. Nor could the fact that the sexual energy *changed its aim at a certain point*, justify the assumption that it loses its main sexual quality, and becomes neutral energy.

Nor could we designate that withdrawn sexual energy as "*sublimated energy*" for the sole reason that it has changed its aim, from the object to the ego. *That change of aim could not in itself result in a loss for that energy of its inherent sexual quality*, especially if the ego may itself be considered as a libidinal object as Freud had suggested. In my view, sublimation should be understood as a process which entails the displacement of an "Affective formation" made of an ideational representation and of its *inseparable sexual affective quality*, and its replacement by some other "Affective formation" made of an ideational presentation and of its *inseparable nonsexual affective quality*.

In those terms only, sublimation could be applied for instance to the intellectual development of the ego, provided that a modification be applied to Freud's statement on this subject to the effect that: "If the intellectual processes are to be classified among these displacements of energy, then the energy for the work of thought itself must be supplied from sublimated erotic sources."[20] The modification in question should be directed to the meaning of the word *displacement*, which should apply not simply to a displaced sexual energy, but to the combination of an ideational representation and its attached sexual quality, that is, to a sexual "affective formation" being displaced in its entirety and replaced by an ideational representation prossessing a nonsexual affective quality that is by a nonsexual "affective formation." In that context there would be no need to resort to any de-sexualization of the energy involved *in the replaced sexual "Affective formation."*

Before closing this chapter, I would like to refer to two questionable statements by Freud which add to the ambiguity of his psychological construction. The first refers to the fact that in 1920 Freud had basically changed his assumption of 1893–94 that the Ego-instincts of self-preservation were the real antagonists to the sexual instincts. In 1921 he identified instead, the Ego-instincts of self-preservation with the sexual instincts and with the "Instinct of life," thus rejecting by implication, his original views of a conflict existing between the sexual instincts and the Ego-instincts of self-preservation. The real antagonism which he now assumed to exist, was that between the sexual instincts which he now had identified with the ego-instincts of self-preservation and with the "Instinct of life," and his newly introduced *"Instinct of death"* which he had identified with the other Ego-instincts, outside those of self-preservation.

By so doing, Freud had therefore altered his basic original conflict between the sexual instincts and *the Ego-instincts of self-preservation*, a conflict which he had considered basic in the development of the psychoneuroses and which implied the conflict between two different specific groups of instincts. Having now identified the Ego-instincts of self-preservation with the sexual instincts, Freud found himself in a difficult position to explain the development of the psychoneuroses in his original terms. It is true that now he had introduced the new "Instinct of Death," as a replacement of the Ego-instincts of self-preservation which he now had identified with the newly introduced Instinct of life, which in turn he had identified with the sexual instinct. But that was done in order to keep alive his own assumption that in governing life, a duality of conflicting instincts was operative. Yet by doing so, Freud had rejected *for all practical purposes* his original views on the psychodynamics of the psychoneuroses based on the conflict between the sexual instincts and the Ego-instincts of self preservation.

Thus, instead of pointing out to what seemed a rejection of his original position, Freud commented on that situation as if nothing had changed in his original views. In his words:

One if justified in saying that the old formula viz. that a psychoneurosis arises out of a conflict between the Ego-instincts and the sexual instincts, *contained nothing that we should have to reject to-day*. Only the difference of the two kinds of instincts, which was supposed originally to be in some kind of way *qualitative*, has now to be defined otherwise, mainly *on a topographical basis*. In particular the transference neuroses, the real object of the psychoanalytic study, is still seen to be the result *of a conflict between the Ego and the libidinous investment of an object*.[21] [italics mine]

Evidently Freud was referring to the Ego as a libidinous Ego.

I cannot help but remark upon the ambiguous way in which Freud introduced an entirely new dynamic concept of the neuroses, by couching it in terms which made it appear as if nothing had to be rejected from his old concept. I feel instead that Freud's shift—from his original approach to the psychoneurotic conflict, as taking place between *two separate and contrasting instincts*, that is between the sexual instincts and the Ego-instincts of self-preservation, each having a separate origin, presumably in some different chemistry, and each being activated by a different type of energy—to his new approach of a conflict taking place between two portions of the same instinct, activated by the same energy, the Libido, but simply operating at two different topographical levels, that is between the libido of the objects and that of the Ego, *constitutes a fundamental change*, which in my estimation deserves more than *an ambiguous semantic treatment*.

The other statement refers to the fact that in spite of all his early assumptions which greatly maximized the importance of the Libido in terms of the energy of the sexual instincts, in the development of the Ego in both its normal and pathological aspects, and in spite of his altered views that the psychoneuroses were the result of an internal conflict between two members of the same family, the Ego-libido and the object-libido, Freud now wished to defend psychoanalysis against the criticism that *it was based upon the dominance of our instinctual life*, by maintaining that it was also based upon considerations of the higher moral and spiritual side of human nature. In Freud's view, the above criticism was doubly unjust, both historically and methodologically. He thus referred to the fact that from the very beginning, he had attributed the function of Repression to morality and conscience. Of course this is true, but what Freud neglected to emphasize in his rebuttal is, that for twenty years, that is from 1894 up to 1914, when he first discussed the Super-ego in his paper *On Narcissism*, the Ego and its derivative the Super-Ego, played a relatively small part in Freud's psychological construction. Furthermore in his publication of 1920–21 *Beyond the Pleasure Principle*, Freud actually reinforced his faith in the importance of our instinctual life, by adding to the play of the sexual instincts, now identified with the "Instinct of life," activated by the Libido, the play of the new "Instinct of death" activated by a separate instinctual aggressive-destructive energy. No discussion of the part played by the Super-ego was undertaken in that publication. It was only in 1923 in *The Ego and the Id* that Freud seemed anxious to answer the criticism that he had made instinctual life, the main spring of our thinking and behavior, and that he devoted himself in that publication to the discussion of the structural super-ego.

Though in his early writings and in his correspondence with his friend Fliess, Freud had already referred to Morality and Conscience and by implication to the spiritual values of these concepts, *yet for many long years he had paid only lip service to these values*, while on the other hand he had proceeded relentlessly in developing and maximizing his "Libido theory." And when it came to the development of the Super-ego, he extolled the role in that development of the sexual Libido. Indeed it was at the time of the resolution of the Oedipal situation that under the threat of castration, the child withdrew his Libido then invested in his parents, into his own Ego, where it resulted in its Identification with the authoritative parental figure, the beginning, the dawn of the Super-ego. It is in that sense that Freud considered the Super-ego as the heir to the Oedipus complex. Thus the Super-ego the guardian of our moral and spiritual values was actually born out of the withdrawal of the sexual libido from the parental figure into the child's own Ego. *The Libido in its connotation of a sexual energy, was therefore essential for the development of the Super-ego.* And it was because of that genetic relationship, an embarrassing one, that Freud had to resort subsequently to his convenient assumption of the *"desexualization" of the Libido*, once it became withdrawn into the Ego.

To maintain therefore that psychoanalysis has given an equal importance to the highest moral and spiritual values, as that given to instinctual life, constitutes in my estimation, a poor rebuttal on Freud's part, considering his belated elaboration, only twenty years later, of those moral values, an elaboration which, only in a very little measure, counterbalanced Freud's entire psychological construction, in which he had extolled the power of our instinctual life.

It may be appropriate at this point to recall also the fact that Freud, as I have already mentioned, *did not believe* in the existence in humans, (*outside of the instincts which aimed only at the return to a previous condition,) of an inborn impulse which aims at progression and perfection*, and which had brought man to his present heights of intellectual prowess and ethical sublimation. In his words:

> I do not believe in the existence of such an inner impulse and I see no way of preserving this pleasing illusion. . . . The development of man up to now and the restless striving towards further perfection which may be observed in a minority of human beings, is easily explicable as the result *of that repression of instincts upon which what is most valuable in human culture is built.* The repressed instinct never ceases to strive after its complete satisfaction, which would consist in the repetition of a primary experience of satisfaction.[22] [italics mine]

In this passage written in 1921, prior to his publication *The Ego and the Id* (1923), Freud was referring to the repressed sexual instincts aiming at satisfaction, inasmuch as he immediately added:

> All substitutions or Reaction-formations and Sublimation, avail nothing towards the relaxing of the continual tension; and out of the excess of the satisfaction demanded, over that found, is born the drive momentum which allows of no abiding in any situation presented to it, but in the poet's words "urges ever forward, ever unsubdued."[23]

Considering that at that time Freud had not discussed Sublimation or Reaction-formations, in connection with the particular instinct of death, it would seem that such a statement referred *mainly* to the sexual instincts. But had that statement referred also to the "Instinct of death," the fact would have remained that the impulse at progress would have been dependent in all cases from the striving of both those instincts and from the repression upon which "what is most valuable in human culture is built."

In the light of the above statement, it follows that Freud's assertion that psychoanalysis is based on the higher moral and spiritual values of human nature, seems to have ignored not only the point that he himself had made when he had denied in man the existence of any inborn impulse towards progression and perfection, but also his newest assumption that any development of man was related to the excess of satisfaction demanded by the instinct over that found, a fact that in spite of Repression did not induce relaxation from the demands of the instincts, but *on the contrary* was responsible for the "ever urge forward," that is for the drive momentum towards perfection and progression.

An observation which I have already made, but upon which I would like to return, is that which concerns Identification. Freud never made the point of differentiating between Identification as it takes place in pathological conditions and that which takes place in the course of the normal development of the Ego, be it at the time of the "Primary Identification," at the time of the resolution of the Oedipal situation, or at a later date in the molding of the adult's character formation. Yet a basic difference exists between the Identification which occurs in pathological situations and that which occurs in the course of the Ego's normal development.

To clarify my statement, I will have to return to my criticism of the dynamics of Identification in the pathological process of Melancholia as presented by Freud, a criticism based on the fact that according to him the withdrawal into the Ego affects only the sexual energy the Libido, the related object of which had been abandoned. In the absence of the combination of the ideational representation of that abandoned object and of its affective quality, i.e. the Libido, to be withdrawn together into the Ego, a point not contemplated by Freud, Identification in my opinion cannot take place. But in whatever terms one were to accept Identification in the pathological condition of Melancholia, the resulting Identification of the Ego with the abandoned object would have to be a total one. That means that the patient's Ego would have *to abdicate the full amount* of its ideational and qualitative attributes and substitute them *completely* for those of the abandoned object leaving nothing for itself. In those terms the designation Identification should be accompanied by the specific qualification of pathological.

This type of pathological identification is in my opinion the same type of Identification which occurs in another pathological condition that of "Paranoiac Megalomania." In this condition the patient's Ego identifies itself entirely with a given person whom he had admired or even feared, and as a result of which he proclaims himself to be God, the Devil, Croesus, or Napoleon. In this pathological condition, the entire amount of ideational and qualitative attributes of the patient's Ego, that is of the total amount of its "affective formations" has been substituted by the full amount of the ideational representations and qualitative attributes of the person whom the patient had loved, admired, or feared. It is a total Identification in which the patient's Ego has abdicated its entire identity. In this case also the designation of Identification should be accompanied by the specific qualification of pathological.

But this is not what happens in the course of the normal development of the Ego where we are dealing with a different situation. The Ego does not abdicate all of its attributes, but retains a great number of them. Only a few traits of his character are substituted for some of the character traits of the parental figure or of that of some other loved person. In that light there can be no question of identification in the strict sense, as it occurs in pathological conditions.

What actually occurs under those circumstances is only an *"alteration of the ego,"* which may vary in extent, but never reaches the stage of identification. That alteration of the ego depends evidently upon the varying degrees of the capacity of resistance of the ego, to external influences which were properly considered by Freud. In his view, the character of the ego was a precipitate of abandoned object-cathexes of which it contained a record of past object choices. He admitted, therefore, that there were varying degrees of capacity for resistance, on the part of the ego, as shown by the extent to which the character of any person accepts or resists the influence of the erotic object-choices through which he has lived. In this connection, he recalled the fact that in women who have had many love affairs, there seems to be no difficulty in finding vestiges of their object-cathexes in the traits of their character.[24]

Evidently such partial modifications of the ego should not be designated "identification" which could imply a pathological state of affairs, but only as "partial alteration of the ego" a condition which allows the ego to exercise, outside of such alterations, all other normal functions of its pertinence. If however one wishes to retain the term identification, one should at least call it "partial identification," and qualify it with adjective "normal" to differentiate it from the total "pathological identification."

The Fallacy of Freud's Distinction Between Sexuality and Genitality

Contents

Freud's Early Formulation of Sexuality in the Development of the Neuroses

Already, in his *Three Essays on the Theory of Sexuality*, first published in 1905, Freud had expressed his views that sexuality should be differentiated from genitality, when writing of thumb-sucking in infants and children, he recalled that Lindner S. in 1879 had clearly recognized the sexual nature of this type of activity, and immediately added: "This view has been most energetically repudiated by number of pediatricians and nerve-specialists, though this is no doubt partly due to a confusion between sexual and genital."[1]

Subsequently, in 1913, in his paper *The Predisposition to Obsessive Neurosis*, Freud made the following important statement:

> *Psycho-analysis stands or falls by the recognition of the sexual-component instincts, of the erotogenic zones, and of the subsequent expansion of the idea of the sexual function as opposed to the narrower one of the genital function.*[2]

In 1935, in his *Autobiography*, reprinted in 1952 by W. W. Norton & Company, under the heading of *An Autobiographical Study*, Freud, referring to the distinction between sexuality and genitality which he had incorporated in the successive editions of his *Three Contributions to the Theory of Sexuality*, wrote as follows:

> I hope it will have been easy to gather *the nature of my extension* (on which so much stress has been laid and which has excited so much opposition) *of the concept of Sexuality. That extension is of a twofold kind. In the first place sexuality is divorced from its too close connection with the genitals, and is regarded as a more comprehensive bodily function having plea-*

*sure as its goal. In the second place the sexual impulses are re-
garded as including all of those merely affectionate and
friendly impulses to which usage applies the exceedingly ambiguous word love. . . .*

The detaching of Sexuality from the genitals has the advantage of allowing us to bring the sexual activities of children and of perverts, into the same scope of those of normal
adults. . . . Looked at from the psycho-analytic standpoint,
even the most eccentric and repellent perversions are explica-
ble as manifestations of component-instincts of sexuality,
which have freed themselves from the primacy of the genitals,
*and are going in pursuit of pleasure on their own account as
they did in the very early days of the libido development. . . .*

The second of my alleged extensions of the concept of
Sexuality, finds its justification in the fact clearly revealed by
psychoanalytic investigation that all of the affectionate impulses were originally of a completely sexual nature but have
become inhibited in their aim or sublimated. The manner in
which the sexual instincts can thus be influenced and
diverted, enables them to be employed for cultural activities
of every kind, to which they bring indeed the most important
contributions.[3] [italics mine]

Finally, in his *Outline of Psycho-analysis* (1940) published posthumously, Freud reiterated that:

1) It is necessary to distinguish between the concepts of sexual and genital. The former is the wider concept and includes
many activities that have nothing to do with the genitals and
2) *That sexual life comprises the function of obtaining pleasure
from zones of the body*—a function which is subsequently
brought into the service of that of reproduction. The two functions often fail to coincide completely.[4] [italics mine]

Having also asserted that: "Sexual life does not begin only at
puberty but starts with clear manifestations soon after birth."[5]
Freud made it clear that his discovery of the sexuality of the children was made at first through the analysis of adults. That means
evidently that at first that alleged discovery was made possible by
allowing a transposition upon the children, of the conclusions which
he had reached in the analysis of adults. It was only later from 1908
on, that according to Freud it became possible for him to confirm
such conclusions in the most satisfactory way and in every detail by
direct observation of children.

With this preamble in mind, let us follow Freud's early steps in
the formulation of his sexual theory of the etiology of the neuroses.
In all his early writings, Freud had made no distinction between

sexuality and genitality, inasmuch as his references to sexuality in his writings and lectures seem to have been related to what at that time was considered genitality. It was in that spirit that in 1894 in his first paper, *The Defence Neuro-psychoses*, Freud had concluded that in his cases of hysteria what the patient had repressed and had translated into clinical symptoms were experiences, ideas, or feelings arousing an affect so painful that the person resolved to forget it, to repress it. Considering that such an unbearable idea or ideas develop in women *chiefly in connection with sexual experiences and sensations*, and that the patients could remember with the most satisfaction and minuteness their efforts at suppressing the recollection of these experiences or ideas, the word "experiences" seems to have included genital experiences, particularly in view of the fact that subsequently, or better soon after, he had considered as of great importance the alleged passive sexual experience of seduction in the early childhood of his hysterics patients.[6]

The importance of sex in the etiology of the neuroses was reiterated by Freud in his paper of 1896, *Heredity and the Etiology of the Neuroses* where he stated that:

> Each of the major neuroses mentioned, has as its immediate cause a special disturbance of the nervous economy and that these pathological functional changes betray as the common source the sexual life of the person concerned, *either a disturbance of his present sexual life, or important events in his* past life.[7]

Again, in 1896, in his paper *Further Remarks on the Defence Neuro-Psychoses*, Freud recalled the fact that Breuer and himself in an earlier publication (1893) had already expressed the opinion:

> That the symptoms of Hysteria can be understood only by tracing them back *to traumatic experiences*, and that these psychical traumas were related *to the patient's sexual life*.[8]

And finally in the same year 1896 in a conference at the Society of Psychiatry and Neurology in Vienna, on the subject of the etiology of hysteria, Freud had again stated that: "Whatever case and whatever symptom we take as our starting point, in the end *we infallibly come to the realm of sexual experience*.[9]

It is at this point that Freud added: "So here for the first time we would seem to have discovered an etiological condition of hysterical symptoms."[10] With that statement one gets the clear impression that Freud *had claimed for himself the discovery of the sexual etiol-*

ogy of the neuroses. This impression was confirmed by a subsequent passage in that same conference, when referring to the opposition which in the medical circle of Vienna had been raised against that view, Freud made the following remark:

> On the actual matter in dispute, I will only remark that in my case at least, there was no preconceived opinion which led me to single out the sexual factor in the Etiology of Hysteria. The two investigators, as whose pupil I began my work on the subject, Charcot and Breuer, *emphatically had no such a presupposition, in fact had a personal disinclination to it, which I originally shared*. Only the most laborious and detailed investigations have converted me, and that slowly enough, to the opinion which I defend to-day.[11] [italics mine]

Thus Freud, while claiming for himself the discovery of the sexual etiology of Hysteria, stated at the same time that his former teachers had a personal disinclination to consider sexuality as the causation of the neuroses, a disinclination which he himself had originally shared.

How can we reconcile such a statement that his teachers Breuer and Charcot to whom he later added Chroback, had a personal disinclination to the sexual theory of the neuroses, a disinclination which Freud himself shared, when we consider that *all three* of his teachers *had been actually the first to initiate Freud to the sexual etiology of the neurosis, in which they themselves explicitely believed*? Nor is there any way to reconcile Freud's implication that he himself had discovered that sexual etiology, when by his own admission in his subsequent publication of 1914 *The History of the Psycho-analytic Movement*, he gave that credit to *those three teachers of his*.

Why did Freud wait eighteen years to admit the truth? Was it because he belatedly felt guilty for having distorted the views of his teachers *who had never been disinclined*, but on the contrary, firmly considered sexuality as a very important factor in the precipitation of a neurosis? Or was it because in the face of the strong criticism and reaction against his views, that had originated in the medical circles of Vienna, Freud tried to soften that criticism by sharing with other prominent physicians his daring theory? Presumably it was because of the latter consideration that Freud in the above publication wrote the following:

> There was some consolation for the bad reception accorded even among my intimate friends, to my contention of the sexual etiology of the neuroses. . . . The idea for which I was

made responsible, *had by no means originated with me.* It had been imparted to me, by no less than three people, Breuer himself, Charcot, and the gynecologist of Vienna, Chroback.[12] [italics mine]

Freud then proceeded to recount their priority. Concerning Breuer, he recalled the fact that one day when he was a young house physician (1882-1885?), he was walking with Breuer through the town, when a man came up, who evidently wished urgently to speak to him. As soon as Breuer was free, he told him that this man was the husband of one of his patients. The wife, he added was behaving in such an extraordinary way in society, that she had been brought to him for treatment. Then Breuer added:

These things are always *"secrets d'alcove."* Astonished I asked him what he meant, and he answered by telling me the meaning of the word alcove (*marriage bed*), for he did not realize how extraordinary his remarks had seemed to me.[13]

As for the reference to Charcot (1885), Freud related that the latter in Paris, was discussing with his colleague, Brouardel, the case of a young married couple from the Far East; the woman was a confirmed invalid, the man either impotent or exceedingly awkward:

"Tachez donc," I heard Charcot repeating, "Je vous assure vous y arriverez." Brouardel who spoke loudly must have expressed his astonishment that symptoms such as the wife's could have been produced in such circumstances; for Charcot suddenly broke in with great animation: *"Mais dans les cas pareils c'est toujours la chose genitale* . . . toujours . . . toujours, and he crossed his arms over his stomach, hugging himself and jumping up and down in his own characteristic lively way.[14] [italics mine]

On his return from Paris, Freud, who had begun medical practice in Vienna as a privatdozent for nervous diseases, had again an opportunity to become influenced by the importance of sexuality in the etiology of the neuroses, this time by a colleague who had been his teacher, Chrobak, whom he highly respected. That circumstance is reported by Freud by recalling the fact that one day, Chrobak asked him to take a patient of his own to whom he could not give enough time, and that when he arrived at the patient's house, he found that she was suffering from attacks of insensate anxiety, and could only be soothed by the most detailed information of where her physician was at every moment of the day. When Chrobak arrived, Freud reported:

He took me aside and told me that the patient's anxiety was due to the fact that although she had been married for eighteen years, she was still *virgo intacta*. The husband was absolutely impotent. In such cases, he said there was nothing for a medical man to do but shield this domestic misfortune with his own reputation, and put up with it if people shrugged their shoulders, and said of him, "He is no good if he can't cure her after so many years." The sole prescription for such a malady, he added, is familiar enough to us, but we cannot order it. It runs as follows:

Rx Penis normalis
dosim
repetatur!

I had never heard of such a prescription and would have liked to shake my head over my kind friend's cynicism.[15]

At any rate, influenced by the views of those three eminent colleagues, Freud began to utilize that newly acquired notion in his private practice and he seemed to have been sold quite rapidly on those views, according to the reports that he himself wrote in his *Studies on Hysteria* which, in collaboration with Breuer, he published in 1895. The first report refers to the medical history of Frau Emmy von N., a patient whom Freud began to treat in May 1888. In that report Freud mentioned the relationship which he had established between the patient's phobias and the fact that she had been living in *a state of abstinence* which in his estimation, could not have left no traces of its influence:

> Thus he wrote: I cannot help suspecting that this woman who was *so passionate* and so capable of strong feelings, *had not won her victory over her sexual needs*, without a severe struggle, and that at times, her attempts at suppressing this most powerful of all instincts, had exposed her to severe mental exhaustion.[16] [italics mine]

Again in the very early 1890s, in the analysis of another patient "Katharina," Freud referred to *the importance of early sexual experiences* in the etiology of her hysteria, and concluded that:

> In every analysis of a case of Hysteria, based on sexual trauma, we find that impressions from the pre-sexual period, which produced no effect on the child, attain traumatic power at a later date, as memories, when the girl or married woman, has acquired *an understanding of sexual life*.[17] [italics mine]

And again in the case of another patient, Fraulein Elizabeth

125

von R., whom Freud analyzed in 1892, *he emphasized the circle of ideas of an erotic nature* which she had to suppress because they came into conflict with her moral ideas.[18] Freud was referring particularly to her feelings towards her brother-in-law, during her sister's life, and to the thought, after her sister died, of being attracted precisely by that man, a thought which she had to repress because it was totally unacceptable to her.

Returning now to Freud's apparent claim that he had discovered the sexual etiology of hysteria, whereas that credit did not belong to him, Freud in his *History of the Psycho-analytic Movement*, (1914) tried to justify that claim of 1896 by stating that:

> These three men had all communicated to me a piece of knowledge, which strictly speaking they themselves did not possess. . . . These three identical opinions, which I had heard without understanding *had lain dormant in my mind for years until one day they awoke in the form of an apparently original idea.*[19]

One can hardly agree with Freud's convenient cryptamnesic explanation for his having forgotten those three important events, when one thinks that it was pretty soon after he had heard these three men, particularly the shocking Chroback, that he began to relate his own cases of neuroses to the sexual factor, as indicated by his first case of Frau Emmy von R. in 1888, after Freud had just returned from Paris in 1886. One must also wonder over the accuracy of Freud's subsequent statement in reference to two of those happenings with Breuer and Chrobak, that both of them: "denied having done so, when I reminded them of the facts."[20]

Indeed, how can we reconcile, at least as far as Breuer was concerned, the fact that according to Freud he had denied of ever having mentioned to him the words "marriage bed," when we consider that in 1895 Breuer, whom Freud a year later had depicted as having had a personal disinclination to consider a sexual factor in the etiology of Hysteria, had published in collaboration with him their *Studies on Hysteria* in which publication Breuer restated his belief in the sexual etiology of the neuroses in the following passage where he used precisely the words "marriage bed": "I do not think that I am exaggerating when I assert that the great majority of severe neuroses, have their origin in the 'marriage bed'."[21] Furthermore "marriage bed" must have certainly implied genitality.

In both his papers of 1896, *Heredity and the Etiology of the neuroses* and *The Etiology of Hysteria*, Freud not only reiterated the sexual etiology of the neuroses, but added an important distinctive factor, always of a sexual nature, for the precipitation of each one of the two neuroses "Hysteria and Obsessive neurosis." In Hysteria, Freud felt that it developed only in those individuals in whom sexual experiences or impulses, at a certain period of later adult life, *reactivated in them the memory-traces of some previous sexual experience of their childhood* which had been forgotten or repressed. In that sexual experience, the child had played *a passive role* having been submitted to a *traumatic painful experience of seduction* at the hands of adults or of other children. Later in life when sexual impulses or thoughts presented themselves to that person, the painful memory of that childhood experience became reactivated, and that recollection was enough to induce the Repression of those recent sexual impulses, and as a result of which, the symptoms of Hysteria developed.

In Obsessive neurosis, it was also the recollection of some sexual experience of childhood which had been forgotten or repressed, that induced the development of its symptoms. But contrary to Hysteria, the childhood sexual experience of the Obsessive neurotic had not been a passive and painful one of seduction, *but an active one perpetrated upon other children and as such associated with pleasure and not pain*. The obscure point in this assumption was the why the reactivation of a pleasant sexual memory, should prompt in later life, the repression of any sexual impulse, even though of a pleasurable nature.

In order to justify repression operating against the reactivation of a pleasant sexual memory, Freud assumed that at still a younger age, prior to the pleasant active sexual experience, the patient in his childhood, must have been subjected to *a passive painful experience of seduction*. In his view, the reactivated memory of the pleasurable sexual experience, converged with the simultaneous reactivation of the memory of the painful passive sexual experience, and in that convergence, it was ultimately the painful feeling which prevailed in the entire sexual recollection. Consequently repression had to be resorted against the ultimate painful feeling, and it was that repression that became operative against any sexual impulse of later life, in the obsessive neurotic.

Things did not end at this point. A great disappointment was in store for Freud. Having proceeded more diligently in the history-taking of new cases of Hysteria and Obsessive neuroses, Freud soon realized that all the incidents of either childhood's painful sexual seduction, or of pleasant active sexual experience, which his patients had reported to him, had not really taken place. That admission he made in a letter to his friend W. Fliess, dated September 21, 1897, in which he expressed the following feelings:

> I no longer believe in my Neurotica.... Now I don't know where I am, as I have failed to reach a theoretical understanding of repression and of its play of forces.[22]

In 1905 in his paper *My Views on the Part Played by Sexuality in the Etiology of the Neuroses*, Freud characterized his error as *"The most momentous of my early errors* which necessitated a change in the concept of hysterical symptoms."[23]

In his *History of the Psychoanalytic Movement* (1914), Freud referred to that error in the following terms:

> When this Etiology broke down under its own improbability and under contradictions in definitely ascertainable circumstances, the result was at first *helpless bewilderment.* Analysis had led by the right path back to those sexual traumas, and yet they were not true. Reality was lost under one's feet. At that time I would have given up the whole thing. *Perhaps I persevered only because I had no choice and could not then begin again at anything else.* At last came the reflection that after all, one has no right to despair, because one has been deceived in one's expectation; one must revise them.[24]

Animated by that resolve and faced with a do-or-die situation, Freud searched for a substitute factor to take the place of the actual sexual experiences of childhood, and thus fell back upon the existence of childhood sexual fantasies, the memory of which could replace the memory of the alleged actual sexual experiences. In Freud's reasoning:

> If hysterics trace back their symptoms to fictitious traumas, this new fact signifies that they create such scenes in fantasy, *and psychical reality* requires to be taken into account along side of *actual reality*. This was soon followed by the recognition that these fantasies were intended to cover up the autoerotic activities of early childhood.[25] [italics mine]

This subject of fantasies had already been taken up by Freud in his Draft M of May 25, 1897, addressed to his friend W. Fliess where he had expressed his views that fantasies arose from an unconscious combination of things experienced and heard, and that they aimed at making inaccessible the memory from which symptoms had been generated. He again repeated his views that fantasies were constructed by a process of fusion and distortions, consisting in a falsification of memory by a process of fragmentation so that a fragment of a visual scene is thus joined to a fragment of an auditory one and made into a fantasy while the fragment left over is linked up with something else. He also reiterated his view that if the intensity of a fantasy increases its intensity, it was repressed and a symptom was generated by a backward drive from the fantasy to its constituent memories.[26]

It is strange to note, however, that while Freud, on the one hand, used the children's fantasies to get him out "of his most momentous error," he on the other hand left us perplexed *by a subsequent statement* that seemed to destroy his own views on the value of the fantasies as a replacement for the actuality of sexual experiences of childhood. That statement was made in a subsequent letter to Fliess dated September 21, 1897 and read as follows:

> *It again seems arguable* that it is later experiences which give
> rise to fantasies which throw back to childhood; and with that
> the factor of hereditary predisposition regains a sphere of in-
> fluence from which I had made my business to oust it, in the
> interest of fully explaining neurosis.[27]

It is also of interest to note that while Freud had recognized his error to Flies on September 21, 1897, he was in no hurry to acknowledge publicly that error. In that letter he stated in fact: "Certainly I shall not tell it in Gath, or publish it in the street of Askalon, in the land of Philistines—but between ourselves I have a feeling more of triumph than of defeat (which cannot be right)."[28] Consistent with that resolve *not to tell*, Freud in his paper *Sexuality in the Neuroses*[29] published a year later (1898), continued to maintain his erroneous view on the actuality of the childhood sexual experiences, and it was only in 1905 in his paper *My Views on the Part Played by Sexuality in the Etiology of the Neuroses*,[30] that he first seemed to have acknowledged his error.

I may conclude this first chapter by stating with reasonable assurance that Freud carried on the earlier analysis of his neurotic patients only after he had been influenced by Breuer, Charcot, and Chrobak, who respectively used the words "marriage bed," "la chose génitale" and "penis in repeated doses" all evident references to genitality. I may also conclude with assurance that Freud in his early writings on the sexual etiology of the neuroses, had therefore made no distinction between "sexuality" and "genitality," thus justifying his early critics who correctly interpreted his references to sexuality as equivalent to genitality.

That Freud had clearly referred to "genitality" in his early writings seems supported also by his views on the etiology of "Anxiety neurosis" and "Neurasthenia" which he called "actual neuroses." In them he evidently referred to genitality when for instance he considered *coitus interruptus* as a major etiological factor in the development of "Anxiety neurosis," and *masturbation* as the major etiological factor in the development of Neurasthenia.

CHAPTER II

Genitality in Dreams

In 1900, in the first edition of his *Interpretation of Dreams*, Freud had not as yet, intended to establish a distinction between "sexuality" and "genitality." It is not my intention here to discuss the many important problems raised in that publication. I am referring to it, for the only purpose of pointing out among other things the fact that from an early beginning of his "Interpretation," when originally Freud *minimized the value of symbols in dreams*, in the subsequent editions of this publication, including the last English edition of 1932, he ended by assigning to symbols a dominant position in the interpretation of dreams. What is also important to note is that most of the symbols in question referred plainly to "genitality."

Freud began his difficult task of dream interpretation in 1897, by first analyzing his own dreams, while at the same time he was reviewing extensively all the existing literature of this subject. In that review he recalled at first the method practiced and held in high esteem by the ancients, that of the symbolic interpretation of the manifest content of a dream. This procedure consisted in the evaluation of the content of a dream *in its entirety*, and of its replacement by some other more intelligible content, though in some respects analogous to the original one. This procedure Freud called "symbolic interpretation." As an example of it, Freud referred to the interpretation of the Pharaoh's dream propounded by Joseph in the Bible: In his view, the seven fat kine followed by the seven lean kine that ate up the fat kines was a symbolic substitute for a prophecy of seven years of famine in the land of Egypt, which would consume all that was brought forth, in the seven years of plenty.[1]

A second popular method of interpreting dreams was described by Freud as that of the *decoding method* since it treated dreams as a kind of cryptography in which each sign had a known meaning in accordance with a fixed key. He then supposed that if he had dreamt of a letter and of a funeral, he would find in a dream book that letter must be translated by "trouble" and funeral by "betrothal." It would have been his task to link together the key words which he had deciphered in this way, and to transpose the result into the future tense.

In the early stages of his investigation, Freud did not assign an important value to the symbolic meaning of dreams. Nor did he accept the meaning of dreams, on the basis of the instructions furnished by the popular dream books available on this subject. He instead accepted for the interpretation of dreams, the interesting modification of the process of *"decoding"* that had been introduced by *Artemidourus of Daldis* (second century A.D.). In Freud's view that method takes into account not only the content of the dreams, but also the character and circumstances of the dreamer. It follows that the same dream-element would have a different meaning for a rich man, a married man, or let us say an orator, from what it would have for a poor man, a bachelor, or a merchant. In his opinion the essence of the decoding procedure however, lies in the fact that the work of interpretation is not brought to bear on the dream as a whole, but on each portion of the dreams content independently. It would seem as if the dream were a geological conglomerate in which each fragment of rock required a separate value.[2]

Though following this modified decoding method of interpretation of dreams, Freud, however, did not subscribe to the use of "dream books," because in them everything depended on the trustworthiness of the keys, and of this he had no guarantee. Nor did Freud, in his early attempts at interpreting dreams, rely on the "symbolic method" because *he found it restricted in its application and incapable of being laid down on general lines.* Instead by his own technique of free association in the analysis of his patient's dreams, he trained himself *to decode each segment of a dream* by asking the patient to refer it to some situation of the immediate present, or of the past, that he had experienced prior to the dream. The patient, operating as a simple observer limited himself to report to him the events of the dream, abstaining from any criticism or from any attempt at suppressing elements of it, simply because they struck him as unimportant or meaningless. In Freud's words: "The material which is in this way freshly obtained from his self-perception, makes it possible to interpret both his pathological ideas and his dream-structures."[3]

On this subject of decoding separately each segment of the dream, Freud felt that if one were *to put the dream as a whole* in front of the patient and ask him what he thought of it, his mental horizon would as a rule become a blank. If however, according to Freud one were to put the dream before him *cut up into pieces*, the patient will give us a series of associations to piece. He considered such associations as the background thoughts of that particular part of the dream. That method of interpretation which he practiced, already differed from the popular, historic, and legendary method of interpretation by means of symbolism, whereas it approximated the "decoding method," which employs interpretation *"en detail"* and not *"en masse"* and which regards dreams as being of composite character, as being conglomerates of psychical formations.[4]

It is this method of decoding each fragment of a dream, that Freud employed first in the analysis of his own dreams and then applied to the interpretation of the dreams of his neurotic patients.

It is not the purpose of this book to go over the various dreams of Freud, which he disclosed and discussed in support of his views of their meaning and mechanisms of production. I will only point to the most important conclusions which he derived from the analysis of his own dreams:

> Dreams are not to be likened to the unregulated sounds that rise from a musical instrument struck by the blow of some external force; they are not meaningless; they are not absurd. . . . On the contrary, they are psychical phenomena of complete validity—*fulfillments of wishes*.[5]

And in his quest to find out if this was a universal characteristic of dreams, Freud ultimately concluded that all dreams represent *"fulfillment of wishes,"* provided the latent contents of the dreams are taken into consideration and not their manifest contents alone.

The question that now presented itself to Freud, was the following: How dreams *with a distressing content* could be resolved into wish-fulfillments? For Freud this was possible if the distressing content of a dream, by virtue of its distortion, serves to disguise something that is wished for. The disguise occurs not only in the gloomiest kind of dreams, that is of those including death, but also in the so-called "anxiety-dreams." As an example of a gloomy kind of dream, Freud reported that of a young girl, a patient of his whose sister had only one boy left, Karl, having lost her elder boy Otto while the patient was still living with her. Otto was the patient's favorite; having more or less brought him up. She was fond of the little Karl too, but not nearly so fond as she had been of the one who died. The dream that she recounted to Freud, in a psychoanalytic session, was that she had dreamed that she saw Karl, lying before her dead. He was lying in his little coffin with his hands folded and with candles all round—he looked in fact, just like little Otto, who had died and whose death had been such a blow to her. How could that be a fulfillment of a wish, she asked Freud, considering that she could not have wished her sister to lose the one child she still had. Did that dream mean that she would have liked to see Karl dead, rather than Otto whom she was so fond of?

Freud assured her this last interpretation was out of the question. After reflecting, Freud was able to give her the correct interpretation of the dream because he was familiar with the whole of the dreamer's previous history, which centered around the fact that his patient had been left an orphan and had been brought up in the house of her much older sister. Among the friends who visited at the house was a man who made a lasting impression on his patient's heart, a man whom she had hoped to marry, though that hope for unexplained reasons was thwarted by her sister. After the breach, the man ceased to visit the home, and the patient herself set up on her own, though she did not however succeed in freeing herself from her attachment to her sister's friend, who was by profession a literary man, a professor involved in lecturing. The patient never missed an opportunity to be in his audience, and managed to see him from a distance on neutral ground at every opportunity she had. The day before her dream, she had told Freud that the professor was going to a particular concert and that she intended to go to it as well, so as to enjoy a glimpse of him once more. The concert was to take place on the day on which she, the patient, told Freud her dream. To construct the correct interpretation of that dream, Freud asked the patient whether she could think of anything that happened at the time of little Otto's death, and she informed him that she had seen that man beside little Otto's coffin. On that basis Freud interpreted the dream of his patient in the sense that if now the other boy Karl were to die, the same thing would happen, and the patient would spend the day with her sister, and the professor would be certain to come to offer his condolences, thus the patient would see him again under the same conditions as the other time. The dream meant no more than the patient's wish against which she was inwardly struggling. Considering also, the fact that she had in her pocket a ticket for a concert to take place the day after the dream, Freud concluded that her dream was a dream of impatience, that anticipated by a few hours, the glimpse that she was going to have of him the day she reported that dream. In Freud's view, his patient in order to conceal her wish she had evidently chosen a situation of grief in which such wishes of love are usually suppressed.[6] It was on the basis of some analogous interpretation of various other distressing or unpleasant dreams that Freud concluded that such dreams represent a disguised fulfillment of a suppressed or repressed wish.[7]

Concerning the anxiety-dreams, Freud, on the basis of the views which he had held in the past, that neurotic anxiety derived from sexual life and corresponded to libido which had been diverted from its purpose and thus found no proper employment, concluded that since this formula had met the test of time, it enabled him to infer from it that anxiety-dreams were also dreams with a sexual content, the libido belonging to which had been transformed into anxiety.[8] Thus at least for the anxiety-dreams, on that basis their latent content expressed the fulfillment of *a sexual wish*. It must be noted, however, that Freud in 1926 rejected his original view of the transformation of repressed libido into the affect of anxiety.

A pupil of Freud, Otto Rank, presumably encouraged by Freud's connection between sexuality and anxiety-dreams, went farther in concluding *that all dreams represent as a rule erotic wishes as fulfilled in a veiled and symbolically disguised shape.*[9] It is true that Freud nowhere adopted Rank's extreme formula as his own, but it must have been Freud's views on the anxiety-dreams that prompted Rank to feel that *it was as a rule* that dreams had a sexual meaning.

In his first edition of *The Interpretation of Dreams* (1900), all of Freud's conclusions concerning the meaning and nature of the dreams resulted from his applying to them *the "decoding method"* of interpretation of their various fragments. He had excluded from his technique the use of the popular historic and legendary symbolic method of interpretation. But in the following editions of his book, Freud allowed gradually the creeping-in of his technique of interpretation of dreams, of more and more of the elements of the symbolic method. The value of symbolic material was added *in the 1909 and 1911 editions* in chapter V (section D) under the heading of "Typical Dreams." It was, however, only *in the 1914 edition* that for the first time a special section E was added to chapter VI under the heading of *"Representation by Symbols in Dreams."*

In that section, Freud stated that at the onset that he had already recognized the presence of symbolism in dreams from the very beginning, but that it was only by degrees and as his experience increased that he had arrived at a full appreciation of its extent and significance, thanks to the contributions of Wilhelm Steckel (1911).[10] Furthermore, he considered that the advance in psycho-analytic experience had brought to his notice patients who have shown a direct understanding of dream-symbols of this kind to a surprising extent, so that when he as others became familiar with the abundant use made of *symbolism for representing sexual material* in dreams, the question was bound to arise of whether many of these symbols do not occur with a permanently fixed meaning, like the "grammalogues" in shorthand, and that we could feel tempted to draw up a new dream book on the decoding principle." He then pursued his view that dreams make use of this symbolism for the disguised representation of their latent thoughts. It follows that if a dreamer has a choice open to him between a number of symbols, he will decide in favor of the one which is connected, in its subject matter, with the rest of the material of his thoughts.[12]

In Freud's experience, he felt obliged in dealing with those elements of the dream-content which must be recognized as symbolic, to adopt a combined technique which, on the one hand rests on the dreamer's associations, and on the other hand fills the gap *from the interpreter's knowledge of symbols*. He was of the opinion that the uncertainties which still attach to our activities as interpreters of dreams spring in part from our incomplete knowledge, which hopefully will progressively improve. However, it springs in part also from certain characteristics of dream-symbols themselves, inasmuch as they may have more than one or even several meanings. The correct interpretation can only be arrived at, on each occasion, from the context.[13]

At any rate, in his later edition of 1914 of his *Interpretation of Dreams*, Freud had made quite a concession to the symbolic interpretation of dreams which in his first edition of 1900 he had labelled as *"restricted in its application and incapable of being laid down on general lines."* Spurred also by his desire of relating dreams to sexual matter as he had done for the clinical symptoms of the neuroses, he must have been quite elated when, following the contributions of Wilhelm Steckel (1911) he could now with that additional strong support, bring also into the *Interpretation of Dreams* his favorite subject of sexuality.

Though expressing reservation to the extensive list of sexual symbols introduced by Steckel, Freud himself extended however his own list of the sexual symbols which he had encountered in the analysis of his neurotic patients. Having first established among the dream symbols, that of emperor and empress, or king and queen, as representing the dreamer's parents, and that of prince or princess representing the dreamer himself or herself (1909), he then assigned a sexual meaning to numerous other dream-symbols. Without entering into a complete enumeration of all the symbols which Freud had associated *with the genitals or with the genital's activities*, I will refer only to the following dream-symbols: All elongated objects such as sticks, tree trunks, umbrellas, and sharp weapons such as knives and daggers, symbolized in his views the male sexual organ (1911). Furthermore, the opening of an umbrella in the course of a dream symbolized the genital erection (1909). In his latest English edition of his *Interpretation of Dreams* (1931), Freud added some more symbols representing the genital organs or the genital activities. Thus: steps, ladders or staircases, or as the case may be, walking up or down on them, represented the sexual act. A woman's hat he often interpreted as a genital organ. In men's dreams a necktie often appeared as a symbol for the penis, so did all weapons and tools and complicated machinery. Playing with a little child, or beating it, often represented according to Freud, masturbation. Sisters represented the breasts, and brothers the larger hemispheres. The number three as confirmed from many sides, became a symbol of the male genitals. The hand or the foot symbolized also the male organ, while the mouth, the ear, or even an eye could represent the opening of the female genital organ. He also felt that many landscapes, especially those containing bridges or wooded hills, mounted to the description of the genitals. Many of the beasts which were used as genital symbols in mythology and folklore among which fishes, snails, cats, mice, and above all snakes, played now the same part in dreams.[14]

All these various sexual symbols, and many more, are to be found in pages from 354 to 357 of Freud's latest English edition of his (*Interpretation of Dreams*) (1931) and in the subsequent pages where Freud reported specific dreams which he had analysed in his patients and where the sexual symbols referred particularly *to the genital organs and to the genital activities*. It must have been on the basis of all the sexual symbols which he and others of his followers had established, that Freud ultimately concluded that, "It was impossible to arrive at the interpretation of a dream if one excludes dream-symbolism, and how irresistibly one is driven to accept it in many cases."[15] At the same time, Freud warned however that one should not rely exclusively on the symbols alone, and that the interpretation of dreams should go hand-in-hand not only with the technique of free associations on the part of the dreamer, but also with the method of decoding the dream by interpreting in detail its various segments. On that basis, Freud regarded the dream from the very first as being a composite character, a conglomerate of psychical formations.[16] It was in this connection that Freud had finally concluded that, he should however utter an express warning against overestimation of the importance of symbols in dream interpretation, that is of restricting the work of translating dreams merely to translating symbols, and against abandoning the technique of making use of the dreamer's associations. In his view, the two techniques of dream interpretation must be complementary to each other.[17]

It was on that broad basis that Freud also concluded that the more one is concerned with the solution of dreams, the more one is driven to recognize *that the majority of the dreams of adults deal with sexual material and give expression to erotic wishes*, inasmuch as no other instinct has been subjected since childhood to much suppression as the sexual instinct with its numerous components. In his opinion, from no other instinct are so many and such powerful unconscious wishes left over, ready to produce dreams in a state of sleep. In interpreting dreams, he felt that we should never forget the significance of sexual complexes, though one should also of course, avoid the exaggeration of attributing exclusive importance to them.[18]

Considering, however, that the third English edition of the *Interpretation of Dreams*, which I have consulted, dates to December 1931, that is eleven years after Freud's publication of his *Beyond the Pleasure Principle* (1920), in which he first introduced his new assumption of the "instinct of death," activated by *a special aggressive "destructive" energy*, one wonders why Freud did not take into consideration in this third English edition, the existence and operation in the course of dreams *of that destructive force* and its related symbols, but instead centered his attention only upon the forces of the sexual instincts.

Had Freud taken into consideration the operation of that destructive force, would he have assigned to all elongated objects, sticks, tree trunks, long sharp weapons such as knives, daggers, sabers, and pikes, the symbolic meaning of a male sexual organs? Would it not have been as valid for him, to assign to those symbols the meaning of weapons of aggression, at the service of some latent aggressive content of the dreams which could be expressing *some pent-up repressed aggressive wish* in the life of the patient? And had he done that, would it not have been possible that his analysis and discussion of the various fragments of his patient's dreams may have followed a different direction and resulted in the uncovering of other forces operating in the unconscious?

It is true that Freud never asserted that all dreams require a sexual interpretation, but he certainly spoke of *the majority of the dreams* and even extended that sexual interpretation to innocent and indifferent dreams which in his views *may embody crudely erotic wishes*. In his words:

> It is also true that many dreams which appear indifferent and which one would not regard in any respect peculiar, lead back on analysis to wishful impulses which are unmistakably sexual.[19] He even asserted that Oedipus dreams, that is dreams "that in disguised form, *refer to the sexual intercourse of the dreamer with his own mother, are many times more frequent than straight forward dreams*.[20] [italics mine]

In all those terms, there was no doubt that the latent content of such dreams dealt specifically with *genitality* and not simply with *sexuality* in terms of some sexual instinct-component in search of its organ-pleasure from areas of the body outside the genital area proper.

We also must not forget that most of the latent content of dreams which Freud interpreted with the help of symbols refer very clearly to either the genital organs, or to the act of copulation or to both. Nor must we forget that up to the last English edition (1931) of his *Interpretation of Dreams*, genitality and copulation constituted for Freud the majority of the dream symbols, leaving no room for possible symbols related to "Sexuality" in terms of its enlarged psychoanalytic concept of organ-pleasure applicable to all organs of the body. No attempt was made by Freud who leaned decisively toward the genital meaning of those symbols, to differentiate possible symbols of Sexuality from those of Genitality.

Thus, in the last edition of his *Interpretation of Dreams*, the English edition of 1931, Freud seemed to have lost track of the fight in which he had become engaged in differentiating sexuality from genitality, a fight which he had carried in his *Three Essays on the Theory of Sexuality* up to its last edition of 1920. It was in that publication that Freud in answer to his critics who accused him of "pansexualism" he in turn accused them *of having failed to differentiate sexuality from genitality*. Freud seemed to have lost track also of the emphasis which he had put over the genital meaning of symbols in dreams, an emphasis which prompted him to devote in his last edition of 1931 a full section to such genital symbols. Considering that emphasis, and considering the fact that the dreams constituted a major key to uncover the unconscious background of the neurotic symptoms, it would seem that Freud at a certain point seems to have lost track of his conclusions of 1913 that:

> *Psychoanalysis stands or falls* by the recognition of the sexual instinct-component, of the erotogenic zones, and of the subsequent expansion of the sexual function as opposed to the narrower one of the genital function.[21]

Evidently that emphasis on genitality by Freud in his interpretation of dreams, an important key to the success of his psychoanalytic method of treatment of the neuroses does not seem to support his very important difference which he claimed should have been established between genitality and sexuality. Indeed that difference seemed to have vanished in Freud's treatment of the dreams in favor only of their pure genital symbolization.

Why did Freud miss the opportunity to establish in his patient's dreams a possible list of symbols representing sexuality in terms of the sexual organ-pleasure related to the various sexual instinct-components, to be differentiated from the symbols of genitality of which he certainly made an extensive and impressive list?

It is possible that in his endeavor to interpret dreams, Freud may have found it difficult to pinpoint symbols representing the manifestations of the various sexual instinct-components in terms of organ-pleasure originating in the mouth in the anus or in the skin and to be differentiated from the genital symbols proper. It is also possible that even if such symbols could have been manufactured, he may have lacked ways and means to separate them from the genital ones, considering how interrelated the alleged various erotogenic zones would have been with the ultimate genital zone, and considering that Freud had originally maintained that the genital excitations, if prevented to discharge properly along the genital route, would overflow for their discharge along the path of those different erotogenic zones.

Aside from these considerations, one could indeed sympathize with Freud's wish to extricate himself from the accusation that his theory of the neuroses was based upon the operation of repressed sexual forces, which in the light of his own early writings and lectures, he had not originally differentiated into the forces of the various sexual instinct-components on the one hand and those of the ultimate genital component on the other hand. In that context it would seem therefore that Freud had no ground for accusing his critics of having failed to make that differentiation which he himself had failed to make in his early writings.

His counterattack began in fact only in 1905 in his *Three Essays on the Theory of Sexuality* where he first assumed the existence and operation of various sexual instinct-components, and all of which originated in separate "erotogenic zones." In these zones, the cessation or removal of the endo-somatic excitations that impinged over them, would elicit a satisfaction which Freud arbitrarily called "a sexual organ-pleasure." Unfortunately this whole concept of the various "erotogenic zones" and related sexual organ-pleasure, rested only upon Freud's own personal conjectures, in support of which he failed to give a valid *observable* proof. And to think that clinical observation had been considered by Freud as paramount in the theoretical construction of his psychoanalytic doctrine. I will discuss at length in the next chapter, this particular subject.

In his publication of 1920, *Beyond the Pleasure Principle*, Freud extended his concept of the "sexual instinct in its totality," made that is of its various sexual instinct-components, by identifying it with the "Instinct of life" and subsequently with the Ego-instincts of self-preservation, and contrasted *them all* with a newly introduced "Instinct of Death" or destructive instinct. The activating energy of the "Instinct of Life" he designated as Libido, the same designation which he had originally applied to the activating energy of *only* the sexual instinct in its totality.

In the same year (1920), in the last sentence of his *preface* to the fourth edition of his "Three Essays," Freud referred to Sexuality in terms of the sexual instinct-components, outside the genital as *"The Eros of the divine Plato."* In his words:

> As for the stretching of the concept of Sexuality which has been necessitated by the analysis of children and of what are called "perverts," any one who looks down with contempt to psychoanalysis, from a superior vantage point, should remember how closely the enlarged sexuality of psychoanalysis *coincides with the Eros of the divine Plato.*

And in his *New Introductory Lectures* (1933), returning to that identity Freud wrote again:

Our hypothesis is that there are two essentially different classes of instincts: the sexual instincts understood in the widest sense—*Eros if you prefer that name*—and the aggressive instincts, whose aim is destruction.[22]

In Chapter V of this Part II of the "Trilogy," I have briefly summarized *Plato's Symposium*, the alleged source of Freud's information, a symposium dedicated to the praise of the "God of Love, but I have failed to find in it any overt reference to its coinciding with Sexuality in Freud's psychoanalytic terms.

Freud's Unsubstantiated Assumption That the Sexual Instinct Is Made of Various Sexual Instinct-Components Originating in Various "Erotogenic Zones"

From the time when he published his views on the sexual etiology of the neuroses (1893-94), Freud found himself under a growing criticism on the part of his colleagues in Vienna particularly, for having advanced such a daring theory which in spite of all, he had expanded in his publication of 1900, *The Interpretation of Dreams*. That criticism was directed mainly against Freud's writings and lectures in which he had given the impression that whenever he mentioned "sexuality," be it in the psychoneuroses, in the so-called "Actual neuroses," or subsequently in his *Interpretation of Dreams*, he obviously referred to "sexuality" in terms of "genitality."

No wonder that under such pressure, Freud was eager to find some convincing way out of that criticism. That way out must have germinated slowly in his mind so as to finally crystallize in his assumption that sexuality should not be confused with genitality, the former being the expression of various individual "sexual instinct-components," seeking sexual pleasure from various zones of the body (the erotogenic zones) while genitality was the ultimate expression of the sexual-instinct-component originating in the sexual organs and seeking its ultimate sexual organ pleasure along the genital path of discharge. That assumption crystallized itself in Freud's mind in the course of his analytic investigations of the sexual perversions frequently encountered in his neurotic patients.

It was in his *Three Essays on the Theory of Sexuality* in 1905 that Freud presented his views on the distinction between sexuality and genitality.

Referring to the "sexual instinct" in its entirety, Freud, to begin with, stated that though popular opinion has quite definite ideas upon the nature and characteristics of this sexual instinct, and that it considered it to be absent in childhood, and the aim of which is presumed to be sexual union, he: "had every reason to believe however, that these views give a very false picture of the true situation and . . . that they contain a number of errors, inaccuracies and hasty conclusions."[1]

Then, on the basis of his analysis of the sexual life of his neurotic adults, Freud became interested in the dissection of the totality of the sexual instinct in various component parts, and advanced the assumption that it seemed plausible to trace back the positive and negative aspects of a neurotic's sexual life to a number of "*sexual instinct-components*," originating in various areas of our body, and which he called "erotogenic zones." He then explained what he meant by instinct, in which explanation he included the various sexual instinct-components:

> By instinct is provisionally to be understood *the psychic representative of an endo-somatic source of stimuli* which are in a continual flux. . . . what distinguishes the instincts from one another, and endows them with specific qualities, *is their relation to their somatic sources and to their aims*. The source of an instinct is a process of excitation occurring in an organ, *and the immediate aim of the instinct is the removal of this organ-stimulus*.[2] [italics mine]

At this point, Freud had therefore assumed that there were several zones of our body (the erotogenic zones) from which endo-somatic stimuli originate, and the proper removal of which resulted in an organ pleasure which he qualified as being sexual. The sexual quality of some of the endo-somatic stimuli (excitations) had been already indicated by Freud when he assumed that he could not escape in the theory of the instincts, the fact that excitations of two kinds arise from the somatic organs, based upon the differences of a chemical nature. One of these kinds he assumed to be *specifically sexual*, and he labeled the organ concerned as "the erotogenic zone" of the sexual component-instinct arising from it.[3] Evidently in Freud's view, it was the *extinction* of those specific sexual excitations that resulted in the related sexual organ-pleasure.

Of course that assumption of a sexual organ-pleasure, originating in the various "erotogenic zones," a pleasure which in those terms represented the essence of what Freud called "sexuality" in contrast with the sexual organ-pleasure originating in the sexual organs, and which Freud considered as the essence of "genitality," represented no more than a conjecture on the part of Freud, a theoretical one lacking any possibility of validation. But Freud needed very badly such a conjecture in order to reply to his critics of the sexual etiology of the neuroses, whom he accused of having failed to establish a difference between sexuality related to the sexual organ-pleasure, elicited from the various "erotogenic zones," and genitality related to the sexual organ-pleasure ultimately elicited from the "genital erotogenic zone."

In the discussion of the various "erotogenic zones," Freud remarked that:

> The character of erotogenicity can be attached to some parts of the body in a particular marked way. These are *predestined erotogenic zones, as is shown by the example of sucking.* The same example however shows us that any part of the skin or mucous membrane, can take over the function of an "erotogenic zone" and must therefore have some aptitude in that direction . . . *Any other part of the body can acquire the same susceptibility to stimulation as is possessed by the genitals and become an "erotogenic zone."*[4] [italics mine] [He further added that] Certain regions of the body such as the mucous membranes of the mouth and anus seem as it were to be claiming that they should themselves be regarded and treated as genitals.[5]

In a footnote to page 62 of his last edition of the "Three Essays" (1920), Freud, after taking other observations into account, ascribed the quality of erotogenicity to all parts of the body, including all the internal organs. In that footnote, Freud must have been referring to what he had written in 1914 in his paper on *Narcissism*, where he discussed "Hypochondria" as a condition which manifests itself in distressing and painful body sensations. In Freud's view, the hypochondriac withdraws both *interests and libido* from the objects of the outer world and concentrates both upon the organ which engages his attention. The activity of any given bodily organ, was then compared by Freud to that of the genital organs in a state of excitation, when they become congested with blood, swollen, moist and the seat of manifold sensations. On that basis, all organs which undergo such changes *without being diseased*, could in his view be considered as "*erotogenic*," acting, that is, as a substitute for the genitals. He thus concluded that he could regard *erotogenicity as properly common to all organs*, and thus feel justified in speaking of an increase or decrease in the degree of it, in any given part of the body.[6]

At this point, one may justifiably ask the following question: On what basis did Freud consider the activity of the various erotogenic zones representing the expression of the activities of various "sexual component-instincts?" To answer that question, I must again refer to what Freud had considered the immediate aim of an instinct and which I have reported previously, that the source of an instinct is a process of excitations in an organ, and that the immediate aim of the instinct lies in the removal of *this organic* stimulus.[7] He then considered the removal of the somatic excitation in that organ, as generating a feeling of satisfaction which he called *"organ-pleasure."* It is this resulting organ-pleasure that Freud assumed to be a *"sexual pleasure,"* the expression of a locally generated and operating sexual component-instinct.

Unfortunately, Freud offered us no plausible argument favoring that conclusion, except that of a personal dogmatic assertion that the organ-pleasure derived from the removal of excitations from all the external or internal portions of our body was of an actual sexual nature. One therefore may rightly question the soundness of such a dogmatic assertion, that defied any possibility of verification.

That unsubstantiated assertion, Freud carried in his paper of 1915 *The Instincts and their Vicissitudes*, where again he restated his views that he no longer considered the existence of a single sexual instinct, but of various sexual instinct-components originating in various "erotogenic zones" and aiming at "a sexual organ-pleasure." In Freud's words, the sexual instincts:

> are numerous, emanate from manifold organic sources, act in the first instance independently of one another, and only at a late stage achieve a more or less complete synthesis. The aim which each strives to attain is organ-pleasure. Only when the synthesis is complete do they enter the service of the function of reproduction, becoming generally recognizable as sexual instincts.[8]

Freud's dogmatic concept of Sexuality was reiterated in his *Autobiography* where he stated that: "Every bodily function having pleasure as its goal is to be considered as the expression of Sexuality."[9] And again in his posthumous publication *An Outline of Psychoanalysis*, Freud restated that:

> *Sexual life comprises the function of obtaining pleasure from zones of the body*—a function which is subsequently brought into the service of that of reproduction. The two functions often fail to coincide completely.[10]

Of course, one might have found some support for Freud's assumption of the "erotogenic zones" operating as generators of individual sexual instinct-components, had he been able to document and prove the notion imparted to him in 1895 by his friend W. Fliess to the effect that at its source sexuality was related to a special chemistry, different from the chemistry that governs the other non-sexual ego-instincts.

To elaborate on this point, I must go back to Freud's belief that excitations of two kinds arise from the somatic organs, based upon differences of a *chemical nature*, and one of which he described as being *specifically sexual*, so that he could speak of the organ concerned as the "erotogenic zone" of the sexual instinct component arising from it.[11]

That chemical theory first appeared in Freud's writings in reference to his interpretation of his own dream of July 1895, in the course of which the formula of *"Trimethylamine"* in heavy type appeared to him in the dream. In analyzing the various fragments of that dream, Freud came to wonder what it was that attracted his attention to the word "Trimethylamine?" His answer was that it had been his conversation with a friend who had confided to him some ideas on the subject of chemistry of the sexual processes, and had mentioned among other things that he believed that one of the product of sexual metabolism was trimethylamine.[12]

In 1920, in the fourth edition of his *Three Essays on the Theory of Sexuality*, Freud returned to the chemical theory of sexuality and pointed out that new investigations had established that the sex-determining influence is not an attribute of that part of the sexual gland which gives rise to the specific cells (spermatozoa and ovum), but of their interstitial tissue, upon which special emphasis is laid by those authors under the name of puberty gland. He also felt that special chemical substances are produced in the interstitial portion of the sex glands and which are taken up in the blood stream and cause particular parts of the nervous system to be charged with sexual tension. How sexual excitations arise from the stimulation of the erotogenic zones when the central apparatus has been previously charged? He felt that such a question cannot be treated even hypothetically in the present state of our knowledge.[13]

That a chemical substance originating in the gonads should be responsible for the erotogenicity and related sexual organ-pleasure in the far distant mucous membrane of the mouth, for instance (the first erotogenic area), or in the eye, as in scoptophilia, or in all the skin of the body as in masochism, seems to me a far-out assumption to the extent that it had been considered by Freud himself as impossible to even hypothesize. Lacking therefore of any possible explanation for his assumption, how could Freud qualify as sexual the organ-pleasure elicited in the various "erotogenic zones," from the removal of the endo-somatic stimuli operating in those various erotogenic zones? Why did he not consider the organ-pleasure related *to the elimination of endo-somatic stimuli* in the various erotogenic zones outside the genitals as representing a pleasure of a nonsexual nature, in terms of a simple hedonistic pleasure? The hedonistic philosophy which originated in ancient Greece with Aristipus the Cyrenaic, preached the view that the "aim of life" was the search for pleasure by the individual man. But nothing in that philosophy indicated that the pleasure to seek was the specific sexual pleasure that could derive, as Freud maintained, from the activity and satisfaction of special endo-somatic stimuli in the course of all our physical and mental activities.

In that respect, Freud was very clear when he assumed that all sorts of physical activities generate sexual excitations, and that this occurs particularly in children. In the latter, he mentioned particularly the mechanical agitation of their body, such as swinging or being thrown in the air, or being shaken in carriages or when traveling by railway. In them, he also assumed that "affective processes" and even emotions of a terrifying quality encroach upon their sexuality. Concerning the sexual pleasure derived from intellectual work in later life, Freud was also quite dogmatic when he stated that: "It is an unmistakable fact that concentration of the attention upon an intellectual task and intellectual strain in general produce a *concomitant sexual excitation* in many young people as well as adults."[14] Later on, in 1914, in his paper on *Narcissism*,[15] Freud elaborated on the point that also in the course of our internal physiological processes, sexual excitations occur. It is in this connection that Freud had already concluded in his "Three Essays" that there are present in our organism contrivances which bring it about that in the case of a great number of internal processes, sexual excitations arise as a concomitant effect, as soon as the intensity of those processes passes beyond certain quantitative limits.[16]

It was on the basis of all these assumptions, none of them possessing any possibility of validation, that Freud ultimately concluded that: "It well may be *that nothing of considerable importance can occur in the organism*, without contributing some component to the excitation of the sexual instincts."[17] One wonders at times how was it, that Freud's followers accepted such assumptions as a matter of faith in their leader and never challenged their accuracy.

Though lacking any documentation in support of his assertion that the "erotogenic zones" were the actual source of various sexual instinct-components, the aim of which was that of eliciting in each of these zones a *sexual organ-pleasure*, Freud addressed himself to the relationship which he had assumed to exist between the above premise and the sexual perversions which he had often encountered in his neurotic patients. Having hypothesized to his own personal satisfaction, as the result of his analysis of those patients, that those sexual perversions were related to the operation of the various sexual instinct-components originating in the various erotogenic zones, Freud easily concluded that if such perversions admit analysis, that is if they can be taken to pieces, then they must be of a composite nature. This gave him the hint that perhaps the sexual instinct itself may be no simple thing, but put together from components which have come apart again in the perversions.[18]

What are the objections that can be raised against Freud's assumption of individual sexual instinct-components originating separately in the various "erotogenic zones" of our body?

To answer properly that question, let me first refer to Freud's following view that most psychoneurotics fall ill after the age of puberty, as the result of the demands made upon them by normal sexual life, and that such illnesses set in later, when the libido fails to obtain satisfaction along normal lines. "In both these cases, *the libido behaves like a stream whose main bed has been blocked. It proceeds to fill up collateral channels which hitherto may have been empty.*"[19] [italics mine]

Such a statement indicates that in Freud's view, it was only after the age of puberty, or later in the adult life of his neurotic patients that the sexual instinct, having manifested itself in the form of sexual genital excitations, the patients because of their inability to obtain a satisfactory sexual organ-pleasure along the genital channel, proceed to fill up with their libido *the collateral channels which hitherto had not been used*. In other words the libido, non-utilized along the genital path, spreads itself over various other anatomic areas, which thus become the seat of sexual excitations.

These are precisely the areas that Freud had called the "erotogenic zones."

It seems to me that, by the above statement, Freud should have found himself in contradiction with his other assumption of the existence of various "erotogenic zones" from where various individual sexual instincts-components actually originated. If indeed the so-called "erotogenic zones" were to be considered as simply collateral zones of discharge for the excitations originated in the genitals, there would be no reason for considering such zones as *generating locally* individual sexual instinct-components. Freud apparently did not take into consideration such a contradiction created by his own writings.

However, had Freud weighed properly such a contradiction and had he therefore modified his original view by accepting now the function of the "erotogenic zones" simply as zones of *collateral discharge for the genital excitations*, and not as individual genetic zones of local sexual excitations, representing individual sexual instinct-components, he would have cut the ground from under his own feet, considering the fact that his major intent was that of establishing various sources for the actual origin of sexuality and related sexual organ-pleasure. He would have been unable consequently to support his contention that sexuality should be differentiated from genitality, a differentiation which had become essential for Freud, so much so that in 1913, as I have already reported he was prompted to conclude that:

> *Psychoanalysis stands or falls by the recognition of the sexual component-instincts, of the erotogenic zones, and of the subsequent expansion of the idea of the sexual function as opposed to the narrower one of the genital function.*[20] [italics mine]

At this point, we meet with an important ambiguity on Freud's part. I am referring to the meaning of the word "Libido" which he had used in explaining how in his patients their Libido having failed to obtain satisfaction along the normal genital path of discharge, behaved like a stream whose main bed had become blocked, and proceeded to fill up collateral channels which may have been hitherto empty. In that sense Libido was intended by Freud as *a movable sexual energy capable of displacement*, along the same lines which he had used in his early writings of 1894 when referring to the Libido in terms of a psychic energy made of "*a sum of excitation and of an amount of affect,*" he assumed that it could attach itself to a given idea, to detach itself from it, and attach itself to some other idea.

That assumption of a movable Libido in terms of a displaceable sexual energy, was carried through by Freud in his discussion of Schizophrenia in 1915 and of Melancholia in 1917. It was always the Libido in terms of a special sexual energy which, having abandoned its object, regressed into the Ego where it either reinforced the ego-narcissism, as in schizophrenia, or contributed to the process of Identification between the abandoned object and the Ego, as in Melancholia.

But in his last edition (1920) of his *Three Essays on the Theory of Sexuality*, Freud spoke of the Libido no longer in terms of only a movable energy, but also in terms of its mental representation:

> The analysis of the perversions and psychoneuroses has shown us that this sexual excitation is derived not from the so-called sexual parts alone, but from all the bodily organs. *We thus reach the idea of a quantity of libido, to the mental representation of which we give the name of ego-libido*, and whose production, increase or diminution, distribution and displacement, should afford us possibilities for explaining the psycho-sexual phenomena observed.[21]

The reference to the mental representation of the Libido brings to the fore something more than a simple movable sexual energy. It seems to indicate a combination of that energy with its own ideational representation. That reference to an idea having become associated with an energic psychic sexual quality changed Freud's assumption of a simple movable psychic energy endowed with a sexual quality. Indeed the assumption of a movable idea in combination with its affective quality, sexual or not, and which constitutes a movable "affective formation," an inseparable unit, an assumption which I have advanced, should have been Freud's ultimate assumption.

It follows that instead of speaking of a libido in terms of sexual psychic energy, which *alone*, having failed to obtain satisfaction along the normal genital path, or instead of speaking of sexual energy (sexual excitations) born locally in various erotogenic zones, we should be speaking of the displacement of a *"sexual affective formation,"* made of the ideational representation of the genital endo-somatic stimuli and of its attached sexual quality. Such a combination, under the energic power of its displaceable ideational representation, *may become associated*, fused, or combined with the *ideational representation* of some other areas of the body to which it imparts its own sexual quality. It is the product of this newly organized sexual "affective formation" which can impart a sexual attribute to those various areas of the body, which proceed to discharge it as such locally. No sexual energy alone is generated in the various areas of the body, nor is the sexual energy alone, generated in the genital organs that travels from the genitals to the various areas of the body in order to find a proper discharge outside the genitals.

However, had Freud considered also the displacement of the ideational representation of the original genital excitation in combination with its attached sexual quality, his view would still have differed from mine, inasmuch as he would have continued to assign to the sexual quality the attribute of the energic force necessary for the displacement of the original genital "affective formation." On the contary, in my view, as I have explained in chapter I of part I of this trilogy, the energic attribute of any old or new "affective formation" belongs to the ideational portion of that formation, and not to its quality, sexual or not.

This view of mine evidently differs fundamentally from Freud's view which he well summarized in his *Interpretation of Dreams* where, speaking of the energy attached to an idea or group of ideas, he emphatically concluded that what we regarded as mobile, *was not the psychical structure but its innervation*. I assume instead that it is precisely the idea or group of ideas which constitute "the psychic Structure," be they with or without any combined affective quality, *that I consider mobile and displaceable.*

Furthermore, the mobility of the ideas (the psychical structure) is not due to the psychic energy, sexual or not, but to that somatic energy which activates the ideational component of any old or new "affective formation." Those ideas are indeed the product of a new "psychic function" which I have discussed in chapter one of part one of this trilogy and which I have assumed to be born automatically out of the synthesis and integration of all the somatic functions already operating at a certain moment of our intra-uterine somatic organization. It follows that this new "Psychic function" is also activated by the same somatic energy which activated the various somatic functions out of which integration and synthesis that "new Psychic function" was born. It also follows that the ideas which are the product of the transformation at the hands of this new Psychic function, of the various somatic stimuli into ideas, must in turn be governed by the same somatic energy which governed the creation of that new Psychic function. (For details see chapter I of part I of this trilogy.) In that same chapter, I have also assumed that once an ideational representation has acquired its own affective quality, sexual or otherwise, it constitutes with that quality an inseparable unit *which does not allow* the quality to detach itself from that unit, and operate separately in terms of a mobile qualitative psychic energy, the Libido as predicated by Freud.

A further contradiction in Freud's assumption that it is not the "Psychical structure" that is displaceable, but its innervation, is found in his concept of what an instinct is. On this point he had stated that:

> By an instinct is provisionally to be understood the psychic representative of an endo-somatic source of stimuli. . . . The concept of instinct is thus one of those lying at the frontier between the mental and the physical. . . . So far as mental life is concerned, it is only to be regarded as a certain amount of demand made upon mind for work.[22]

In other words the instinct is the result of the somatic demands made upon mental life.

It is in that sense that Freud must have assumed that the endo-somatic stimuli generated in the genital zone, as well as in all other alleged erotogenic zones, become a sexual instinct after they first operate upon mental life. That this seems to be the case is confirmed by Freud in his posthumously published *An Outline of Psychoanalysis* (1940) where he restated his views on the nature of the instincts: The force which we assume to exist behind the tension caused by the needs of the Id are called instincts: *They represent the somatic demand upon mental life.*[23]

In that light, the extension of the genital excitations to other channels of discharge, i.e., to the so-called "erotogenic zones," should not be considered in terms of the simple displacement of a sexual energy. Once they have originated in the genital organs, these sexual somatic stimuli, by effect of their demands upon mental life, must first become transformed into their ideational representation which carry with them the sexual quality of the genital stimuli. Having thus become sexual mental representations by virtue of the operating new Psychic function, their function in filling up collateral channels cannot be envisaged in the terms of a simple sexual energy, but in terms of the ideational representations of the genital excitations and related sexual quality. It is that combination which undergoes displacement towards other areas of the body, to the ideational representation of which they impart a sexual meaning, and which areas can be then utilized as sexual areas of discharge.

Approached from that angle, the above considerations would seem to support my concept of *the mobility and displacement of ideational formations and related affective qualities* i.e. of "Affective formations," rather than Freud's concept of the mobility and displacement of a sexual energy. It would also seem in the light of the above considerations that if the analysis of psychoneurotics were to uncover, in their Unconscious, sexual impulses which Freud considered to be at the basis of their sexual perversions, that finding should not have been considered as supporting his assumption of the existence, development and operation of individual sexual instinct-components originating in the alleged "erotogenic zones." On the contrary, his analytic findings could have been used in support of the different view that the stimuli generated in the sexual organs, become first transformed into sexual ideational representations. That would have harmonized with Freud's own views that the instincts represent the somatic demands upon mental life. It is only when those sexual ideational representations i.e. "Affective formations" are faced with Repression, or with some other inability to express themselves along the intended genital route of discharge, that they displace themselves over other anatomical areas of the body which are therefore utilized as areas of discharge for the genital representations.

To conclude, it would seem therefore that the various areas in question should not have been called as Freud did *"erotogenic zones"* but simply as *"erotic areas"* in the sense that they simply represent areas of discharge for the mental (ideational) representations of the genital sexual stimuli. As for the energy which governs the displacement of the original sexual ideational representations, it is in my view the same somatic energy which I have called "Organismic energy," the same energy which presided over the development of the new "Psychic function." It is that new function and related somatic energy that presides over the first translation of the somatic stimuli into ideational representations. (See chapter I of part I of this trilogy.)

Freud never changed his mind on the subject of the existence of various sexual instinct-components originating locally in the various "erotogenic zones," so much so that in 1933 in his *New Introductory Lectures*, he still maintained that:

It is not the case then that we recognize a sexual instinct which is from the first the vehicle of an urge towards the aim of the sexual function—the union of the two sex-cells. *What we see is a great number of component-instincts arising from different areas and regions of the body which strive for satisfaction fairly independently of one another, and find that satisfaction in something we may call "organ-pleasure."* The genitals are the latest of these erotogenic zones and the name of sexual pleasure cannot be withheld from their organ-pleasure. These impulses which strive for pleasure are not all taken up into the final organization of the sexual function. Some persist in minor role and serve for the performance of introductory acts, for the production of fore-pleasure.[24] [italics mine]

Of course, against this latest statement by Freud that the organ-pleasure derived from the satisfaction of the endo-somatic stimuli originating in various areas of the body (the so-called erotogenic zones) *is actually a sexual organ-pleasure*, I raise the same objections which I have already raised in discussing Freud's previous statements on this same subject. To state in fact that *out of the extinction of* the endo-somatic stimuli originating in various areas of our body, a certain organ-pleasure follows, may be evidently an acceptable statement. *But to maintain that such an organ-pleasure is of a sexual nature* and as such represents the aim of a sexual instinct-component generated locally in those areas, is quite a dogmatic and unsubstantiated assertion. Before making such statement one may have wished that Freud had undertaken a closer investigation on the appropriateness to call these various areas "erotogenic zones" and that he had better explored the significance of these zones, not as generators of sexual instinct-components, but as zones for the discharge of the sexual excitations and related sexual ideational representations which originate primarily and exclusively in the genitals. But had Freud done that, he would have destroyed his own dogmatic assumption of the existence, origin, and operation of various sexual instinct-components, the ultimate aim of which was that of a "sexual organ-pleasure" elicited in various areas of the body.

My alternate approach to the operation of various locally generated sexual instinct-components, that of the discharge of sexual ideational representations of the stimuli originating in the genital organs through the ideational representations of various areas of our body, seems particularly applicable to our teenagers in the present era of permissiveness, when young boys and young girls having reached puberty, seek every opportunity to get together away from parental supervision. Their purpose is among others to give vent somehow to their normal genital excitations, the ultimate aim of which they have learned to be that of the union of the genitals. However on these occasions, no sexual intercourse in that specific sense is intended, or if intended may be repressed, but many other activities such as the looking at, the holding, the squeezing, the embracing, the caressing of the body of the partner, and above all the passionate and prolonged kissing of the mouth are indulged in. All such activities may very well be viewed as alternate avenues for the discharge of the genital stimuli in terms of a displacement of the sexual affective formations made of the sexual ideational representations of the genital stimuli and related sexual quality upon various ideational representations of body areas with which they associate and to which they impart their sexual quality and which are then used in their necking activities and which thus become areas of discharge for their genital excitations.

In that light, the sexual organ-pleasure resulting from the discharge from various body areas of the displaced sexual representations of the genital excitations, should not differ in quality from the sexual organ-pleasure related to the discharge of the original mental representation of the genital excitations along the regular genital path of discharge. What may differ indeed is not the quality of the sexual organ-pleasure but simply *its intensity*, being more marked if discharged along the genital pathway, and generally less intense along the various other areas of discharge.

What happens at puberty in the teenagers, applies also to adults, who find themselves in the same situation of having to refrain from the proper route of discharge of the mental representation and attached sexual quality of their genital excitations, because of morality or fear of retribution. They too try to find some collateral avenue of discharge for the ideational representation and related quality of their genital excitations, by utilizing various parts of their body and particularly their mouth, as substitutes for the direct genital organ-pleasure, no matter how less intense that substitute sexual pleasure may be.

These various activities, common to adolescents and adults and which I have considered as substitute activities for the discharge along various areas of the genital sexual excitations, had been lumped by Freud under the designation of "fore-pleasure." In his view, that pleasure then leads to an increase in tension which in its turn is responsible for producing the necessary motor energy for the conclusion of the sexual act which is of the highest intensity, which is wholly a pleasure of satisfaction and which *is brought about entirely by discharge*.[25]

However, while Freud had assigned to these preliminary stages of sexual pleasure the designation of fore-pleasure, he assigned to the last one the designation of end-pleasure, the only pleasure which he related to the function of discharge. The fore-pleasure he differentiated from the end-pleasure because in his view, *the former were generated locally in the various erotogenic zones* by the simple extinction or removal of the local endo-somatic stimuli, whereas the latter resulted from the confluence of the organ-pleasure related to the various sexual instinct-components, including that of the genital instinct-component itself.

We are again confronted with the fundamental difference between Freud's assumption that the erotogenic zones constitute zones from where various sexual instinct-components originate and from which local sexual-organ pleasure is elicited, and my assumption that Freud's various erotogenic zones constitute only the zone of discharge of the sexual ideational representations of the somatic stimuli originating only in the genital organs. The resulting sexual organ-pleasure in these various areas is of the same qualitative nature as that elicited in the genital organs, but less intense quantitatively. It in turn may contribute to an ultimate discharge through the genital pathway.

In the light of my assumption that in all the so-called "erotogenic zones," we are dealing with simple phenomena of discharge of the sexual ideational representation of the endo-somatic stimuli originating exclusively in the genital zone, there could be no difference between genitality and sexuality, the latter in the terms advocated by Freud. Yet such a distinction was introduced and defended by Freud who arbitrarily assumed the existence and operation of separate individual sexual instinct-components, originating in various parts of our body and capable of inducing a sexual-organ pleasure independently from the sexual excitations and related sexual organ-pleasure originating in the genital organ themselves.

But Freud failed to substantiate his dogma that the "erotogenic zones" represent areas from which sexual excitations originate locally as the expression of the operation of various sexual-instinct-components, and because of that failure, he also failed to establish a difference between Sexuality and Genitality. In my view, Sexuality and Genitality are interchangeable concepts of expression for the one and only sexual ideational representation of the endo-somatic stimuli originating primarily and exclusively in the genital organs. *Such ideational representations and attached sexual quality which may be called a "Sexual Affective formation"* represent the mental units which can undergo displacement upon the ideational representation of various areas of our body with which they become associated and to which they impart their sexual quality and from which they can be discharged locally. These areas should be therefore designated "erotic areas" and not "erotogenic areas" in the meaning attributed to them by Freud.

If we were to accept my assumption that the various "erotic areas or zones" as I call them, represent zones for the discharge of the mental representation of the sexual excitations originating in the genitals only, a question would evidently arise: At what point should we call *"perverts"* those individuals who use collateral avenues of discharge for their genital excitations? The answer would be: only if the use of those collateral channels of discharge were *to substitute and supplant entirely* the accepted popularly view of the discharge of the sexual excitations along the genital route. But such an answer would still leave room for some ambiguity, because it does not take into consideration *the possible inability* of an individual for whatever reason, it may be constitutional or acquired, to make use of the genital route of discharge, nor does it answer the question of what makes normal only the genital route of discharge for the mental representation of the genital excitations.

It may be relevant in this connection to recall Th. Szasz' comments on Freud's views of the normal aim of the sexual instinct "as being the union of the genitals in the act known as copulation, which leads to a release of the sexual tension . . . In Szasz' view:

> What Freud did here was to set down the rules that he believed govern or should govern sexual behavior. Thus speaking of a *normal sexual aim*, implies certain correspondingly *"abnormal aims."* This usage makes it seem as if he were talking about a medical problem; as if for example he were saying that the number of white blood cells per cubic millimeter, was such and such, and thus proceeding to set forth the various abnormalities of white blood-cell formation. However sexual behavior, as Freud knew only too well, has much more

to do with social learning and convention than do most medical matters. Consequently I believe that Freud was closer to describing what I suggested was analogous to rules governing games rather than to the description of sexual normality and abnormality . . . To illustrate, Freud wrote: "perversions are sexual activities which either a) extend in an anatomical sense, beyond the region of the body that are designated for sexual union or b) linger over the immediate relations of the sexual object which should be normally traversed rapidly on the path towards the final sexual aim." This I submit is simply a description of what Freud considered to be the proper (on medical grounds of course) form of sexual behavior. Logically this description has a closer affinity to a set of rules setting forth how to dance the Viennese Waltz, or how to play chess, than it does to those describing the pathological anatomy and physiology of a disease syndrome of the body, such as pulmonary tuberculosis for example. To say that male and female are so constructed as to fit together in sexual union, is to make a medico-scientific statement; however to say that this is the manner in which they should be used, and that other uses are pathological, is to render a normal-normative judgement, couched and disguised in the idiom of medicine.[26]

Only if one were to subscribe to Freud's views of what the normal sexual aim or sexual object should be, one could designate as *perversions in the derogative sense* all forms of sexual discharge through the various alternate routes for the mental representation of the sexual excitations generated only in the genital organs. It is true that popular acquiescence makes the union of the genitals of two persons of the opposite sex as constituting what is supposed to be the natural outcome of the sexual instinct, but this does not justify *the labeling of "sexual perverts" in that derogatory meaning* for those who utilize other avenues of discharge for their genital excitations, considering that obscure organic conditions or environmental influences related to childhood upbringing, may be at the basis of their inability to discharge their sexual excitations along the genital route. Those who utilize different avenues of discharge for their genital excitations, and I speak of those who substitute entirely the collateral ways for the genital route, should be more appropriately labeled "sexual deviants," so as to avoid the depreciative meaning of "sexual perverts."

Such deviations, if properly investigated, could lead to their correction and even elimination, unless as I have stated, genetic factors of which we know very little at the present may be at the basis of such deviations.

It may be worth repeating that *my assumption of the various avenues of discharge* from the various parts of our body, for the sexual excitations originated in the genitals, through the formation in those parts of new "Sexual Affective formations," as presented by me in part II of this book, applies only to those individuals children who have already developed to the stage of genitality. In young children, it can apply only to those who have reached the so called "Phallic stage of the sexual development," the stage that Freud called "the stage of infantile genital organization" around the fourth year of life. It follows that in infancy, prior to that stage that is at the so-called "oral" or "anal" stages of the sexual development in Freud's term, my assumption expressed in the above terms cannot be applied. The reason is that prior to that "Phallic stage," no ideational representation of the genitals and related sexual quality attached to it has as yet begun its operation in infants or very young children. More on this important subject in the following chapter.

It has occurred to me as it must have occurred to many others who however have remained conveniently silent, that Freud in order to support his arbitrary views of the existence and operation of separate "sexual instinct-components," may have neglected to look into the meaning of the word which long before him was called "sensual." Had he thought of applying that word "sensual" to all of our senses, he might have avoided the assumption of his various *"erotogenic zones"* as zones being generators of individual sexual instinct-components to replace the unity of the "sexual instinct."

The *Oxford Universal Dictionary* (1933) describes the word *"sensual,"* derived from the Latin "sensus," as meaning the carrying or transmitting various sensations pertaining to our senses; as an adjective, it applies not only to the physical sensation of the senses, *but also to the appetite and pleasure connected with the gratification of the senses."* Now gratification of one of our senses, let us say the sense of touch, of any part of our body must be called, according to the dictionary, simply *sensual.* No hint of sexuality is involved in that definition that could justify Freud's designation of that pleasurable gratification as "Sexual organ-pleasure."

Of course, had Freud made use of the word "sensual" in that accepted meaning, he would have had no reason to introduce his arbitrary assumption of the existence and operation of various "erotogenic zones" as zones of origin of various "sexual instinct-components" responsible for the development of "a sexual-organ-pleasure" whenever a gratification of any sensory stimulus occurred, in whatever area of our body. Freud could have limited the designation of "sexual organ-pleasure" only to the gratification of the stimuli originating in the genital organization. The genitals themselves (penis and clitoris) constitute indeed the sense-organs of the only sexual instinct as popularly understood, and at the same time they constitute *the original and natural pathway* for the ultimate discharge, once the genital stimuli have obtained complete gratification.

But as I have repeatedly stated, Freud had to find a way out of the impasse in which he had put himself when he assumed that sexuality was already present and manifest in the infant, in the course of what he called "the oral stage of his sexual development" and when he assumed that immediately after that stage, sexuality developed in the infant in the course of the "anal stage of his sexual development." Such assumptions were so highly criticized by his colleagues that Freud had to concoct in a hurry his new assumption that there are several sexual instinct-components and not a single sexual instinct. He furthermore added that these various sexual instinct-components originate in various areas of our body and which he called "erotogenic zones!" These sexual instinct-components when gratified induced in those various areas an organ-pleasure, which Freud arbitrarily qualified as sexual.

These assumptions remained unchanged until the time of Freud's death, and up to the present have not been modified by his faithful followers.

Freud's Unsubstantiated Assumption of the Sexual Development of the Child by the Means of Successive Constitutionally Determined Stages Each One Representing the Activity of an Independent Sexual Instinct-Component.

Why did Freud in his publication *Three Essays on the Theory of Sexuality* (1905) proceed first to discuss his theory of the sexual perversions before discussing the sexual development of the child? It would seem that it was because in that publication he wished to introduce first his own assumption that the sexual instinct was not a single instinct, but was constituted by the amalgamation of various sexual component-instincts, each one originating in different areas of the body which he called "erotogenic zones!"

Freud's theory was revamped in 1915 in his paper *Instincts and their Vicissitudes* where he stated that

> an attempt to formulate the general characteristics of the sexual instincts would run as follows: they are numerous, emanate from manifold organic sources, act in the first instance independently from one another, and only at a late stage achieve a more or less complete synthesis. *The aim which each strives to attain is organ-pleasure*; only when the synthesis is complete do they enter the service of the function of reproduction. At first appearance they support themselves upon the Ego-instincts of self-preservation, from which they only gradually detach themselves.... Some of them remain throughout life associated with these latter, and furnish them with libidinal components.... They have this distinctive characteristic—that they can readily change their objects. In consequence of the last mentioned properties they are capable

of activities widely removed from their original modes of at-
taining their aims (sublimation).[1] [italics mine]

That view of the sexual instincts gradually detaching themselves from the Ego-instincts of self-preservation was later rejected by Freud or so it may seem, when in 1920 he equated the sexual instincts with the Ego-instincts of self-preservation, both operating in terms of the instinct of life both activated by the same and only sexual energy, the libido.

The various somatic zones from where endo-somatic excitations originate, and the aim of which was the extinction of those excitations, Freud called "erotogenic zones" that is, *zones of origin* of various sexual instinct-components. Furthermore he called *organ-pleasure* the pleasure derived from the attainment of their aim, that is the extinction of the endo-somatic stimuli. In consequence of his assumption that those endo-somatic stimuli in the various organs of our body are the actual source of the various sexual instinct-components and that the aim of those components is the extinction of those stimuli, Freud concluded that the resulting organ-pleasure for each instinct-component is of a sexual nature. Unfortunately, all that theoretic formulation, was the product of Freud's imaginative mind, and lacked of any possibility of verification.

But Freud needed that formulation of various sexual instinct-components and related "erotogenic zones" in order to support his very convenient assumption, that the development of sexuality takes place prior to and independently from the functioning of the genital zone, and that consequently "sexuality" should be distinguished from "genitality" a distinction which in his view, the critics of his sexual theory of the neuroses, had failed to take into account. Furthermore without the assumption of the "erotogenic zones" as the genetic source of his various "sexual instinct-components," Freud would have been unable to advance and develop his own theory of the sexual development of the child. It was indeed on the basis of the gradual development and operation of the several independent sexual instinct-components that Freud formulated his own theory of the successive developmental stages of the child's sexuality, which he designated as: the oral stage, the anal stage, the phallic stage, the oedipal stage, the latency stage, and the stage of the genital supremacy.

In Freud's view, the first oral stage represents the manifestations of *the first sexual instinct-component*, which develops at the time of birth and lasts for over a year, overlapping gradually the second anal stage of the child's sexual development. During that first stage, the infant experiences endo-somatic excitations in his oral organization, as the manifestation of his immediate need for nourishment. Though such an extinction of the oral stimuli satisfies mainly the need of the ego-instincts of preservation, it also satisfies, according to Freud, the demands of the first sexual instinct-component which he arbitrarily assumed to originate also in the same oral cavity. Without discussing the nature and further development of the organ-pleasure related to the satisfaction of the first Ego-instinct of preservation, Freud paid attention *only* to that portion of the organ-pleasure that in his view resulted from the satisfaction of the concomitant first sexual instinct-component. The oral stimuli become satisfied only with the introduction in the mouth of food which in the case of the infant is represented at first by the milk from the mother's breast or from the milk bottle. It is the extinction of those oral stimuli that according to Freud, induces the first organ-pleasure, which he considered as *sexual organ-pleasure* because he related it to the demands of the concomitant first sexual instinct-component, originating from the activity of the endo-somatic oral stimuli. It was the sexual component of the oral organ-pleasure that most interested Freud.

Having experienced his first *sexual organ-pleasure* through his sucking activities, the child subsequently, in the absence of his feeding mother, searches for some other means that may induce in him the extinction of his endo-somatic oral stimuli and at the same time induce in him the repetition of the same organ-pleasure which he had already experienced, and which he now remembers, an organ-pleasure which Freud *unfortunately characterized as sexual in nature*. The infant therefore resorts for that purpose to the use of whatever object may be at his nearest disposal, such as his own thumb or fingers, his own tongue, a portion of his lips or the skin of any other part of his body, or even his big toe. These various manifestations of sucking on the part of the infant, Freud called *"sensual sucking," the expression of sexuality in early childhood*.

According to Freud, Lindner S. in 1897 had already recognized the sexual nature of this activity of thumb-sucking, and supported it without reservation. This view, writes Freud: "has been most energetically repudiated by numbers of pediatricians and nerve specialists, *though there is no doubt that this is partly due to a confusion between 'sexual' and 'genital.'* "[2] [italics mine] It is at this point that Freud asked himself the question, "What is the general characteristic which enables us to recognize the sexual nature of the above activities in children?" Unfortunately without any satisfactory documentation outside of his own conjecture, Freud all inclusively answered to the effect that thanks to the insight given to him by the psychoanalytic investigation, he was justified in regarding thumb-sucking as a sexual manifestation and in choosing it for his study of the essential features of *infantile sexual activity*.[3]

It was the persistence and dominance in later life of that form of infantile sexual activity and related sexual organ-pleasure, the expression of early sexual instinct-components, that Freud considered to be a *sexual perversion* in his neurotic patients. By obtaining for instance his sexual organ-pleasure from the satisfaction of his oral sexual instinct-component, the pervert had no longer need to search for that pleasure in the ultimate operation of the genital instinct-component. It was upon this alleged theoretical concatenation of events alledgedly uncovered in his opinion, in the analysis of his neurotic patients, that Freud had concluded that the oral sexual perversion could be related back to the operation of a first sexual instinct-component.

By introducing the new assumption of the existence and operation of various sexual instinct-components, the first of which made its appearance with the birth of the child through endo-somatic excitations in his oral organization and the satisfaction of which induced a first sexual organ-pleasure, Freud seemed to have deviated from another of his assumptions. I am referring to the one by which he had explained how the genital excitations in terms of a sexual energy, the libido, could extend the field of its operation from the genital zone of discharge, over several other zones of discharge, whenever the normal genital path of discharge was blocked for one reason or another.

In a statement to which I have already referred in a previous chapter, Freud had precisely maintained that most psychoneurotics fall ill only after the age of puberty as the result of the demands made upon them by normal sexual life, and where they particularly exercise repression. On the other hand, illnesses of this kind may set in later, when the libido fails to obtain satisfaction along normal lines. In both these cases, he reiterated his previous assertion that libido behaves like a stream whose main bed has been blocked and therefore *proceeds to fill up collateral channels which may hitherto have been empty*.[4]

In that light, the libido, in terms evidently of sexual energy, having been blocked from its discharge along the genital pathway, would discharge itself along other collateral avenues such as the oral pathway. But, in those terms, that collateral discharge of the libido implied evidently an operation which could not have taken place prior to the development of the latest genital activities, and therefore could not apply to the infant prior to the phallic stage of his sexual development. Thus, what was applicable to his psychoneurotics could not be applied to infants or young children.

Faced with that difficulty, Freud had to discard his earlier general assumption and rely now on his new assumption of the existence and operation of various individual sexual instinct-components which originate independently from the genital instinct-component, in various areas of the body, the first one originating from the endo-somatic stimuli of the oral organization. This new assumption I have discussed and rejected in the previous chapter.

If now I were to reject, in infancy and early childhood, not only Freud's assumption of the existence of various sexual *instinct-components* and related sexual organ-pleasure, but evidently also the alternative that in infancy, prior to the development of the phallic stage, the mouth represents a substitute collateral zone of discharge for the genital excitations, the question which arises again to my mind is the following: What qualification should I apply to that oral organ-pleasure in infancy and early childhood? To answer that question, I would have to enter into the discussion of the entire philosophical concept of the nature and meaning of "pleasure" in general, a discussion that would take us far away into for instance the philosophical views of the "Hedonistic School,"[5] from its founder in ancient Greece, Aristippus the Cyrenaic, to Epicurus, to Hobbes, to Locke, to Hume, to Bentham, to John Stuart Mill, and to Herbert Spencer. That school contemplated as the goal of life the search for pleasure in all human endeavors, be they of a phisical or of mental nature, but never relating them to a primary search for sexual pleasure.

I will satisfy myself with a more pragmatic approach to the question of pleasure by simply stipulating that there must be different forms of pleasure outside the sexual pleasure, which makes itself known according to Freud as soon as life itself begins. But to identify, as Freud seems to have done, all sorts of organ-pleasure resulting from all sorts of activities, including the very first oral activities as a sexual organ-pleasure, constitutes in my views an extreme, arbitrary, and unfounded assumption.

It is only if one were to accept such an arbitrary assumption that one could agree with Freud's definition of 1905 that sexuality is a bodily function having pleasure as its goal, and that sexual life comprises the function of obtaining pleasure from various zones of the body. And it is only if one agrees with him on that definition that one may subscribe to Freud's view that it may well be that nothing of considerable importance can occur in the organism without contributing some component to the excitation of the sexual instinct. And only if one agrees with him on that statement could one light-heartedly subscribe to his view that no one who has seen a baby sinking back, satisfied from the breast, and falling asleep with flushed cheeks, and a blissful smile, escaped the reflection that this pleasure persists as the prototype of the expression of sexual satisfaction in later life.[6] How much more convincing Freud could have been had he used the appearance of the infant following a satisfactory feeding, as the prototype of the pleasure *evidently nonsexual* in my estimation, enjoyed in adult life by some epicurean who, after an abundant and delicious meal, doused down by some fine gourmet wine, relaxes blissfully into a welcome post-prandial siesta.

The second stage of the child's sexual development is, according to Freud, the "anal stage," so-called originally but subsequently called the "anal-sadistic stage." That stage manifests itself in the course of the second year of life and is related to the endo-somatic excitations in the anal region generated by fecal material and to the sexual organ-pleasure which follows the removal of those excitations by the expulsion of the fecal material. Freud's arbitrary assumption of a sexual organ-pleasure induced by the relief of the rectal tension produced by the fecal material, became the more puzzling when one considers the fact that subsequently Freud and his followers seem to have assumed that it was *the same sexual organ-pleasure* that the child experiences in retaining his feces, at the time of his toilet training, when he defies his parental authority. Retention evidently does not relieve tension and could not therefore elicit sexual pleasure in Freud's original terms.

The objection against the "anal stage" of the sexual development as constituting the genetic source of another independent sexual instinct-component is therefore the same as that which I have raised against the genetic origin, in the oral organization of the first sexual instinct-component and related sexual organ-pleasure.

These two early "oral and anal stages" of the alleged sexual development of the child and which according to Freud represent the functional activities of the first two sexual instinct-components, were originally considered by him as representing what he had originally called "*the pre-genital organization*."

Then in 1923, in his paper, *The Infantile Genital Organization of the Libido*, Freud having recalled his previous statements that the coalescence of the various sexual instinct-components and their concentration under the primacy of the genital organs, was not effected in childhood or very imperfectly so, made the following new statement:

> I am to-day no longer satisfied with the statement that the primacy of the genitals is not effected in the early period of childhood, or only very imperfectly. That approximation of childhood sexuality to that of the adult goes much further and it is not limited solely to the establishment of an object-attachment. Even if perfect concentration of the component impulses under the primacy of the genitals, is not attained at any rate at the height of the development of the childhood sexuality, *the functioning of the genitals and the interest in them reaches predominant significance which comes little short of that reached in maturity*. The difference between the two, the infantile genital organization and the final genital organization of the adult, constitutes at the same time the main characteristic of the infantile form, namely that for both sexes in childhood, only one kind of genital organ comes into account. . . . The primacy reached therefore is not a primacy of the genital but *a primacy of the phallus*.[7]

From then on, Freud added to the stages of the sexual development of the child that of "*the stage of the infantile genital organization*," which develops between the ages of three and four and which he called "*the phallic stage*."

It would seem therefore that it is only at that stage of the infantile genital organization, that in my opinion, the first excitations of the phallus are experienced by the child, and that in order to extinguish them the child may resort to manipulation of the organ (penis for the boy, clitoris for the girl). The organ-pleasure which results from these manipulations is in my opinion the real first organ-pleasure *that should be called sexual*. It is only at this stage that the genital sexual excitations may extend themselves beyond the area of the genitals, over the mouth, the anus, the thumb, the skin, or any other part of the body, so that in addition to the phallus as a route for the discharge of the genital excitations, these other areas may now be utilized as collateral avenues of discharge for the one and only genital excitations in terms of ideational representations and related sexual quality and subsequent sexual organ-pleasure.

This is the assumption that I would favor and which by the way harmonizes with one of Freud's own statements that when the libido is for some reason or another, blocked from discharge along the genital path, it proceeds to fill up collateral channels of discharge. Had he continued to support that line, Freud would have had no reason to resort to his assumption of the existence of various sexual instinct-components which he designated "erotogenic zones," the two first of which were the mouth and the anus.

But Freud needed such an assumption of various sexual instinct-components originating outside the genital zone, in order to support his new differentiation between sexuality and genitality, a differentiation which he manufactured for the purpose of silencing his critics who, in his view, had failed to take in consideration such a difference. Unfortunately Freud failed to bring forward convincing arguments in favor of the multiplicity of sexual instinct-components originating from the activity of various body-areas, independently of the genitals. In the absence of any validation for his far-out speculation, call it philosophical if you wish, of the origin of a sexual-organ pleasure in the various activities of our somatic functions, one can hardly agree with Freud's distinction between sexuality and genitality. The designation of "erotogenic zones" for the various alleged areas of origin of the various sexual instinct-components should have been more appropriately that of "erotic zones" in terms of collateral zones for the discharge of the basic genital sexual excitations.

Evidently, Freud's concept of what *he had once* viewed as various areas of discharge for the genital excitations, would have become still more acceptable, had he, instead of discussing the sexual excitations in terms of a movable and displaceable sexual energy, discussed those excitations in terms of ideational representations of the genital excitations and attached sexual quality, a combination capable of undergoing displacement toward other areas of the body represented also by their own ideational formation and with which they establish associations. In that light, the ideational representations of the genital excitation and attached sexual quality, constitute what in Part One Chapter I of this trilogy I have called an *"affective for-*

mation" capable of displacing itself in its entirety.

It would be again a matter of *the displacement of ideas and related affective qualities*, a basic concept which I have tried to carry through this entire book, *and not of the displacement of a qualitative psychic energy* as maintained by Freud who opposed the concept of displacement of psychic structures.

One point still remains to be discussed: If, as I have assumed, it is the sexual genital excitation, in whatever form that may be, which from the genital zone extends itself over the oral or anal zone of discharge, *such an extension could not occur in the child before the development in it, of what Freud called "the phallic stage," at which stage only the genital excitations begin to operate in the child in a manner which Freud himself considered to be "little short of the genital functioning at maturity." It follows that, at this point, we are still faced with the obligation of qualifying the nature of the organ-pleasure elicited in the mouth and the anus of the child prior to the development in him of the "Phallic stage."*

We can only state logically that such a pleasure cannot be sexual, considering that the "phallic stage," the reservoir of genital sexual excitations, had not as yet developed in the child. A philosophical discussion of the nature of pleasure in general could be helpful, but transcends the confines of this presentation. Of course Freud resolved this problem to his own advantage by resorting to the assumption of a separate sexual instinct-component originating in the mouth as well as in the anal region, and the related organ-pleasure of which he considered to be sexual.

Because, at the time of the "phallic stage," the genital excitations of the little child are directed towards a definite object, the mother or the substitute mother, who takes care of all his needs, including the manipulation of his genitals in the course of bathing and other hygienic ministrations, a further stage of the child's sexual development comes into existence: the "Oedipal stage," so designated by Freud. This stage coincides with the time at which the child's libido, according to Freud, changes from an "auto-erotic" position in which it involves portions of the child's body itself, and which Freud called ego—libido or narcissistic—libido, to that of object-libido: involving first of all the mother or the substitute mother.

This Oedipal stage was first introduced by Freud in his letter to his friend Fliess dated October 15, 1897. At that time, Freud had already initiated his own analysis, and because of his childhood recollections and on the basis of the interpretation of his own dreams, he became interested in the Greek legend of Oedipus, which he thought applicable to his own personal situation. In his search for confirmatory data, he fell upon Shakespeare's *Hamlet,* and advanced the assumption that Shakespeare himself may have been influenced in the creation of the character of Hamlet, by some personal unconscious Oedipal complex, which in turn he transferred into the character of his hero. In Freud's interpretation, Hamlet was being tormented by the obscure memory, that he had once wished the suppression of his own father, because of his own sexual desire for his own mother, a wish of suppression which he later transferred upon his uncle. It is on account of that obscure memory, that Hamlet hesitated to avenge his father by killing his uncle, the assassin of his father. This at least was Freud's interpretation of Hamlet's line: "Thus conscience doth make cowards of us all."[8]

The earliest reference to the Oedipal situation, Freud had found in the Greek legend and in Sophocles' play *Oedipus Rex.* In that legend, Oedipus had been abandoned at birth by his father the King of Thebes, because an oracle had predicted that the boy would some day kill him and then marry his own mother. In the course of his wanderings as a young man, Oedipus met his father whom he did not know, entered into an argument with him, and in the course of a fight killed him. He then reached Thebes where the legend claims that he succeeded in solving the riddle of the Sphinx which had tormented the Thebans, or succeeded in killing the latter, according to another version, and thus liberated the city from a pestilence. In return Oedipus was proclaimed king, and subsequently married the queen, his own mother, with whom he had four children. Later on, when the truth was known, Queen Jocasta committed suicide, and Oedipus in desperation blinded himself and ever after lived a wandering and miserable life, according to one version, and a peaceful one according to another version.

The importance of the Oedipal stage in the sexual development of the child had been so greatly emphasized that in one of the most recent textbooks of psychoanalysis, Ch. Brenner, its author, considered that phase of a crucial significance for many individuals. In his words:

> The most important fact to underline in relation to the Oedipus complex is the force of the feelings which are involved. It is a real love affair which for many individuals, represents the most intense event of their entire existence.

During that phase intense passions, storms of love and hate, of desires and jealousies, and of fury and fears, develop within the child.[9]

Evidently that view harmonizes with the importance that Freud himself attached to that complex in a footnote in the 1920 edition of his *Three Essays on the Theory of Sexuality*, as I have already reported, where he had stated that it had justly been said that the Oedipus complex is the nuclear complex of the neuroses and constitutes the essential part of their content. . . . Every new arrival in this planet is faced with the task of mastering the Oedipus complex; anyone who fails to do so, falls victim to neuroses. . . . Its recognition has become the shiboleth that distinguishes the adherents to psychoanalysis from its opponents.[10]

And to think that when Freud first hit on the idea of the Oedipus complex, he considered that idea so daring as to prevent him from communicating it to other colleagues, except to his friend Fliess, according to his letters to him dated October 15, 1897 and the other dated November 5, 1897, in which latter he so expressed himself:

You have said nothing of my interpretation of Oedipus Rex and Hamlet. As I have said nothing to anyone else, because *I can imagine in advance the hostile reception it would meet*, I should be glad to have some comment on it from you. Last year you turned down a number of my ideas with good reasons.[11] [italics mine]

One wonders how often that Oedipal stage actually develops and actually reaches the dramatic intensity which the analysts attribute to it. Even admitting the sexual nature of some of the feelings of the child towards his own mother, sexual feelings that could not develop prior to the "phallic stage," how important actually is their role in influencing the child's development, compared with the so many other elements *of a nonsexual nature* that had already been established with the mother prior to the "phallic stage" and which continue to develop after that stage had been reached?

Unfortunately, in his presentation of the psychosexual development of the child, Freud did not differentiate sufficiently between the erotic and non-erotic aspects of that child-relationship to his mother, taken as he was with his new assumption of the existence and operation of various sexual-instinct-components that the child's mother was in a position to satisfy.

However, having rejected, as I have, Freud's assumption of the operation of various sexual instinct-components and related sexual organ-pleasure in infancy, and having rejected the possibility in the child, of the discharge of his genital excitations prior to the development in him of his *"phallic stage,"* I feel justified in concluding that all the feelings of attachment of the child to the mother *prior to that "phallic stage"* must all have been of a non-sexual nature. Furthermore I feel that after the "Phallic stage" had developed, those nonsexual feelings *of affection*, trust, and attachment of the child to the mother, feelings which constitute an important part of the fabric of the child-mother relationship continue to exist, to develop and to operate.

It seems to me that the non-erotic aspects of the child-mother relationship *by far overpower* in their extent and significance the occasional sexual pleasure that the child, after his "phallic stage" may experience toward his mother, particularly in the course of the brief hygienic sessions when direct genital stimulation may take place. One wonders therefore if, as Freud maintained, that during that Oedipal stage, the child actually considers his father as an important rival for the attachment to his mother, and that he fears to be punished by him by means of castration, (anxiety-castration) a fear out of which the desire is born to eliminate him as a dangerous rival.

Freud divided the Oedipal stage of the sexual development of the little boy into two phases: the positive and the negative. The positive phase is the first to develop and refers to the sexual attachment of the little boy to his mother. The negative phase which follows, refers to the subsequent libidinal attachment of the little boy to his father, a phase which involves ties of both affectionate and sexual nature, though Freud did not elaborate on the distinction between the nature of such ties. This is why in the negative phase, there develops an ambivalent attitude of the boy for his father, its being made not only of a combination of libidinal and affectionate attachment but also of fear of punishment by that rival for his attachment to his mother. In the little boy however, the positive Oedipal phase of libidinal attachment to his mother constitutes in Freud's view, the most important and prominent situation, whereas the subsequent negative phase plays in him a minor role, except in pathological situations derived from what Freud subsequently considered as possibly an excessive inborn "feminine attitude" of the little boy.

The Oedipal stage, as well as all the other stages of the psychosexual development of the child had been *constitutionally de-*

termined and therefore of a universal occurrence. If this were the case, one should find traces of it in all parts of the world and in all civilizations. The fact remains however, that according to known anthropologists this is not the case. In the so-called primitive societies of Australia, South Africa, and the Pacific islands, Ford and Beach[12] wrote that one rarely finds among these tribes traces of sexual interest on the part of the child towards his own mother, which results into the alleged Oedipal situation and related fear of retribution on the part of the father. In those societies, the very early promiscuous opportunities which are available to children, direct their sexual interest away from the mother and towards children of the opposite sex, with whom they are free to practice various sexual activities, from masturbation to voyeurism, and to early coitus under the approving parental eyes. In Kazak, a nomadic tribe of central Asia, adults who play with small children excite the young one's genitals by rubbing them and playing with them. Among the Chewa, a tribe of British central Africa, mother, father, and parents believe that unless children begin to exercise themselves sexually early in life, they will never beget offspring. In Ifugao, in central Luzon of the Philippines, boys are urged by their fathers to begin sexual activities early. In these primitive tribes, taboo against incest may be found, but it refers to adult relationship and not to the growing child.

It is in connection with Freud's introduction of an alleged Oedipal phase in the course of the psychosexual development of the child that Kardiner, Karush, and Ovessey directed also at him the following criticism:

> In the absence of historical evidence for a primal Oedipus complex *Freud invented a self-designated scientific myth*, to account for it. He expounded this thesis in *Totem and Tabu* and postulated a primal horde or family, which sons killed their fathers to keep the mothers and daughters for themselves. The sense of guilt which arouse from this primal parricide was recapitulated in each succeeding generation as the incest-barrier.[13] [italics mine]

On the subject of the sexual character of the whole attachment of the child to his mother, Freud was very explicit when he felt that there may be perhaps an inclination to dispute the possibility of identifying a child's affection and esteem for those who look after him *with sexual love*. He felt, however, that a closer psychological examination may make it possible to establish that identity beyond any doubt. In his view, a child's intercourse with anyone responsible for his care *affords him an unending source of sexual excitations, and satisfaction from his erotogenic zones.* . . . This is especially so, since the person in charge of him is his mother. The mother, in Freud's view, regards the child as a substitute for a complete sexual object.[14] Though Freud himself had considered that statement as one *that some people would rate as sacrilegious,* that consideration did not deter him from making what he considered sexuality, an important link in the early mother-child relationship.

Of course, by continuing to designate as "sexual" the organ pleasure resulting from the unending "sexual excitations and related satisfaction" which the child experiences from his various alleged "erotogenic zones" without any distinction between early childhood and puberty and adulthood, Freud seemed to have again shifted away from his original assumption that *these various areas represented various areas of discharge for the excitations originated in the genitals,* and relied instead upon the newly introduced assumption of the existence of independent sexual instinct-components originating in the mouth, the anus, the skin and other body areas of the infant and young child.

On the basis of that arbitrary assumption, Freud, having avoided any satisfactory discussion of other nonsexual pleasures outside the sexual one, now could claim with impunity *the sexual nature* of the infant and young child organ-pleasure derived from the satisfaction of his various endo-somatic stimuli at the hands of his mother. He could thus differentiate the various sexual organ-pleasure derived from the various erotogenic zones, from the genital sexual organ-pleasure. Evidently that line of separation of sexuality from genitality was quite an elusive and arbitrary one which Freud needed, however, in order to defend himself against his critics who in his estimation had failed to make such a differentiation. In his view, the friendliness, the attachment, and the affection of the child for his mother were the expression of sexual impulses initiated from sources other than the genitals, that is, from the various sexual instinct-components in the child's various "erotogenic zones" mouth, skin, etc. . . . Freud therefore continued to ignore the great value of any other nonsexual origin upon which the relationship of the child to his mother could have been established.

In my opinion, Freud should have divided the child-mother relationship into two groups, the group that developed prior to the establishment of the child's "phallic stage," and the group that developed after that stage, at puberty and in adulthood. The first group of the child-mother relationship should not have been considered by Freud as involving sexuality, in terms of the extension of the genital excitations along various other areas of discharge, because as I have already argued, the child prior to the "phallic stage" (the stage of the infantile genital organization) had not as yet experienced genital excitations. Nor, in line with the criticism which I have advanced in the previous chapter against the concept of Freud's "erotogenic zones," could these zones represent, as Freud maintained, genetic areas for the various sexual-instinct components responsible for the development of the child's feelings of attachment and affection for his mother. These alleged "erotogenic areas" represent areas of discharge for genital excitations, but only in the terms of substitute "affective formations" and furthermore not before the development in the child of what Freud called the "phallic stage." In that perspective, those alleged "erotogenic" zones could be designated simply as "erotic zones" in the sense that they represent areas in which endosomatic excitations, if satisfied, would induce a pleasurable feeling, but certainly not a sexual pleasure.

It is only in the second group, when the child-mother relationship becomes enhanced after the development of the "phallic stage" had been established in the child, that Freud could have considered the child's affection and attachment of the child to his mother as the expression of "sexual love," as he called it, to be distinguished from the manifestation of "genitality." Unfortunately Freud's concept of "sexual love" unrelated to genitality, and which he had distinguished from the former, seems to have been contradicted by Freud himself in his paper of 1915, *Instincts and Their Vicissitudes*. In that paper speaking of love in relation to the ego to its sexual object, he had stated that:

> Since *we do not* customarily say *that the single sexual component-instinct loves it object*, but see the most appropriate case in which to apply the word "love" in the relation of the Ego to its sexual object, we learn from this fact that the application of the word in this relation, *begins only with the synthesis of all the component sexual instincts under the primacy of the genitals*, and in the service of the function of reproduction.[15] [italics mine]

How then could Freud designate as sexual, *the love that the infant or young child feels for his mother at a time prior to his "phallic stage"* (the stage which he called the stage of the infantile genital organization) which follows the "oral" and "anal" stage of the child's sexual development according to Freud? At those two stages, no synthesis has as yet occurred between the various so-called sexual instinct components and the ultimate genital component. To designate therefore as *"love"* and what is more as *"sexual love"* the feelings of the child in his young affectionate attachment for his mother, prior to the "phallic stage" must have been an unfortunate slip on Freud's part. At the oral or anal stage, the feelings of affection and attachment of the young child for his mother, prior to the "phallic stage" should not have been qualified as "love" and in particular as "sexual love," because in Freud's own view the earlier oral and anal sexual instinct components could have no love for their object, and thus the child's ego should have no sexual love for his mother. And yet the child's ego could not help to love, in the general meaning of the word, without any intonation of sexuality, those objects or persons who are responsible for the cessation of his unpleasant stimuli of hunger and thus induce what Freud had arbitrarily called an oral sexual organ-pleasure.

Furthermore, it would seem that in Freud's view, based only on speculative intellectual thinking, the word love for an inanimate object, whatever this may be, or for animate objects such as parents, children, relatives, or even friends, must rely for its development upon the synthesizing power of the genital component instinct from which the ultimate word "love" depends. If this were the case, it would seem quite a strange position to assume, considering the great value that Freud himself had assigned to each individual sexual instinct-component, aiming at what he called "sexual organ-pleasure" from which the "feeling love" can be eliminated only arbitrarily.

Let me now return to the Oedipus stage, a stage which as all other stages of the sexual development, Freud had considered to be constitutionally determined, and therefore of universal occurrence. That stage, which occupies a determined position in the sexual development of the child, must at a certain moment come to an end in order to leave room for the subsequent stage. As Freud had put it in his paper: *The Passage of the Oedipus Complex*:

> The time comes for its dissolution just as the milk teeth fall out when the permanent ones begin to press forward. Although *the majority of human children* individually pass through the Oedipus complex, yet after all it is a phenomenon determined and laid down for him by heredity, and must decline when the next pre-ordained stage of development arises.[16] [italics mine]

Unfortunately, Freud, though using the word "majority" must have actually meant "all human children," if one were to abide by his other statement that: *Every new arrival on this planet* is faced with the task of mastering the Oedipus complex or fall a victim to neurosis."[17] Irrespective of the method by which the positive Oedipal stage disappears in the little boy, be it by its exhaustion, by repression, or by its hopeless longing for the mother, the fact remains that Freud made of that *sexual attachment* of the child for his mother an obligatory stage constitutionally determined. It is this approach by Freud that seems to me particularly dogmatic. That only a group of children may actually pass through an actual Oedipal stage in Freud's important meaning might be an acceptable proposition, provided that it refers to that minority of children who may become victim of a neurosis.

But what about the group of children who subsequently develop a neurosis without having necessarily passed through that alleged constitutionally determined Oedipal stage, and whose neurosis might become related, after analysis, to some other nonsexual factor, among which for instance, the influence of the destructive impulses representative of the instinct of death? And what about the group of children in whom the dominance of their constitutional proneness to anxiety makes them unable to stand for their rights or beliefs, for fear of scorn or retribution, and who subsequently develop a neurosis? Are there statistics on these groups?

Following the Oedipal stage, the child's sexual organization enters into what Freud had called the stage of "latency." In the course of that stage which begins around the fifth year of life, and lasts up to puberty, the "infantile genital organization" is brought to a standstill according to Freud.

During that stage, the infantile nature of the sexual object-choice undergoes a marked change. Because of the repression of the Oedipal complex, the sexual aims become tamed and undergo transformation. In Freud's view:

> Those sexual aims have been mitigated and they now represent the affectionate current of sexual life. Only psychoanalytic investigation can show that behind this affection, admiration and respect, there still is concealed the old sexual longing of the infantile components of the sexual instincts. The object-choice of the puberal period is obliged to dispense with the object of childhood, and to start afresh as a new sensual current.[18]

Freud thus conceived two changes of the sexual development occurring at puberty, one dealing with the sexual object and the other with the sexual current. Concerning the latter I fail to see any change, considering the fact that it is the same sexual current which is operating at first at the "phallic stage" and not before, and which extends itself uninterruptedly into the puberal stage without the need for a new sensual current to develop. As for the change in the sexual object, it would not be very difficult to follow in a growing boy, the gradual extension of the sexual object of his "infantile genital organization" from the mother or substitute mother upon other object-choices of the same sex. This is particularly observable in our present day culture where the coeducational system from kindergarten to all grades of public schools allows a smooth transition from the mother-object to other female schoolmates, at a very early period of life.

Nor do I see the need for Freud's concept of the taming of the "infantile sexual current" during latency, as a necessary step for the creation and development of the "affectionate current of sexual life." *An affectionate current which I do not consider as "sexual" already operates in full swing during infancy and early childhood prior to the "phallic stage" of the sexual development as conceived by Freud.* It is precisely that "affectionate nonsexual current" that Freud unfortunately ignored or minimized.

The affectionate current of puberty may well be nothing more than the continuation and extension of the same nonsexual current of attachment to the mother which was already operating in early childhood, prior to the development of the "phallic" stage. On the other hand, the sexual current of puberty may well be nothing more than the continuation and extension of that sexual current which had begun to operate in the child at the time of the "phallic stage" or stage of "the infantile genital organization" as Freud designated it, and which led the child into his Oedipal situation. Thus the affectionate current and the sexual current may be able to run concurrently at the "phallic stage" and subsequently at the pubertal stage. It follows that there would be no need to assume that the affectionate current conceals behind it any old sexual longing, inasmuch as this affectionate current is capable to develop and operate independently from the sexual current.

Evidently, my disagreement with Freud on the subject of the affectionate current which he had related to sexuality, is based on his views on sexuality as he expressed them in the various editions of his "Three Essays" and in his *Autobiography* (1935) where he made the following statements:

1) *Sexuality is a bodily function having pleasure as its goal.* 2) Sexual impulses include all affectionate and friendly impulses to which the ambiguous word "love" applies. 3) All the affectionate impulses are originally of a complete sexual nature, but have become inhibited in their aim, or sublimated, and employed for cultural activities of every kind, 4) *Sexual life comprises the function of obtaining pleasure from various zones of the body.*[19] [italics mine]

All these statements are evidently related to Freud's arbitrary assumption that the organ-pleasure, elicited from whatever organ or zone of our body *is of a sexual nature*, the expression of various individual sexual instinct-components generated locally. Evidently on the basis of such an unsupported conjecture, Freud found no difficulty in establishing a difference between sexuality and genitality. Yet though lacking any documentation that outside of the genitals, the organ-pleasure derived from the removal of endo-somatic stimuli in those organs and areas of our body was of a sexual nature, that conjecture became the foundation upon which Freud established that alleged difference between sexuality and genitality.

And it was on the basis of that unfounded conjecture that Freud could further state that *all affectionate impulses were originally sexual impulses which had become inhibited*, tamed, or sublimated. It was unfortunate however that Freud, from the very start, failed to make a distinction in the infant and very young child, between two types of impulses, the early affectionate ones and the later sexual ones, considering that the early affectionate impulses develop in the child prior to the "phallic stage" of his sexual development. And it was unfortunate also that Freud in order to support his assumption of the operation in young children of sexuality in terms of a sexual organ-pleasure related to individual sexual instinct-components, had considered those first alleged sexual impulses as constituting the fabric of the first child-mother relationship and in later life the fabric of father-daughter or mother-son, or of brother-sister relationship, without counting the fabric of the relationship among devoted friends. It is sad indeed to feel that all those beautiful feelings should have been related by Freud to the initial operation of sexual instinct-components, and subsequently to some mitigated or inhibited expression of the same sexual instinct-components.

Strange, however, that while Freud assumed that all affectionate and friendly impulses represented tamed or concealed sexual impulses, he on the other hand identified sexuality with *Plato's divine Love!* On this subject, Freud in one of his passages gave us the impression that he had found substantiation to that view in "*Plato's*

Prior to becoming a neutral energy, the original sexual libido, according to Freud's latest views on ego-libido (1923), (views which he later changed again,) was at first all stored in the id from where it is directed upon various objects which thus became sexual objects. It is the ego which, when necessary, withdraws that libido from the sexual objects and invests it into itself. It is this withdrawal of the libido from the object onto the ego, which according to Freud involves an abandonment of the sexual aims on the part of the ego, inasmuch as that withdrawn libido into the ego represents now a desexualized energy. Freud then added: "If that displaceable energy is *desexualized libido*, it might also be described as '*sublimated energy*' for it would retain the main purpose of Eros—that of uniting and binding."[24] [italics mine] It is with the introduction of this concept of withdrawal and desexualization of the sexual energy that Freud disposed of the sexual excitations originating from the various sources of sexuality, the various erotogenic zones, by assuming that the ego would undertake their discharge along other special outlets, for its nonsexual activities, a process which Freud called sublimation.

This line of reasoning rested unfortunately upon compound assumptions lacking any possible way of validation, particularly in connection with the point that an energy which at its origin was of a sexual nature, could divest itself from that sexual quality and become neutral energy, by the mere fact of its withdrawal into the ego and of its becoming utilized for the activation of some nonsexual ego-function. Could there be a magic wand for that transformation of a sexual energy into a neutral one?

Of course, there is an alternative to Freud's conjectural concept of the existence, operation and vicissitudes of an elusive displaceable sexual energy, be it utilized for sexual activities or following its desexualization, for intellectual and creative activities. That alternative I have presented in Part I of this trilogy. In it I have disagreed with Freud's concept of a movable psychic energy in terms of a sexual energy, and presented instead my own concept of *displaceable ideational formations made of simple ideas or of ideas and attached affective quality, be it sexual or otherwise.* An ideational formation and attached affective quality I have called "affective formation," an inseparable unit capable of displacement in its entirety, and capable to replace other "affective formations." I have also assumed that the activating energy of the ideational formations is not a psychic energy, no matter if neutral or sexual, but a somatic energy which I have called "organismic energy."

That energy in my view is the same somatic energy which had presided over the development of the new "psychic function" born initially out of the integration and synthesis of all the somatic functions already operating at a certain moment of our intrauterine somatic organization.

On that basis, I feel that an interpretation of the process of "sublimation" would be better served if we were to consider that process as the result of *a displacement of a given sexual "affective formation" and its replacement by some other nonsexual "affective formation,"* all displacements being governed by the only operating somatic energy, which is in a state of constant production through our chemical and biological processes. That approach would evidently dispose of the necessity for resorting to the obscure and elusive concept of a sexual energy, undergoing now and then, desexualization.

Evidently, my views of displaceable ideas and displaceable "affective formations" representing psychic structures, contrast fundamentally with Freud views of a displaceable "psychic energy" but not of *psychic structures*. Freud's views on this subject were clearly expressed in the latest edition of his *Interpretation of Dreams* (1932), when, as I have already reported, speaking of thought processes, he referred to images derived from a set of ideas. Such ideas may tempt someone to suppose that it is literally true that a mental grouping in one locality may be brought to an end and replaced by a fresh one in another locality. In Freud's view, such metaphors should be replaced by something more real, and thus we should be speaking instead of particular mental grouping which had a *cathexis of energy attached to it or withdrawn from it*, so that the structure in question comes under the sway of a particular agency once that cathexis becomes withdrawn from it. He again repeated that what he was doing here is once again to replace a topographical way of representing things, by a dynamic one and what he regarded as mobile was not the psychical structure but its innervation.[25] In a footnote on page 537 of that same publication, the editors explain the meaning of innervation as intended by Freud, that of a transmission of energy to indicate a process towards discharge.

Contrary to Freud's view, while I also support the dynamic concept in mental activities in the sense, however, that our mental processes operate at different levels of strength but not of topography, what I consider as essential in the operation of our "psychic apparatus," *is the movement in it of the psychic structures*, ideas, and "affective formations" and not the movement of an alleged "psychic energy."

Freud's Unsuccessful Attempt at Equating Sexuality With the "Divine Love of Plato"

I have already pointed out the fact that in order for Freud to extricate himself from under the criticism that in his earlier writings in dealing with sexuality he had implied genitality, in his later writings he defended his new concept of sexuality as being different from genitality on the basis of his new assumption that the sexual instinct was a compound instinct made of many individual sexual instinct-components, which were independent of genitality, the ultimate functional sexual instinct-components.

To enhance that difference, Freud went as far as to state that sexuality as intended by him, coincides with *the Eros of the divine Plato.* In the preface to his latest edition of *Three Essays on the Theory of Sexuality* (1920), Freud so stated:

> As for the stretching of the concept of Sexuality which has been necessitated by the analysis of children and what are called perverts, any one who looks down on psychoanalysis from a superior vantage point, should remember how closely the enlarged sexuality of psychoanalysis coincides with the Eros of the divine Plato.[1]

Continuing along a different line in the subsequent publication *Beyond the Pleasure Principle*, Freud approached first the problem of the instincts from the new philosophical angle. That *an instinct would be a tendency innate in living organic matter impelling it towards the reinstatement of an earlier condition*, and that such a condition it had to abandon under the influence of external disturbing forces.[2]

As a result, in Freud's view, we are obliged to place the organic development, to the credit of external, disturbing, and distracting influences. He also felt that the conservative organic instincts thus present the delusive appearance of forces striving after change and progress, while they are merely endeavoring to reach an old goal, by ways both old and new. He then added:

> The final goal of all organic striving, must rather be an ancient starting point to which it harks back again, by all the circuitous paths of development. . . . If we may assume that everything living dies from causes within itself, and returns to the inorganic, we can only say: *The goal of Life is Death, and casting back: The inanimate was there before the animate.*[3] [italics mine]

Therefore, according to Freud, there was at first an inanimate lifeless matter into which the properties of life were subsequently awakened by some conjectural force, the force of life. Once the force of life had aroused tension in the lifeless matter, that matter strove to return to lifelessness. In other words, there was at first an inanimate matter which became animate by the forces of the "instinct of life" and which matter subsequently strove to return to its inanimate lifeless condition, under the tension of the destructive force of the instinct of death.

Freud then assumed that in the human organism there are present some cells which retain the original structure of the early living substance, and which later on detach themselves from the parent organism, charged with all the inherited and newly acquired instinctive dispositions. One portion of the substance of these cells carries its development through to a finish, while another part, as a new germinal core, again harks back to the beginning of the development. These cells possessing the "reproductive attribute" are the cells which in Freud's views: "Operate against the death of the living substance, and are able to win for it, what seems to us to be the potential immortality, although perhaps it only means a lengthening of the path to death."[4]

The destiny of these elementary organisms which survive the individual being, is taken care of by a group of instincts which according to Freud, *constitute collectively the sexual instincts*, which not only shelter these cells, but govern also their conjunction with other reproductive cells. At this point, Freud identified that group of protective sexual instincts with his newly conceived "instinct of life" in the following words:

These sexual instincts are conservative in the same sense as the others are, in that they reproduce earlier conditions of the living substance . . . they show themselves specially resistant to external influences . . . and preserve life itself for a longer time. *They are the actual life-instincts.*[5] [italics mine]

It also followed, according to Freud, that there was, as it were, an oscillating rhythm in the life of an organism as the one group of instincts that press forward to reach the final goal of life, as quickly as possible, the other the sexual instincts fly back at a certain point on the way to traverse the same stretch once more from a given spot, and thus to prolong the duration of the journey.[6] Also in his view, these opposing groups of instincts, the ones impelling towards the preservation of life, the sexual instincts, and the ones impelling towards death are possibly present in an organism from the very beginning.

This is not the place to indulge into a philosophical discussion of Freud's assumption of an "instinct of death" which he did not relate to some inherent quality of the living substance "but rather to a purposive contrivance to a phenomenon of adaptation to the external conditions of life."[7] Too much has already been written in favor or against Freud's assumption of an instinct of death as opposed to an instinct of life. Freud is himself in support of the operation of these two instincts referred to E. Herring's theory of the processes occurring in living matter. According to that theory, there course through the living matter two kinds of uninterrupted processes of opposite direction, one anabolic assimilatory, and the other catabolic disintregrative. It was in that light that Freud asked himself if he should not venture to recognize in these two directions of our vital processes, the activity of two instinctive tendencies, the life-instinct and the death-instinct.

I will not indulge either in the details of Freud's report of two groups of experiments, such as on the one hand the experiment of S. Woodruff who by means of cultures of a "ciliate infusorium" succeeded in following its reproduction by division into two individuals, up to the 3029th generation at which time he discontinued his experiment. That experiment seemed to have favored the existence and operation of an instinct of life. On the other hand, the contrary data of Maupas, Calkins, and others, who reported that the infusorium, after a certain number of division became weaker, decreased in size, lost a portion of its organization, and finally died after a phase of senile decay, just as the higher animals do. That experiment could favor the assumption of an operating instinct of death.

Commenting on these contradictory data, Freud remarked that taking the net results of these two researches together, he noted two facts which seemed to afford him a firm foothold. Indeed, if the animalculae at a time when as yet they show no signs of age, have the opportunity of mingling with each other, of conjugating and afterwards again separating, then they remain exempt from age, they have been *rejuvenated*. The conjugation is doubtless the prototype of the sexual propagation of higher organisms; yet it has nothing to do with multiplication, being confined to the mingling of the substances of both individuals (Weismann's Amphimixis). Such invigorating influences of conjugation, which do not involve as yet propagation, seemed in his view, to be governed by the forces tending to preserve life, forces which could obscure the instinctive forces which endeavor to conduct life to death.[8] Such forces governing "conjugation" and related "rejuvenation" representing the prototype of sexual propagation, and therefore the expression of the sexual instincts, Freud concluded that they could be identified with the forces of the instinct of life.

At this point, Freud, having equated the sexual instincts with the instinct of life, he subsequently stated that such forces coincided *with the forces of the Eros of the ancient Greeks, the Eros of the divine Plato*. That view, which as I have already mentioned was to be found in the last edition (1920) of his *Three Essays on the theory of Sexuality*, was reiterated by Freud in his *New Introductory Lectures* (1933) and again in his *Outline of Psychoanalysis* posthumously published (1940), where having again identified the sexual instincts with the instinct of life, he assigned the name of Eros to both those instincts.

What impressed me in that reference of sexuality in the psychoanalytic sense of sexual instinct-components coinciding with *"the Eros of the divine Plato"* is that Freud never discussed any particular passage of Plato's writings, except in one passing mention of simply "Plato's *Symposium*."[9] I have tried to locate in that *Symposium* any reference to the "God of Love" as the god of sexuality or of the purveyor of the energy of life, but I have failed in my intent. What instead I found in that *Symposium* was an interesting reference by Aristophanes, a participant in that *Symposium,* who discussed the fate of men at the hand of Zeus. To punish them for their arrogance for having dared to attack the gods, Zeus split each man in two, so as to diminish his original strength. Subsequently these two separate halves of man *longed for each other and wish to become reunited again.*

That statement by Aristophanes was presumably picked up by Freud who paraphrased it in terms that indicate that human nature was once quite other than now; beside the male and the female, there existed a third sex which had an equal share in the two first ... and thus such beings had four hands and four feet, two faces, two genitals and so on. Then Zeus allowed himself to be persuaded to cut these beings in two, as one divides pears to stew them. ... When all nature was divided in this way, to each human being came the longing for his own other half, and the two halves embraced and entwined their bodies and desired to grow together again.[10]

What Freud may have derived from the speech of Aristophanes in Plato's *Symposium*, and from his elaboration of it, may have been an inspiration for his already stated assumption that an instinct would be a tendency innate in living matter, impelling it towards the reinstatement of an earlier condition.[11] Aristophanes himself (400 B.C.) may in turn have been influenced by the Hindu philosophy of the Upanishad or of the Veda (800 B.C.) according to which the creation of the world from the Altman (the self) was described. Freud, who mentioned the Altman, reported that the Altman (the self, the ego) experiences no joy, for the reason that no one has joy when he is alone. This is why he longed for a partner. He (the Altman) was as big as a woman and a man together when they embrace, so that he divided himself into two parts which made a husband and wife. This body, therefore having consisted of one half of the self, consequently longed for its other half so as to reconstitute the original Altman.[12]

While the above references, as well as the one extracted, from Aristophanes speech in the above mentioned Plato's *Symposium*, could be considered as an inspiration for Freud's assumption of *an instinct representing a tendency in living organic matter towards the reinstatement of an earlier condition,* There was nothing in that *Symposium,* the intent of which was simply to praise the God of Love as the purveyor of "Beauty and Goodness" that indicates to me that Sexuality viewed in modern psychoanalytic terms was among the attributes of that god.

I have attempted in the Addenda that follows to summarize very briefly the Dialogue which constitutes "Plato's special Symposium" so that the reader may judge for himself. In that symposium, however I found nothing that seemed to support Freud's speculation that:

> with the discovery of narcissistic libido, and the extension of the libido concept of the individual cells, the sexual instinct became transformed *into the Eros God of Love and Beauty that endeavors to impel the separate parts of living matter to one*

In my opinion, Freud's view that the psychoanalytic concept of sexuality, and its equivalent "instinct of life" coincide with Plato's divine love could be interpreted differently. Instead of interpreting Plato's divine Eros, as the expression of sexuality in the psychoanalytic sense, independently, that is from genitality, one could interpret Plato's divine Eros now equated with the sexual instincts and with the instinct of Life, as simply the force which brings together and reunites separate portions of the living matter.

But such an interpretation would come pretty near to assigning to Plato's divine love the meaning of genitality, inasmuch as genitality is still a part of sexuality representing the last analytic sexual instinct-component intended for reproduction. This last sexual instinct-component, the genital component can operate individually, independently from the amalgamation of the other sexual instinct-components. In that light it is the genital sexual instinct-component, a part of sexuality as intended by psychoanalysis, that presides over the function of reproduction, by means of reuniting portions of the living matter belonging to two individuals of the opposite sex in the process of fecundation. In that light genitality could as well be interpreted as also a part of Freud's alleged "Plato's divine Love."

To conclude, from all that I have discussed in the various chapters of this Part II of the trilogy, it would seem that whatever assumptions Freud may have advanced in connection 1) With the existence and operation of various sexual instinct-components originating from various areas of the body which he called "erotogenic zones." 2) With his characterizing "sexuality" as a bodily function having pleasure as its goal, that is of obtaining through it "a sexual organ-pleasure" from the various zones of the body. 3) With his attempt at differentiating sexuality from genitality, and with his views that the psychoanalytic concept of sexuality coincided with "the Eros of the divine Plato,"—all these assumptions were nothing else but formulations of his philosophical mind, which unfortunately lacked of any possible way of verification.

It would seem therefore that Freud must have been unable to support his basic tenet of 1913 that:

Psychoanalysis stands or falls by the recognition of the erotogenic zones, and of the subsequent expansion of the idea of the sexual function as opposed to the narrower one of the genital function.[14]

ADDENDA
A VERY BRIEF SUMMARY OF PLATO'S *SYMPOSIUM*

In that *Symposium*, Appolonius reported to Glaucon, what he had heard from Aristodemus concerning the banquet given by Agathon who was celebrating the prize he had won for his first tragedy. At that banquet, Socrates was present, as well as Aristodemus who accompanied Socrates.

At the suggestion of one of the guests, the physician Eryximachus, it was decided that a discussion should take place to honor the great and glorious god "Love," Eros. That suggestion was seconded by Socrates and the first to speak was Phaedrus, who actually was the one to have proposed to Eryximachus the subject for discussion. Phaedrus began by stating that "Love" is the oldest of the gods, of whose parents there was no trace, no poet nor prose writer having ever affirmed that he had any.

Phaedrus then continued:

> Love is not only the eldest of the Gods, he is also the source of the greatest benefit to us. For I know not any greater blessing to a young man and who is beginning life, than a virtuous lover, or to the lover than a beloved youth . . . neither kindred, nor honour, nor wealth, nor any other motive is able to implant so well as love.[15]

In that statement, Love, in its spiritual meaning of inspiration, affection, and courage that the god breathes into the soul, might have become somewhat ambiguous when Phaedrus referred to the love of Patroclus for Achilles, two persons of the same sex. But that ambiguity between lover and loved disappeared once Phaedrus next referred to the lover simply as the one who imparts advice, guidance, and protection to the loved one, and the loved one as the beneficiary of that love coming from a wiser and more experienced person.

The next speaker, Pausanias, remarked that in praising love we must establish which aspect of Love deserves praises, there being more than one love. In his view, Love was inseparable from Aphrodite, and if there were one Aphrodite, there would be only one Love, but as there are two goddesses, there must have been two loves. The elder Aphrodite, who had no mother he called *the heavenly Aphrodite*, daughter of Uranius. The younger one, who was the daughter of Zeus and Dione, he called *common Aphrodite*, and the Love who was her fellow-worker *was rightly named* common, while the other Love he called *heavenly*. The Love who is the offspring of the common Aphrodite he considered essentially common, inasmuch as it was the love of the body rather than of the soul.

In Pausanias' view, the offspring Love of the heavenly Aphrodite derived from a mother in whose birth the female had no part, being from the male only (Uranius). He also felt that those who are inspired by this love turn to the male. However, having praised the love of an older man for a younger man, Pausanias added that the love of young boys should be forbidden by law, because "Evil is the vulgar lover who loves the body rather than the soul, whereas the love of the soul and of its noble disposition is life-long and everlasting."[16]

Eryximachus, the physician who spoke next said that Pausanias had rightly distinguished two kinds of love, and that he had gathered and learned from his own art of medicine, how great and wonderful and universal *is the deity of love* whose empire extends over all things divine as well as humans. Then referring to the heavenly love and common love as discussed by Pausanias he added that:

> There are in the human body two kinds of love which are confessedly different and unlike, and being unlike they have love and desires which are unlike; and the desire of the healthy is one, and the desire of the diseased in another.[17]

Aristophanes, whose turn came next, spoke by stating that, mankind judging by the neglect of "Love" has never at all understood the power of Love. For if they had understood him, they would surely have built noble temples and altars, and offered solemn sacrifices in his honor. For him, of all the gods, the god of love is the best friend of men, the helper and the healer of the ills. He then proceeded to discuss the nature of man, and what happened to him pointing out that:

> The original human nature was unlike the present, different, inasmuch as the sexes were not two as they are now, but originally three in number and that there was a man, a woman, and the union of the two having a name corresponding to this double nature, Androginius who had four hands and four feet, one head with two faces looking opposite ways, four ears, two

privy members, and the remainder to correspond. . . . Terrible
was the might of strength of the primeval men, and that the
thoughts of their heart were great, so that they dared to scale
Heaven and make an attack upon the Gods.[18]

After a good deal of reflection, Zeus, according to Aristophanes,
had a plan to humble their pride and improve their manner. He allowed them to continue to exist, but he cut them in two so as to diminish their strength and increase their number. But after the division, the two parts of man, each desiring his other half, came together entwined in mutual embraces as they longed to grow again
into one.

In another passage of his speech, Aristophanes, referring to the
division of the human male, added,

> But they who are a section of the male, follow the male, and
> while they are young, being slices of the original man, they
> hang about man, and embrace them and they are themselves
> the best of boys and youths because they have the most manly
> nature. . . . But, the intense yearning which each of them has
> towards the other does not appear to be the desire of lover's
> intercourse, but of something else which the soul of either
> evidently desires and cannot tell. . . . The pursuit of the whole
> is called love. . . . If we were to praise him who has given us
> that benefit, we must praise the *God Love* who is our greatest
> benefactor.[19]

Even though the first part of Aristophanes speech may have left
room for ambiguity, he soon clarified again his thinking when he
had stated that the yearning for each other to which he had alluded,
*should not be construed as the desire for lover's intercourse, but of
something else which the soul of either evidently desires.* Thus, sexuality in Freud's terms and least of all of individual sexual instinct-
components, had no room in that desire of the souls of each part of
the original whole.

When Agathon's turn came, rather than to speak first of the
benefits which the God Love conferred upon men, he first wished to
praise that god and only then speak of his gifts to men. He felt that
of all the blessed gods, he is the most blessed because he is the
fairest and best and the youngest, for Agathon views the fairness of
the complexion of the God Love resulted from his habitation among
the flowers and scents where he sat and abode. And since the birth
of Love, and from the Love of the beautiful has sprung every good in
heaven and earth and that at the touch of him, everyone becomes a
poet, he concluded as follows: "Love is a good poet and accomplished

in all the fine arts. And as to the artists do we not know that he only of them whom love inspires, has the light of fame? He whom Love touches, not walks in darkness."

When Socrates' turn to speak came, he first recalled that all previous speakers had attributed to Love every imaginable form of praise which can be gathered anywhere, making him appear the fairest and best of all those who know him not. But, if the speakers liked to hear the truth about Love, he was to speak in his own manner.

He then stated that love *is the love of something which is wanting to a man*. He subsequently reminded Agathon as having said that it was the love of beautiful that had set in order the empire of the gods, and that there was no love for the deformed things. Thus love is the love of beauty and not of deformity. Having them recalled also the fact that he and Agathon had agreed on the point that *love is something which is wanted*, he could conclude that *love wants but has no beauty*. Thus, how can Love be called beautiful when he wants the beauty which he does not possess? Having further recalled Agathon's statement that Love is also good he asked, "Is not the good also beautiful? And if so in wanting the beautiful, Love wants also the good. Thus how can we say that Love is good and beautiful if it wants beauty and goodness?"

At this point, Socrates recalled a similar discussion on the God Love, which he had sometime in the past with a woman, *Diotima of Mantineaia*, who at that time having listened to Socrates' reasoning, questioned how a God can be who has no portion in what is either good or fair. Thus she felt that Socrates was denying the divinity of Love. In her view God was neither mortal nor immortal but a great spirit and like all spirits, he is intermediate between the divine and the mortal. And in her view, the power of God consisted in the fact that: "He interprets between Gods and men, and that *he is the mediator who spans the chasm which divides* them, and therefore in him all is bound together."[20] Parenthetically, in this passage, one may find what inspired Freud in considering Eros, alias "sexual instincts" alias "instinct of life," as the forces that bind things together.

The last speech was that of Alcibiades who praised Socrates for his wisdom, his knowledge, his courage, and his great influence on youth. With that speech, Plato brought to an end his famous *Symposium*.

From my reading of Plato's *Symposium* on Eros, *nothing in my opinion transpired that could have any relation with Freud's enlarged concept of "Sexuality" based on the operation of various independent sexual instinct-components which originated in his so-called "erotogenic zones."* The identification made by Freud of his enlarged concept of sexuality with Eros, the God of Love, a love of the soul, and which he referred to as the Eros of the divine Plato, lacks of any support. That identification impresses me as no more than a philosophical conclusion formulated by Freud's brilliant mind, carried away by his admitted ambition of being considered also a philosopher.

PART THREE

The Fallacy of Freud's Concepts of "The Conscious" and of the Origin, Structure and Characteristics of "The Unconscious"

Contents

C H A P T E R   I

Flaws and Vacillations in Freud's Concept of "Consciousness"

Faced with Freud's initial acceptance of Lipps' views that whatever is conscious has had a preliminary unconscious stage, I consider it of interest to contrast such an acceptance with Freud's subsequent views on how the conscious first developed. These views he elaborated in 1900 in his *Interpretation of Dreams*, a few years after he had expressed to his friend Fliess his belief in Lipps's approach to "consciousness." To follow chronologically Freud's evolution of his concept of "consciousness," I have to recall his very early views on this subject, even though these were originally formulated in what is known as his posthumously published *Project for a Scientific Psychology*, a project soon after repudiated (1895). Though in 1895 in a letter to his friend, Freud had subscribed to Lipps's views, the subsequent year (1896) in a letter of June 12 to the same friend, he expressed his views on the functioning of the "psychic apparatus," views which did not seem to fit very well with those of Lipps inasmuch as they entailed the operation of "memory traces," the origin of which must have implied the operation of a previous "psychic function" responsible for those memory-traces which must have operated first at a conscious level, a function which Freud had not as yet contemplated as such.

In that letter of June, Freud had in fact stated that he was working on the assumption that the psychical apparatus came about by processes of stratification and that the material present in the shape of memory-traces was from time to time subjected to rearrangement, as if it were transcribed. What he considered now essential in his theory was the thesis that memory was present several times, being registered in various species of signs. It followed that

200

the transcripts were also separated, in respect to the neuron which were their vehicles. Such an assumption, though not an essential one, he considered as the simplest, and he felt that it was provisionally admissible.[1] Then returning to his neuronal theory he referred to the *"perceptual neurones"* (Pcpt) on the basis of which he outlined his first schematic representation of our psychic apparatus, in terms of at least *three systems of sign-registration*: The Pcpt-s (the perception signs), the Uc-s (the unconscious signs), and the Pc-s (the preconscious signs).

The perceptual neurones (Pcpt), *to which consciousness was attached*, were the neurones incapable of retaining any trace of excitations which passed through them. The perceptual signs, Pcpt-s, represented the first registration of the perceptions, arranged according to associations of simultaneity. The Uc-s signs constituted the second registration of the perceptions, according to causal relations, corresponded to conceptual memories, and were inaccessible to consciousness. The preconscious signs (Pc-s) represented a third transcription of the perceptions attached to the verbal images. The cathexis proceeding from this Pc. transcriptions would become conscious by activating *the neurones of consciousness, that is the perceptual neurones*.

At this point, therefore, Freud had clearly considered consciousness as being an initial phenomenon originating in the perceptual neurones (Pcpt.) That view was a reiteration of what Freud had already expressed to his friend Fliess in his letter of January 1, 1896 where he had considered the perceptual processes as representing consciousness. In his words:

> *On this view perceptual processes would eo-ipso (from their very nature) involve consciousness*, and would only produce further psychical effects after becoming conscious. The psychic processes could in themselves be unconscious and would only subsequently acquire a secondary artificial consciousness, by being linked to discharge and perception.[2] [italics mine]

In that letter, Freud had also stated that the perceptual neurones received excitations from our terminal sense-organs.

Freud's position at this point was to say the least an ambiguous one. How could he indeed remain faithful to his belief that as Lipps contended, all mental processes were at first unconscious, before becoming conscious, when he now admitted the direct origin of consciousness from excitations of our sense-organs of perception, which *eo-ipso* involve consciousness? Of course Freud may have meant by "psychic processes being in themselves unconscious" that it was only the mechanism leading to the transformation of the excitations of our sense-organs of perception into conscious processes, that was unconscious, that is taking place outside our own awareness. But such a semantic ambiguity could hardly support his adherence to Lipps's views that all mental processes are unconscious in their first stage, that is that they are existing and operating as such in the unconscious, prior to becoming conscious at a subsequent stage. In my view, mental processes (see part One of this trilogy) are being created by a new "Psychic function" born at a certain moment of our ontogenetic intrauterine development, from the synthesis and integration of all somatic functions already operating at that moment. The task of that new "Psychic function" is to translate the various somatic stimuli related to the operation of the various somatic functions, into ideational representations which from their very onset constitute conscious formations (apperceptions of the old philosophers).

Returning now to the first letterings of the transcription signs of the functioning of our psychic apparatus which Freud first introduced in 1896, they were evidently the precursors of the ultimate lettering of Cs. Pcs. and Ucs. used by him in his subsequent letter to Fliess dated May 31, 1897, and in chapter VII of his Interpretation *of Dreams* (1900). In the latter Freud modified his first graphic illustration of our psychic apparatus, into a linear model at which left end (the sensory end), he placed the Pcpt. system which received the proper excitations. However, the elements of that system could not retain their excitations, "but could provide consciousness" with the whole multiplicity of sensory qualities. That version seemed to be an enlarged version of his previous statement that "perceptions eo-ipso involved consciousness" but in which statement no mention was made of any special quality. At the right end of the linear representation, Freud placed another system (M) which opened the gateway to motor activities and to other forms of conscious discharge. In that light it would seem that it was consciousness which had developed at the perceptual end (Pcpt.) that induced all conscious activities at the other end (M). At the same time, it was an indication that consciousness in terms of a psychic process, manifested a sense of direction.

That first directional system was supported by a second system which "transformed the momentary excitations of the first system into permanent traces."[3] In that second system which he called "the unconscious," Freud included the memory-traces of the momentary conscious excitations, as well as the associative links which became established among them, all of them underlying the function which he called memory. It was no longer a matter therefore of different neurones, the permeable and the impermeable ones, presiding over the registration of temporary or permanent excitations, but of a transformation of momentary conscious excitations into permanent ones, in terms of some different forms of ideational presentation taking place into a separate system, the unconscious. No clarification was given by Freud as to the mechanics of that transformation. Was it actually a change of venue undergone by those temporary conscious perceptions in their passing into a different system, the Ucs.? Or was it a simple loosening of the associative connections between the conscious as a system, and some of its formative components? Were we dealing with a latent operation of some of those formative ideational conscious representations, which however remained within the functional boundaries of the Cs. system, though their activity was masked by the more dominant elements of that same Cs. system?

At any rate, once the so-called memory-traces of past ideational formations had become, according to Freud, established in the Ucs. system, these elements could reenter the first system and become conscious again. In order to return in consciousness, these elements would have to pass through a third system which Freud placed between the Ucs. system and the Cs. system, but in closer relation to the latter, a system in which the memory-traces underwent certain modifications, such as that of acquiring a certain intensity, by attracting the cathectic energy of attention. That system Freud designated as the preconscious (Pcs.), a system for the obligatory passage for the elements of the Ucs. before they were allowed to enter consciousness. No access to consciousness for unconscious elements could take place except via the preconscious. In later writings Freud made exception for the affects which in his view enter consciousness directly.

Already, in connection with *the Pcs. system*, we meet with vacillations and even contradictions on Freud's part. At first he had considered that system to constitute a portion of the Ucs. system. Subsequently he considered it a part of the conscious system, Cs., and no longer a part of the unconscious as a system. It took him a long time however to change his mind, once he had realized the inconsistency of his earlier position. In retrospect, it would seem therefore that Freud's earlier introduction of the Pcs. as a formative part of the system Ucs. had been premature as well as superfluous. Indeed the designation of the Pcs. as a part of the Ucs. system was not justified because Freud on his own accord had stated that in the Pcs. traces were left of the perceptions which impinge upon our psychic apparatus. Now if in the Pcs., traces were left that belonged *to the perceptions which eo-ipso involved consciousness*, I do not see how conscious perceptual elements could belong to the unconscious as a system. Even if one were to consider such left-over portions of the conscious perceptions as memory-traces, these memory-traces should have retained with the Cs. system sufficient associative connections, and as such could hardly have been considered as forming a portion of the entirely different Unconscious (Ucs.) system. There should be some other way to properly evaluate the relationship of these traces of conscious perceptions to the system to which they should legitimately belong. I will return to this important subject in the following chapters.

As another indication of Freud's vacillating position on the origin and nature of consciousness, I will refer to the new assumption which with the greatest of ease he had introduced on this subject in his *Interpretation of Dreams*. While up to 1900 he had considered consciousness as a mental quality derived *eo-ipso* from the activity of the various perceptions (Pcpt.), he now in 1900 assumed the existence and operation of two different processes giving origin to consciousness. On the one hand, he kept unaltered his view that perceptions *eo-ipso* involved consciousness and on the other hand he assumed the existence and operation of "*A special organ of Consciousness for the perception of mental qualities*" and to which he attributed the development of consciousness. Parenthetically, on this point, Freud's new position seemed to be the acceptance of what Lipps had already postulated and which Freud had communicated to his friend W. Fliess in his letter of August 31, 1898, where he wrote, "Lipps regards Consciousness *as only a sense-organ*, the contents of the mind as ideation, and all mental processes as unconscious."[4]

Elaborating now on the qualities of that "*special sense-organ of consciousness*," Freud, in his *Interpretation of Dreams*, regarded it in its mechanical properties as a system resembling the perceptual system, but incapable of retaining traces of alterations, that is to say, having no memory. He also felt that such a system, by perceiving new qualities, made a new contribution *to directing the mobile quantity of cathexes*, and distributing them in an expedient fashion. In addition, he felt that with the help of its perceptions of pleasure and unpleasure, it influenced the discharge of the cathexis in the unconscious by means of the displacement of quantities.[5]

Yet, Freud had attributed practically the same functions to the perception system, "Pcpt.," when he assumed that the perception by our sense organ has the result of directing a cathexis of attention to the paths along which the incoming sensory excitation is spreading. In his view, the qualitative excitations of that system acted also as a regulator of the mobile quantity in the "psychical apparatus."[6] Thus Freud attributed also to the Pcpt. system the same function which he now attributed to his *new special sense-organ of consciousness.* At this point, one cannot help consider the fact that perceptions by our various sense-organs, be they tactile, thermic, or vibratory, must involve also an ideational qualitative representation of their operation, at the hand of the new "Psychic function." (See part I of this trilogy.) In that light, one could hardly see the need for a second special organ of consciousness for the perception of mental qualities.

At any rate, Freud had viewed the Pcpt. system and the new "special organ of consciousness" as constituting two different systems. The only point which in my estimation supported Freud's alleged distinction between these two systems was his vague reference to the fact that the more discriminating regulation of the special sense-organ of consciousness, could oppose the earlier regulatory function of the perceptual system (Pcpt.). But such a distinction would have to rest upon a very flimsy and artificially introduced discriminatory function assumed to belong to that alleged new *"special organ of Consciousness."* Altogether therefore, Freud's position in 1900 was quite at variance with that which he had taken in January 1895 when he had simply maintained that the perceptions by our sense-organs *eo-ipso* (by their very nature) involved consciousness, and pointing to no exclusion of the psychic qualities of these perceptions.

The ambiguity of Freud's differentiation between the special sense-organ of consciousness and the perceptions by our various sense-organs was not made clearer in his subsequent reference to the "pleasure-principle" that governs the quality of our conscious mental processes, since that principle according to him operates at first in the Ucs., the original source of mental processes according to Lipps. This view of Lipps Freud had shared with the only variance that in the Ucs., he had also relegated mental processes which having been conscious at first were subsequently rejected in that Ucs. by repression.

If, therefore, all mental processes are operating at first in the Ucs., it should be natural in my estimation, that it would be in the unconscious that those mental processes should acquire *the elements* that impart to them their pleasurable or unpleasurable qualities, considering that in Freud's view, *the pleasure-principle reigns sovereign in the unconscious*. It would make no difference if those primordial elements are subsequently registered by the ego. Under those circumstances it becomes difficult if not impossible to conceptualize the role of that "special organ of consciousness for the perception of psychic qualities" that includes evidently that of pleasure or unpleasure, as operating in the unconscious. If thought-processes at their first unconscious stage, are governed by the pleasurable or unpleasurable element that accompanies their unconscious formulation, one is therefore justified in asking the following question: "Is there in that Unconscious some other special organ responsible for the registration of such elements of pleasure or unpleasure, an organ which is not that of the special organ of Consciousness for the perception of mental qualities?

That point was indeed raised but not solved by Freud in his posthumous publication *An Outline of Psychoanalysis* where he stated that:

> The Unconscious Id cut off from the external world *has its own world of perceptions* though it is hard to say by what means and with the help of what sensory terminal organs *these perceptions come about*. But it remains certain that self-perceptions, *coenesthetic feelings of pleasure-unpleasure*, govern events *in the Id with despotic forces*.[7]

The ambiguity of the feelings of pleasure-unpleasure operating in the unconscious, feelings which should involve consciousness, was subsequently extended by Freud to the Preconscious system (Pcs.) which originally constituted the other portion of the Ucs. system, though later he identified that Pcs. with the Cs. system. In that Pcs. system, the memory-traces retain some residues of psychic qualities so that in Freud's subsequent formulation that in order that thought-processes may acquire quality, they are associated in human beings with verbal memories whose residues of qualities are sufficient to draw to them the attention of consciousness. Such an association endows the process of thinking with a new mobile cathexis from consciousness.[8]

In that context a point remained clear: If the verbal memories contained in the preconscious possessed instead "residues of mental qualities," these memory-traces must have been already operating in that Pcs. under the influence of the *"special organ of consciousness."* If that special sense-organ of consciousness were still operative in a residual form in the Pcs. which Freud considered now no longer as belonging to the system Ucs., but operating nevertheless in what he termed a "descriptive unconscious," the fact still remained that the "special organ of consciousness" was operating outside our own awareness. One cannot help note some basic inconsistency in that situation, considering also the fact that later in 1915, Freud stated that affects, of which evidently pleasure and unpleasure are formative components, can be felt and registered only by a conscious ego, and could not be felt in the unconscious.

As for the reference to the function of attention capable of drawing presumably "the special organ of consciousness" upon perceptions, which it endows with psychic qualities, I must point out that in his various assumptions on this subject, Freud had neglected to consider the other important assumption, that of the intervention at a certain moment of our ontogenesis, of a new "psychic function" born of the integration and synthesis of the various somatic functions operating at that moment. It is that "Psychic function" that governs the first translation of the various functional somatic stimuli into their respective ideational representations. It is this newly developed "psychic function" which from its very onset involves consciousness that registers and directs all the ideational representations of the various perceptual stimuli. The operation of that function supersedes evidently the need for resorting to a superfluous *special organ of consciousness for the perceptions of psychic qualities.* The acquiring of psychic affective qualities on the part of the ideational representation of the various somatic stimuli is dependent from other factors than the alleged intervention of a special organ of consciousness. I have dealt with this subject in chapter I of part I of this trilogy.

Though Freud never considered the origin and function of a new "psychic function" capable of translating into ideational representations the various functional somatic stimuli and capable of presiding over their acquiring an affective quality, he nevertheless spoke of a psychic function of "attention" with, however, no mention of its special task in relation to the ideational representations, nor to its relation to a more general "psychic function."

A first reference to that special "psychic function of attention" is found in Part III of Freud's "Project" where discussing the mechanisms which cause the ego to follow perceptions and influence them, he wrote:

This mechanism lies I believe in the fact that according to my

> hypothesis, a perception invariably excites the perception sys-
> tem, that is *passes indication of quality*. Here we seem to have
> the mechanism of *psychical attention*. I find it hard to give
> any mechanical explanation of its origin. I believe therefore
> that it is biologically determined; that it has been left in the
> course of psychical evolution. . . . The effect of psychical atten-
> tion is to cathect the same neurones which are the bearers of
> perceptual cathexis.[9]

Note that in this statement Freud referred to that special function of
attention as that which imparts psychic qualities to the various perceptions, and not to the special organ of consciousness which he introduced only later in 1900. It was that same psychic function of attention that now governed and directed the activities of all perceptions.

In the *Interpretation of Dreams*, Freud returned to this function
of attention, but now seemed to favor the point that it was no longer
the psychic function of attention that was responsible for the direction of the perceptual cathexes, but on the contrary that it was instead the cathexes of the sense-organs of perceptions which directed
the cathexes of attention along the path of the incoming stimuli:

> We know that perception of our sense-organs has the result *of
> directing the cathexis of attention* to the path along which the
> incoming sensory excitation is spreading. The qualitative ex-
> citation of the Pcpt. system acts as a regulator of the dis-
> charge of the mobile quantity in the psychical ap-
> paratus. . . . We can attribute the same function to the overly-
> ing sense-organ of the Conscious system. By perceiving new
> qualities it makes a new contribution to directing the mobile
> quantities of cathexis and distributing them in an expedient
> manner.[10]

Thus both the Pcpt. system and the special organ of consciousness,
though similar but not identical in Freud's views, were responsible
for directing the function of attention.

Freud's position on the question of the function of attention continued to remain ambiguous when Freud assumed that becoming
conscious was connected with the application of a particular psychic
function, that of attention, which in his view was only available in a
specific quantity. This quantity may be diverted from a train of
thought onto some other purpose. However if we come upon an idea,
which still bears no criticism, the cathexis of attention was
dropped.[11] This statement seems to go contrary to Freud's earlier
statement that it was the special sense-organ of consciousness that

directed the course of attention, inasmuch as he now assumed that it was attention that directed the train of thoughts in their path to consciousness. One must also keep in mind the fact that a train of thoughts is the product of past and present perceptions that have been translated into ideational formations and subsequent thought-formations, so that the proposition of their being directed now by the function of attention, runs contrary to Freud's previous statement that perceptions were the ones to guide attention.

What also seems a flaw in connection with Freud's relationship between attention and a train of thoughts, is the fact that in my opinion, for a train of thoughts to be formulated and operative, it requires the operation of *an already active general psychic function* from which that formulation depended. But Freud never discussed the relationship of the particular function of attention to any general psychic function already in operation, and therefore deprived us from the possibility of evaluating "attention" in terms of *a particular facet of that general psychic function*, which latter was first entrusted with the translation of all stimuli originating in our various sense-organs of perception into their corresponding ideational representations and subsequent thought formations over the activities of which it from then on presided.

In *The Interpretation of Dreams*, the function of attention was further discussed by Freud, in connection with the hallucinatory character of the dream formation. Contrasting with the waking state of *normals*, in the course of which *the regulatory function of attention* prevents a hallucinatory development, in dreams the hallucinations result from the fact that the cathexes at work during sleep are prevented from following their normal directional course, from the perceptual end of the psychic apparatus to the memory-traces of the perceptions in the Pcs. system and to their ultimate discharge in thoughts or in motor activities. As a consequence the cathectic flow is forced to follow a retrograde, regressive course from the Pcs. system to the Ucs. system, and back to the perceptual excitations which latter become vividly activated by that regressive cathectic flow and thus generates the hallucinatory content of the dreams. In the waking state, "attention," because of its controlling function upon the perceptual excitations, prevents the regressive movement beyond the mnemonic traces, and thus prevents hallucinations. Here again it is attention that governs the perceptions and not vice versa as Freud had originally maintained: another instance of his vacillation.

Freud's assumption that becoming conscious was connected with the application of the psychic function of attention, became complicated by the fact that "attention" had been involved by him into the operation of the Pcs. which at that time (1900) he had considered as a formative part of the Ucs. system. In that Pcs. system, Freud had stated that its processes could enter consciousness: "only if other conditions are fulfilled: for instance that they reach a certain degree of intensity, and that the function which can be described as Attention be distributed in a particular way."[12] We were thus presented with two different systems, the Cs. and the Pcs., the latter being considered at that time (1900) as an integral part of the Ucs. system, though both of those systems made use of the conscious function of attention. The operation in the unconscious system of a conscious function was in those terms an evident contradiction. It was only years later that Freud identified the Pcs. system with the Cs. system and thus erased that contradiction.

This entire concept of consciousness as dealt with by Freud, and which he at first considered to be the inherent function of the perceptual system of our various sense-organs of perception which *eo-ipso* involved consciousness; Freud's subsequent addition to the perceptual system of a new "*special organ of consciousness for the perception of psychic qualities*"; Freud's concept of attention which he at first considered as a cathectic energy which was governed by both our various sense-organs of perception and by our special sense-organ of consciousness for the perception of psychic qualities; his considering later "attention" as a cathectic energy which *governs* the direction of all perceptions *instead of being governed by them* as he first assumed; his earlier ambiguous position of the conscious function of attention operating in the Ucs. system; his failure to correlate that function of attention with a more general "psychic function" of which it could have represented only a special facet; all these considerations seem to reflect in their ensemble the evident difficulties encountered by Freud in dealing with a so nebulous and elusive concept as consciousness, a fact which accounts for his flaws, contradictions, and vacillation on this subject.

Faced with the obscurity of his special function of "attention" operating within the Cs. system and the Pcs., formerly a portion of the Ucs. system, Freud quietly refrained himself from referring any longer to that function, *so that no mention at all* is to be found of that function in all his subsequent writings. At the same time also, without any fanfare for the change, he abandoned his views on the existence and operation of the new system which he had introduced in 1900, that of "*the special organ of consciousness for the perception of psychic qualities.*"

Thus, in 1916, in his paper *The Metapsychological Supplement to the Theory of Dreams*, Freud returned to his original assumption that perceptions from our various sense-organs, *eo-ipso* (by their very nature) involve consciousness. In my estimation that return to his original assumption should have been introduced by Freud much sooner, considering that "the special sense-organ of consciousness" for the perception of psychic qualities, should have been interpreted not as a special sense-organ, but as a refinement of the function of the various sense-organs of perception, presided over by the new "psychic function" born of the synthesis and integration of all somatic functions, already operating at a certain moment of our early intrauterine somatic organization. (see chapter I of part I of this trilogy).

At any rate, it was in 1916, that Freud officially returned to his original unitarian views of perception and consciousness, in the above mentioned paper where he stated that:

> Already in the "traumdeutung" it became necessary to decide upon regarding conscious perceptions as a function of a special system to which we have ascribed certain remarkable properties and shall be justified in attributing other characteristics as well. This system there called the Pcpt. (Perception), we now identify with the system Cs. upon which normally the operation of becoming conscious depends.[13]

Thus no more mention of the special organ of consciousness, no more distinction between the Cs. system and the Pcpt. system, but an identity between these two systems as indicated by his final lettering of the system Cs. as the Cs.-Pcpt. system, a reiteration of his very early views that perceptions *eo-ipso* involved consciousness.

Three years later (1919), in a footnote added to page 541 of *The Interpretation of Dreams*, Freud returned to that identification when, referring to the linear schematic representation of our psychic apparatus, he wrote:

> If we attempt to proceed with the schematic picture, in which the systems are set out in linear succession, we should have to reckon with the fact that the system beyond the Pcs. is the one to which consciousness must be attached. In other words that Pcpt. = Cs.[14]

In connection with Freud's equating in 1916 the Pcpt. system with the Cs. system, I must also recall that the previous year, in his paper *The Unconscious*, he had reached another important equation:

conscious = preconscious. I am referring to this conclusion that the Pcs. system could be equated with the Cs. system, since he had lettered the representation of both systems in a single unit Cs.-Pcs. Considering that he had already identified the Pcpt. system with the Cs. system and that he now had designated the Pcs. as a unified Cs.-Pcs. system, we would then be justified in considering as *a single system the Pcpt.- the Pcs.- and the Cs. systems* and inquire as to what effect such a unification could have had on the formulation of a possible different approach to the structure of our psychic apparatus. One should keep in mind the fact that the Pcs., though identified by Freud with the Cs., operated according to him, outside the field of our awareness.

One wonders indeed how little attention has been paid by Freud and followers to the possible elaboration of some other formulation of the structure of our psychic apparatus, a formulation which if pursued could have resulted not only in the cancellation of any difference between the Pcpt. the Pcs. and the Cs. systems, but also the possibility that whatever mental process was in operation in that apparatus, even though outside the field of our awareness, could have been nothing else but the function of the Cs. system itself operating at a subordinate level, and constituting what I will propose to call "the Subordinate conscious." As a matter of fact in the following chapters, I will even propose "Subordinate conscious" as a substitute for Freud's entire concept of the unconscious.

In *The Ego and the Id* (1923), where Freud dealt with our psychic apparatus in the structural terms of an ego, an id, and a super-ego, consciousness in his new graphic scheme represented the most external surface of our mental apparatus, possessing the function of a *surface organ of reception*, receiving excitations from without in the form of sensory perceptions and from within in the forms of sensations and feelings. Whereas ideas which originate in the unconscious had to establish connections with the verbal images in the Pcs. in order to become conscious, sensations and feelings considered in terms of "a quantitative and qualitative element in the mind" could reach directly the system Cs. In that context Freud seems to have adopted a twofold approach to consciousness. On the one hand, he still could adhere to Lipps's views that mental processes, at least those inherited, pass through a first unconscious stage before becoming conscious, while on the other hand he admitted of consciousness as originating also in the most external surface of our psychic apparatus, i.e. in the areas of perceptions and receptions. These presumably were the mental processes which having been conscious at first, could become relegated subsequently in the Ucs. by means of repression. In this latter approach to consciousness, Freud evidently returned to his original concept that perceptions *eo-ipso* involve consciousness. He disregarded again however his earlier views of 1900 that consciousness was related to the operation of *"a special sense-organ for the perception of psychic qualities."*

As for the description of the Pcpt.-Cs. itself was concerned, Freud added very little information to what he had already given in his paper *The Unconscious* and that of the *Metapsychological Supplement to the Theory of Dreams*. Outside of adhering to his concept that the Pcpt.-Cs. systems constituted a single system, he simply added:

> The term Conscious, is to start with a purely descriptive one, resting on the perception of the most direct and certain character. Experience shows next, that a mental element (for instance an idea) is not as a rule permanently conscious; an idea that is conscious now, is no longer so a moment later, although it can become so again under certain conditions. What the idea was in the interval we do not know. We can say that it was *latent*. And by this we mean that *it was capable to become conscious at any time*. Or if we say that it was *unconscious* we are giving an equally correct description. Thus unconscious in this sense of the word coincides with latent and capable of becoming conscious.[15]   [italics mine]

He subsequently added that the mind could be conceived as an unknown and unconscious id, upon whose surface rests the ego developed from its nucleus, the Pcpt. system. He did not elaborate further, though in his diagram of page 29 he lettered the latter system by combining it with the lettering of the Cs. system in the form of a single Pcpt.—Cs. system.

In the *New Introductory Lectures* (1933), Freud was even clearer in that respect:

> As regards a characterization of the Ego we shall get on better, if we turn our attention to the relation between it and the most superficial portion of the mental apparatus which we call the Pcpt.-Cs. (perceptual-conscious system). This system is turned towards the external world—it is the medium for perceptions arising thence, and during its functioning the phenomenon of consciousness arises in it. *It is the sense-organ*

of the whole apparatus, receptive moreover not only of excitations from without, but also of such as proceed from the interior of the mind.[16] [italics mine]

In this passage there was no more distinction between that sense-organ of the whole apparatus and the special sense-organ of consciousness *for the perception of psychic qualities*, which Freud had first introduced in 1900, but since forgotten. What was reaffirmed instead was his original unitarian concept of what he now considered the most superficial portion of the mental apparatus, the Pcpt. system, which alone constituted the sense organ of the whole apparatus and the activity of which involved *eo-ipso* consciousness.

In his *Outline of Psychoanalysis*, Freud limited himself to reiterate in a general manner, that the process of a thing becoming conscious, is above all linked with the perceptions which our sense-organs receive from the external world. Concerning the feelings which originate from the inside, Freud felt that it was possible also to maintain that their becoming conscious is linked with the perceptions of the external world: "It need only be said by way of distinction, *as regards the terminal organs of feelings* the body itself takes the place of the external world."[17] This mention of the terminal organs of feelings was indeed however quite an obscure and elusive reference, if one considers that at some point Freud had stated that the id: "which is cut off from the external world has its own world of perception. . . . It is to be sure, hard to say by what means and with the help of what sensory terminal organs these perceptions come about."[18] Freud never clarified that statement.

At this point, I would like to return for a moment, to two statements made by Freud in one of which he had characterized the Cs. system as a system similar to the perceptual system and susceptible to excitations by qualities, but incapable of retaining traces, that is, as having no memory, and to the other statement in which he had said that in the psychic apparatus, memory and the quality that characterizes consciousness are mutually exclusive. The assumption of the existence of two separate functional systems, based on the attributes of retaining or not retaining excitations, goes back to Freud's original *Project for a Scientific Psychology* (1895), where he considered the existence of two systems of neurones. To one system, *the permeable one*, he assigned the function of receiving excitations and of getting rid of them immediately so as to be ready to receive new excitations. To the other system, *the impermeable one*, he assigned the function to receive and retain the traces of those excitations. From this he derived his concept on the one hand of sensory and perceptual neurones, and on the other hand of memory neurones, and reached the conclusion that one single neurone could not perform both functions, one function excluding the other.

My reaction to this theoretical distinction between neurones, which allow the passage of excitations without any modification of their content, and those which become modified by such a passage, is that such a concept might have been valid only if the involved neurones were to be considered as neurones performing an individual isolated function, independently from any connections with other neurones. But this is not the case in the nervous system, where not only structural connections bind one neurone to another, but where the dynamic and functional connections of each neurone makes it an integral part of some wider structural and functional group of neurones.

The passage or the blocking of the passage of excitation through a given neurone becomes then related to the whole chain of structural and functional connections of that neurone. In any case, one cannot assume that a neurone allows the passage of an excitation without undergoing some sort of functional modification, even if limited only to what mysteriously underlies in a living neurone, the facilitation in it for the passage of a subsequent excitation of the same nature. This *functional tracing* of the passage of a given excitation in individual neurones contributes to the creation of a wider system of tracings which involves a given group of neurones and their neural connecting paths. From that group, the resulting excitation extends itself along new systems of tracings, to other groups of neurones. In this context of extensive functional tracings, it therefore becomes difficult to conceptualize in living matter, the existence of neurones which are exempted from functional modification related to the passage of given excitations.

The assumption of neurones retaining traces of the passage of excitations and of neurones incapable of doing so, and from which assumption Freud evolved his concept of a Pcpt.-Cs. system, which permits only the passage of excitations, as opposed to the Ucs. (unconscious system), the neurones of which retain the traces of excitations in the form of memory-traces, *is untenable in those terms*. The phenomenon of conscious perceptions in living matter is related to both the passage of excitations and their leaving functional traces of their passage in all neurones, be they perceptual neurones or otherwise. If furthermore one considers the existence of a two-way directional current for the excitations in the tracing systems, between the perceptual neurones and the receptive neurones, as well as the network of interrelated connections between the perceptual neurones and the various other neuronal groups, one could hardly differentiate the Pcpt.—Cs. system *on that simple basis* of neurones not retaining and neurones retaining traces of the passage of excitations.

Evidently, all the considerations advanced by Freud in his discussion of the workings of our psychic apparatus, consciousness included, were based upon his personal theory of the existence and operation of a "psychic energy," the excitations of which possessed various affective qualities and which were capable of displacement from one mental formation to another, or capable of being withdrawn at any time from that given mental formation.

At no time did Freud assume the existence and operation of mental formations in terms of ideational representations, which themselves were capable of independent displacement and replacement by some other ideational formations, and the energy for which activity was not a "psychic energy." It is in this connection that in *The Interpretation of Dreams*, speaking of conscious ideas that are subsequently taken in the unconscious, that Freud admonished that instead of speaking of a mental grouping in one locality brought to an end and replaced by a fresh one in another locality, one should feel it more appropriate to consider that any particular mental grouping which has had a cathexis of energy attached to it may have that cathexis withdrawn from it, so that such a psychic structure may come under the sway of some particular agency or may be withdrawn from it. What he was doing here was only to replace a topographical way of representing things by a dynamic one. *What he regarded as mobile was, he repeated again,* not *the psychical structure but its innervation.*[19]

Thus, Freud's entire concept of the operation of our psychic apparatus is based only on a displacement of a "psychic energy" which can be withdrawn from a conscious idea or group of ideas and thus relegated them into the unconscious. I, on the other hand, consider of major importance, not the displacement of energy, but the displacement itself of ideas or group of ideas or of "affective formation" made of ideas and related affective qualities, independently from the operation of an alleged "psychic energy." I have discussed in detail my views in chapter I of part I of this trilogy.

I do not mean to say however, that the displacement of an idea or group of ideas implies their passage from one system to another such as for instance from the Cs. system to the Ucs. system. In my view, an idea or group of ideas, even though operating outside the field of our awareness, may continue to belong to the Cs. system with which they retain their structural and functional connections. What may take place in a conscious idea is that while at a certain moment it operates at a *dominant conscious level*, it may at a subsequent moment become relegated into a subordinate position in that same conscious system with which it retains however the privilege of belonging to it. There has been no passage of that idea from the Cs. system into the Ucs. system. I will return to this important subject in the following chapter.

The above comments which I have made concerning Freud's original attempts at establishing *a neuronal basis* for his new brand of psychology, a basis which he soon after had repudiated, did not seem superfluous to me because of Freud's return in 1925 to that repudiated subject of the functions of the neurones, some of which retain permanent traces of the passage of excitations and some of which do not retain such traces. The revival of that subject seems to have been undertaken by Freud in his paper *The Mystic Writing Pad* (1925). He described that pad as a small contrivance consisting of a slab of dark brown resin or wax, over which is laid a thin transparent sheet, made itself of two layers, a transparent celluloid layer superimposed upon a thin translucent waxed paper. To make use of the pad, one writes upon the celluloid portion of the covering sheet which rests upon the wax slab. Writing is performed with the use of a pointed stylus which scratches the external surface upon the wax slab.

If one wishes to destroy what has been written on the covering sheet, all that is necessary is to raise the covering sheet from the wax slab. The marks created by the writing stylus on the covering sheet then disappear. When again the covering sheet is replaced upon the slab, it is now ready to receive fresh writing notes, but the permanent traces of what was written is retained upon the wax slab itself, and is legible under suitable light. Thus concluded Freud:

The writing Pad provides not only a receptive surface that can be used over and over again, but also permanent traces of what has been written, like an ordinary paper pad. It solves the problem of combining the two functions by dividing them between two separated but interrelated component parts or systems. This is precisely the way in which our mental apparatus performs its perceptual function. The layer which receives the stimuli, the system Pcs.-Cs. forms no permanent traces; the foundation of memory comes about in other adjoining systems.[20]

The comparison brought out by Freud of the perceptual and of the memory systems, with the mystic writing pad, lacks to say the least a sound conceptual basis. In the mystic writing pad, we are dealing with two entirely different components, which structurally may at will become separated and disconnected. It is only following that separation that the covering sheet may again receive new impressions. In the mystic pad, the receiving system, if not lifted, would in due time undergo a state of saturation of graphic impressions, and its usefulness would therefore end at a certain point. Therefore it cannot be compared with the Pcpt. system which allows excitations to pass continuously without any limitation. As for the wax slab compared by Freud with the memory system, one wonders what structural changes would result ultimately in it, if the many impressions received and retained would reach it, not only from a single horizontal plan, but at the same time from a vertical or from a diagonal plan. Evidently a jumbled undecipherable transcript would result from that multidirectional transcript of impressions, a situation which hardly occurs in the memory system though it receives excitations from many directions.

To press further this comparison of the mystic writing pad with that of the Pcpt. system and with that of the memory system, Freud then resorted to the elaboration of a theory which in his own words he had hitherto kept to himself. It consisted of the notion that a current of cathectic innervation, was sent out and withdrawn in rapid periodic impulses from the unconscious into the previous Pcpt.-Cs. system, and as long as this system is cathected in that manner, it receives excitations which are accompanied by consciousness, to be subsequently passed to the unconscious. One cannot fail to perceive in this assumption by Freud the reflection again of Lipps's view that all that is conscious had a preliminary unconscious stage.

In my estimation, however, this whole comparison of permanent and transitory impressions by incoming excitations, be they in relation to the perceptual system or to the memory system, rests upon an unsatisfactory evaluation of the analogy of the mystic writing pad with either one of these systems. Considering that Freud himself had to acknowledge the fact that there must be a point at which the analogy between an auxiliary apparatus of this kind, and the organ which is its prototype, will cease to apply, one wonders what useful purpose had been served by him, in introducing the very unsatisfactory comparison between the mystic writing pad and both the very complex Pcpt. system and the memory system of a living organism, a comparison based on his original views, later repudiated, of the existence and operation of permeable and impermeable neurones.

Because of Freud's reference in this paper to both the contrasting concepts that perceptions *eo-ipso* involve consciousness and the concept of Lipps that an unconscious stage *precedes* the conscious stage of our mental processes, a concept partially accepted by him, it would seem that Freud in 1925 was still vacillating and ambiguous, in his evaluation of the origin of consciousness.

Chapter II

Alternatives to Freud's Concept of Consciousness

My Own Alternative

In the preceding chapter I have mentioned the role that Freud attached to the "special function of attention" in relation to consciousness. His presentation on this point was unfortunately very fragmented and unsatisfactory. Its proper elaboration could have disposed evidently of the superfluous and elusive operation of what he had called "the special organ of consciousness for the reception of psychic qualities." On the other hand, a proper elaboration might have reinforced Freud's own original assumption that the perceptions from our various sense-organs *involved eo-ipso consciousness.*

To offer now my own alternative to Freud's flaws and vacillations in his concept of consciousness, I must return to what I have already discussed in chapter I of part I of this trilogy. In that chapter, I had asked myself two questions: 1) Is there indeed some other alternative to that of Freud who viewed the "psychic energy" as being different from the somatic energy, and who conceived that "psychic energy" in terms of a movable energy possessing an affective quality (a sexual quality in the case of the libido), and capable of attachment to a given idea, detachment from it, and subsequent attachment to some other idea, or capable of discharging itself in some other appropriate manner? 2) Is there instead a special function which develops at a certain moment of our intrauterine somatic and biological organization, a so-called *"psychic function"* which could account for the first appearance of mental life, independently from the operation of that alleged "psychic energy"?

Leaving aside the answer to the first question concerning the existence of a separate "psychic energy" which I have already discussed and refuted in that first chapter of part I of this trilogy, I will answer again the second question. In that first chapter of part I, I had expressed myself as follows: To answer the question if there exist a function that could account for the first appearance and for the further development of mental processes, I will have to go further back than when Freud had introduced his first assumption of a "psychic energy," capable of activating ideas *already present in our mind*. I will have to take into consideration first of all the origin of those ideas. *How did such ideas come into existence?*

To answer that question, I had assumed that those ideas represented the product of a newly developed *"psychic function"* which had made its appearance automatically at a certain moment of our intrauterine somatic and biological organization, in the form so to speak, *of a super-function born out of the integration and synthesis of all the somatic functions* which at that moment were already operating in that organization. Furthermore I had assumed that once that "psychic function" had made its appearance, its first task was that of translating *into some sort of "ideational representation,"* the stimuli related to the activity of those already operating somatic functions.

These ideational representations were in my views, the ideas to which Freud had referred in 1894 when he had considered them as the recipients of the "psychic energy." But at that time, Freud unfortunately failed to address himself to the origin of those ideas. My assumption of the development of a new "psychic function," responsible for the origin of those ideas filled the gap left open by Freud. I had further assumed that the product of that new "psychic function," that is, the ideational representations of the various somatic stimuli, *were eo-ipso conscious representations*, in other words the result of a conscious operation of that psychic function.

In that first chapter, I had also discussed the nature of the energy involved in the appearance and development of this new "psychic function" and had assumed that energy to be the same somatic energy that activated the various somatic functions. That somatic energy which I had assumed to be of a bio-physical nature I called "Organismic energy."

In that same chapter, I had also raised the following question: At what stage of man's structural and biological intrauterine organization does that new "psychic function" develop and become operative? I could not answer that question because of our ignorance of the time at which the human fertilized egg may be considered structurally and biologically a complete functional unit. And yet there must be a time at which the human fetus develops its new "psychic function." That moment I had assumed to be the moment when, so to speak, a synthesis and integration of the various somatic functions takes place in that intrauterine organization.

Evidently, my assumption of the development of a new "psychic function" out of the integration and synthesis of the various somatic and biological functions already operating in that intrauterine organization, *entails a definite leap from the soma to the psyche*. But so was the important conjecture by Freud of the development of the "instinct of life" which at a certain moment, out of nowhere, transforms the inanimate matter into a living organic matter. In Freud's words: "At one time or another *by some operation of forces which still baffles conjectures* the properties of life is awakened in lifeless matter. Perhaps the process was a prototype resembling that other one which latter *in a certain stratum of living matter gave rise to consciousness*."[1] [italics mine] What more leap could there be than that of consciousness arising all of a sudden in the living matter?

By the same token, I had therefore assumed that *by some operation which also baffles conjectures*, a "psychic function" develops out of the integration and synthesis of various somatic functions already operating at a certain moment of our intrauterine organization. This conjectural force could have been the one that Freud had inferred to become operative when in his letter to his friend W. Fliess (January 1, 1896) he had stated that: "Perceptual processes would *eo-ipso* involve consciousness and would only produce further psychical effects after becoming conscious."[2]

At this point, apart from any other consideration on the nature or origin of consciousness, Freud in the above statement to Fliess, seems to have assumed that conscious mental processes could originate directly from somatic perceptual stimuli, which by their own nature involved consciousness. That assumption contrasts evidently with Freud's original complete acceptance of Lipps's thesis that all mental processes are unconscious in their first stage, and become conscious only in a subsequent stage.

That brings me back again to the question of the special psychic function of "attention" which Freud at one point in 1900 in his *Interpretation of Dreams* assumed to be governed by our various perceptual processes, while at another point he had considered that same function of attention as being governed instead by those perceptual processes. Apart from the contradiction of these two points of view, Freud at this juncture missed the opportunity of elaborating on the origin of that psychic function of attention, having stated only that it had been biologically determined and that it had been left in the course of psychical evolution, a statement which in those simple terms was quite unsatisfactory.

Had Freud assumed that out of the synthesis and integration of the stimuli originating from the activities of the already operating somatic functions, a new "psychic function" had developed and which had been entrusted with the translation into some sort of ideational representations of those somatic stimuli, he could have taken a more substantial position on the question of the origin of conscious life. He naturally may have been in a better position to support his own assumption of 1895 *that perceptions eo-ipso involve consciousness*. He also would have been in a better position to consider the function of attention as a special facet of a more general "psychic function."

With the assumption of a new "psychic function," Freud may have been able also to present us with a working hypothesis on the origin of the structural ego in the sense that the new "psychic function" once in operation could have elicited in our developing intrauterine organization *a first awareness that is a first consciousness of its own existence as a whole*. Such a first awareness could have been construed in terms of a *"primordial or protopathic conscious ego!"*

This is exactly the position which I have taken in chapter I of part I of this trilogy where I called this "primordial conscious ego" the "protopathic ego." Altogether my position was at variance with that taken by Freud who on the one hand spoke of a special psychic function of attention with no reference to a prior "general psychic function," and who did not subscribe to the existence and operation at birth of a functioning ego.

It goes without saying, however, that with the accumulation after birth of additional new experiences, the "protopathic ego" would gradually develop into what I have called the "epicritic ego." However when I speak of "epicritic ego," I refer to it as representing only a certain more advanced ontogenetic stage of its development, inasmuch as an ego can be considered "epicritic" only in relation to a certain given period of Life, that is in relation to a given age. At each age there corresponds a sum of experiences and influences related to new internal activities as well as to new environmental influences which are pertinent to a given particular age. What one may consider "epicritic ego" at seven would not be the same at fourteen, twenty-one, or forty-one.

With the introduction of a first mental expression of consciousness *in the course of our ontogenetic intrauterine development* and subsequent modifications related to age and environment, under the aegis of that newly developed "psychic function," we could also dispose of the necessity of invoking in that initial "protopathic ego," the participation in it of any pre-individual inherited mental components as advocated by Freud. What we actually inherit is only our structural and biological organization governed by genetic laws, and from which our psychic organization develops ontogenetically, in subsequently more complex stages.

Concerning the spatial disposition of the various formative stages of the ego as alleged by some writers to take place in the form of a stratification of layers upon layers, I do not agree with them inasmuch as in my view, the ego does not develop by a simple process of superimposition of strata upon strata of the newer ego-formations upon the older ones. I assume that the "epicritic ego" of any given period of life, derives from the *functional absorption* within itself (be it in its ontogenetic development, in the course of its intrauterine, or in that of its extrauterine period of life) of its own preceding protopathic stage, which thus contribute to its further epicritic developmental stage.

In other words, in connection with the gradual development of the functional ego, we may apply to it what I would like to call the principle of *"Intussusception"* from the Latin "intus = inside," and "suscipere = taking up," which is the principle that in my view governs also the development of the structural nervous system in the course of phylogenesis. I will discuss this particular point in a subsequent chapter. For the moment it will suffice for me to state that in my opinion that same principle of "intussusception" that applies to the structural nervous system applies also to the gradual development of the ego, that is to say, that the more advanced "epicritic ego" develops from the absorption in it of the lesser developed elements which represented the "protopathic ego." These absorbed "protopathic elements" become therefore formative elements *of the more advanced "epicritic ego"* and in that sense, they occupy in the latter a subordinate position. It goes without saying that the "epicritic ego" develops also through all that it acquires from its new perceptions of the environment.

To summarize: With the introduction of my own alternative assumption for the development of consciousness by means of a "new psychic function" governing the first development of conscious ideas in the terms which I have discussed, there would be no need to resort to the existence and operation of *a special organ of consciousness for the perception of mental qualities* as advocated by Freud. Nor should there be the need to resort to the operation of a *primal func-*

tion of attention, unrelated to some sort of a prior general "psychic function," and which attention in terms of Freud's vacillating terms either governed, or was governed by the perceptual system.

Consciousness in my assumption would be the expression of the activity of a "new psychic function" born of the synthesis and integration of the activity of the various somatic functions already operating in the course of our intrauterine life. That new function, because of its task of translating into ideational representations all somatic stimuli related to the operation of those somatic functions involves *eo-ipso* (by its very nature) Consciousness.

That consciousness is therefore not simply related to the operation of our various sense-organs of perception, which according to Freud were the ones which *eo-ipso* involved consciousness; the attribute of consciousness belongs to the new "psychic function" which translates into ideational representations the various somatic stimuli and which function is consequently responsible for imparting to those ideas their conscious attribute. It is the operation of that function which *eo-ipso* (by its own nature) involves consciousness and not simply the operation of the various organs of perception.

This approach to the origin of consciousness, varies basically from Freud's approach because the latter had not taken into consideration the intervention of a primal general "psychic function," a function entrusted with the translation into ideational representations of the various somatic stimuli, a function which itself *eo-ipso* involved consciousness, and which therefore imparted that attribute of consciousness to those resulting ideas. The various organs of perceptions *are only the conveyor of somatic stimuli* and do not *eo-ipso* involve consciousness.

The reference to the psychic function of attention was in fact introduced by Freud in terms of a simple cathecting energy activating the neurones, bearers of perceptions. That was quite an obscure approach, which had neglected a discussion on the origin of that function to which no conscious attribute had been assigned. That function could not therefore impart that attribute of consciousness to the various somatic perceptions. Furthermore Freud had failed to discuss the relationship of that function of attention to a more general "psychic function" of which it could have represented a subsequent functional aspect, but not a principal one.

My assumption of an operating new "psychic function" that *eo-ipso* involves consciousness in its resulting ideational representations, seem to me a clearer and more complete approach than that of Freud who limited himself to assume that perceptions *eo-ipso* in-

225

volved consciousness, without discussing the important mediation of a "new psychic function" in that involvement, in the terms which I have contemplated. My own assumption would also eliminate the need for resorting to the operation of an alleged "psychic energy."* If indeed one considers the fact that my assumed "psychic function" is the product of the synthesis and integration of the various somatic functions, that "psychic function" must be activated by the same somatic energy which had activated the various somatic functions from the integration and synthesis of which it derived, and not by some different alleged "psychic energy."

With the introduction of ideational representations conscious from their very onset, and with the subsequent acquisition by these ideas of their affective qualities in relation to the factors which I have discussed in chaper I of part one of this trilogy, the functioning of our psychic apparatus need not depend as Freud maintained upon the displacement of his "alleged psychic energy." We would be dealing with ideas or group of ideas and related affective qualities, capable of displacing themselves under their own energic force, the same somatic energy that presided over the development of the new "psychic function," and capable of associating themselves with other ideational formations, or replacing each other. This concept of the working of our "psychic apparatus" by displacement and replacement of ideas or group of ideas by other ideas or group of ideas, instead of the displacement of a "psychic energy" was rejected by Freud, as I have repeatedly stated.

Alternatives to the Concept of Consciousness Offered by Other Investigators

Before entering into the presentation of these alternatives and in order to establish a background to the principle of "intussusception" to which I have referred, I think it necessary to devote some space to the important subject of the *central reticular formation* so often mentioned in present day literature in connection with the problem of consciousness. We of course know that the interest of the scientific world on this subject developed only after Freud's death, so that he could not have benefited from that knowledge. Yet a brief summary of the data related to this important formation, seems to me in order, so as to justify the different approach other investigators have pursued on this subject of consciousness, and the utilization of which formation I have also used in the formulation of the development of the conscious system other than the more limited one pursued by Freud.

According to the various diagrams drawn by modern neuro-anatomists and neuro-physiologists, the reticular formation constitutes a central cellular mass in association with an intricate fiber structure, located in the central portion of the brain-stem extending from the rostral portion of the diencephalon to the pons, medulla oblongata, and spinal cord. Within that central cellular mass, one can individualize according to Olzewski, more than one hundred separate nuclei, without counting numerous isolated nerve cells, the processes of which, extremely long at times, can reach, according to the Scheibels, far distant caudal or rostral areas. The central reticular formation contributes to the activity and integration of various systems of projection, such as those governing motility, sensitivity and endocrine activities. It particularly contributes to the very important regulation of our state of wakefulness, thus representing a basic factor in our state of consciousness.

Personally, I subscribe to the opinion that the elements of the reticular formation are not all contained in its massive central portion, but extend themselves and infiltrate, so to speak, many other areas of the central nervous system. Indeed phylogenetically speaking, as I will elaborate in a following chapter, the nervous system originates in the invertebrates (coelenterates) in the form of a simple neural reticulum which envelops the whole body of the animal, and in the intersection of which, the first nerve cells are to be found. The subsequent growth of the nervous system, in higher species, takes place through the development of additional new structures which not only surround, but also incorporate in them the more primitive structures. It follows that neural elements belonging to the original neural network of lower animals are to be presumed present in various quantities mixed within the more recently developed neural structures of the higher animals.

Experimental data, to which I will refer later, point indeed to the presence in the cerebral cortex, a more recently developed neural structure, of areas which display the same functional attributes of the central reticular formation, thus justifying the conclusion that in the cortex, cellular elements belonging to the original reticular formation, have been incorporated in it. The incorporation of neural paleo-structures into neo-structures makes it easier to understand the very close relationship between old and new structures and functions, in the course of the ascending phylogenetic development of the nervous system.

227

The investigation of the structure and function of the Central reticular formation, originated with the basic studies of Hess[3] in Switzerland, Bremer[4] in Belgium, and Bard,[5] Ranson,[6] Dempsey and Morrison, in the United States. As a starting point they reported that, following experimental lesions of the thalamo-diencephalic area in cats and monkeys, the animals manifested torpor, sluggishness and somnolence, whereas electrical stimulation of the same area re-established the alertness and vigilance characteristics of the waking state, and in addition, elicited certain emotional reactions.

However, it was the contribution of Moruzzi[7] of Pisa, Italy, and Magoun[8] of Los Angeles in 1949, that actually stimulated the most fruitful, anatomical, neuro-physiological and psycho-biological investigations of the central reticular formation. Magoun and Moruzzi, in their elaboration of previous data of Jaspers and Rheinberg, established the fact that the electrical stimulation of the reticular formation in animals was followed by manifestations of electrical activities in various cortical areas of the brain, in the form of electric waves characteristics of the waking state, and that conversely the destruction of the same areas of the reticular formation resulted in observable manifestations of diminished alertness and motor sluggishness in the animals. They located the areas responsible for the activating portion of the reticular formation, in the ventro-medial area of the thalamus, in the so-called reticular nuclei of that formation and in the hypothalamic area.

Such an activating function of the central reticular formation, they attributed to centrifugal nerve fibers which from that formation, were directed towards various cortical areas. In addition to these centrifugal fibers, they established that the reticular formation receives from various cortical areas centripetal fibers that reached various segments of that reticular formation, thus establishing a two-way system of communication between the cerebral cortex and the central reticular formation. In more detailed investigations by Jasper and Aimone-Marsan,[9] Bremer and Terzuolo,[10] French,[11] and French et al[12] and Segundo and collaborators,[13] it was established that the cortical areas involved in this two-way system of exchange, were predominantly the orbital cortex, the frontal cortex, the cingulum, the para-central and paraoccipital cortex, and particularly the superior temporal convolutions. They also established that the central reticular formation, receives from and sends to, connecting fibers to the nuclear systems governing the general sensibilities, via the medial lemniscus, and to the systems of the specific sensibilities, via the cochlear, vestibular, trigeminal, optic, gustatory, and olfactory nuclei.

Of particular interest was the fact that the central reticular formation was not the only source of activating function, inasmuch as the electrical stimulation of the above mentioned cortical areas resulted also in the activation of other cortical areas, an activation which was of the same electrical character as that which followed the direct stimulation of the central reticular formation itself.

We are further indebted to Magoun and Rhines,[14] for having established that the reciprocal influence of cortex and reticular formation is not limited only to the phenomenon of activation. In 1947 they established that when simultaneously with the electrical stimulation of the motor cortex, they stimulated also the most caudal portion of the central reticular formation, that is its mesencephalic portion in the brain, the expected motor manifestations did not occur. Other investigators brought out the fact that such inhibition could also be registered in connection to specific sensibilities. Thus Hagbarth and Kerr,[15] Eccles and associates,[16] Green and Mancia, and Baumgarten[17] succeeded in suppressing the electrical conductivity normally associated with the stimulation of the medial lemniscus, or with the stimulation of the second cochlear or trigeminal neurones, or with the olfactory tracts, whenever simultaneously with the stimulation of these structures, they also stimulated electrically the central reticular formation. What is particularly interesting is that experimentally it was established that in the cerebral cortex itself there were also areas, the stimulation of which resulted in the same type of inhibitory function that followed the direct stimulation of the caudal portion of the central reticular formation, and that these cortical areas were in general the same areas from which activating impulses originated.

Thus, in the cortex, there exist areas governing both phenomena of activation and inhibition of the same type of those resulting from the direct stimulation of certain areas of the central reticular formation. These data may evidently be construed as supporting my contention, that incorporated in the midst of new structures, remnants of older neural phylogenetic structures may be found still capable of exerting a complementary or even independent function of their own. I will deal with this specific concept of incorporation of older neural structures by new structures in a following chapter devoted to the phylogenetic development of the nervous system.

I will now mention in passing only, the additional functions attributed to the central reticular formation, such as that of its intervention in the function of attention and concentration, as documented by the findings of Hernandez-Peon, Scherer and Jouvet;[18] in the process of conditioning as inferred by the data of

Jouvet[19] and Gastaut;[20] in that of the regulation of the whole neuro-endocrine system as outlined by Magoun; and in that of the regulation of certain emotional reactions as documented by the experimental work of Hess, Ranson, Bard, Magoun, Masserman,[21] Delgado and collaborators.[22]

The reasons for my indulging in the presentation of data related to that "central reticular formation" will become clearer in a following chapter where I will discuss the development of our mental apparatus in terms of the gradual development of both its structural and mental functioning.

And now for those other alternatives to Freud's exclusive psychological approach to the problem of consciousness.

In the second decade of this century, psychiatrists in the United States began to move away from the descriptive type of Kraeplinian type of psychiatry. Following the teachings of Adolf Meyer, they focused their attention on psychobiology, while at the same time following Brill's translation of Freud's original contributions, they became interested in the psychoanalytic movement, which found ultimately its permanent place in American Psychiatry.

Very little was done at the onset of that movement in terms of investigating the soundness of Freud's many theoretical assumptions, inasmuch as there seems to have been a sort of blind acceptance of his views particularly concerning his libido theory, the seual etiology of the neuroses, and the structure of the unconscious. Then, strangely enough, a group of neuro-physiologists, and not psychiatrists, became acutely interested in carrying on investigations intended to clarify some of the physio-dynamics of mental activity.

Though, already in 1939, the Annual meeting of "The Association for Research in Nervous and Mental Diseases" had for its main topic of discussion "The Interrelationship of Mind and Body,"[23] it was only after the earlier studies of Magoun and Rhines (1946) and those of Magoun and Moruzzi (1949), that a feverish activity of research in that direction developed, particularly in the United States, a trend which carried in its wake a revived interest in the problem of consciousness.

Meeting after meeting, at which clinical neurologists, pathologists, neuro-physiologists, neuro-anatomists, and biochemists, participated, were organized for the specific discussion of consciousness, and of the relationship of psyche to soma. Among them I will mention at random the five annual Conferences from 1950 to 1954 of the Macy Foundation, on "The Phenomenon of Consciousness,"[24] The Moosehart Symposium on "Feelings and Emotions" (1950), The Hixon Symposium on "Cerebral Mechanisms and Human Behavior" (1951),[25] The First International Congress of Neurological Sciences on the topic of Consciousness[26] (1957), the three conferences of the Macy Foundation on "Central Nervous System and Behavior" (1958–60),[27] The Symposium of The American Association for the Advancement of Science, "The Evolution of the Nervous System" (1959,[28] the Kaiser Symposium on "The Physiology of Emotions,"[29] the Oxford Symposium on "The Cerebral Mechanisms and Learning" (1961,[30] the First Conference of The Brain Institute of Research of California (1961),[31] The International Congress of Genoa (Italy) on "States of Consciousness" (1963)[32] and finally the first Conference on "Learning, Remembering, and Forgetting" held in Princeton also in 1963.[33]

Evidently, it would be presumptuous for me to even attempt to summarize all the important contribution that were presented and discussed at those meetings. I feel however that a very condensed reference to only some of the most appropriate contribution particularly related to consciousness, might prove useful for the purpose of this book.

Let me now summarize some of these contributions and begin with that of Kleitman[34] who at one of the meetings of the Macy Foundation, after having presented his views on the states of being awake and of being asleep, concluded that the state of being awake should not be considered as being synonymous with the state of consciousness. In the waking state he maintained that, in order to create a state of consciousness, animistic activities are added to the state of simple vegetative functioning, and that such an activity is itself dependent upon the presence of cortical activity. Consciousness which in his view resulted from the intervention of the cerebral cortex, he designated as "wakefulness of choice." In the absence of cortical participation, he designated the existing waking state as "Wakefulness of necessity."

In my estimation, the weak part of Kleitman's argument is that it implies that in *decorticated animals* one should subscribe unreservedly to his views that a "state of wakefulness of choice" could not exist, and that it is the simple state of "wakefulness of necessity" which in them governs all activities. Experimental data do not seem to support that contention. A decerebrate frog for instance, as reported by E. von Hartman, in his *Philosophy of the Unconscious*[35] having remained quiet for a long time after the operation, suddenly began to make natatory movements, and hopped away, and having taken a fixed direction in its hopping, tried with marked obstinacy, to constantly regain that direction, while creeping away under a cupboard, or into old corners, manifestly to seek protection from its persecutors. In my opinion these activities seem to indicate that some mentation of choice must have been exercised by that animal, notwithstanding the removal of cortical structures.

A wakefulness of choice seemed also to be implied in Flourens's report that hens, from which he had removed the cerebrum, sat motionless as a rule, but on going to sleep, tucked their heads under their wings, and upon waking shook themselves and preened their feathers; or when he reported that decerebrated pigeons endeavored to avoid a hand which was trying to grasp them, and carefully avoided obstacles in their flight. The same considerations may be applied to the various reports on decorticated dogs by Rothman,[36] Zeliony,[37] Dusser de Barenne, Brouwer,[38] and others,[39] concerning the directional movements of these animals towards the location of their food; or to the report that decorticated dogs, who usually swallowed a certain food, refused to ingest that same food if it were rendered bitter by the addition of quinine.

Nor did Kleitman improve his position when in support of his thesis he stated that at birth and for several months after, the human infant is not endowed with conscious activities, so that functionally speaking, he does not differ from a decorticated animal. It seems to me that even though at birth and in early infancy, the cerebral cortex is not as yet mature structurally and functionally, as indicated by the incomplete myelination of its fibers, and the lesser number of cellular dendrites, we cannot discount the functionality of the unmyelinated fibers, nor can we arbitrarily deny to an immature cortex its participation in the phenomenon of consciousness.

Another unsubstantiated statement by Kleitman is that *at birth, memory is absent in both its aspects of retention and recall, thus rendering impossible the development of consciousness.* Memory, according to him, does not develop before the seventh month of life. I do not subscribe to the absence of memory and consciousness at birth, and for that matter, I assume that to a certain extent memory is even operating in the course of intrauterine life. In this connection I may point out that Kleitman did not consider, even from a hypothetical standpoint, that the function of memory may be exercised by older neural structures, let us say for instance by the central reticular formation which in the course of phylogenesis in animals and ontogenesis in humans, may have been presumably responsible for the exercise of that function prior to the development of the cortical structures. It is in virtue of that situation that the decorticated animals which I have mentioned could still resort to that old neural structure for the exercise of that conscious function.

In fact experimental data, such as those of De Snook in 1937,[40] seem to indicate the presence of conscious activities during the course of intrauterine life. In twenty pregnant women suffering from polyhydramnios, that is of increased quantity of amniotic fluid, which resulted in an excessive and painful distension of the abdominal walls, De Snoo suspected that the fetus refused somehow to swallow that fluid because its chemical composition had altered and became distasteful to him. He then resorted to the device of injecting into the amniotic fluid a small amount of saccharine, thus modifying its taste and rendering it more palatable to the fetus. He then observed a gradual diminution of the abdominal distension in his patients, a fact which he attributed to the resumption on the part of the fetus of its intake of that fluid.

While Kleitman centered his discussion of consciousness around his expert knowledge of the waking and sleeping states, Piaget[41] in his discussion of consciousness, relied on his expert knowledge of the intellectual cognitive development of children. In his opinion consciousness is constituted by the grouping together of *"individual meanings of things and objects"* so as to form from their aggregate various *"systems of cognitive and affective meanings."* Up to the sixth or seventh year of life, these elementary cognitive and affective systems of meanings constitute *simple systems of conscious knowledge,* related to perceptual configurations, and are somewhat unstable in their combinations. Later on to these *"elementary cognitive systems"* more complex systems are added, the *"systems of logic consciousness"* or better designated *"systems of conscious implications,"* which develop gradually up to the twelfth or fifteenth year of life. These more complex systems acquire in turn, in the course of further development, a higher meaning and values *in terms of moral and social* significance.

According to Piaget, between these various cognitive systems from which consciousness depends, and our structural and biological organization, there comes to exist an intimate relationship, which must not be conceived however in terms of causality, that is of the somatic component creating the mental ones, but simply in terms of intimate connections between the two systems and which Piaget designated as "isomorphism." He added however that, though the systems of neural and biological organization are independent from the systems of logic consciousness and interpretations, such an independence is however somewhat uncertain in view of his feeling that in the future, a relationship of dependency, a very close one, between the two systems may be established. On this count Piaget's position seems to me somewhat ambiguous. He indeed on the one hand very explicitly stated at one point that consciousness possesses a structure of its own, the function of which is original, not replaceable, having no relation with the neuro-biological structures, while on the other hand he foresees that the future may furnish us with data of interdependence of the two elements, the equation of which eludes us presently.

Lashley[42] took a more decisive position in his belief that the phenomenon of consciousness derives strictly from neural structures by the means of "mnemonic systems of tracings" organized within the central nervous system. These systems can be induced into a state of "specific tonic activity" by the stimuli which are specific for each system. A tonic state of activity by its persistence may manifest itself in the form of a drive and may stimulate other systems of tracings. The systems, in a state of tonic excitation, determine the direction of the tension, and of the flux of our thoughts in other systems. The systems which are in a state of weaker tonicity, activate our mental processes during sleep or anesthesia. The lowering of tonic activity destroys partially the organization necessary to the maintenance of memory, as well as to that of consciousness, by allowing the interaction of partial systems of tracings, which result in their reciprocal contamination, an event which occurs during sleep. These assumptions Lashley considered to be speculative, but not inconsistent with what was known at that time in the field of cerebral physiology in relation to structure and function of the cerebral cortex.

Grimker[43] was more practical in his comments at one of the meetings of the Macy Foundation, when he expressed his opinion that the difficulties met in the discussion of the problem of consciousness spring from the fact that we try to simplify the subject beyond its limits of simplification, and from the fact that we try to approach it from the point of view of our personal competence in whatever that special field may be. In his opinion, taken separately each special field may be inadequate to accomplish the ultimate task inasmuch as we do not as yet possess a proper scale of values capable of establishing the hierarchical position of each individual field. This is why he recommended that the proper value be given also to the field of environmental factors, which through family, cultural, and social influences, are in some way capable of modifying our conscious activities.

At the First International Congress of Neurological Sciences in Brussels (1957), Alajouanine[44] made a very interesting summation of the problem of consciousness, when he stated that consciousness represents a quality of the functioning of the nervous system which permits a) the perceptive experience of the facts related to our surroundings, as well as the ones related to our own body, and b) the cognition of the reactions which follow such experiences of perceptions, as well as the memory of their having occurred. With such a definition, which Alajouanine considered comprehensive, he felt that he had taken into consideration two orders of phenomena, the phenomenon of perception in the broad sense of the word, and that of its psychological nature. The phenomenon of the first order he designated as "alertness or vigilance," and the phenomenon of the second order as "consciousness proper." In his opinion the structural mechanisms related to perceptions and to the state of alertness or sleep, are known to us, whereas the substratum of what constituted consciousness eludes us.

In establishing such a distinction, Alajouanine based his reasoning upon the fact that conscious activities are possible in persons whose electro-encephalogram registers the tracings of a coma, that is of a state of "clinical unconsciousness," while on the other hand, normal electrographic tracings indicating a waking state, may be registered in individuals in a comatose condition. Thus from his point of view, there is no absolute parallelism between a "waking state" of alertness or vigilance, and a state of consciousness proper, considering that an indication of alertness may be present during comatose states, and vice versa. However, in the future, stated Alajouanine, it may be possible with the help of electrograms taken from deeper regions, and with the help of more sensitive instruments, to establish a correlation between the waking state of alertness and the state of consciousness proper. But for the time being, he concluded that:

> On the basis of our avaiable data and instrumentation, and differently from what possibly occurs in animals, we cannot ignore in humans the fact that on top of the activities related to the state of wake or alertness dependent from structural and biological elements, there is superimposed a psychological phenomenon which constitutes precisely the "conscious state proper."

Alajouanine felt also that some simple reactive manifestations
to perceptions, such as the automatic movements of posture or of
walking, or of certain muscular synergic activities, can originate at
a subconscious level, but that these reactions to perceptions must
later on become integrated at a higher level with intellectual and
volitional activities. It is only at this superior level of integration
that all perceptions become conscious. In Alajouanine's words:

> Consciousness does not constitute either a function or an en-
> tity. It represents a corollary to the normal functioning of
> nervous activities at the summum of perceptual and volitional
> integration. This is why there does not exist a localization for
> Consciousness. But Consciousness cannot exist outside of the
> mechanism of alertness.

Alajouanine's presentation in my estimation was not convincing
because, to begin with, he had considered what he had called "state
of alertness or vigilance" as a state generated by perceptions in
terms only of structural and biological values, and thus seemed to
consider perceptions as being all along devoid of a conscious mental
quality. In fact he differentiated them from the phenomenon of cognition of those perceptions, that is from "consciousness proper" out of
which memory is built. But in view of the fact that he had designated the effect of perceptions as a state of "alertness or vigilance,"
that designation must have implied I presume, a mental representation of those perceptions, a representation in the absence of which no
state of alertness could have developed. Alajouanine did not seem to
have been concerned with this point, and attributed instead the
phenomenon of consciousness to the elaboration of these perceptions
by the cortical formation, without however discussing the time at
which the cortical structure and related function develop in relation
to the first appearance of the perceptual function.

The relationship of the perceptions to their first mental representation prior to the ontogenetic development of the cortex seems
to have been missed by him. In other words, contrary to what I ad-
vocate, Alajouanine had not considered at all the development and
operation at a certain moment of our intrauterine structural and
biological organization of a new "psychic function" born of the
synthesis and integration of the various somatic functions already
operating in that organization, and entrusted with the translation of
all perceptual stimuli into conscious ideational representations,
which at first could operate independently from the developmental
stage of the brain cortex.

In addition, Alajouanine statement that consciousness is to be considered as a psychological phenomenon superimposed to the state of "alertness or vigilance" gives unfortunately the impression that he considered soma and psyche to be two separate entities, though that impression was somewhat attenuated by his subsequent statement that consciousness is not an entity, but that it represents a corollary to the normal functioning of nervous activities at the summum of perceptual volitional and intellectual integration.

As for the automatic reactions to perceptions originating at a subconscious level, Alajouanine did not clarify his meaning of subconscious, having failed to take into consideration the fact that such reactions could be the expression of earlier conscious reaction which in the course of the ontogenetic development of the conscious system, may have been absorbed into the fabric of higher conscious formations of which they constituted subordinate formative elements. In that sense, they are part and parcel of the Cs. system, though in a subordinate conscious position. In that light the observable automatic reactions to perceptions, could represent the expression of those subordinate conscious formative elements of what Alajouanine considered as "consciousness proper." The cerebral cortex which presided over the highest forms of the conscious development, only subsequently becomes entrusted with the task of integrating all the subordinate conscious formative elements.

Had Alajouanine, in his discussion, referred to data of comparative anatomy, and had he descended quite low in the zoological scale, he might have found himself embarrassed in upholding his distinction between alertness-vigilance and consciousness proper, the latter only related to cortical activities, considering that he had not faced the situation where animals not possessing a cerebral cortex or basal ganglia, and animals endowed with the most elementary nervous system, made up of only a reticulum of nerve fibers and of few interspersed nerve cells as for instance, the coelenterates are capable of activities to which we cannot deny the attribute of consciouness proper.

As for the electro-encephalograms typical of the waking state in the course of a comatose state, we cannot exclude in humans that they represent the residual activity of the lower functional and structural neural centers which have contributed by means of their incorporation into higher centers to the higher development of the latter higher conscious activities. In that light, elements of the central reticular formation itself which would have been incorporated into the new structural neural formations, may be responsible for such an occurrence.

Consciousness proper is not therefore the prerogative of the cortical structures alone, performing at the summum of integration, but the expression of many lower structural and mental formations, which at various ontogenetic levels of development in humans as well as in very low animals, have operated at more elementary levels, and which have been subsequently incorporated into and absorbed by higher neural structures and related higher mental functions. The function of these subordinate conscious formations, may, under certain circumstances reacquire their original functional capacity and operate independently from the newly developed cortical structures and functions.

At the same International Congress of Neurological Sciences (Brussels 1957), W. Penfield[45] summarized his views on the problem of consciousness on the basis of his extensive experience in brain surgery, during the course of which, beginning in 1938, he became particularly interested in the correlation between neural and mental functioning. In his view, the psychic phenomenon of consciousness constitutes the final product of a dynamic process, derived from electrical potentials which runs along nerve fibers or systems of fibers organized in various neural systems, and which presides over the recall of past experiences stored in the brain. The nervous activity which takes place between the reception of various sensory-sensorial stimuli, and the resulting corresponding motor expression, represents the physical basis of our mental processes. Penfield avoided however any final commitment on his part on the relationship of cause and effect between neural structures and mental activities.

Penfield was not satisfied with the accepted view that the organizational activity of our nervous system took place to a large extent, by the means of intracortical associative fibers that pass from one hemisphere to the other through the corpus callosum, so that in 1938, he developed his concept that the integrative organization of the two cerebral hemispheres was dependent upon the activies of various centrally located *sub-cortical regions*. In 1952 he suggested the designation of "centrancephalon" to indicate the sum total of the normal circuits which connect the centro-cephalic portion of the brain with the two cerebral hemispheres.

The "centrencephalon" grossly corresponds to an area which includes diencephalon and mesencephalon, and also the central reticular formation in its diencephalic and mesencephalic portions. However, in his views, the "centrencephalon" must not be construed as a new anatomical formation, but simply as a certain topographical area of the brain-stem which he considered essential for the organization of inter-hemispheric functional relationship upon which the state of consciousness depends. From the "centrencephalon" nervous impulses originate, which following the long efferent fibers, are directed towards various cortical areas of both hemispheres, while in return the "Centrencephalon" receives impulses that originate in both hemispheres, and are discharged in the various nuclei of that formation.

The importance of these cortico-subcortical connections presented itself to the attention of Penfield in the course of various surgical interventions on the brain, when after he had isolated by incisions, the motor, the sensory, and the Broca's cortical areas from all the surrounding tissues, but leaving intact the straight downward deep connections of these areas with lower structures, he failed to observe any motor, sensory, or aphasic symptoms. From these findings Penfield concluded that the functional association of the two hemispheres, or the association between the various lobes of the same hemisphere could not be exclusively dependent from transcortical associative fibers, but also from fibers originating in the depths of these isolated cortical areas, and which had not been affected by the surgical procedure. These fibers so spared, evidently established connections between the related cortical areas and some sub-cortical structures, central reticular formation included. From these observations the concept of "Centrencephalon" became crystallized and applied to the theoretical discussion of the problem of consciousness. In his estimation, it provided the structural neural basis for that phenomenon, the expression of which was also determined by the various modalities of those connections. Though Penfield assigned to the "Centrencephalon" an important role in the development of conscious phenomena, he never minimized the value of the cortex, and always maintained that it played an important part in the final integration of conscious mental processes.

Though I am in general agreement with his approach, I feel that Penfield should have also considered the initiation of elementary conscious processes and of their early integration, as taking place in the "centrencephalon" itself. It is only in order to become integrated at some higher functional levels that these elementary processes may require the intervention of the cerebral cortex. But that does not prevent them, under certain circumstances, from exercising an activity of their own, independently from the cortex.

In connection with the integration of memories of past events, Penfield assigned a special importance to the temporal cortex, which he designated as "interpretative cortex," the boundaries of which included the external and medial surface of the temporal lobes, the insula of Reil, the Hippocampus, and the periamygdaloid area. In his estimation, the temporal cortex presides over two distinct functions in relation to conscious phenomena. In the first group, he included the phenomena of "psychic hallucination" or "experiential hallucination" which consists in the reactivation of a band of fragments of memory in the flux of conscious phenomena. In the second group, he included the phenomena of "psychic illusion" or (interpretative illusion,) consisting of the alteration of the perception of the present moment.

In the course of 273 neurosurgical interventions on the brain, Penfield and associates, by using the method of electrical cortical stimulation in patients under local anesthesia, succeeded in establishing the existence of an area in the proximity of the anterior pole of the superior temporal convolution, at the depth of approximately one centimeter, and precisely of area 17 and 20, the stimulation of which resulted in the recall by the patients of certain events of the past. Also following the surgical removal of the superior and lateral portions of the temporal lobes, the stimulation of the exposed medial surface resulted in the recall of fragments of past episodes. Contrasting with the memory recall following electrical stimulation, Penfield reported that the surgical removal of the Hippocampus or of its temporal gyri resulted in defects of memory if the removal was unilateral, and of a very serious impairment of memory if the removal was bilateral.

Now, in contrast with the phenomenon of "experiential hallucination" resulting from electrical stimulation in depth of various areas of the temporal cortex, Penfield obtained different results from the stimulation of the superficial surface of the same temporal cortex. That stimulation resulted in a special phenomenon which he designated "phenomenon of psychic illusion" or "interpretative illusion," which consisted in an alteration of the conscious perceptions of the present. A patient was questioned while Penfield stimulated the superficial areas 14 and 15 of the temporal lobe, and was asked to report what he was actually experiencing. The patient reported that he felt that the entire surgical procedure to which he was being subjected at that time, was familiar to him, inasmuch as in the past he had already been submitted to that procedure. In reality the patient had never before been subjected to that surgical intervention. Such an interpretation of present events, as having already occurred in the past, Penfield considered in the same light as the phenomenon of "deja vu," often encountered in temporal epilepsy. Among the phenomena of "interpretative illusion" Penfield also included illusions possessing an affective coloring such as the feeling of strangeness, disgust, sadness, and even anxiety. Confirmatory data to Penfield's findings were reported by Bickford R. C. and collaborators.

According to Penfield, the phenomenon of consciousness related to both the experiential hallucination and interpretative illusion, depended upon the neural connections established between the temporal cortex and the wide complex of the "centrencephalon," reticular formation included. The recall of situations that occurred in the past, established according to him, the fact that within the various neural ganglionic structures and related neural associations, there is stored some sort of a permanent record or file of registration of our continuous conscious activities. He did not know in what way that mnemonic material was stored and preserved. But it seemed evident to him that a model of the ganglionic activities, which did accompany some previous experiences must exist, and that such a pattern of organization can be reactivated by a single electrical stimulation which thus lets loose the chain reaction of the original neural model, and evokes the related memory.

The only comment I would like to make to Penfield's conclusions is that in his wordings, he seemed to have favored somehow the concept of the storage of memory-traces in some sort of permanent record or file of registration. In my estimation no actual store of memory-traces exist in terms of a deposit of concrete visual, auditory, gustatory, or olfactory images. The recall of past activities or sensations, depends only upon dynamic relationships between the perceptual neurones, the ganglia of the respective sensory nerves, the central reticular formation, the sub-cortical ganglia, and the various cortical areas, in a continuous exchange of excitations to and from these various structures. These structures are functionally and structurally related, and the passage of a current from one to another *creates a sort of functional tracing, a beaten path*, for the passage of subsequent excitations similar to the original ones. This repeated passage of current results in a facilitation for the activities of the whole network of associated structures, in the manner in which servo-mechanisms operate, but do not imply a storage of actual memory-records.

Of course, no structuro-functional organization of the nervous system can be conceived as being independent from local or general biochemical processes. It became natural, therefore, for biochemists and biologists to disclose interest in the biochemical processes underlying the neural activities, just as neuro-physiologists had become interested in their electro-physical aspect. Numerous individual contributions on this subject may be found in the literature of the last three decades, not counting those discussed at the various combined national or international meetings, in which both neuro-physiologists and biologists participated. Without attempting to summarize all of the presented data, I will simply refer to some of them particularly of those discussed at the "Hixon Symposium" on "Cerebral Mechanisms in Behavior" (1951) and at the Symposium on "Learning, Remembering and Forgetting" held at The National Foundation of Science and published in book form in 1966, under the title *Anatomy of Memory*.

At the "Hixon Symposium," for instance, W. McCulloch emphasized particularly the mechanism of "reverberating neural circuits," a mechanism first advocated by Lorente de No, in the activation of memory and in other facilitating functions of the nervous system. In his view, reverberating circuits or positive feedbacks, are based on the presence of numerous interrelated connections in the extensive neural network, by means of which neurones receive, at a given time, a signal in the form of an impulse which becomes reverberated along the entire closed system of the network. That reverberating activity is patterned after something that happened previously, and which had retained its building form. That reactivated form exists as long as the reverberation endures. When that ceases, the form is no longer anywhere.

Evidently, I cannot enter into the details of that concept nor of the discussion that followed. I only wish to add that McCulloch considered also the existence of neural circuits of "negative feedbacks" as a result of which an action starting in some part of the perception system, sets up impulses to the central nervous system, from where they are reflected and redirected toward the structures from which they originally arose. This process of inverse feedbacks is reminiscent in my mind of Freud's concept of the origin of the hallucinatory dreams and of V. M. Buscaino on the retrograde excitation of the perceptual visual system.

In 1958, Lashley[46] reiterated his view that any theory of neurone interaction must be couched, not only in terms of the activity of individual cells, be it at a molecular level or otherwise, but in terms of mass relation among cells. Even the simplest bit of behavior requires the integrated action of millions of neurones. Memory in his opinion, is not a single item that can be filed in a single neurone or reverberating circuits; it involves the activity of millions of cells. Differential behavior is determined by a combination of cells acting together, rather than by cells which participate only in particular bits of behavior. The same neurones which maintain the memory traces, and participate in the revival of a certain memory, are also involved in different combinations in thousands of other memories and acts. The memory-trace is the capacity of many neurones to work together in certain permutations.

Weiss,[47] in his presentation raised what I consider a very important, but sadly neglected point, that of the existence in us of inborn basic patterns of action or response, which we inherit at birth on the basis of our structural and biological organization. In Weiss's words:

> No theory of the neuronal system can claim to represent the facts, if it ignores the central autonomy of the basic patterns of motor performance. . . . The fact is that frequently we suspect a given neuronal precision set up as being relevant for a particular neural function, but often find that in an earlier stage of development this function will be performed in essentially the same way without that particular structural precision scheme having even developed as yet. . . . We know from the lower organism that the working of the central nervous system is a hierarchic affair, in which functions at a higher level do not deal directly with the ultimate structural units, such as neurones, or other units, but operate by activating lower patterns that have their own relatively autonomous structural unity."[48] . . . It is a fact that most of the basic motor patterns of behavior are developed within the nervous system by virtue of the laws of its own embryonic differentiation, without the aid of, and prior to the appearance of a sensory input from the outside world. The basic configuration of the motor pattern therefore, cannot possibly be a direct product of the sensory input.[49]

Leaving aside the implications contained in Weiss's remarks concerning the relative importance of the sensory input, which he considers only as a regulatory of inborn reactive patterns, Weiss's views bring into prominence the same important concept advanced by Lorenz and his school of ethology. To Weiss's remarks I would like to add as a complement, the concluding remarks of Lashley when he stated that: "I am convinced more and more that the rudiments of every human behavioral mechanism will be found far down in the evolutionary scale, but also represented even in primitive activities of the neurones themselves."[50]

At the "Princeton Symposium of Learning and Remembering,"[51] Hyden[52] first reminded us of the general meaning of the nucleic acid DNA and RNA and of the fact that in the nucleus of the nerve cells, DNA acts as a primary coding molecule from which RNA originates, it being a copy of a part of the DNA, and RNA becomes the messenger carrying the specific DNA informations. The RNA is carried from the nucleus into the cytoplasm of the nerve-cell, and is ready to offer its instructions for the formation of proteins. RNA appears in the form of a thin folded structure to which two to six ribosomes are attached. The RNA molecule is now called the polysome, and contains almost eighty nucleotides. To this structure various amino-acids, which constitute the building blocks to the protein, become attached, and occupy a given place in the sequence of the protein formation.

In the course of his investigation of the biochemical aspect of learning and memory, Hyden established the fact that during these activities there always occurred an increase in the amount of RNA in both nerve-cells and glia-cells, and that the nucleotides of the RNA molecules of the glia-cells are constantly transferred to the nerve-cells where they activate the enzymes necessary for the synthesis of an additional RNA production. Hyden was the opinion that both nerve-cells and glia elements constitute a functional unit which, by regulating the induction of RNA synthesis, become an integral part of the memory mechanism. Though so many unknowns still exist, Hyden felt that the RNA mechanism of coded instructions cannot be excluded from the process of learning and memory.

Gerard R. W.[53] also expressed his opinion that the various perceptive informations received by a given nerve-cell are presumably transmitted to the various nucleotides, which constitute the RNA molecule, and which are always present in the cytoplasm of the cell, because of their continuous production by means of local synthesis. The electrical current originating from the various stimuli which reach the nerve-cells, either directly from the periphery, or from the electrical magnetic fields of other nerve-cells of the neighborhood, can influence and modify the grouping of the nucleotides of the RNA molecule, determine the deployment of one of the many chains of the RNA, and thus create various patterns of activity, each chain being activated by a certain type of molecular grouping. For Gerard also, memory would thus depend from these various grouping of molecular impressions involving the RNA. In order for the mnemonic impression to create a so-called mnemonic image any molecular activity, if taking place in a single cell, would evidently be insufficient.

To obtain a satisfactory functioning of the memory process it is indispensable to secure the intervention of many other cells of the vicinity or of various distantly located areas connected to each other either directly or by means of relay stations.

To the development of the biochemical and electro-physical aspects of the memory concept, numerous investigators have contributed. Of necessity I must limit myself to present the point of view of very few of them. Eccles[54] for instance, emphasized particularly the point that in order to account for the activities of our nervous system, one must take into consideration not only the changes occurring in the cell body itself, but also those which take place at the synaptic level, from which area the neural impulses are transmitted to other cells. These changes begin to occur in the pre-synaptic structure where so-called transmitter substances, contained in numerous small vesicles, burst open into the synaptic cleft, and act upon the post-synaptic membrane, change its ionic permeability, and thus allows the transmission of the impulse across the synaptic cleft. In one large pyramidal cell alone, Eccles suggested that there might be as many as 10.000 synapses contained in the spines of its dendrites, and as far as the property of the transmitters is concerned, he considered them mostly of the excitatory type though two of them at least are known to be inhibitory in their function.

The importance assigned by Eccles and co-workers to the circumscribed synaptic formations should not however minimize the importance of the neural impulses tracking around various pathways of associations in the complex neural network underlying memory-processes. It is in that light that Kruger[55] felt that because of the complex and extensive interconnections of nerve-cells and groups of nerve-cells, the brain may be considered analogous *to a most complex computer*, with the difference that because certain connections of nerve-cells are lost in the course of time, and new connections are acquired, as suggested by his own experiments with ionizing radiations, the brain would be analogous to a computer only one instant at a time.

R. W. Sperry[56] was also of the opinion that a structural theory of memory and learning, based only on the theory of synaptic transmission and of molecular coding, could not if so limited in scope, explain the memory features at a behavioral level. In his opinion, memory must also involve patterning in the whole network of the nervous system. The molecular coding alone is not sufficient and would have to be translated or expressed in the language of neurophysiology. In this context the mnemonic information is not coded directly into an engram form, but is carried through the dynamic patterns of the excitations always needed to activate any particular engram. In other words the engram of memory, the excitatory situation in which it is aroused and its transmission, are co-functions and are mutually interdependent. The coding comes then out in terms of that combination. It is a higher level kind of coding, not only coding at a molecular level. Much of the information does not have to be put in a static tracing system; it comes out by reactivation of the combination of the transient excitatory phenomena added to the engram effect.

In all the discussions of the problem of consciousness and memory, to which I have referred in connection particularly to neural structures and bio-electrical processes, in the course of the various scientific meetings which I have mentioned, I have failed however to find any discussion dealing even in some hypothetical manner with the origin of mental life. All the discussion centered around the structural basis and of the biological phenomena which develop in the course of conscious mental life. None of the participants dealt with the phenomenon of consciousness itself in terms of what I have called the new "psychic function" itself, the mother-hen of the conscious processes which I have assumed to originate from the synthesis and integrations of all somatic functions, already operating at a certain moment of our ontogenetic intrauterine development.

That failure I consider regrettable because it deprived the various discussants to reach the source of that mental life in terms of a newly developed "psychic function," the expression of which, by its very nature, was a conscious one.

CHAPTER III

Freud's Fallacy on the Origin, Structure, and Characteristics of the Unconscious

Working in collaboration with Breuer on his early paper of 1893 *On the Psychical Mechanisms of Hysterical Phenomena*, Freud published in it his first concept of the two main groups of mental phenomena, those which constitute the conscious system, and those which existed in the form of certain memories not at the disposal of the patient's individual consciousness, and which only under hypnosis, could be recollected and thus brought back into consciousness. But it was in his subsequent paper *On the Defence Neuropsychoses* (1894) that Freud, having introduced his concept of "defense" resulting from a deliberate effort of a patient, to forget some objectionable and dangerous ideas, he delineated more clearly his concept of the "unconscious."

It was in the course of the development of that concept that in December 1896 (letter 52 to W. Fliess) that Freud introduced his first sketch of "our psychic apparatus," in which he distinguished the perception system (pcpt.) to which *consciousness was attached*, the Uc. (the unconscious) designated by two letters only in those days and the Pc. (the preconscious) designated also by two letters only. To the Uc. he assigned the transcription of conceptual memories, and to the Pc. the transcription of verbal images, and which corresponded to the official ego.[1]

In 1900, in his *Interpretation of Dreams*, Freud discussed in more detail his view on what he considered conscious and what he considered mental. He elaborated upon his division of our mental apparatus into the three topographical systems of Cs., Pcs., and Ucs., the two latter being now designated by three-letter signs. Concern-

247

ing the relationship of what is mental to what is conscious, he was convinced that as long as psychology dealt with this problem by a verbal explanation to the effect that "psychical" meant "conscious," to speak of unconecious psychical processes was palpable nonsense, and that any psychological evaluation of the abnormal mental states was out of the question. He was of the opinion that the physician and the philosopher can only come together if they both recognize that the term "unconscious psychical processes," is the appropriate and justified expression of a solidly established fact.[2]

In Freud's view, it was essential to abandon the over-evaluation of the property of being conscious, before it becomes possible to form any correct view of the origin of what is mental. On this subject, Freud relied heavily upon the writings of Lipps in which he had become deeply interested in 1898 (letter 94 to Fliess), and according to whom the unconscious had to be assumed to be the general basis of psychic life. In Freud's words:

> I have set myself the task of making a bridge between *my germinating metapsychology* and what is in the books, and I have therefore plunged into the study of Lipps whom I suspect of being the best mind among present day philosophers. So far, he lends himself very well to comprehension and translation into my own terms.[3]

In his subsequent letter to Fliess, dated five days later August 3, 1898, Freud added:

> *Lipps regards consciousness only as a sense-organ*, the contents of the mind as ideation, and all mental processes as unconscious. In details the correspondence is close too; perhaps the divergence on which I shall be able to base my own contribution, will come later. I have read a third of him.[4] [italics mine]

Note here, the mention of consciousness as only a *"sense-organ of perception,"* a concept which Freud exploited later, with no further mention of Lipps.

In 1900, Freud in his *Interpretation of Dreams*, quoted again Lipps as having stated that the unconscious is the larger sphere which includes within it, the smaller sphere of the conscious, and that everything conscious has an unconscious preliminary stage. Lipps felt also what is unconscious may remain at that stage and nevertheless claim to be regarded as having the full value of a psychical process. In Lipps's view, *the unconscious is the true psychic reality* and in its innermost nature, it is as much unknown to us as the reality of the external world, presented by the data of consciousness.[5] In that light the mental processes were to appear first in the unconscious in terms of a system, whereas the conscious mental processes represented a subsequent stage of their development in the conscious as a system.

At this point, I wish to anticipate in a restricted capsule form, that which I will develop in the next chapter, that is contrary to Lipps and Freud, I consider mental life as being originally a conscious one. I furthermore assume that what Freud considered as the "unconscious" in terms of a system, I consider as representing no more than the activities of a "subordinate conscious" that never loses its attribute of belonging to the conscious system, though it is capable of operating outside our own awareness, in a so-to-speak "subliminal capacity."

Returning now to the particular subject of the topographical division of our mental apparatus in the three Cs., Pcs., Ucs. systems, Freud had claimed as his own discovery the fact that the unconscious itself was to be considered as being formed by two separate systems. In his words:

> The Unconscious, that is the psychical is found as *a function of two separate systems*, and that this is the case in normal as well as in pathological life. Thus, there are two kinds of unconscious, which have not as yet been distinguished by psychologists. Both of them are unconscious in the sense used by psychologists; but in our sense one of them which we term the Ucs. *is inadmissible to consciousness* while we term the other, the Pcs. because its excitations, after observing certain rules, it is true, and perhaps only after passing a fresh censorship, are able to reach consciousness.[6] [italics mine]

That division of the unconscious system into two separate systems was not further pursued by Freud in his paper of 1912 *The Unconscious in Psychoanalysis* where discussing its content, *he spoke only of "latent ideas"*:

> We were accustomed to think that *every latent idea* was so because it was weak, and that it grew conscious as it became strong. We have now gained the conviction that there are some latent ideas which do not penetrate into consciousness however strong they may have become. Therefore we may call the latent ideas of the first type *preconscious*, while we reserve the term *Unconscious (proper)* for the latter type which we came to study in the neuroses. The term unconscious

which was used in the purely descriptive sense before, now
had come to imply something more, *that is not simply ideas in
general*, but especially ideas with a certain dynamic character,
ideas keeping apart from consciousness, in spite of their intensity and activity.[7] [italics mine]

Thus, while in 1900 Freud spoke of the unconscious in terms of
the function of *two separate systems*, the Pcs. and the Ucs., in 1912
he no longer referred to separate systems but simply to the activity
of preconscious and unconscious ideas in terms *of latent ideas*, some
of which could penetrate consciousness, and some of which could not.
Yet in 1912 though Freud no longer referred to two separate systems in the unconscious, but simply to the activity of preconscious
and unconscious ideas in terms of latent ideas, some of which could
penetrate and some of which could not penetrate consciousness, his
description of the unconscious as being formed by two different
groups of latent ideas, amounted to the same thing as when he originally maintained the division of the unconscious into the two separate systems of the preconscious, and of the unconscious (proper).

In a following paper of 1915, *The Unconscious*, Freud elaborated
further on this subject of the latent ideas in the unconscious when
he stated that:

> There are mental acts of very varying values which yet have
> in common the characteristic of *being unconscious*. The Un-
> conscious comprises on the one hand, processes which are
> merely latent, temporarily unconscious, *but which differ in no
> other respect from consciousness*, and on the other hand pro-
> cesses as those which have undergone repression, and which if
> they came into consciousness must stand out in the crudest
> contrast to the rest of the conscious mind.[8] [italics mine]

It was indeed the first time that Freud had maintained that latent
ideas *though being unconscious*, differed in no way from the conscious ones. These are the unconscious latent ideas that Freud subsequently considered as belonging to the conscious system, and later
he even identified them with it.

It is in this connection that Freud had remarked that:

> We cannot escape the imputation of ambiguity in that we use
> the words conscious and unconscious sometimes in a systema-
> tic and sometimes in a descriptive sense, in which former they
> signify inclusion in some particular system and possessing
> certain characteristics. . . . Perhaps we may look for some as-
> sistance from the proposal to employ, at any rate in writing,
> the abbreviation Cs. for consciousness and Ucs. for the uncon-

scious when we are using the two words in the systematic sense.[9]

However, no matter how Freud tried to overtake that ambiguity, one cannot help noting that in this publication of 1915 *The Unconscious*, he spoke of the unconscious as comprising not only mental processes which are latent, but which differed in no other respect from conscious ones. It follows that if the unconscious of Freud comprised also mental processes which could not enter consciousness, Freud by the word unconscious must have referred to the Ucs. as a system. Thus it is in that Ucs. system, that he had included also the latent preconscious processes which constituted the Pcs. system, and the content of which differed in no other respect from the content of the Cs. system. It would seem therefore that Freud failed to solve the ambiguity in question by the mere use of the word unconscious as a description, as opposed to the use of Ucs. as a word for the description of a system.

The ambiguity in question became more accentuated when Freud, in his further elaboration of the unconscious Ucs., generalized the two stages of development of all mental acts by asserting *that a mental act goes through two phases*, between which is interposed a kind of testing process (censorship.) In his view, the mental act is unconscious and belongs to the system Ucs. If on the scrutiny of the censorship it is rejected, and not allowed to pass into the second phase, Freud felt that it is considered as being repressed and as such must remain unconscious. If, however, it passes this scrutiny, it enters upon the second phase and henceforth belongs to the second system which Freud called the Cs. He added however that the fact that it so *belonged*, did not unequivocally determine its relation to consciousness. *It was not yet conscious but it was certainly capable of entering consciousness.* In other words it could now without any special resistance become the object of consciousness. It was in consideration of this capacity to become conscious, that Freud *also called the system Cs. the preconscious*, a system that shared the characteristics of the Cs.[10]

Apart from the fact that in the last portion of that statement, Freud admitted that a preconscious act, belonging to the Cs. system and sharing its characteristics, could operate in the unconscious that is outside our own awareness, a point to which I will return in the next chapter there is another consideration to be made concerning Freud's two phases of a mental act. Indeed, Freud's reference to a mental act going through two phases, the first of which is unconscious followed by its conscious phase, constitutes a return to Lipps's view that *all* mental acts are unconscious in their first stage. However it would seem to me that such a return by Freud's to Lipps's view, should have been limited to those unconscious mental acts that may have been inherited, and which at first may have expressed themselves in some primordial unconscious manner. But Freud included in that first unconscious stage, when he had stated that a mental act, with no specification, goes through the two phases of first, the unconscious stage and then the conscious one, *all mental acts*, that is, not only the preconscious ones that Lipps himself had not contemplated, but also those acts which had been conscious at one time, and which had been rendered unconscious only subsequently by the means of repression.

It would seem, therefore, that a certain contradiction existed in Freud's statement that a mental act (with no further specification) goes through two phases, the first of which is unconscious, when in that reference to a mental act in general he seemed to have referred to all acts, including inadvertently maybe in that expression, also the acts that at one time had already been conscious, prior to the intervention of repression. Furthermore, it would seem that with such an ambiguity, Freud had lost track of what he had stated in 1900 in his *Interpretation of Dreams* in clarifying his position on Lipps's views of the unconscious, when he referred to "*our unconscious*" and when he underscored the fact that it was not the same as the unconscious of the philosophers or even the unconscious of Lipps. At this point, for the first time, he noted that Lipps carried things farther with his assertion that the whole of what is psychical exists unconsciously and that a part of it also exists consciously. In Freud's view, the new discovery of psychoanalysis rested upon the fact that the unconscious was found to be a function of two separate systems . . . so that there are two kinds of unconscious which had not yet been distinguished by psychologists. Both of them were unconscious in the sense used by psychology, but in the psychoanalytic point of view, one of them which he termed the Ucs. was also inadmissible to consciousness, because of repression.[11]

Thus, it would seem that Freud accepted Lipps's views of a first operational unconscious stage of mental acts, in terms only of those allegedly inherited ones, to which he added now the unconscious operational stage of mental acts which had been first conscious at one time. Freud therefore had exceeded his own belief when in 1915 in his paper *The Unconscious*, he had stated that a mental act, *with no other specification*, goes through a first unconscious phase, considering that this could not be the case for the Pcs. as well as for the repressed unconscious.

Freud's calling the system Cs. also the preconscious became more complicated in his subsequent publication *The Metapsychological Supplement to the Theory of Dreams* (1916), where he had identified the Cs. system with the Pcpt. system by designating the two systems with the common lettering *Cs.-Pcpt. system*. Such an identification was subsequently confirmed in a footnote dated 1919 in page 541 of his *Interpretation of Dreams* where he had equated consciousness with perceptions, by designating in a single lettering the two systems Cs.—Pcpt. Considering now that Freud had identified the Pcs. with the Cs. under the common designation of Cs.—Pcs. system, the ultimate representation of that entire chain of relationship between these three identical system should have been lettered more correctly as the *Pcpt.—Cs.—Pcs. system*, the expression of a single conscious system.

As a result of this unification, one could also argue the point that if the Pcs. system belonged to the Cs. system and if the latter represented also the Pcpt. system, there would hardly be the need for the existence as predicated by Freud of two separate censors one between the Ucs. and the Pcs., and the other between the Pcs. and the Cs. system, representing also the Pcpt. system. The operation of a censor between the Cs. and the Pcs. would evidently weaken Freud's unitarian concept of a Cs.—Pcs.—Pcpt. system. Yet in Freud's view: "If it should turn out that a certain censorship also determines whether the Preconscious becomes Conscious, we shall discriminate more sharply between the system Pcs. and the Cs."[12]

Some ambiguity in Freud's views of the relationship of the Cs.—Pcs.—Pcpt. system still persisted when having maintained that consciousness regards the whole sum of its mental processes as belonging to the realm of the preconscious, he then added that though a censorship existed between the Ucs. and the Pcs., and that the content of the Ucs. could have no access to consciousness except via the Pcs. he made an exception for the affects, which at that time he considered to be "affect formations"[13] which from the unconscious could circumvent that route and reach consciousness directly. Of course it all depends upon what Freud considered the "affective formations" to be, that is if made of *a simple cathectic qualitative energy*, or of some cathectic somatic energy attached to some inseparable ideational representation, which by the way is my interpretation of an "affective formation." In the first case if one could theoretically subscribe to a direct passage of a qualitative energy, but in the second case some of the ideational component of the "affective formation" could constitute objectionable material, and therefore should become subject to the operation of the censor between

the Ucs. and the Cs-Pcs. system. That point was never touched on by
Freud.

To the preconscious system, Freud had assigned at first only the
transcription of the verbal representation of memory-traces, but subsequently he referred also to the presence in it of visual memory-
traces. In 1923, in *The Ego and the Id*,[14] Freud stated his opinion
that some individuals may formulate conscious thought-processes by
means of visual residues, though this form of thought-formation is
an incomplete and more primitive one. Later in his posthumous publication *An Outline of Psychoanalysis* (1939), Freud, having considered the fact that the thinking process in animals must take place in
the absence of verbal-memory-traces in the Pcs, felt that it would
not be right, however, to assert that a connection with memory-
traces of speech is a prerequisite of the preconscious condition.[15]

This concept of verbal images of objects and persons had been
first introduced by Freud in his paper *The Unconscious* (1915),
where he resorted to the assumption that the representation of conscious processes are stored partly in the preconscious (pcs.) in the
form of the idea of the word (*the verbal idea*) and in part in the unconscious (Ucs.) in the form of the idea of the thing (*the concrete
idea*). In order for an unconscious mental process to become conscious, a combination of the idea of the thing with the idea of the
word, must take place in the preconscious, and only then the process
could become conscious.

This whole subject of the distinction between the idea of the
word and the idea of the thing was brought into discussion by Freud
in the above-mentioned paper where Freud had assumed that following repression, in the pathological condition of schizophrenia: "The
withdrawn libido does not seek a new object but retreats into the
Ego; that is to say that here the object-cathexies are given up and a
primitive objectless condition of narcissism is re-established."[16] In a
following page of the same paper, Freud stated that he must modify
that assumption in the sense that the cathexis of the ideas of the
words corresponding to the object *is retained*. He then introduced his
view that what we call the conscious ideas of the object could now be
split up *into the idea of the word* (verbal idea) *and the idea of the
thing* (concrete idea); the idea of the thing consisted in his view, of
the cathexis if not of the direct memory images of the thing, at least
of remoter memory-traces derived from these. By so assuming, Freud

felt that now he knew what is the difference between a conscious and an unconscious idea, inasmuch as the conscious idea comprised the concrete idea plus the verbal idea corresponding to it, while the unconscious idea was that of the thing alone.[17]

In schizophrenia, what repression denies to the rejected idea, is according to Freud, the conjunction of its verbal representation which is retained in the preconscious, with the idea of the thing, its concrete idea, which remains repressed in the unconscious. There could be much to be asked of these assumptions on the part of Freud in relation to schizophrenia, such as why in the Pcs. the verbal idea of an object should persist, considering that the verbalization of an idea should be presumably the first to suffer from the impact of repression. And why in melancholia, Freud, referring to the regression into the ego of *the libido alone*, did not take also into consideration the regression also into the ego of the concrete image of the abandoned object, thus making more acceptable the resulting identification between the ego and the abandoned object.

Another question relates to the fact that if in the unconscious there is retained the ideational representation of a thing in terms of the concrete image of that thing, does it not follow that such a concrete representation implies the operation of *a cognitive evaluation of that thing*? A cognitive evaluation implies I would say a conscious appreciation of the shape, size, and consistency to say the least, of that thing. In that case couldn't there be operating *in what we call the unconscious* some sort of a subordinate conscious function, responsible for that evaluation? With the passing introduction of such an assumption, I have actually anticipated what I will discuss in detail in the subsequent chapter as an alternative to Freud's entire concept of the unconscious.

Returning to Freud's conjectural separation of the ideational representation of an object into its verbal representation and its concrete representation, it would seem that Freud needed that particular assumption for various purposes, first to theorize on what the difference consisted of between a conscious and an unconscious idea. Secondly, to theorize upon the fact that in the transference neuroses repression operating by means of the withdrawal of the Cs.-Pcs. cathexes, involved both the concrete and the verbal representation of the thing, whereas in the narcissistic neuroses, the cathexis of the verbal idea to be repressed was retained in the preconscious. Thirdly, in schizophrenia, a narcissistic neurosis, when the hypercathexis of the verbal representation of a lost object that has maintained its cathexis in the preconscious, in spite of repression, and is therefore capable at a certain moment to make its appearance in the clinical picture in various forms of verbalization, it indicates in Freud's view the first attempt of the patient at recovery, by regaining that lost object by first reacquiring the cathexis of the word belonging to it.

Here, as in all his other writings, we meet again with Freud's fundamental approach to the functioning of our mental apparatus in terms only of a displaceable cathexis (psychic energy), instead of relying upon the displacement and replacement of ideas and of "affective formations" under the power of their own somatic energy, an approach I strongly favor.

The difficulty of conceptualizing Freud's unconscious which he ultimately called the id, became greater when in that deepest structure of our mental apparatus, he included that inherited portion made of archaic remnants of previous ego's and super-ego's formations, as well as of precipitates of pre-individual affective states and above all of the elusive various instincts. Evidently such an inherited transmission of mental processes from the donor to the recipient, in the absence of supporting data, could be conceived only in spiritual or metaphysical terms.

There is indeed no need to agree to the concept of inherited mental processes in the sense of a genetic transmission from generation to generation of unconscious mental processes representing atavistic formations. In my opinion all that is present at birth in terms of a mental endowment, is not inherited, but the product of a gradual ontogenetic development of a new "psychic function," born at a certain point of our ontogenetic somatic growth, in the course of our intrauterine life, from the integration and synthesis of the various somatic functions already operating at that point. These mental processes are to be considered simply as inborn processes and not inherited in the strict sense of that word.

As for the content of the *acquired unconscious* in which Freud at first had included only its repressed portion, it was extended later by him when he elaborated on his concept of the resistance exercised against the reentry in consciousness of the repressed material. It was in *The Ego and the Id* (1923), that he pointed out that those resistances operated in the unconscious, without the patient being aware of them, though one could guess it by the patient's discomfort at a certain point of his free association. Since in his opinion, there could be no question that the resistances emanated from his ego and belonged to it, he concluded that: "We have come upon something in the Ego itself, which is also unconscious, which behaves exactly like the repress, that is which produces powerful effects without itself being conscious."[18]

It would seem, therefore, that Freud's unconscious in terms of a system did not now coincide with only that which was *inherited* and with what had been *repressed* because objectionable, but also with that portion of the ego which according to him operated dynamically as a repressed force. Freud however gave us no inkling as to the complete nature of that unconscious ego. Did he include in it some atavistic portion as well as portions of previous egos? And in that case wouldn't that unconscious portion become deprived of its critical function in terms of resistance, by the mere fact that such portions may have lost their conscious attribute of a discerning agency.

Freud had also considered as belonging to the Ucs. some special derivatives of the instinctual impulses, which in themselves unite opposite features. On the one hand they are organized, having made use of acquisitions from the Cs. system, while on the other hand they are unconscious and are incapable of becoming conscious, thus operating as repressed formations. In Freud's view, *they belong according to their qualities to the system Pcs. but in actual fact operate in the Ucs.* They constitute the fantasy formations of normal persons as well as of neurotics which, in spite of their high degree of organization, remain repressed. In my estimation, the fact that Freud referred to those fantasies *as being repressed*, had put them as a formative portion of the Ucs. in the systematic sense. Yet Freud considered them as enjoying in that system the same characteristics of the Cs.—Pcs. system to which in his views they actually belonged.

It would seem that by so assuming Freud revived the old ambiguity between what we term conscious and what we term unconscious, the latter dealt at times in a descriptive sense, and at others in a systematic sense. *Is there actually a way to speak of only one single system, the Cs. system, operating at various levels of our awareness in terms of subordinate levels of consciousness, and which could replace Freud's entire concept of the unconscious?* I will attempt to give an answer to this question in the following chapter.

Let me continue now with the content of Freud's unconscious. To the elements already included in it, Freud subsequently added all the useless and discarded mental processes of childhood. Curiously enough he considered them to be of the same nature of those mental processes which are inherited. In his words:

> If inherited mental formations exist in the human be-
> ing . . . these constitute the nucleus of the unconscious. Later
> there is added all that is discarded as useless during child-
> hood development, and this *need not differ in its nature from
> what is inherited.*[19] [italics mine]

On this subject of the useless and discarded processes of childhood, one cannot help remark on the obscurity of Freud's views.
Why did he consider these mental processes as being of the same nature as of those which have been inherited and as such deeply rooted
in the unconscious (Ucs.) as a system? Why did he not consider them
as simply "latent processes" which had lost their childhood utilitarian value, and the memory-traces of which could however easily
reenter consciousness, not differently from the latent processes
which according to Freud constituted the preconscious (Pcs.)

In connection with those discarded mental processes of childhood, we may also assume that rather than considering them of the
same nature of the inherited mental processes, which according to
Freud operate at first in their unconscious stage, we could consider
them as the expression of processes which at one time had operated
in a dominant capacity in the conscious system, but later had assumed a subordinate position in that same conscious system because
of their having lost their immediate utilitarian value. I will elaborate this point also in the next chapter.

This may be the proper place for some remarks on the subject of
inherited mental processes. I would like first to restate my personal
assumption that *mental processes are ontogenetically created and
therefore not inherited.* They originate in the course of our ontogenesis from the operation of the newly developed "psychic function," born of the synthesis and integration of all somatic functions
operating at a certain moment of our intrauterine organization. That
new function is thus already operating at the time of birth. But
being inborn does not mean being inherited. Details and discussion
of this assumption of mine will be found in chapter I of part I of this
trilogy.

What I consider inherited are simply our structural and biological formations and related functional activities which are governed
by genetic laws, but not mental processes as such. Evidently in the
course of our intrauterine life and subsequently after birth, the development of that new "psychic function" parallels the development

of our inherited structural and biological organization. In that sense only, the ontogenetic development of our mental life is related to our inherited soma, that is to say that, as our developing structural and biological endowment becomes further established, special mental aptitudes may develop.

In connection with the development of our structural ego, I must recall what I have already stated in that chapter I of part I of this trilogy, that the new "Psychic function" which develops at a certain moment of our intrauterine life, has for its main task that of translating into ideational representations the various stimuli originating from the activity of our various somatic functions already in operation. As a result, with the development of that new "psychic function," there appears at a certain moment of our intrauterine organization, a first global awareness of our own existence. That first awareness I have assumed to be the first functional expression of an operating "primordial ego" which I have designated as *"Protopathic Ego."*

To correlate the ontogenetic development of our "psychic function" with our inherited structural and biological organization, I will advance certain assumptions. It can very well be that in humans, in the case for instance of the optic system, the following reasoning could apply: A particular structural retina endowed with a particularly fine neural composition, and thus capable of establishing neural connections of a particularly fine nature, with the primary and secondary visual cortical centers of the brain, and which centers are themselves endowed hereditarily with a particularly fine neural structure and the functionality of which is particularly sensitive to biological processes, could explain why a certain individual born with that special endowment to perceive, transmit, discriminate, and react to shadows of light, outlines of forms, and perception of colors and related shades, could develop a special talent for drawing and painting, a talent which may be erroneously interpreted as the expression of an inherited mental organization.

By the same token, an individual endowed with a particularly delicate and sensitive well integrated inherited structural neural organization, of both the peripheral and the central auditory system, may develop the gift of perceiving and integrating various combinations of sounds and rhythm, as a result of which he will disclose a special talent for music and harmony, a talent which could be erroneously interpreted as the expression of some inherited mental organization.

Even in the field of "affective development," a certain inherited structural and biological organization, particularly of the nervous system, could influence in certain individuals more than in others an unusual tendency to anxiety, the most basic of our affects. Indeed, a certain inherited structural sensitivity of our sense-organs of perceptions to visual, tactile, or auditory stimuli, in combination with a very sensitive functioning of our inherited system of internal secretion, could more easily result in the course of our ontogenetic development, into some unusual states of nervous tension, which as such, could evidently generate a first conscious reaction of "unpleasure." In turn if that "unpleasure" is strong enough, it may evoke a sense of dreadful expectation. Under such circumstances, "anxiety" which is the expression of that "dreadful expectation" could more easily develop in those individuals, either automatically or in anticipation of a situation of danger, and be responsible for the development of various types of anxiety states.

Always on this subject of the inherited portion of the unconscious (Ucs.) in terms of the instincts, which Freud considered as the kernel of the Ucs., I must remark that Freud considered that "kernel" as made of "instinct-presentations": "whose aim is to discharge their cathexis, that is to say that they are 'wish-impulses.' "[20] The question now arises: What is that determines the transformation of somatic excitations, and the latter into wish-impulses? There must be in operation a "psychic function" capable of translating at first those somatic excitations into *ideational representations*. That new "psychic function" I have assumed to be born of the synthesis and integration of the various somatic functions already operating at a certain moment of our intrauterine structural and biological organization.

In Chapter I of Part One of this trilogy, I have endeavored to establish the fact that such a new "Psychic function" which is entrusted with that translation, involves *eo-ipso* consciousness. That assumption follows Freud's original one of 1895, that the perception of a stimulus involves *eo-ipso* consciousness. That new "psychic function" is in my view entrusted not only with the translation of the somatic stimuli into ideational representations, but also by means of their association with other ideational formations already operating in our mind, with the endowing of those representations with some affective quality. That combination of an ideational representation and its related affective quality I have called "Affective formation." Such a formation because of the cognitive implication of its quality, could be construed as a "wish-impulse." In that light wish-impulses, contrary to Freud's considering them as the "kernel" of the Ucs. system, could be construed as the kernel of a conscious awareness of the wishful aim of those "affective formations."

Let me now proceed to the discussion of the two main rules which according to Freud, govern the activities of mental processes in the unconscious, that of *"displacement"* and that of *"condensation."* In undertaking that task a first important question presents itself to my mind: To what portion of the unconscious had Freud intended to apply those rules? Was it to the entire content of the unconscious which included also its acquired repressed portion, or was it only to its inherited portion, the real core of the unconscious according to him? Unfortunately Freud never addressed himself to that distinction.

Let me first approach the law of "condensation." It was in his *Interpretation of Dreams* (1900), that Freud elaborated in a special segment of chapter VII the subject of "condensation" in the course of the dream-work. In this connection he stated that: "The great lack of proportion between the dream-content and the dream-thoughts *implies that the psychical material had undergone an extensive process of condensation* in the formation of the dream."[21] [italics mine]. That Freud was referring only to psychical material and not to a mental energy, is supported by a footnote added to that page in the 1914 edition of that publication where he again stated that:

> The occurrence of condensation in dreams has been hinted by many writers. Du Prell (1885) has a passage in which he says that it is absolutely certain that there has been a process of condensation *of the group of ideas in dreams.*[22]

It would seem to me that, by this reference, Freud was actually referring to "condensation" in terms of ideas or group of ideas which Du Prell at that time had contemplated only in those terms, and not in terms of energy. Freud himself at this point was not referring specifically to "psychic energy." That inference was supported by Freud's own subsequent statement that:

> A dream is not constructed by each individual dream-thought, or group of dream-thoughts finding (in abbreviation) separate representations in the content of the dream. . . . A dream is constructed rather, by the whole mass of dream-thoughts being submitted to a sort of manipulative process in which those elements which have the most numerous and strongest support, acquire the right to entry into the dream-content.[23]

Here again we evidently deal with a manipulative process of mobile ideas undergoing association and condensation and which becomes the dominant factor in the construction of a dream. There was no implication of the operation in this manipulation of an alleged "psychic energy." The role of energy in that construction seemed to have been of secondary importance.

The same remarks seem to be applicable to the other rule governing in the unconscious the construction of a dream, that of "displacement." In the four pages which Freud subsequently devoted to this subject, he at first referred again to the displacement of ideas or group of ideas, with no mention of the displacement of a "cathectic energy." That was quite different from what he had originally assumed in his "project" of 1895, where he spoke only of a displaceable energy activating both the perceptual neurones representing "consciousness" and the "impermeable neurones" representing the unconscious. In fact in 1900 he seemed more concerned with the value of the dream-thoughts in terms of the ideas themselves, and much less with their activating energy:

> In the course of a formation of a dream, the essential elements charged as they are with intense interest may be treated as though they were of small value, and their place may be taken in the dream by other elements of whose small value in the dream-thoughts, there can be no question. . . . What appears in dreams, we might suppose, is not what is important in the dream-thoughts, but what occurs in them several times over. . . . *The ideas which are most important among the dream-thoughts* will almost certainly be those which occur most often in them, since the different dream-thoughts will, as it were, radiate out from them.

Up to now, Freud seemed therefore mainly concerned with the play of the ideas themselves. It was only later, as if only on second thought, that Freud referred now to the intervention in that condensation and displacement of ideas, of a psychic force, a psychic energy:

> It does seem plausible to suppose that in the dream-work *a psychical force is operating*, which on the one hand strip the elements which have a psychical value, of their intensity, and on the other hand, by means of over-determination creates from elements of low psychical value, new values which afterwards find their way in the dream-content. . . . The process which we are here presuming is nothing less than the essential portion of the dream-work and it deserves to be described as dream-displacement. . . . The consequence of the displace-

ment is that the dream-content no longer resembles the core of the dream-thoughts, and that the dream gives no more than a distortion of the dream wish, which exists in the Unconscious.[24]

In all this alternating reference now to the ideas and now to the psychic force, one need not however subscribe to Freud's assumption of a "psychical force" responsible for the displacement of the various ideas, an acceptance which would imply subscribing to Freud's concept of an operating "psychic energy." Instead one could subscribe to the view which I have advanced, that the displacement of thought-processes by other thought-processes, that is of a group of ideas by some other group of ideas, is governed by the new *"psychic function"* (not to be confused with "psychic energy") which is born out of the synthesis and integration of the various somatic functions already operating at a certain moment of our intrauterine organization. I have discussed in details that view in chapter I of part I of this trilogy.

It is the content of the thought-processes made of ideas or group of ideas that after all constitutes the essential fabric of our psychic apparatus, be it at work in the course of dreams or in the course of our waking life. The *energy* that activates the "displacement" or the "condensation" of those ideas or group of ideas, becomes in my views a matter of lesser importance. *Indeed it is not a psychic energy at work in those processes*, but the same somatic energy which had presided over the creation and operation of what I have called the new "psychic function." That energy does not differ from the somatic energy which had presided over the activity of the various somatic functions out of which that "psychic function" was born, an energy which I have designated as *"organismic energy."* (See chapter 1, part I of this trilogy.)

But Freud seemed impervious to any other assumption that dealt with the displacement and condensation of an idea or of a group of ideas under their own power of somatic energy, and maintained that in the unconscious, one idea may surrender to another idea the whole volume of its mental cathexis, thus resulting in its displacement, or that an idea may appropriate for itself the whole mental cathexes of several ideas, thus giving access to the process of condensation. It is within that frame of reference that Freud built his entire psychological construction *and refused to ever acknowledge* the concept of the displacement of the ideational formations themselves and their possible replacement by some other ideational formations. What he considered displaceable was only the cathexis of a psychic energy in both the process of "displacement" and in that of "condensation."

That unshakable belief of his, was well expressed in section F of chapter VII of his *Interpretation of Dreams* where, referring to somebody's supposition that a group of ideas in one locality may be brought to an end and replaced by a fresh one in another locality, Freud felt that one may say instead that some particular mental grouping either has had a cathexis of energy attached to it or withdrawn. In that case, the structure in question may come under the sway of a particular agency or been withdrawn from it. What he regarded as mobile was not the psychical structure itself but its innervation.[25]

Having assumed that the rules of "condensation" and "Displacement" govern the activities of our mental processes in the unconscious, Freud seemed to have disregarded the fact that the same rules may well govern the activity of our mental processes in the course of our conscious mental life. Had he, however, acknowledged this point, he would have lost the advantage *of seemingly assigning only to the unconscious processes* the use of those two governing rules. But in my view, those rules apply also to the operation of our conscious system, which in my opinion includes also the activities of its "subordinate portion" which I call *"the subordinate conscious"* (see the following chapter).

Thus, for instance, let us take the situation which may arise when a certain person re-visits a very poor and unsanitary section of a city where he once had lived. In the course of that visit, his attention may become attracted by a particularly dilapidated house which reminded him of a similar house which once had been his home. The sight of that house was indeed a conscious one and as such, it elicited in his conscious mind a long chain of conscious ideational representations and associations, made of various displaceable ideas which made him relive at that moment, past ideational situations and past "affective formations" related to poverty, humiliation, and frustrations of early past years, all feelings which became reactivated at that moment in his conscious mind. No one could doubt the conscious nature of those revived ideas and related affective qualities, nor the fact that because of the displacement of those ideas and their condensation into a new group, that new group may present itself in consciousness. That group of thought-processes may appear in terms of some determination of the part of that visitor to devote himself from now on, to some social endeavor leading to the correction of the unsanitary conditions of this particular area, as well as of other similar areas existing in that city. The formulation of this succession of displaceable ideas and resulting thought-formations *was consciously registered* by that visitor, *though the mechanics of that displacement and condensation was unknown to him.*

It would seem, therefore, that Freud was not justified in considering the process of displacement of ideas as a rule governing mental activities only in the Ucs. viewed as a separate system. *To equate ignorance of a mechanism* with that of a governing rule does not evidently contribute to clarity.

The same considerations which I have presented concerning the rule of "displacement" operating in the unconscious, can now be applied to the rule of "condensation" which, according to Freud, governs also the mental processes operating in the unconscious. Without entering in superfluous repetitions, we only have to remember how under certain circumstances the sight of a national flag, the sight of a military parade, the sound of a military band may result in a condensation of ideas and of thought-processes and of various "affective formations" which present themselves at first separately at *a conscious level*, but ultimately converge into the conceptual terms of country, honor, duty. We know nothing of the mechanism of such a condensation of separate thought-processes, a mechanism which escapes our own awareness, yet the ultimate conceptual result is a conscious one and cannot be viewed as the result of a special operating rule governing mental processes in the Ucs. system alone, as predicated by Freud. In my opinion that mechanism which Freud designates as "rule" operates also in the Cs. system.

In addition to the rules of displacement and condensation which, according to Freud, govern the mental processes operating in the Ucs. system (the ID), that system is endowed with certain special characteristics. These characteristics were described by Freud in his paper of 1915 *The Unconscious* in which he stated that in the unconscious, the mental representations are coordinated with one another, that they exist independently side by side, and that they are exempted from mutual contradictions. When in the Ucs. two wishes, the aim of which may appear as incompatible, become simultaneously active, they do not detract from each other, but combine to form an intermediate aim, a compromise. In that description however, there was no indication of Freud's part, to which particular portion of the unconscious ultimately called the id, these various characteristics were to be applied, to its inherited portion alone, to its acquired portion or to its entire structure. It is therefore in that ambiguous sense that Freud added that in the unconscious, there is no negation, no dubiety, no varying degrees of certainty . . . and that in that system the processes are timeless, i.e., they are not ordered temporarily, are not altered by the passage of time, inasmuch as they bear no relation not only to time but are also little related to reality; the fate of those unconscious processes depended only upon the degree of their strength and upon their conformity to regulation by pain and pleasure.[26] This last characteristic was restated by Freud in the *Ego and the Id* (1923), where he asserted that in the id, the pleasure principle reigns sovereign and that: "The task of the Ego is to bring the influence of the external world to bear upon it, and endeavor to substitute the reality-principle for the pleasure-principle."[27]

In his *New Introductory Lectures* (1932), Freud returned to the characteristics of the unconscious, which by now he had designated the id. He included in that id all the elements which he had already included in his earlier unconscious and in particular the repressed impulses, that portion of the ego which had been withdrawn from its own knowledge and regarded as unconscious in the truly dynamic sense, the discarded and useless processes of childhood, the nature of which did not differ from the inherited portion, and last but not least all that which had been inherited at birth, and especially the instincts. Still no distinction was made by Freud as far as characteristics were concerned, between what he had considered as its inherited portion and what he had considered as its acquired portion. As a matter of fact, when speaking of *timelessness* he assigned that characteristic to all the wishful impulses, with no distinction between the repressed ones and the inherited ones which had never passed beyond the id. In his words: "Wishful impulses which have never passed beyond the Id, but impressions too which have been sunk into the Id by repression, are virtually immortal; after the passage of decades they behave as though they had just occurred."[28]

Another confusing reference concerning the characteristics of the unconscious, was Freud's statement that the unconscious ego, as I have already stated, was to be regarded as unconscious in the truly dynamic sense, implying that it has all the attributes of the repressed and consequently, as well as those of its inherited portion.

Strange enough however, he seemed to have established some contradiction to that statement by assuming at the same time that some difference existed between the repressed ego and the rest of what he called "the irrational unconscious" meaning presumably its inherited portion, when he added that: "You can recognize the possibility of portions of the ego and of the super-ego, being unconscious, without possessing the same primitive and irrational characteristics."[29] Evidently Freud had lost track of the fact that in his views, the unconscious ego had included most of its archaic atavistic nuclei-components, the characteristic of which he had not discussed. If so, in what way this important components of the unconscious ego could avoid possessing primitive and irrational characteristics? And if so, how could one differentiate indeed between the characteristics of the repressed ego which at one time had been conscious and the characteristics of some primitive and irrational portion of the unconscious ego.

And if that differentiation were not possible to make, then the question arises again: Do the various characteristics of the unconscious as formulated by Freud, apply actually to the entire content of the unconscious, that is, to both its acquired and inherited portion? And if they apply to the whole content of the unconscious, how should we qualify that portion in it, which originates from all that has been discarded as useless in the course of the child's development and which portion, contrary to Freud's view, should naturally be considered different in its nature from what has been inherited?

No clarification of this point is found in Freud's latest posthumous publication, *An Outline of Psychoanalysis* (1939), where he reiterated the characteristics of the unconscious with no distinction between its inherited and its acquired portion. He again simply reiterated his views that the governing laws of logic have no sway in the unconscious that may be called the kingdom of the illogical, where impulses with contrary aims exist side by side, without any call being made for an adjustment between them, having no effect upon each other, considering that a senseless compromise comes about, which embraces mutually exclusive elements. It follows that in the manifest dream, any element may stand for its contrary.[30]

Since this was referring to the unconscious activities in the course of dreams, and since the characteristics of these activities do not differ from those same unconscious activities operating outside the dreams, it is evident that Freud did not feel the need to establish a distinction between the characteristics of the inherited unconscious and those of its acquired portion. However, considering the important part played by the acquired portion of the unconscious in the development of the neuroses, a role which in my estimation *by far outpoints that of its alleged inherited portion*, it is unfortunate that in establishing the characteristics of the unconscious, Freud gave the impression that in dealing with the above-acquired portion, he assigned to it most of the qualities which past philosophers had attributed to their "universal unconscious," in terms of their metaphysical concept.

That impression receives support when one compares the characteristics of the unconscious as outlined by Freud with those attributed to it, for instance, by the philosopher E. von Hartmann,[31] the most articulate student of the unconscious, in his classical original three volumes on *The Philosophy of the Unconscious*, published in its first edition in 1868, and succeeded by many others. In that treatise, Hartmann, who presumably was not interested in the clinical application of his views, dealt with the unconscious from a pure universal, metaphysical, and spiritual points of view, and attributed to it the same characteristics attributed to it by Freud, who included in that unconscious its acquired portion made mainly of its repressed elements. In Hartmann's views which should have been known to Freud's philosophy teacher, the unconscious has no dubiety, does not vacillate, does not err, is timeless and has no memory. Other qualities assigned by von Hartmann to his unconscious differ however, *and even clash* with those assigned to it by Freud. Thus, for instance, in von Hartmann's views the unconscious is capable of discerning with intellectual intuition *and with infinite penetration of the pure logical*; that in it the instincts are endowed with a special knowledge, *that is of clairvoyance*, and that it is in the unconscious that the direction of the ideas is established. On this point his views evidently did not coincide with those of Freud who in his *Interpretation of Dreams* had maintained that it was the conscious system by the means of "the special sense organ of consciousness for the perception of psychic qualities," that directed our various perceptions and related ideational formations, and not the unconscious system.

However, what stands above all in sharp contrast with Freud's concept of the unconscious, from that of von Hartmann, is the fact that according to the latter, the instinctive activities which predominate in the unconscious, *are not at all governed by the pleasure-principle* as maintained by Freud. In von Hartmann's words: "What is grand and awe-inspiring in instincts, is that its behests are obeyed with utter disregard for all personal well-being; *if it really proceeds from the endeavor after bodily pleasure, it is not true instinct and can only be deemed as a mistake.*" von Hartmann's position is a far cry from Freud's position that in the unconscious, the pleasure-principle reigns sovereign and governs in it despotically.

Freud's views of the pleasure-principle governing despotically the mental processes in the unconscious which included its inherited portion and above all the instincts, created indeed an ambiguous and obscure relationship of the "affects" to that system. If as Freud maintained in 1915, that to speak of "unconscious affects" is out of the question, one wonders how the pleasure-principle and its related feelings could operate in the unconscious at the time when no differentiation had as yet been established between the unconscious and the conscious, as in the case of the instinctual activities, and as in the case of Freud's "primal repression" occurring at a time when no "anxiety" could have been felt by a *non-existing ego.*

It is true that Freud had circumvented that difficulty by speaking of the "affects" as being present in the unconscious, only as a *potential disposition*, an obscure concept, and by describing what becomes conscious in the shape of pleasure or unpleasure as an *undetermined quantitative and qualitative element in the mind, which behaves like a repressed impulse*, another obscure concept. But Freud does not seem to have taken into consideration the fact that for an "undetermined qualitative element" to be registered, it needed at first the operation of the conscious ideational representation of any given somatic stimulus and capable also of acquiring a given affective quality, and that such an ideational representation is, as I have repeatedly argued, the product of a "psychic function" operating at a conscious level from its very onset. Such a qualitative element could not have been therefore related to some undetermined element in the mind operating as a repressed impulse or as a simple potential disposition.

Had Freud avoided the inclusion in his unconscious, of that inherited portion, he might have directed more of his attention to the relationship existing only between the acquired unconscious and the system conscious. By so doing, Freud might have reached the conclusion that the unconscious could have represented no more than the expression of various degrees of functional differentiations in the operation of a unique conscious system, some of the activities of which operated at a conscious level, while others operated at a "subordinate conscious level." I will develop this important concept in the following chapter.

Had Freud done that, he could still have remained faithful to his views that:

Our mental topography has for the present nothing to do with anatomy; it is concerned not with anatomical location but with regions in the mental apparatus, irrespective of their possible situation in the body.[32] [However the same cannot be said of his other statement that:] The transition from one system to another is not effected through the making of a new record, but through a change in its state, *an alteration in its cathexis*. The functional hypothesis has here *routed* the topographical.[33] [italics mine]

Concerning that alleged route, it would seem to me that though relying only on the alteration of the cathectic energy responsible for the activation of the various ideational presentations, Freud had not routed his original topographical approach to the functioning of our psychic apparatus. Indeed no matter how important he had considered the shift of the psychic energy, the situation ultimately ended in the displacement of a given ideational representation, at different levels of its functioning. Those various level of functioning do not seem to me to be different from Freud's original topographical designation of the operation of the ideational contents at the Cs., Pcs., and unconscious levels. All that Freud now accomplished by emphasizing the function of the displaceable psychic energy, was to emphasize again his basic views of that "psychic energy" operating at various levels of strength, but did not actually change the topographical result of its operation.

Irrespective of who or what was responsible for the displacement of the ideas, be it a "psychic energy" as Freud maintained, or the ideas themselves operating under their own energic somatic power as I maintain, *the fact remains that such a displacement of the ideas resulted in their allocation to different functional levels from which they operate*, be it at a conscious, preconscious, or unconscious level. I wonder if one could easily conclude as Freud did, that the topographical concept of the functioning of our mental apparatus, had actually been routed.

Chapter IV

My Own Alternative to Freud's Concept of the Unconscious

Can we improve on Freud's concept of the unconscious made partly by an inherited portion and partly by what is designated in general as its acquired portion? Can we also avoid the ambiguities of Freud's original distinction of three separate level of registration of a given mental perception in the three separate conscious, preconscious, and unconscious systems, a topographical concept, which he subsequently replaced by his dynamic concept of a displaceable mental energy capable of simply altering with its charge, the conscious, preconscious, or unconscious nature of any mental formation? My answer would be in the affirmative.

Having already presented in part One, chapter I, of this trilogy, my assumption on the origin of mental life by means of a newly developed "Psychic function," and having furthermore assumed that mental life from its very onset is a conscious life, I will now anticipate in a capsule form my own alternative to Freud's concept of his entire unconscious, with the exception of its inherited portion, to which I do not subscribe with my own concept of what I propose to call "the Subordinate conscious."

In support of my proposed alternative of a "subordinate conscious" substratum for Freud's unconscious, I will present in this chapter data from comparative anatomy, and data from experimental material. For the moment it will suffice for me to repeat again that contrary to Freud's views that mental life operates at first at an unconscious level, I consider mental life as operating from its very onset, at a "conscious level" out of which the "subordinate conscious" (Freud's acquired unconscious) subsequently develops.

In my view, as I have elaborated in chapter I of part One of this trilogy, once the new "psychic function," born of the synthesis and integration of the various somatic functions already operating in our intrauterine organization, has fulfilled its task of translating into "ideational representations" the various somatic stimuli related to those somatic functions, these "ideational representations" constitute *the first conscious system* operating in our incipient "psychic apparatus." As new individual conscious ideational representations or groups of them, in terms of ideational formations, develop, and as some of them acquire an affective quality, thus becoming "affective formations," the earlier ideational formations become incorporated, or better absorbed in this case, by the new incoming perceptions and related ideational representations of which they now become formative elements. In that sense, they evidently contribute also to the functional expansion of the very original conscious system.

In my view, whatever has been once conscious, in terms of ideas or of "affective formations" (see part I of this triolgy, on the meaning of "affective formations") never disappears completely, but becomes a building block for the more advanced conscious formations. In that capacity all past conscious formations absorbed into the more advanced conscious ones, occupy in that conscious system a "subordinate position" in relation to the newly acquired ones, which latter constitutes at the time of their acquistion *"the Dominant conscious system."*

In my view, it would also follow that these subordinate formations could never lose completely their genetic and associative relationship with the now "dominant conscious" of which they have become formative elements. That relationship I assume to be in terms of a functional one entered between the earlier ideational formations and related affective qualities, and the new dominant conscious elements. In my opinion that relationship could be expressed in terms of displacements, associations, replacements, and condensations of the old ideational representations themselves which so to speak become absorbed by the new dominant conscious, to which development they now contribute as formative elements. These absorbed elements which now occupy in the new dominant conscious a subordinate position I call the "Subordinate Conscious."

In that subordinate position, these absorbed elements retain their attribute of building blocks of the conscious system as a whole, and do not become a part of a different system. As subordinate conscious elements, they retain their genetic ties with the dominant conscious, some of which ties are stronger than others, and it is in

described in the *Coelenterates* (Hydra Marina), that is from its neural reticulum and interspersed never-cells. However, while in the latter, the existing nerve-cells are sparse and diffusely spread within the enveloping neural reticulum, in the starfish there begins to develop *a first grouping of nerve-cells into a single conglomerate, a first ganglion* located in the central and dorsal portion of the animal's body. That grouping of nerve-cells represents evidently the precursor of the chain of ganglia which makes its first appearance in the more evolute animal species. In the starfish, that single dorsal ganglion is sufficient for the coordination of the activities of the trunk and of the various tentacles of the animal. Its appearance however does not indicate that the nervous reticulum and related interspersed nerve-cells of the lower *Coelenterates* have disappeared or ceased to operate in this ganglion. It may only mean that structurally speaking, a portion of the old neural elements, cells and reticulum, have been incorporated in that central ganglion, to which they may now delegate their original function.

In that position, the incorporated elements in the ganglion may be presumed to exercise their original function, in a subordinate capacity to the entire function of the ganglion. At the same time those incorporated elements could now in their structural capacity be considered as formative blocks of the ganglionic structure itself.

Some portions of the neural and cellular reticular formations of the lower animal scale, must also be presumed to be still operating in some areas of the animal's body, outside the dorsal ganglion itself. Thus a more complex neural structure comes into being, in connection with the higher demands of that Phylum, for the regulation of the functions between body and tentacles. Yet under certain circumstances the functional activities of the tentacles could be exercised independently from the central regulating function of the ganglion, relying for that independence, upon the older neuro-reticular elements which have not as yet been incorporated in the ganglion, and which may be still operating independently in certain localities.

In the phylum "Annellides," of which the *"Platelminthes"* are a good representative, the global activity of the "Flatworm" for instance, depends from a thin chain of small ganglia which are individually circumscribed and incapsulated. These ganglia form a thin chain of small structures located on each side, along the medial line of the elongated animal, each ganglion connected with each other from side to side and also with those located above and below them.

The upward connection extends up to the cephalic end of the animal, where for the first time there appears two special ganglia, one on each side of the middle line. In certain specimens of the "Annellides," the two cephalic ganglia are fused into a single medial one.

In the "Annellides," in the course of their structural phylogenetic development, the new chain of the lateral ganglia has incorporated in it some portion of the original neuro-reticular system of the lower group of the *Ecchinoderms*, while the one or two cephalic ganglia have incorporated the single dorsal ganglion of the previous species. The new lateral chain of ganglia and the new cephalic ganglion or ganglia, have therefore established structural and functional connections with whatever portions of the older neural structures have been incorporated in them. It follows that from the functional standpoint the activities of the flatworm are governed not only by the more recently developed chain of lateral or cephalic ganglia, but also by whatever portion of the older neuro-reticular structures that has been incorporated in them. Last but not least however, the activities of the *Plathelminthes* are also governed in part by whatever portion of the old neuro-reticular structures that has not been incorporated in the newly developed neural ganglionic structures.

It goes without saying that from the structural standpoint the older structures may be considered as subordinate structures operating *as formative blocks* of the new structures, while from the functional standpoint the function of the old elements may be considered as a subordinate function to the newly acquired function, of which they represent formative functional elements. These assumptions seem to be supported by experimental data: Following a surgical transverse division of a *Planaria Dorotocephalica* in such a manner as to separate the cephalic portion of the animal from its caudal portion, the cephalic portion retains the cephalic ganglia, while the caudal portion retains only the chain of the lateral ganglia. Both portions retain however the formative structural neural elements which had been incorporated in them. Both segments of the separated animal were now found capable of regeneration, to the point that the cephalic portion regenerated a complete caudal portion, while the caudal portion regenerated a cephalic portion, leading in both instances to the reconstruction of a complete new worm.

Leaving aside for the moment the all important considerations of a biochemical nature which seem to preside over the embryonic development and the process of regeneration in lower animals, and which have made the subject of special studies by J. Brachet,[3] M.

C. Niu[4] and others I will limit myself to note that in the course of the regeneration of the cephalic portion of the *Planaria*, its caudal portion which includes its lateral chain of ganglia, must have contributed to the regeneration not only of the cephalic ganglion or ganglia themselves, but also to the regeneration of all the subordinate neural elements which had been originally incorporated in them, and to which development they had contributed in terms of formative structures.

By the same token, the cephalic portion of the animal separated from its caudal portion, must have retained in it those neural structures as well as those functional attributes which it had previously incorporated, and which allows now that cephalic portion to govern the neural structural and functional reconstruction of its caudal portion.

In the phylum "Mollusca" (snails, polyps, oysters, etc.,) the nervous system is composed of numerous ganglia variously distributed and among which the best developed are the cephalic and the podalic. It is in this phylum that the visceral parietal and pleural ganglia appear for the first time. In the phylum "Arthropoda" which includes the bees, the ants, the flies, the wasps etc. . . . the nervous system becomes more specialized and is represented by two very dominant ganglia, the cephalic designated supra-esophagus destined to receive stimuli from all the sensory organs of the head, eyes, antennaes, mouth etc. . . . and the infra-esophagus ganglion connected with the supra-esophagus ganglion by numerous fibers, and itself destined to the activities of the antennae, of the jaw and of the mouth. Both these cephalic ganglia are connected with the lower bilaterally located thoracic ganglia destined to the sensory and motor innervation of the limbs and of the wings if the latter are present. The thoracic ganglia are in turn connected with the bilateral abdominal ganglia from where the nerves of the abdominal walls and for the stingers originate. In the higher species of Arthropods, the ganglia of the lateral chain constitute a single chain occupying the middle line of the animal's body. In all this phylum, the same principle of the structural and functional development of the nervous system is here operative, that is the one which governs the incorporation of older neural structures into the new ones, and that of the taking up of the lesser neural functions by the more complex newer ones.

Passing over the anatomical data related to the development of the nervous system in the "Chordates," I will say only a few words concerning that development in *the lower vertebrates*, and specifically of the phylum pescis (fish). In the *Amphioxus* as well as in the *Petromyzon Marinus*, for instance, the nervous system has already reached an outstanding development. In them we not only meet with what in the lower animals was represented by the cephalic ganglia, but with a larger representation of them in the form of a common trunk in which we can already distinguish some diencephalic, mesencephalic, and bulbar structures which in still higher forms constitute the brain-stem. As a representative of the cortical structures, there appears for the first time a circumscribed formation at the rostral end of the brain stem, the so-called olfactory lobes. From this point on, the phylogenetic development of the nervous system consists in the gradual appearance and development of more pronounced cortical structures which assume greater extent as we progress upwards to the reptiles, the amphibia, the birds, and the mammals, *structures which incorporate in part and in part surround the older phylogenetic structures*. The gross appearance of the human brain is too well known to justify even its summary description.

In all the stages of the phylogenetic development of the nervous system, the older neural structures may still be present here and there in their original location, in the midst of the newer ones, and in which position they seem to retain their former structural and functional attributes, as formative elements of the structure and function of the more advanced neural formations and organization. However, under certain circumstances, when for instance, the new structures are so to speak functionally impaired, these former structures can again assert their independent functional activity.

In humans, we find in their nervous system remnants of earlier structures functioning at their earlier level of activity. I am referring to the presence in it of the characteristic *perivascular network of neural fibers* which is reminiscent of the neural reticulum which surrounds the entire body of the *Coelenterates*; the presence of *intramural neural plexi* in the walls of the small intestine reminiscent of that same earlier reticulum of nerve fibers; and the presence of autonomic neural ganglia in the cardio-muscular system, reminiscent of the very early central dorsal ganglion of the *Ecchinoderms*. Even the location of the central reticular formation in humans all along the central portion of the brain-stem, surrounded by all the new nervous structures, seems to indicate that in the course of phylogenesis the old original reticular structures prominent in the *Coelenterates* may have been surrounded and incorporated by the newly developed thalamic structures. Along these lines I have already referred to the fact that in the brain cortex elements of the central reticular formation have been incorporated in it, and are still capable of exercising in that position the same functions of the central reticular formation, which operates outside the brain cortex itself.

A typical example of the development of the human brain along the lines of incorporation of older neural structures within newer ones, is the limbic lobe of Broca, a further development of the olfactory lobe of lower animals, and which now surrounds the corpus callosum, losing itself rostrally in the mesial surface of the frontal lobe, and caudally in the lower region of the hippocampus. A part of that limbic lobe was originally designated "rhinencephalon" by Turner, and allegedly governed the mechanism of olfaction. Recently it was designated "limbic system" or "visceral brain" by McLean who included in it an intricate neural system incorporated in or surrounded by both neo-cortical and paleo-cortical structures. The latter such as the hippocampus, is in turn surrounded by the neo-cortical portions of the temporal lobes.

The phylogenetic principle of the structural and functional development of the nervous system by means of the incorporation of older structures and related functions into new ones, I would like to call *the principle of "intussusception,"* from the Latin "intus" = inside, and "suscipere" = taking up. Intussusception would thus designate the process of incorporation of less developed structures and functions into newer and higher structures and functions.

In my view, my concept of "intussusception" comes near to Ariens Kappers concept of "neurobiotaxis." In this author's view, "hodogenesis," from the Greek, hodos = path + development, is governed by the law of "neurobiotaxis," according to which a developing axis-cylinder has a tendency to establish connection with a neural center already in operation. Irrespective of who first attracts who, the end result would seem to be that at a certain moment, older and new structures come together, the new ones incorporating the older ones.

This process of "intussusception," I would like to differentiate from the concept of pure and simple *"stratification" or "structuration"* as advocated by Hughlings Jackson and more recently by Henry Ey,[5] which I consider less integrative, inasmuch as they simply imply *a hierarchical superimposition* of structures and functions at various stages of their development. In the process of "Intussusception," the original formative elements do not become so to speak stratified, deposited in other words into a lower layer upon which new structural and functional layers become superimposed. In the process of "intussusception" the various formative elements in my view, become incorporated with each other, or at least they become surrounded by the newer ones, so as to establish among them a single structural and functional unit. In that sense, the simpler and older structures and functions become an integral part of the new higher structures and functions which they have thus contributed to create.

Because structural ontogenesis repeats phylogenesis, one expects to find in the well developed and well functioning nervous system in humans, some remnants of individual structural and functional elements incorporated into the newer structural and functional formations, reminiscent of the earliest stages of the structural and functional development of that system. I have illustrated this point in the previous chapter II of this part Three of the trilogy.

SECTION B

While in connection with the structural development of the nervous system, the principle of "intussusception," in terms of incorporation of old neural structures and related functions into the newer ones in the course of phylogenesis, may be considered a starting point for its application, not the same can be said concerning its application to the development of our psychic apparatus, the origin of which can only be conjectured. It is indeed the problem of the origin of our psychic functioning that should concern us before considering the application to the development of our mental processes of that same principle of "intussusception." That principle may evidently play its role, but only after the "psychic function" has made its appearance in the course of our ontogenetic development.

To clarify my views on this subject, I must go back to the assumption which I have developed in chapter I of part One of this trilogy, that is, the assumption that at a certain moment of our intrauterine somatic and biological organization, there suddenly develops a new function, the "psychic function," which is born out of the integration and synthesis of the various somatic functions which are already operating at that certain moment of our somatic and biological organization. The main task of this new "Psychic function" is that of translating the various somatic stimuli which originate

282

from those somatic functions into some sort of primordial ideational representations. It is in that context that I have also assumed *that mental life is from its very onset a conscious one*, contrary to Freud's position that at their onset mental processes are unconscious.

To clarify my assumption of the conscious nature of our mental processes at their onset, I must recall Freud's views on the nature of what he had considered to be the deepest inherited unconscious layer of our mental apparatus and which he called the "instincts." In his words: "The forces which we assume to exist behind the tensions caused by the needs of the Id are called instincts. *They represent the somatic demands upon mental life*."[6] [italics mine] Leaving aside for the moment the nature of those forces which Freud ultimately assumed to be, on the one hand the energy of the sexual instincts which he also equated with the energy of the instinct of life, and on the other hand the destructive forces which he related to the instinct of death, the fact remains that by the above statement, Freud had implied that a mental life must already have been in operation *at the time when those instinctual forces made their demands upon it*.

He, in fact, in his posthumous publication *An Outline of Psychoanalysis* tried but unconvincingly to establish the fact that at the onset of life, there was an uninterrupted line of operating somatic processes and that: "*It seemed natural to lay stress in psychology upon these somatic processes, and to see in them the true essence of what is mental*."[7] [italics mine] It seems therefore that what was mental must have already been operating at the same time, in order to allow the somatic processes to make demands upon it.

But Freud never indulged even in a speculative manner, upon how and in what way those somatic processes represented at the same time the essence of what is mental. I, on the other hand have assumed that it was through the synthesis and integration of the already operating somatic functions, *that a new psychic function developed*, and attributed to that new function the first task of translating the various somatic stimuli related to the activity of those somatic functions, into some sort of mental representation in terms of ideational formations.

I have further argued that Freud's views that those somatic processes constituted the true essence of what is mental, did not authorize him however to consider the early mental processes as being unconscious at their first stage of operation. His considering them as such, was in my view a dogmatic philosophical assertion derived from Lipps's philosophy that at their very onset, mental processes are unconscious. There is much to say for the opposite view.

I, in fact, assume *that mental life is from its very onset a conscious life* inasmuch as the *new "psychic function"* which in my view
originates from the synthesis and integration of the already operating somatic functions resolves itself in a conscious mental function
which at its onset expresses itself in terms *of a first awareness on
the fetus's part, of its own existence.* That the operation of this new
"psychic function" involves consciousness does not seem to me any
different from what Freud had originally maintained when he first
stated in 1895[8] that perceptions of stimuli *eo-ipso* (by their own nature) involve consciousness. The main difference between the two
situations is that at the time of Freud's original statement, he had
failed to take into consideration the point that in order for a perception to involve *eo-ipso* consciousness, there must have been already
at work a "psychic function" capable of translating those somatic
stimuli into conscious ideational formations.

I may add at this point that Freud's assumption that the forces
operating behind the tensions of the somatic needs and related demands upon mental life, should be considered in terms of a simple
operating energy, the psychic energy, without taking first into consideration the development of the ideational representations of these
somatic stimuli at the hands of a newly developed "psychic function," constitutes a serious gap in Freud's reasoning. This is another
instance of Freud's resting his entire psychological construction upon
the mobility an operation of an alleged "psychic energy." He thus
neglected and even refuted the mobility and displacements of the
ideational formations themselves, the activities of which need not
have depended upon the existence of a mobile "psychic energy."

I, on the other hand, have relied on my own assumption that it
was the ideas and their related affective qualities which were themselves endowed with an energic attribute, allowing them to undergo
displacement. That energy was not of a psychic nature, but of the
same somatic nature of the energy that activates the "psychic function" which was born out of the synthesis and integration of the various somatic functions which themselves were activated by a somatic
energy (the organismic energy as I called it) which had presided
over the development of that new "psychic function."

Evidently, my assumption of a newly developed "Psychic function" born of the synthesis and integration of the various somatic
functions, a function which operates at a conscious level, *entails an
obscure leap from the Soma to the Psyche.* But that leap does not differ from a similar obscure leap taken by Freud in connection with
the first appearance of the "instinct of life." I have referred to this

fact in chapter I of part One of this trilogy in the following terms: Evidently my assumption of the development of a new "psychic function" out of the integration and synthesis of the various somatic and biological functions already operating in a constituted organism in the course of the intrauterine life in humans, is a conjectural one which constitutes a leap from the soma to the psyche and which is beyond any means of verification. But so were the similar assumptions introduced by Freud in connection with the development of consciousness and of the development of the "instinct of life" which latter transforms the inanimate matter into a living organic matter. In Freud's words:

> At one time or another *by some operation of forces which still baffles conjectures, the properties of Life awakened in the lifeless matter. Perhaps the process was a prototype resembling that other one which later, in a certain stratum of living matter gave rise to Consciousness.*[9] [italics mine]

By the same token I have conjectured that by some operation which baffles conjectures, a new "psychic function" develops out of the integration and synthesis of the various somatic functions already operating at a certain moment of our ontogenetic intrauterine somatic organization. My conjecture, contrary to the barren conjecture of Freud, has at least the advantage of having offered on this subject the support of the working hypothesis of a new "psychic function" responsible for the generation of all ideational representations.

Do unicellular animals enjoy a mental life? Let me state here that I consider the observable activities of a unicellular animal, the product not only of its somatic and biological endowment, but also of its mental functioning. That mental functioning had even been related according to some investigators, to no more than the molecular and biological activities of its simple proptoplasma. G. E. Coghill[10] for instance stated that: "The living matter once it has become organized, possesses structural and functional as well as psychic qualities, be the animal represented by *a unicellular animal*, or by an animal possessing a highly developed brain."

In reference to a constituted organism, Wheeler,[11] in his *Essays on Biological Philosophy* (1939) stated also that:

> An organism is represented by a system of cells organized in one unit, and capable of securing from its environment, the

necessary substances capable to protect the integrity of its organized system and to reproduce its own species.

By substituting in Wheeler's definition the word "unit" with the word "cell," his definition could apply perfectly well to the unicellular animal.

H. Bergson,[12] referring also to the activity of a living protoplasma, stated that:

> Neither mobility nor choice, nor consciousness require as a necessary condition the presence of a nervous system which canalizes in a certain direction and leads to a higher degree of intensity, the vague rudimental activity which lies diffusely within the mass of organized substance.

And E. W. Sinnot[13] commenting on the process of development stated that:

> It is difficult to establish a clear cut difference between the process of development in embriology and those of physiology from the psychological processes designated as behavior. All three processes represent manifestations of *a regulating activity of the protoplasma.*

Indeed, in the *Protozoa*, we meet with all the functional expressions of life, though that organism is operating within the boundaries of a single cellular limiting membrane. In that single cell, we find the structural and biological elements which constitute its nucleus, its protoplasma, its nucleic acids, and its nutritional and water vacuoles. In that unicellular animal, we observe its functional ability to provide for itself the nutritional elements necessary for its survival. In it we also observe its functional ability to absorb oxygen, to eliminate carbon dioxide, and the ability to reproduce its own species. We also observe its ability to move adequately by the means of pseudopodia or cilia, in order to proceed forward or to retreat from unfavorable or dangerous surroundings, and finally the ability to protect itself by means of incapsulation and incrustation against inclement weather. Last but not least, according to L. Day and M. Bentley[14] and L. K. Losina-Lozinski,[15] also a certain ability to learn and retain.

In connection with the vital activities of the unicellular animal, I will now refer briefly to the problem of "tropisms" where two different schools of thought prevail, that of J. Loeb[16] for whom all instinctual activities of the lower animals do not represent the result of mental processes, but of simply a collection of "tropisms" (phototropisms, chemo-tropisms, and thermo-tropisms) and the school of M. Rose[17] who favors the opinion that even admitting that tropisms may exercise a certain function in the activities of the animals, to reduce the whole essence of the instincts and of the innate functions of the lower animals to a series of more or less complex tropisms, would mean pushing such an exaggeration to the limit of the absurd.

A compromise position has been taken by Viaud[18] who divided the tropisms into "positive tropisms" and "negative tropisms." By *negative tropisms* or *pseudo-tropisms*, Viaud G. referred to the negative activities of an animal, already under the influence of a "positive tropism," to withdraw from that influence, and spontaneously retreat towards a lesser stimulating environment, to which it can adjust itself. A "negative tropism" according to Viaud implies *a psycho-physiological function* of which the procedural elements of adaptation constitutes the clearest expression.

How can we indeed conceive the sum total of the activities of even a unicellular animal, without considering that somehow in this animal there must exist a functional operating state of which the animal is aware of. At this level "consciousness," "awareness" or "vigilance" are identical states. To differentiate at this point as Kleitman[19] suggested, a state of "wakefulness of necessity" from a "state of wakefulness of choice" or to differentiate as suggested by Th. Alajouanine[20] between a "state of alertness" and a "state of consciousness proper would certainly be quite difficult. At the same time to deny to the many activities of the unicellular animal a quality of consciousness, that is of choice, inherent to the development of a new "psychic function" derived from the integration of various somatic functions, would be tantamount to subscribe to some other not-as-yet-established spiritual and animistic concept of the origin of mental life.

Indeed, if we subscribe instead to the view that the total activities of a fully organized unicellular animal include also the manifestation of a "psychic function" derived *ontogenetically* from its structure and biology, we could also dispense with the concept of an "inherited unconscious mental life" as advocated by Freud. In my opinion, as I have repeatedly stated, the moment that the various somatic functions of an animal or human, have become synthesized and integrated, mental life appears automatically in the form of a new "psychic function," the task of which is to translate into some sort of conscious primordial ideational representations, all stimuli related to the functioning of its various somatic activities.

As Dethier[21] also justly remarked:

> If we subscribe to the idea of a lineal evolution of behavior,
> there is no reason for failing to search for adumbration of
> higher behavior in animals. If on the other hand we believe in
> a behavioral dichotomy, in the idea that the invertebrates dif-
> fer, it behooves us to put that belief to test.[22]

If we were to accept the operation of conscious mental processes in the unicellular animal, we could evidently accept the development of more complex conscious mental processes in the higher forms of animal life, as we gradually proceed from the *Protozoa*, to the *Metazoa*, the *Ecchynoderms*, the *Annellides*, the *Mollusca*, the fish, the reptiles, the amphibia, the birds, and the mammals.

How can we conceptualize that gradual development? By applying to it the same principle of "intussusception" which I have applied to the progressive development of the structural nervous system in the ascending zoological scale. By virtue of that principle, the lower mental processes *become gradually absorbed by the higher mental ones*. The word absorbed fits better in the case of mental processes, than the word "incorporated" which I feel applies better to the neural structures.

Indeed, as we proceed upward in the phylogenetic zoological scale, the conscious mental processes of the lower step of the ladder become absorbed into the newer and more complex ones of the higher species. As it was the case for the old neural structures which having been incorporated by the new structures became formative parts of the latter, the old mental processes which are absorbed by the newer and more complex ones, become formative blocks of the latter. In that sense the function of these formative blocks becomes a "subordinate function" to the newer conscious functions which constitute the dominant portion of the conscious system. It is in that sense that these formative elements of the dominant conscious, represent what I have called the "Subordinate conscious." In their capacity of "formative blocks," these subordinate conscious elements are evidently in a position to influence the activities of the Dominant conscious in which they have been absorbed and with which they retain from now on some permanent genetic and functional connections.

The main difference between the "intussusception" related to the structural development of the nervous system and that related to the development of the psychic apparatus, is that while in the phylogenetic development of structures I assume the operation of processes governed by inherited genetic laws, in the development of the psychic apparatus no genetic laws seem to be operative. The *psychic development is in my view an automatic one related only to the ontogenetic somatic development of an animal's organism* and yet not necessitating on its own, of the intercession of any genetic law that we know. The first appearance of a "psychic development" in the terms of a *"new Psychic function"* is in fact, I repeat, the product of the integration and synthesis of the various somatic functions already operating in a constituted organism. It has nothing to do directly with genetic laws that govern the structural and biological development of an animal's organism. It simply appears at a certain moment of our somatic and biological organization in the course of our intrauterine life. The appearance of that new "Psychic function" which represents the leap from the soma to the psyche, defies all conjectures.

From that elusive beginning, the more complex ontogenesis becomes in the animal's ascending phylogenetic scale, the more complex the development of that "psychic function" becomes. But its first appearance is not related to the position occupied by any animal in the zoological scale and is always the same in all species of animals. However, as we proceed higher in the zoological scale, the more complex the ontogenetic structural and biological development of the animal species becomes, the more complex the expression of that new "psychic function" becomes in terms of its continuous translation of more and more somatic stimuli into ideational representations.

With increasing number of ideational representations generated by the ever more complex "psychic function" in the course of the ever more advanced ontogenetic development in each ascending species of animals, it would follow that the further development of that "Psychic function" becomes more and more related directly to that ontogenetic development which can reach only a certain maximal degree in each species. It is in that context that we must now consider the development of various levels of the conscious ideational representations. Some of the old ones which I have considered as formative stages of the newer and more complex conscious formations (in which they assume a subordinate position) must gradually lose more and more of their original independence and become entirely absorbed by the new conscious formations. By virtue of this process which is intended also to leave room so to speak, to the new ideational support to the dominant conscious, the old ideational formations assume a more and more subordinate position in the field of consciousness, in proportion to the degree of their absorption by the new conscious presentations.

In what way do the old ideational conscious representations become a formative portion of the new ones in the sense that they become absorbed by the latter? We may assume that this process of absorption takes place by the means of association of conscious ideas, an operation which entails not only displacement, but also condensation of ideas. *It is this operation that epitomizes my concept of what I call "the absorption" of older ideational conscious formations by the new ones.* Association, displacement, and condensation of ideas may evidently occur outside our own awareness, but this fact does not mean that in order for the ideas to undergo such changes, they need to become displaced so to speak into an entirely different system: the unconscious system.

It is because of that displacement, association, and condensation, of conscious ideas which *epitomize* my concept of "absorption," that I have applied the same principle of "intussusception" which I have already applied to the structural development of the nervous system, to the gradual development of our psychic apparatus. Indeed the process of "Absorption" of older ideational formations by the newer ones, parallels the process of incorporation of older structural neural elements into the newer ones.

Once the old conscious ideational elements have been absorbed in the new "dominant conscious" they occupy in the latter a subordinate position, in which position these subordinate elements and related affective qualities become overshadowed in their function by the function of the new Dominant conscious. In that "subordinate position," those elements may to a certain extent continue to exercise some influence over the operation of the dominant conscious. It follows that even though that influence is exercised outside our own awareness, this fact does not justify our considering that influence as taking place in the unconscious viewed as an entirely different system.

In connection with the fact that a portion of the conscious system, its subordinate portion, can operate outside our own awareness, let us not forget that Freud himself held that precise view when he had established the existence of two types of *latent ideas*, one type of which he considered as belonging to the unconscious system, while the other type (the preconscious ideas) which operate also *outside the field of our own awareness*, he considered it as belonging to the system Cs., and later even identified that type of latent ideas with the system Cs.

It is along a similar line that I have developed my concept of a "subordinate conscious," as constituting an integral portion of the conscious system (Cs.) with which it retains a permanent functional relationship, which however may vary in degrees. That relationship is effected outside our own awareness, and in that sense it constitutes an unconscious operation, though only from a descriptive and not systematic standpoint. And this descriptive approach applies to all subordinate processes operating in the whole of the Cs. system irrespective of the strength and extent of the ties which these subordinate conscious formations, maintain and retain with its dominant portion.

It is on this point that my concept of what is descriptively unconscious differs from Freud's concept of the "unconscious" as a system. In my opinion the designation of "Subordinate conscious," the operation of which takes place outside our own awareness, applies *to all latent* ideational processes which operate in the Cs. system. It makes no difference in my opinion, if those processes became subordinate conscious, by virtue of their representing original formative blocks of a developing dominant conscious, or if they became subordinate because these formative blocks had been relegated involuntarily into that position by "amnesia," or because willfully relegated in that subordinate position by the defensive process of repression.

In that position, these "subordinate formations" made of ideational formations and related qualities, which once had been conscious and now relegated in a subordinate capacity, continue to maintain, as I have already stated, various degrees of connecting ties to the *present* dominant conscious born itself originally from their contribution, and as such never lost their right to consider themselves as belonging to the system Cs. *I therefore do not subscribe to Freud's views* that any portion of them, such as that portion which has been repressed, has relinquished its right to be labeled as "latent conscious processes" and that they have become instead a part of an entirely new system, Freud's unconscious system.

In connection with my concept of the "subordinate conscious," as a system operating outside our own awareness, though belonging to the conscious system, it may be appropriate at this point to recall some of the facts related to the so-called "subliminal perceptions." There is no denying in my mind that mental processes could be divided into conscious processes of which we are naturally aware, and conscious processes, the operation of which we are not aware.

Both types originate in our various sense-organs of perceptions some of which are known to us, while some others may be vestigia of phylogenetically older ones, that have been incorporated within our present perceptual organs. Irrespective of the presence of such primordial instruments of receptions, there are indeed perceptual stimuli which may be rapidly registered in some fleeting conscious way, but without us being aware of this happening. And yet that registration should not be denied the quality of a conscious registration, which seems to fade away immediately from a first conscious position into that of a subordinate conscious position.

The registration of such perceptions which had been designated as "subliminal" had been discussed by Binet in 1896,[23] in the course of the following experiment: In a hysterical woman, he applied upon her neck which was one of her anesthesic areas, and therefore a supposedly non-reporting area, a round mental disk, having on its surface some embossed marks. Because of the anesthesia, the patient did not react to the pressure of the disk against her neck. Subsequently when the patient was asked to recall the properties of that disk, and draw them on a sheet of paper, she reproduced to the surprise of every one the outline of the disk and of some of its details.

During the same year, Urbanschitsch V.[24] reported the result of some of his experiments, in the course of which he subjected certain individuals to visual stimuli represented by various graphic illustrations. As the illustrations were presented, they were asked to describe them as they looked at them. After the illustrations were removed from their visual field, they were then asked to recall by memory the details of their earlier visual description. To everyone's surprise, the subjects succeeded in recalling not only the original details mentioned when the illustrations were in front of their eyes, but some new details which they had omitted at first. In recent years the study of these phenomena of "subliminal perceptions" has been pursued and early experimental results have already been reported by J. C. Miller,[25] and others.

In our daily life, we could indeed find instances of subliminal perceptions which contribute to the recollection of past conscious ones. Take the instance in which arriving in a new city, we wish to orient ourselves in finding again the location of a certain street which we had previously traveled. In that search when we retrace our steps, we first recall certain visual perceptions which will guide us in establishing the landmarks of one particular street. These will indicate to us whether to proceed north or south, east or west, from that perceived point. At times however at a certain intersection, we hesitate and become undecided as to which way to proceed. Then while we concentrate and look around, we all of a sudden perceive a store, a sign, or a poster, which we had not consciously noted when we first had traveled that street. Yet it is that perception registered only subliminally at first, that will indicate to us the final and proper direction to follow.

Now, if such unexpected perceptions of which originally we had not been aware, appear subsequently as a definite recollection, they evidently must have been registered, if only for a fleeting second, as conscious perceptions, the first time we studied that street, after which they must have become immediately relegated into a subordinate position into what I call the "subordinate conscious." These must have been the perceptions which in the course of our first attempt at orientation seemed less important in their utilitarian value for that purpose. But when needed in an emergency, when the other conscious perceptions fail us, so to speak, these perceptions become reactivated by a particular effort of "attention" called into action in our effort at recollecting, and which as such contribute as formative elements to the ultimate conscious reconstruction.

A possible support to my assumption that more elementary mental formations contribute to the development of more complex ones in my terms of "intussusception" may be found in the experimental work of Thompson and McConnell.[26] These investigators succeeded in conditioning a *planaria* while submerged in water in a through, which had inserted at each one of its two extremities, an electrode which allowed the passage in the water from one extremity to the other, of a weak electrical current. At the top of the trough, two electrical bulbs of 100 watts each were installed. Under normal circumstances, the worm navigated freely from one extremity to the other of the trough. In the experimental condition, the two electrical bulbs were suddenly lit for three seconds. After the two first seconds, an electrical current was discharged in the water. To this discharge, the worm reacted with a sudden lateral deviation of the head and a sudden contraction of its entire body. Following 150 to 200 repetitions of the same procedure, the worm became conditioned to the light stimulus, so that afterwards, following the simple lighting of the electrical bulbs, but not accompanied by the electrical discharge, the animal reacted immediately with the deviation of its head and the contraction of its body.

Having thus established the technique of the conditioning of a normal intact worm, McConnell and co-workers in 1959[27] used an animal already conditioned, in order to establish if and in what measure, the memory of the learned reaction persisted in the two portions of the worm which was subsequently divided in two. Their investigation established the fact that following the surgical transverse division of a "conditioned *planaria*" the regenerated animal which developed from the caudal portion of the separation, elicited a more rapid inclination to a new conditioning. The investigators reported in fact the very interesting observation that in contrast to the intact original animal that required the exposure to 150 to 200 light stimuli followed by electrical discharge, in order to become conditioned, the new animal which had regenerated from the caudal portion of the originally conditioned animal required now only 40 exposures to the light and related electric stimuli. One could well interpret such results by assuming that the caudal portion of the original conditioned animal, following its separation from its cephalic portion, must have retained, as the expression of a still functioning mental life in that caudal portion, many conscious primordial ideational elements in the form of "subordinate conscious elements," which may have been now absorbed by the new perceptions of the reconstructed cephalic portion and which may have been utilized by it in the course of the new conditioning experiment. The old "subordinate conscious elements" of the caudal portion may have acted as formative blocks of the new conscious perceptions experienced by the new cephalic portion, and thus facilitated a more rapid acquisition of a conditioned status by the reconstructed animal.

SECTION C

Up to the present I have discussed the constructive aspect of the "subordinate Conscious" in terms of ideational representations which by virtue of their having been absorbed into the higher conscious representations, participate as formative blocks to the development of the latter.

There is now another aspect of the evaluation of these subordinate formations which is the reverse of the process of "intussusception" which I have assumed to preside over the development of the conscious system. That reverse approach involves the shedding, the casting off on the part of the dominant conscious, by means of its operating arm, the ego, of some of its formative elements by relinquishing voluntarily or involuntarily most of its associative connections with some of its earlier ideational representations which thus become relegated to a state of "functional latency" for various periods of time. Even though these cast-off elements lose some of their connections with the dominant conscious, they still retain enough of them to allow them eventually to subsequently re-enter consciousness under certain procedures.

There seems to be two major ways by means of which the ego may cast off its associative connections with earlier ideational formations which have been a part of its conscious expression. One way is that at a certain moment of the ego's conscious activities, some of these earlier formative elements lose their utilitarian value, as a result of which the ego loses its incentive to maintain operative their function, and allows them through amnesia, to fade away so to speak, into a latent position by means of their discontinued usage, a process which takes place by default, with no active intervention on the part of the ego. These forgotten elements retain, however, the capacity of being recalled into consciousness whenever the ego senses again the usefulness of their function.

In that interval between their having faded away and forgotten and their being recalled by the ego, what has become of these representations? One can theorize that these elements have assumed a latent position in the conscious system, or theorize also that they have become what may be called in a descriptive sense memory-traces. However in view of the fact that they eventually can be recalled in consciousness, they need not have occupied in that interval a position in some different system, the unconscious, but should be considered still as subordinate elements of the conscious system in terms of its latent components.

Thus, in relation to the "subordinate conscious," we are faced with different processes. On the one hand we are dealing with earlier conscious formations which contribute in terms of formative elements, to the development of further advanced conscious formations by means of displacement, replacement, associations, and condensation of ideas, *which I have epitomized in the concept that they have been absorbed by the newer conscious formations*. It is in that context that I have considered these absorbed formations as constituting "the subordinate conscious" in its constructive expression.

On the other hand, we are dealing with ideational formations that originally contributed to the development of the dominant conscious and which subsequently the ego casts off. These can now be grouped into the group that has lost its immediate utilitarian value for the ego, and which the latter shed through involuntary amnesia, and the group which the ego repressed. The formations that have lost their immediate utilitarian value for the ego and thus cast off, occupy from then on a latent position in our psychic apparatue. That position may also be called *a passive latent subordinate conscious position*, because in that position these formations, though eventually available for use by the ego, remain inactive, though retaining their potential energic attribute for mobility.

In that position, they do not however lose their main feature of belonging to the conscious system (Cs.), considering that they are subject to a possible recall in consciousness, whenever the ego decides to apply for that recall the services of its special psychic function of attention, which it has at its disposal whenever it deems it necessary, by means of harking back to past memory-trace.

Another group that the ego casts off, if he so decides, is also made of ideas and of "affective formations" that is of ideas and attached affective qualities, that once operated as subordinate formative portions of the dominant conscious and which the ego may have now subjected to repression for one reason or another. By the intervention of repression, the ego not only rejects, at first deliberately, this group of formations because they are unacceptable to it but because also they are dangerous to its integrity. Not only the ego rejects these formations, but also prevents actively their return to consciousness by the means of its continuous resistance to that return. In that rejected situation, these formations also become "latent formations," which however, contrary to the forgotten presentations, are in *an active latent position*, inasmuch as they utilize their potential energic attribute in their struggle for their reentry in consciousness, opposed as they actively are, by the resistances of the ego. In that latent position, they too have not lost however all connections with the dominant conscious, inasmuch as they eventually can reenter consciousness, provided we can apply for that return the services of the special psychoanalytic technique. In that context I consider these rejected formations as still belonging to the conscious system, in terms of its "subordinate portion."

This whole group of latent ideas which I have divided into active and passive, constitute precisely what originally Freud had assumed the case to be, when he spoke of two types of "latent" ideas, the one which can reenter consciousness and the other that cannot. The only important difference is that initially Freud had considered both types as belonging to a different system, the unconscious. It was later that Freud made a distinction between the group of latent ideas that can eventually reenter consciousness, and which he called "preconscious," and the latent ideas that cannot, and which he called the "repressed." However he ultimately ended by considering the latent ideas capable of reentering consciousness, as belonging to the conscious system, and still later he identified them with the conscious system. As for the repressed ideas that could not reenter consciousness, Freud retained his view that they belonged to a different unconscious system.

Contrary to Freud's distinction between the latent formations, so that some of them belong to the conscious system and some others to the unconscious, I assume that all mental processes belong from their onset to the conscious system in which they never cease to operate though in the various terms of either formative elements of the dominant conscious, or later as latent subordinate conscious formations. In both those terms, these formations represent the activities of the subordinate portion of the conscious system.

Returning again to the subject of the "latent ideas," the only difference that could be assumed to exist between the two groups of latent ideas that have resulted from their being shed by the ego, is that of the procedure utilized for their reentry in consciousness. The group of latent ideas that can easily reenter consciousness depends for that operation from the utilization by the ego of its special psychic function of "attention" the efforts of which are sufficient for that purpose. The group of latent ideas which have been repressed by the ego, in order to reenter consciousness, must overcome the resistance on the part of the ego. It is for the purpose of reaching that goal that Freud introduced his special psychoanalytical method of free associations.

In Freud's view, that method is the only efficient way for the recall of the repressed material, inasmuch as that material had been pushed out of the conscious system and relegated into another system, the unconscious. It is in this connection that my approach to this latent portion of our psychic apparatus differs from that of Freud. While in my view, all latent ideas continue to belong to the conscious system, irrespective of their source, be it from forgotten or from repressed material, Freud instead considered the repressed material as having practically severed all connections with the conscious system, and entered into close relation only with the new unconscious system, a view which I do not share.

Unfortunately, in that unconscious system ultimately designated the id, Freud had included in addition to the repressed material all the formations which had been forgotten such as the discarded impressions of childhood and the fantasies of both neurotic and healthy individuals. To that content he added also that inherited portion which included the instincts, the pre-individual ego-nuclei, some archaic super-ego formations, some precipitates of pre-individual affective states, and even the elements of some primal repression which operated at a time when no differentiation had as yet occurred between the conscious and the unconscious. That made of the unconscious a caldron of formations, in which the elements of an alleged acquired portion mingled with the inherited elements that old philosophers considered only in terms of a universal metaphysical and even spiritual point of view.

What the unconscious was assumed to be by Freud, I propose to substitute with my own assumption of a "subordinate conscious" as an integral portion of the conscious system. Though the "subordinate conscious system" operates outside our awareness, I differentiate however that operation from that of an alleged different unconscious system. My concept of the unconscious in terms of a "subordinate conscious" implies a continuity of genetic and functional relationship with conscious system, the first and only functional system of our psychic apparatus, and from which the subordinate conscious derives. Evidently this type of chronological dependency had not been considered by Freud who subscribed to Lipps's views that all conscious processes represent a subsequent developmental stage, thus upholding an initial operating unconscious stage.

Evidently, however, in my view, the functional relationship of the "Subordinate conscious" to the Dominant conscious or conscious proper, varies according to the utilitarian value of those subordinate formations. That value is unquestionably at its maximum for those subordinate formations which, useful at one time, have become temporarily latent in a passive way, by virtue of the ego's amnesia. They however remain at hand so to speak, for their eventual reentry in consciousness, because of their having retained most of the associative connections with the dominant conscious. On the other hand the value of those formations which by virtue of repression are relegated in a latent subordinate position because of their objectionable or dangerous nature, may not only be at the lowest scale of associative connections with the dominant conscious, but may also become a hindrance to its normal functioning. This is the group of latent processes which I have qualified as "active" because they continuously struggle for their reentry in the Dominant conscious.

To conclude: In my view, there is one single operating mental system in our psychic apparatus and this is the conscious system. That system becomes established the moment the "new psychic function" develops out of the synthesis and integration of the various somatic functions already operating in the course of our ontogenetic intrauterine life. That "psychic function" is entrusted with the translation into some sort of ideational representations of the stimuli originating from those somatic functions. Those ideational representations are from their onset conscious and constitute the first functional expression of an incipient psychic apparatus. They automatically represent the dawn of the conscious system which at this point is the only system in operation and in that sense may be designated as the Dominant conscious, the first functional expression of which is that of an incipient operating protopathic ego.

As the somatic ontogenetic development of the intrauterine creature proceeds, all new somatic stimuli become translated into new ideational representations at the hands of that new "psychic function." These new ideational representations entering our psychic apparatus from both our internal organization, as well as from the ever developing environment, meet in that apparatus the older ideational representations and related affective qualities. Out of that encounter an association of the older ideational representations with the new ones, becomes established in terms of displacement, replacement, and condensation of ideas. In virtue of that operation, the older ideational representations become so to speak *absorbed* by the more complex newer ones, a process which in my mind *epitomizes the nature of that absorption.*

Because of the "absorption" of older representations into the newer ones, I have assumed that the older ones become the formative elements of the newer more complex ones. Because of their function of formative elements, I have also assumed that the older ideational formations occupy in the newer ones a "subordinate structural and functional position." At this point we are presented therefore with the existence (1) in the conscious system of two operating portions a) the Dominant conscious and b) the subordinate structures representing the formative elements of the Dominant conscious as well as the dominant elements that are subsequently relegated in a latent subordinate position. That second portion I have called "the Subordinate conscious." The elements of the latter, do not however constitute a different system, but only a portion of the conscious system which because of that organization, may now function at two different levels, that is, as part of the Dominant conscious and eventually as an independent "Subordinate portion."

That process of absorption of old ideational formations by the newer complex ones, goes on and on, as long as the ontogenetic development of both our somatic and psychic apparatuses continue to proceed onward. From the standpoint of the "psychic apparatus," there takes place a continuous synchronic gradual development of both the Dominant conscious and of its subordinate conscious portion.

How such an operation of *absorption* of the older ideational representations by the newer and more complex ones takes place, is evidently unknown to us and in that sense we may also assume that these operations occur outside our awareness, not differently however from the operations which govern the many various neurobiological activities which preside over our many metabolic and endocrine functions. But the fact that the process of absorption in terms of displacement, association, and condensation of ideas and "affective formations" takes place outside our awareness, does not justify our considering these subordinate formations, *as belonging to and operating within an entirely new system,* the Unconscious system, governed by special laws, and possessing special characteristics. Such characteristics had been unfortunately assigned to that system by philosophers and thinkers who viewed that system *not from a clinical standpoint, to which they never addressed themselves,* but from a metaphysical and spiritual point of view.

In my opinion, the Subordinate conscious either in its aspect of a formative structural portion of the Dominant conscious, or in that of latent mental processes cast off by the ego, constitute simply a part of the conscious system. No portion of that system has the roots in the Unconscious as Freud maintained when he first subscribed to Lipps's views that every conscious mental process has an unconscious preliminary stage. Furthermore in my opinion, a mental formation belonging to the Dominant conscious, may be subsequently cast off in a subordinate latent position, in which position however, it never loses its attribute of belonging to the conscious system, nor that of potential mobility and therefore need not be considered as having become a part of some entirely new system.

To summarize: Because of my concept of the "Subordinate conscious" as the sole representative of what Freud had considered "the Unconscious"; because the "Subordinate conscious" originates only from mental formations which once had been conscious, and which in their subsequent subordinate position contribute to the development of new conscious formations, thus making the "Subordinate conscious" a part of the conscious system; because the Conscious system through its operating arm, the ego, can subsequently cast off, i.e. shed and relegate into a "latent position" some of its formative

elements either by means of amnesia or by that of repression; because in my view the "Subordinate conscious" never loses completely
its genetic-associative connections with its dominant portion when it
refers to both the formations which have been forgotten or to those
which have been repressed; because contrary to Freud I do not subscribe to the concept of an inherited portion of the Unconscious; because of my position, contrary to that of Freud, that from their very
onset mental processes are conscious; because I see no reason to invoke a different set of laws governing the conscious system and its
subordinate portion as Freud did for his alleged Unconscious, and because I see no reason to assign different characteristics to the Dominant conscious system and to its "Subordinate portion" as Freud
did for only his alleged Unconscious; and because Freud applied to
that *repressed portion* of the unconscious, which he had considered
as an acquired portion, the same laws and characteristics which the
old philosophers had applied to their inherited Unconscious, which
they had conceived in transcendental and spiritual terms—I feel justified in having considered Freud's concept of the origin, structure,
and characteristics of the Unconscious (Ucs.) *as constituting one of
his major fallacies.*

Summary

This book is intended as a critique of Freud's "Three Major Fallacies," and as an introduction to my personal alternative to each one of them.

The first part of this book, which I consider of a particular value, deals with the "Fallacy of Freud's Libido Theory." In it I refer to Freud's fundamental concept that there exists in operation a special energy which he called "psychic energy." That energy, in his view, is a mobile and displaceable energy which may attach itself to a given idea, detach itself from it, and attach itself to some other idea which it then activates. In most of his writings up to 1923, when Freud introduced his concept of *desexualization*, he considered that energy as *a sexual energy*. In 1921, however, he equated the sexual energy in question with *the energy of the instinct of life*, and even with the energy of *the ego's instincts of self-preservation, which up to that time* he had considered as the antagonists of the sexual instinct, an antagonistic conflict which in his early thinking, was the pathogenic cause of the neuroses.

It is on the basis of the existence and operation of that psychic energy of "a sexual nature" that Freud built up his "Libido Theory," which in turn was based upon his distinction and operation of a sexual energy, *having a special chemical origin* and which he called "Libido." It differed from the nature of the energy that activated all of the Ego's other instincts of self-preservation. That sexual libido varied in production increase or decrease, distribution, and *displacement*, thus affording it various possibilities for explaining the psychosexual phenomena observed.

That sexual libido, which Freud originally considered as constituting a reservoir in the ego, could be put to the use of objects, thus becoming sexual object-libido. In his words:

> We can then perceive it concentrating upon objects, becoming

fixated upon them, or abandoning them, moving from one object to another, and from these situations directing the subject's sexual activity, which leads to the satisfaction, that is to the partial and temporary extinction of the Libido.[1]

Freud then added:

> We can follow the object-libido through still further visissitudes. When it is withdrawn from the object, *it is held in suspense in peculiar conditions of tension*, and is finally drawn back into the Ego, so that it becomes Ego-Libido once again.[2]

It was evident that his entire concept of a sexual mobile energy, later on equated with the energy of "the instinct of life" was made up of a mobile and displaceable "psychic energy" capable of activating objects and ideas, to be withdrawn from them, and to become attached to and activate other objects, or ideas or group of ideas.

Convinced as he was of *the mobility only of the psychic energy,* Freud *denied any mobility to any psychic structure*, that is to say to any idea or group of ideas and their related affective qualities. In his view, it was the libido alone, that special psychic energy which, because of its attributes of mobility and displacement, could detach itself from an object or from an idea and attach itself to some other idea, which it would then activate. *The psychic* structure, made up of ideas or ideas having already acquired a certain affective quality, sexual or not, in his view, *had no attribute at all of mobility, displacement or replacement. It was only the psychic energy* which possessed such attributes.

The position on Freud's part on this subject was clearly expressed in his latest edition of *The Interpretation of Dreams* first published in 1900 in Section F of his chapter VII. In that section, referring to the formation of new thoughts forcing their way into consciousness, Freud felt that he did not have in mind the forming of a second thought situated in a new place, and that the notion of forcing a way through consciousness must be kept carefully free from any idea of changing its locality. Rather than supposing that a mental group in one locality has been brought to an end, and replaced by a fresh one in another locality, Freud proposed to assume instead that some mental grouping has had a cathexis of energy attached to it or withdrawn from it. By so doing, the structure in question would come under the sway of a particular agency, or be withdrawn from it. What he was doing was therefore to replace a topographical way of representing things by a dynamic one. *"What we regard here as mobile is not the psychical structure itself, but its innervation."*[3] [italics mine]

It would seem as crystal clear that Freud denied to the *psychical structures* (ideas and related affective qualities) any attribute of mobility, displacement, and replacement. In his assumption, it was the mobility and displacement of the *psychic energy* that would result into the swaying into another agency, the unconscious for instance, of any idea or group of ideas and their related affective qualities that would not be allowed to remain in consciousness. I, on the contrary, refute that basic view of Freud and advance instead the assumption *that it is the psychic structure*, that is the idea or the group of ideas with their attached affective qualities, *that are endowed with the attribute of mobility, idsplacement, association, and replacement by other ideas* and their attached affective qualities, the latter forming with the idea an inseparable unit which I have called an "affective formation."

If I consider as movable and displaceable the psychic structures, that is, the ideas or group of ideas and related affective qualities, but not the psychic energy as advocated by Freud, the following question arises: What is the energy that activates such "psychic structures?" To answer that question, I must refer the reader to chapter I of part One of this trilogy, where I have assumed and discussed the development of a new function *"The Psychic Function,"* not to be confused with "psychic energy." That new "psychic function" develops automatically at a certain moment of our intra-uterine somatic organization. *Out of the functional integration and synthesis* of all the operating somatic functions at that moment, there develops *automatically that new "Psychic Function."*

Considering that in my view the energy which activated the various somatic functions is a chemico-physico-biological energy, I assumed as evident that it would be the same somatic energy which activated the synthesis and integration of those various somatic functions, out of which the new "psychic function" automatically develops. The main task entrusted to this new psychic function is the transformation of the various and numerous somatic stimuli, resulting from the activity of the various already operating somatic functions, *into some sort of "ideational representation"* of those somatic stimuli: that is, into some sort of idea.

The ideational representations (the ideas) of those somatic stimuli, which in final analysis constitute the fabric of our new burgeoning psychic apparatus, acquire an affective quality, first of all from the quality of the organ or function from which the somatic stimuli primarily originate. Subsequently, additional qualities are imparted to those ideas, as the result of *their association and combination* with ideas already born of the somatic stimuli, related to the activity of all other somatic functions, operating at the time of our initial intrauterine somatic and functional organization.

Once an idea or group of ideas have acquired their "affective quality," sexual or not, they constitute *a unity* which cannot become separated into the idea and its affective quality. That unit becomes *an inseparable unit* which I have called *"affective formations."* These represent the "psychic structures," the fabric of which our mental apparatus is formed. They represent the *mobile displaceable and replaceable elements* of that apparatus. For their mobility, displacement and replacement, they evidently need an activating energy. But that activating energy *need not be any new special psychic energy* that imparts a quality to the idea. It must be the same energy which had activated the entire complex of the somatic functions, in operation at the time of our intrauterine organization, an energy that had no mental quality, and out of which the new psychic function had originated. By the same token, the product of that new function, the ideas or group of ideas, continue to receive and benefit for their activation and for their combination, association, and displacement *from that same general energy* which had activated all the various somatic functions of our early developing somatic organization. This is why I have introduced the name of *"organismic energy"* for that unique general somatic energy which, at a certain moment of our intra-uterine organization, governs all the somatic functions already in operation in our developing somatic functional organization, and from the synthesis and integration of which the new "psychic function" itself develops. At no point did I find any reason to resort to the concept *of a new psychic energy* endowed with mental qualities and capable of mobility, advance, or withdrawal, from our various psychic structures.

These considerations on the nature of what is mobile and displaceable and what is not, have evidently a considerable bearing upon what Freud assumed to be his "libido Theory" founded upon its two major pillars: *repression and regression*, both based in turn on the mobility, displacement, and withdrawal of the psychic energy from the various "psychic structures, to which Freud had denied these attributes which he had assigned only to the "psychic energy."

In part I of this trilogy, I have discussed at length Freud's views on repression and regression, both based on the fallacious mobility, displacement, and withdrawal of the "psychic energy." I have then concluded that with the substitution of Freud's assumption of the mobility of the so-called "psychic energy" with my assumption of the mobility, displacement, association, and combination of the various numerous *"psychic structures"* which constitute the fabric of our complex psychic apparatus, Freud's "libido theory," as well as his dual foundation for "repression" and "regression," would automatically, particularly in the terms advanced by Freud that these two processes constituted the pathogenesis of the neuroses, fall of their own weight. Concerning the fall of "regression," I was referring *only* to that aspect of the regression which Freud called *"the regression of the libido."*

Regression of the ego, as first described by Freud in his *Interpretation of Dreams, stands on solid ground*, because it is based on the ego's voluntary or involuntary recollection of feelings and experiences which a normal person, as well as a neurotic patient, may have endured in his more recent or remote past (the harking back on the part of the ego to past reminiscences), a process which is the most valuable instrument of the *psychoanalytic interview*.

Part Two of this trilogy deals with Freud's fallacy of having attempted to differentiate "sexuality" from "genitality."

In 1895, the date of his collaborative work with J. Breuer on *Studies on Hysteria,* where Freud summarized some of the cases which he had treated in 1888 on his return from a visit to Charcot in Paris in 1886, Freud gave us no inkling of his aim at differentiating between "sexuality" and "genitality." As a matter of fact, in summarizing in his *Studies on Hysteria* one of his three cases, that of Frau von Emmy,[4] suffering from phobias, Freud made the point that this woman had lived for three years in a state of *sexual abstinence* and that he could not help suspecting that this woman, *who was so passionate,* and so capable of strong feelings, *had not won her victory over her sexual needs* without a severe struggle ... and that her attempts at suppressing this most powerful of all instinct had exposed her to severe mental exhaustion.

Again, in the early 1890s, in the analysis of another patient, "Katharina," Freud, in the same book, referred *to the importance of early sexual experiences* in the etiology of her hysteria, and again in the case of another patient, Fraulein Elizabeth von R., whom Freud analyzed in 1892, he emphasized, always in that same book, the "circle of *ideas of an erotic nature* which she had to suppress."[5] One can hardly think that in these three cases Freud had made any attempt at differentiating between sexuality and genitality.

Furthermore, in the section written by J. Breuer in *Studies on*

Hysteria, a section which Freud *must have read*, in his function of collaborator, Breuer, speaking of the quantity of excitations which activates a given idea in hysteria, speaks of *excitations liberated by the sexual instinct*, so that ideas become gradually an affective idea. In Breuer's view, when that idea is actively foreseen in "consciousness," it "sets going the increase of excitations which actually originated from *"the sex glands."* In his concept, these ideas, being the most powerful source of persisting increase of excitations, are consequently the cause of neuroses. Freud did not object at this point to the interchangeability between sexual excitations and genital excitations as intended by Breuer.

That Freud did not object to the equation, sexuality = genitality, is also established by the fact that as early as possibly 1882–1885, as he reported in *The History of the Psychoanalytic Movement* (1914), Breuer, as I have reported in detail in part Two of this Trilogy, in one of his conversations with Freud, used the word "secrets d'alcove" in referring to *marriage bed*, as the cause of a neurosis in one of his patients. *Marriage bed clearly implies genitality*, but Freud never thought to establish at that time any difference between sexuality and genitality. The same applies to Freud not objecting to the remarks of Charcot, made in his presence in Paris, when discussing the causes of a neurosis, in a patient of his colleague Brouardel, Charcot stated emphatically to the latter *"mais dans des cas pareils, c'est toujours la chose génitale, toujours . . . toujours . . ."* No difference was construed in Freud's mind, at that time, of a possible difference between sexuality and genitality. And finally, when Chrobak, one of Freud's instructors, referring to a patient of his who was suffering from attacks of insensate anxiety, told Freud that in such cases the sole prescription that a physician could order, was as follows: *"Penis normalis, dosim repetatur,"* no objection was raised by Freud to the genital meaning of that prescription.

And both in his papers of 1896 *Heredity and the Etiology of the Neurosis*, and *The Etiology of Hysteria*, Freud spoke of, as a precipitating factor for both hysteria and obsessive neurosis, *sexual experiences of either an active or passive role at an early age*, but there was no doubt there that he was referring to experiences involving the sexual organs. Chapter II of part Two of this trilogy deals with the symbolism of *genitality* in dreams *but not of sexuality*, a symbolism which Freud brought up and emphasized gradually in the most recent edition of his *Interpretations of Dreams*, in relation to the manifest content of the dream with its latent content. I wrote sufficiently on this subject in that chapter II.

It was only later, in 1905, under the pressure of the general criticism raised by his colleagues in Vienna, against his theory of sexuality, which up to then had dealt only with *genitality*, that Freud felt the need to pass to the counterattack, and with this intent in mind, he introduced *his new concept* that *"genitality"* should be distinguished from *"sexuality,"* a point which in his view, his critics had overlooked. He thus proceeded to repudiate his original concept that there was *a single sexual instinct*, and advanced his own assumption that the sexual instinct is not a single one, but was made of various components, of several independent sexual instincts, each one having *origin* in different portions of the body. He thus included the mouth and the anus as the two earlier areas of origin of the oral and anal sexual component-instincts, to justify particularly his views that sexuality originated and operated *in very early infancy*.

It is really astonishing that Freud, with no material to substantiate his assumptions, but only a defensive philosophical argument, introduced this *revolutionary concept* of the various zones of origin of what he called "sexual instinct components" and spoke of those areas as *erotogenic zones*, meaning that the sexual instinct components, for instance of the mouth, of the anus, of the skin, and of all parts of the body, including our internal organs, were to be considered as "erotogenic zones" in the sense of *"source of origin of sexual component-instincts."*

For a while, Freud, also maintained that these so-called erotogenic zones could also be considered as areas through which the *mainstream of the sexual instinct, originating in the sexual organs, could serve as areas for the collateral discharge* of the sexual stream, blocked *at its only genital source*, for one reason or another. But soon after he abandoned that theme and concentrated again on the separate origin of sexual instinct-components, the main purpose of which was to induce *"an organ pleasure"* by eliminating the disturbance that any endo-somatic stimulus generated in any one of our external or internal organs or portions of our body.

But where did Freud get the idea to call all sorts of *organ pleasure*, originating in all sorts of the organs of our body, *a sexual pleasure*? Couldn't Freud have used the general term of pleasure used by the hedonists without involving himself into the impossible task of justifying his assumption that the source of an instinct is a process of excitation in an organ, and that the *immediate aim of the instinct lies in the removal of these organic stimuli*? He further made more difficult his justification when he added that the removal of the somatic excitations in question generates a *feeling of satisfaction* which he then unfortunately and *arbitrarily* considered a *sexual organ pleasure*.

And yet with nothing to substantiate his assumptions, Freud had concluded that every bodily function, having pleasure as its goal, was to be considered as the expression of sexuality, and that sexual life copmprises the function of obtaining pleasure from zones of the body, a function which is subsequently brought into the service of that of reproduction.

A discussion of these various points and of the *alleged special chemical origin* of the sexual instinct, is also discussed in part Two of this book. *But what special chemistry* could in itself originate in the mouth or in the anus, or anal organization of the infant, or for that matter, subsequently in all the other zones of the body of an adult, and thus release ultimately *an alleged sexual organ pleasure*?

My alternate proposition to Freud's assumption of innumerable *erotogenic zones* meant to generate the organ-pleasure, which Freud arbitrarily qualified as sexual organ-pleasure, is that those various zones, called *erotogenic* by Freud, are nothing but *areas of discharge of the sexual ideational representations of the stimuli originating in the genital zone and only there*. In other words, of what in part One of this trilogy I have called an "affective formation," which in the case of the genital sexual stimulus, would be represented by the ideational representation of the genital stimulus *and of its related sexual quality*. Such an *"affective sexual formation"* would then be capable of *displacing itself and associate and combine itself* with the ideational representation of various areas of our body, to which ideational representation they impart their sexual quality. Such associative product, possessing now a sexual quality, would allow then the original ideational representations of those various areas to be discharged *as sexual ideational formations*, without the need for these areas to be considered as *generators of independent sexual instinct-components (erotogenic zones)*.

In part Three of this trilogy, I have discussed Freud's fallacy of the origin, nature, and characteristics of the "unconscious" where, on this subject, Freud followed originally the line of thinking of Th. Lipps and even of E. von Hartman, two philosophers who approached the problem of the unconscious from a metaphysical and spiritual point of view, but not from a clinical standpoint, and for whom the unconscious in terms of a *"universal unconscious,"* governs the development of the *conscious*, which only subsequently makes its appearance.

On the contrary, I have advanced the assumption *that from its very onset, mental life is conscious.* I have presented my case in detail in part One of this trilogy, where I have advanced the assumption, in chapter I, that conscious mental life is the original product of what I have called the *"psychic function,"* a new function, the product of which (the ideational representations) constitutes the *conscious formative elements,* of what may be considered *an elementary Protopathic Ego,* the first mental expression of our intra-uterine organization, *which thus, for the first time, becomes aware of its own existence.*

In part Three of this trilogy, I have also advanced the assumption that from its onset, our mental life, being conscious from its very beginning, represents the expression of only one mental system, *the conscious system,* which at its onset I have named *"The Dominant Conscious"* which constitutes through the intercession of the new "psychic function" the conscious ideational representation of all the somatic stimuli which the functioning of our somatic intra-uterine organization induces. I, therefore, disagree with Freud and Lipps that the first stage of our initial mental life is an unconscious life, and I maintain instead that conscious life *is the primary form of mental life,* and what Freud and other philosophers called the unconscious, constitutes a secondary stage of the first stage of the conscious development of our mental apparatus.

What actually happens when a group of ideas belonging to the "dominant conscious" becomes mobilized in the intricate and complex fabric of our psychic apparatus and undergoes displacement association and combination with or replacement by some older or new ideas and related affective qualities, is that such combinations or replacements *retain their original ties* with the "dominant conscious system" but assume in that system a *"subordinate conscious position."* The functional placement of a combined or displaced idea, in that subordinate conscious position, varies according to the reasons why they have been relinquished into that subordinate position. If it is because of some involuntary process of the ego they have been forgotten and thus relegated into a subordinate conscious position, on account of their having temporarily lost their utilitarian value in the workings of the cominant conscious, these subordinate conscious elements are capable, usually under a minimum effort of *concentration of attention,* of re-acquiring their original position in the dominant conscious.

If, on the other hand, some of the original dominant conscious elements prove to be dangerous to the integrity of the ego, they are

gradually forced, by an effort of the ego itself, to assume a subordinate position, but always in the Conscious system as a whole. Because of the effort exercised in this instance by the ego, their subordinate position in the conscious system will encounter strong resistance on the part of the ego before it allows to these subordinate
elements their original return in the dominant conscious. These are
the "subordinate conscious ideas or processes," which Freud had
qualified *as being repressed* and which require for their resurfacing,
his special analytic technique, in overcoming the resistances of the
ego.

I have considered all portions, of the Subordinate conscious as
constituting *a segment of the dominant conscious*, which latter is the
earliest psychic system which governed our mental life from its very
beginning. All subordinate segments of the conscious system, *The
"subordinate conscious"* as I call it, retain I repeat their genetic original ties to the dominant conscious and never lose them. In this connection, we must remember that at one time Freud considered the
preconscious as a portion of what he had originally called the *unconscious*. Later on, he modified his view and considered the *preconscious* as having close genetic ties with the conscious system. And
finally, he ended by considering the *preconscious as an integral part
of the conscious system* and indicated that integration *and even identity* by designating that integrated unit with the single name the
Cs.-Pcs. system.

To conclude, in part Three of this book, I have suggested that
*there is only one system that governs our mental life, the Conscious
system,* which at its onset may be called the *Dominant conscious,*
and that the Subordinate conscious constitutes a second but integral
portion of the original and only Conscious system. I have thus endeavored to eliminate the subdivision of our mental apparatus in the
three ambiguous systems of Cs., Pcs., and Ucs. as established by
Freud.

In support of the existence of a single mental system, the dominant conscious system of which the subordinate conscious is the
derivative and at the same time a *formative portion* of the further
developing "Dominant conscious," I have submitted in chapter III of
part Three of this trilogy, anatomical, developmental, and experimental data which could support my concept that the Subordinate
conscious constitutes both a formative and a derivative integral portion of the only conscious system which originally and subsequently,
with the help of its subordinate portion, governs ultimately our
psychic apparatus.

These data I have discussed in three separate sections: A, B, and

C, in chapter IV of this part Three. These data I have integrated into the *principle* which I have called *"Intussusception,"* from the Latin *Intus = Inside* and *Suscipere = To take up.* I have dealt with that *principle* first in connection with the structural development of our nervous system where I have discussed the point that portions of the older neural structures are incorporated in the newer ones to which development they contribute but that, under certain circumstances, these older structures may re-acquire their original independent function.

That same principle of *Intussusception* I have applied to the development of our psychic apparatus, in the sense that older conscious formations may become, so to speak, absorbed by the new ones to the development of which, through associations, combinations, or fusion, they also contribute. These older conscious formations under certain circumstances, can also free themselves from said associations, and exercise again their original independent position, prior to their having been absorbed into the newer conscious formations.

To support my assumption in the field of the structural development of the nervous system, I have made extensive use of the development of *"The Central Reticular Formation,"* because *traces of it* can be found still operating independently in various somatic structures of our adult body, and because traces of the reticular formation of lower animals are still present and operating in various areas of our brain embedded in and surrounded by the great mass of our newly developed cerebral structures. These portions of the original reticular structure, can also be stimulated in the midst of those new cerebral structures and exercise anew part of their old original function which was their prerogative in the lower animals.

In support of my view of the development of our psychic apparatus by the process of absorption of old mental structures into newer ones under the principle of "Intussusception," in part Three, chapter IV, subdivision C of this trilogy, I have referred to the experimental data of Thomson R. and of McConnell J. V., and collaborators, on the *"Planaria Dorotocephalica"* which they succeeded in conditioning to the effect of an electric current and concomitant flash of a light bulb, which resulted in certain motor activities of that worm. The same condition reactions were then reported by those authors after they surgically divided the *"Planaria"* into a cephalic and into a caudalic portion. The same type of conditioned reaction was reported to be still possible in the two regenerated separate segments of the *"Planaria"* and furthermore, the time involved in reconditioning *the regenerated caudal portion* was smaller than the original time involved in conditioning the original intact animal. The assumptions which I expressed on this subject are discused in that section C of chapter IV of part Three of this trilogy.

My assumption cf the origin of our psychic life by means of a "new" function, the *psychic function*, born at a certain moment from the synthesis and integration of all the activities of the various somatic functions operating in the course of our intra-uterine organization, is an original one. That new *"psychic function"* is entrusted from its start with the translation of those various somatic stimuli into some sort of "ideational formations," the first expression *of our psychic life*. That new psychic function is activated by the same somatic energy that activates the various somatic functions operating in our intra-uterine organization. That physico-biological energy I have called *"organismic energy."* That entire assumption of mine which I consider to be creative and imaginative was never advanced by any critic of Freud's "psychic energy," nor was it advanced by anybody who should have been curious *of the origin of the first ideas mentioned by Freud*, and upon which, according to him, the alleged "psychic energy" were to first exercise its energic and qualitative function. My assumption of the origin of the ideas fills that gap.

Freud's denial in 1905 of the existence of *a single sexual instinct*, which he replaced by a multiplicity of *various "sexual instinct-components"* born in various areas or organs of our body, external or internal, in the so-called *"erotogenic zones"* and the function of which he discussed in the arbitrary and elusive terms of "sexual organ-pleasure" is not acceptable to me. I submit instead *my own substitute assumption* of the operation in the various portions of our body of various *ideational formations* representing mentally these various areas of our body. These ideational representations of our body, as I have already stated, in the course of the activities of our mental apparatus, may acquire their own affective qualities, thus forming what I have called *"affective formations,"* an indivisible unit. In the course of the same activities inherent to the working of our mental apparatus, they may become combined or associated with the original "sexual affective formations," that is, with the appropriate ideational representation of the genital organs and their attached sexual quality, related to the nature of the stimuli originating from the activity of the genital organs, thus constituting *"sexual affective formations."* Through the association or combination of the "affective formation" representing the various parts of organs of our body, with the *"sexual affective formations"* representing the genital, new sexual "affective formations" in the various parts of our body may develop, inasmuch as they acquire the new sexual meaning through the above-mentioned association with the original sexual "affective formations" of the genitals.

My alternative assumption, as above summarized, would permit various parts of our body to operate as *"areas of discharge"* for all sorts *of newly constituted "sexual affective formations,"* thus giving a sexual meaning to the utilization of these various areas in any passive or active form of activities. There would be consequently no need to resort to the existence and operation of Freud's various "erotogenic zones" as *generator* of some elusive "partial sexual instinct-component," meant to substitute the concept of a unique sexual instinct. That assumption of mine, which I consider also creative and imaginative, was never advanced, and least of all hypothesized, by any of the previous students or critics of Freud's theories.

It must be noted that the above reasoning of mine applies to all cases where the original "sexual affective formations" of the genitals, having become activated *by either physical or mental stimuli*, are incapable of finding their way toward their natural discharge along the genital path, because that way is blocked to them, by whatever somatic or psychological obstacle is operating. In that case, those "sexual" or more precisely "genital affective formations" are compelled to search for some other way of discharge through various other parts of our body. It is at this junction that those "sexual affective formations," in their mental travel so to speak, in our psychic apparatus, may become associated with the ideational formation or with the "affective formations" of other areas of our body with which they combine or fuse in the sense which I have already discussed, and which new formations have acquired their sexual quality out of that combination. So qualified, they can now utilize those various areas of our body, as areas of sexual discharge.

It must be said, however, that in certain cases where *no impediment exists* to the discharge of the "genital affective formations" along the normal genital channel, but where the "genital sexual affective formations" are built *in excessive amount*, that excessive amount can utilize simultaneously both the genital path of discharge, as well as other areas of our body for that discharge, thus increasing the resulting sexual pleasure by the intervention of these additional areas of sexual discharge.

Evidently, my views would put to rest once and for all Freud's assumption that the first stage of the sexual development of the infant originates in his "oral organization," particularly the mouth, or that the second stage of the infant's sexual development originates in his anal organization (the anal stage), because at that time *the infant had not as yet reached*, what Freud called subsequently the *third phallic stage* of his sexual development, that is, the stage which he also called *"the stage of the infantile genital organization."* It is only at this "phallic stage" and not before that, that the child begins to feel the working *of the ideational representations of his genital stimuli, which for the first time carry to the child the sexual quality attached to them.* Hence, in his alleged oral or anal stage of his sexual development, as formulated by Freud, the child could not have associated the ideational representation of his oral or anal organization, with the ideational representations of the genitals and attached sexual quality, because that phallic stage had not as yet been reached by the child.

Finally, my alternative assumption, which I also consider to be imaginative, of *a unique conscious system, the dominant conscious* system, and its related and dependent *subordinate conscious* portion, which alone governs our mental life, has never been suggested even by those who, like Ellenberger H., have made an extensive and historical study of the development of the unconscious, but offered no alternative to Freud's origin, structure, and characteristics of what Freud called "the unconscious," a separate and independent system, which in his view, *at least in part, preceded* the development of the conscious system.

As a paradigm in support of my view of the mobility of the "psychic structures" and not of "psychic energy," I found no better example than that of chapter VII of Freud's *Interpretation of Dreams*,[8] in which he discussed the problem of "Regression." In that chapter he stated that regression does not occur only in dreams but also in the course of our normal thinking when it involves recollection of past thinking or affective experiences. *Normal recollection, in his opinion, involves a retrogressive movement in the psychical apparatus* from a complex ideational act, back to the raw material of the memory-traces underlying it. That process he later labeled as a "Regression of the Ego" in terms of its harking back from the present ideational content to the memory-traces of its related past experiences.

Also in *The History of the Psychoanalytic Movement*, I found support to my concept of the mobility of *"psychic structures"* when

Freud referred to the need in the course of an analysis of a neurotic patient, to bring to the surface the memory-traces and associated affects of past events. That "regression" of the patient's mental processes he considered as an important character of the psychoanalytic treatment, so much so that he felt that psychoanalysis could explain nothing current, *without referring back to something past.*

In my opinion this "Regression of the Ego" in both the above references by Freud, I consider to be the result of the mobility of the individual's "psychic structures" made of ideational representations and related attached affect (Affective formations) which become displaced in our psychic apparatus and which are capable, in their regressive course to reactivate by associations the memory of their underlying ideational representations.

Such a dynamic process of the "Regression of the Ego" as formulated by Freud, does not seem to me as requiring the intervention of *some mobile specific psychic energy* which abandons the present thought-processes to direct itself towards underlying memory-traces of past ideational formations which it then reactivates. In my view that dynamic process is satisfactorily explained by my basic concept of the mobility and displacement of *"psychic structures"* (ideas and attached affective qualities) retrogressing in our psychic apparatus.

The Ego itself intentionally or under guidance, can perform that function of harking back from his present thought content to its underlying memory-traces, and I see no need to resort to Freud's view that such a regression needs to take place under the sway of some psychic energy mobilized by some particular agency of our mind. My concept of the "psychic structures" being activated by what I have called "Organismic energy," would provide the energy necessary for the mobility and displacement of our "psychic structures."

My concept of mobile psychic structures can also explain the perception, by what I have called the *"Psychic function,"* of the ideational representation *of the various stimuli of the environment.* The mobility of such ideational representations and related affective quality of the environment, once formulated by that "psychic function" may influence the activity of our present thought-processes. That influence may be accepted by the Ego, if constructive in its object of enlarging the field of its knowledge, or be rejected by the Ego because of the danger that such an influence may represent to its integrity.

It is not, therefore, the mobility of any qualitative psychic energy, but the mobility, displacement and associations of various and numerous "psychic structures," be they of *internal or of external origin* that constitutes in final analysis the key to the activity and development of our Ego in the course of its constructive and protective functions or in the course of its pathological deviations.

In an attempt at harmonizing my view of the mobility of the "psychic structures" with the neurophysiological data of the nervous impulses and nervous conduction, one may accept my assumptions that the *"psychic function,"* which I have discussed in the first chapter of this book, governs the initial translation of all the stimuli emanating from our internal or environmental milieu, into various ideational representations (our *first psychic structures*).

Once that transformation has occurred, the "psychic function" may utilize such ideational representations as *psychic signals* which, whenever necessary, can be transmitted and distributed along the numerous neural channels available, along their nodal structures and along their various branching directions.

Such a functional operation which involves mobility and displacement of ideational representations and related affective qualities may lead to their association and combination with other ideational formations already representing other portions of our somatic organization. That initial transmission of psychic signals may be conceived in the same manner as the signals which are transmitted in a very refined computerized system, though its extreme complexity, as far as our nervous system is concerned, is beyond any artificial duplication at this moment in time of our scientific knowledge. It is in this master computerized system that the original signals released by our "psychic function" are scanned, spaced, codified and coordinated.

It is along such lines that one can assume the manner in which displaced ideational representations and related affective qualities are capable on one hand, through their association and combination, to increase the field of our acquired knowledge and, on the other hand, to influence the ideational representations of other parts of our body to which they impart a given affective quality which the former did not possess originally.

I have illustrated that second point in part Two of this book when dealing with Freud's fallacy of the existence of numerous sexual instincts born locally in various "erotogenic zones."

Notes

A Trilogy of Freud's Major Fallacies
Notes by Chapter

PART ONE

Chapter I

1. Sigmund Freud, *The Defence Neuro-Psychoses* (New York and London: The International Psychoanalytic Press, 1924), vol. 1, p. 75.

2. Ibid., p. 62.

3. Ibid., p. 63.

4. Ibid.

5. Ibid., p. 66.

6. Ibid., p. 67.

7. Sigmund Freud, *The Justification for Detaching From Neurasthenia a Particular Syndrome: The Anxiety Neurosis* (London and New York: The International Psychoanalytic Press, 1924), Vol I, Collected Papers, p. 97.

8. Freud, *The Defence Neuro-Psychoses*, p. 63.

9. Ibid.

10. Sigmund Freud, *Repression* (London: Hogarth Press and the Institute of Psychoanalysis, 1934), Vol. IV, Collected Papers.

11. Ibid., p. 91.

12. Sigmund Freud, *An Outline of Psychoanalysis* (New York: W. W. Norton & Co., Inc., 1949), p. 35.

13. M. Ostow, "Attempt at the Systematic Restatement of the Libido Theory," *Annals of the New York Academy of Sciences* 76 (5959): 1038–65.

14. Freud, *An Outline of Psychoanalysis*.

15. Sigmund Freud, *Beyond the Pleasure Principle* (London: Hogarth Press and the Institute of Psychoanalysis, 1948), p. 47.

16. Sigmund Freud, *The Origin of Psychoanalysis: Letters to William Fliess* (New York: Basic Books, Inc., 1954).

17. Ibid., p. 417.

18. Sigmund Freud, *The Interpretation of Dreams*, trans. J. Strachey (New York: Basic Books Inc., 1955), p. 593.

19. Ibid.

20. Ibid., introduction.

21. H. A. Modell, "The Concept of Psychic Energy," *The Journal of the American Psychoanalytic Association* Vol. 11, No. 3 (July 1963).

22. Ibid., p. 608.

23. Freud, *Repression*.

24.. Sigmund Freud, *Mourning and Melancholia* (New York and London: Hogarth Press and the Institute of Psychoanalysis, 1934), Vol IV, Collected Papers.

25. Sigmund Freud, *Three Essays on the Theory of Sexuality* (London: Imago Publishing Co. Ltd., 1949), p. 94.

26. A. Kardinet, A. Karush, and L. Ovesey, "A Methodological Study of Freudian Theory," *International Journal of Psychiatry* 2, No. 5 (September 1966), p. 497.

27. Freud, *Three Essays on the Theory of Sexuality.*

28. R. W. Waelder, "The Concept of Psychic Energy," *The Journal of the American Psychoanalytic Association* 11, No.3 (July 1963).

29. M. Ostow, "The Concept of Psychic Energy," *The Journal of the American Psychoanalytic Association* 11, No. 3 (July 1963).

30. Ibid., p. 609.

31. R. Holt, "The Concept of Psychic Energy," *The Journal of the American Psychoanalytic Association* 11, No. 3 (July 1963).

32. L. Kubie, "The Concept of Psychic Energy," *The Journal of the American Psychoanalytic Association* 11, No. 3 (July 1963), p. 610.

33. W. S. McCullough, "The Systematic Restatement of the Libido Theory," *Annals of the New York Academy of Sciences* 76 (July 23, 1959), p. 1046.

34. Holt, "Psychic Energy," p. 617.

35. D. Beres, "The Concept of Psychic Energy," *The Journal of the American Psychoanalytic Association* 11, No. 3 (July 1963), p. 618.

36. E. Pumpian-Mindlin, "The Systematic Restatement of the Libido Theory," *Annals of the New York Academy of Sciences* 76 (July 23, 1959), p. 1050.

37. L. von Bertanlaffy, "The Systematic Restatement of the Libido Theory," *Annals of the New York Academy of Sciences* 76 (July 23, 1959), p. 1091.

38. Beres, "Psychic Energy," p. 617.

39. Freud, *The Justification for detaching from Neurasthenia a Particular Syndrome: The Anxiety Neurosis.*

40. Freud, *The Interpretation of Dreams.*

41. Freud, *The Defence Neuro-Psychoses.*

42. "A New Symposium on the Question of Psychic Energy," *Journal of the American Psychoanalytic Association*, 25, (1977), pp. 529–667.

Chapter II

1. Freud, *The Origin of Psychoanalysis.*

2. Sigmund Freud, *Further Remarks on the Defence Neuro-psychoses* (New York and London: The International Psychoanalytic Press, 1924).

3. Ibid., p. 155.

4. Sigmund Freud, *Comments on Jensen's novel "Gradiva."*

5. Sigmund Freud, *The History of the Psychoanalytic Movement* (New York, London, and Vienna: The International Psychoanalytic Press, 1924), Vol. I, Collected Papers.

6. Freud, *Comments on Jensen's novel "Gradiva."*

7. Freud, *The History of the Psychoanalytic Movement.*

8. Ibid., p. 297.

9. W. Riese, "The Pre-Freudian Origin of Psychoanalysis," *Science and Psychoanalysis* (New York: Grune and Stratton, 1958) p. 42.

10. Freud, *The Origin of Psychoanalysis*, p. 122.

11. Ibid., p. 123.

12. Ibid., p. 126.

13. Ibid., p. 129.

14. Ibid., p. 131.

15. Sigmund Freud and J. Breuer, *On the Psychical Mechanisms of Hysterical*

Phenomena (New York, London, and Vienna: The International Psychoanalytic Press, 1924), Vol. I, Collected Papers.

16. Freud, *The Origin of Psychoanalysis*, p. 127.

17. Ibid., p. 149.

18. Ibid., p. 160.

19. Freud, *Repression*.

20. Freud, *The Defence Psycho-Neuroses*, p. 63.

21. Freud, *Repression*, p. 95.

22. Freud, *The Origin of Psychoanalysis*, p. 215.

23. Freud, *The History of the Psychoanalytic Movement*, p. 299.

24. Freud, *The Origin of Psychoanalysis*, p. 209.

25. Ibid., p. 216.

26. Sigmund Freud, *Sexuality in the Theory of the Neuroses* (New York, London, and Vienna: The International Psychoanalytic Press, 1924).

27. Ibid., p. 243.

28. Sigmund Freud, *My Views on the Part Played by Sexuality in the Etiology of the Neuroses* (New York, London, and Vienna: The International Psychoanalytic Press, 1924) vol. 1, Collected Papers p. 276.

29. Freud, *The Origin of Psychoanalysis*, p. 217.

30. Freud, *The Defence Neuro-Psychoses*, p. 63.

31. Ibid., p. 66.

32. Ibid., p. 63.

33. Freud, *An Outline of Psychoanalysis*.

34. Freud, *Repression*, p. 91.

35. Ibid.

36. Freud, *My Views on the Part Played by Sexuality in the Etiology of the Neuroses*, p. 279.

37. Sigmund Freud, *A Case of Paranoia* (New York and London: The Hogarth Press and the Institute of Psychoanalysis, 1936), Vol. III, Collected Papers, p. 453.

38. Freud, *Repression*, p. 86.

39. Sigmund Freud, *The Unconscious* (New York and London: The Hogarth Press and the Institute of Psychoanalysis, 1936), Vol. IV, Collected Papers, p. 113.

40. Ibid.

41. Ibid., p. 118.

42. Freud, *Repression*, p. 95.

43. Ibid., p. 96.

44. Freud, *The Unconscious*, p. 114.

45. Ibid.

46. Ibid.

47. Ibid.

48. Freud, *Repression*, p. 87.

49. Sigmund Freud, *Inhibitions, Symptoms, and Anxiety* (London and New York: The Hogarth Press and the Institute of Psychoanalysis, 1936) p. 26.

50. Sigmund Freud, *New Introductory Lectures* (New York: W. W. Norton & Co., 1933).

51. Ch. Brenner, *The Nature and Development of the Concept of Repression in Freud's Writings: The Psychoanalytic Study of the Child* (1957).

52. Anna Freud, *The Ego and the Mechanisms of Defence* (New York and London: Hogarth Press and the Institute of Psychoanalysis, 1937).

53. Freud, *The Defence Neuro-Psychoses,* pp. 61–62.

54. Freud, *Repression*, p. 87.

55. Freud, *Further Remarks on the Defence Neuro-Psychoses*, p. 155.

56. Freud, *The Defence Neuro-Psychoses*, p. 67.

57. Freud, *Repression*, p. 88.

58. Ibid., p. 90.

59. Freud, *New Introductory Lectures*, p. 90.

60. Freud, *Repression*, p. 87.

61. O. Fenichel, *The Psychoanalytic Theory of the Neuroses* (New York: W. W. Norton & Co., 1946) p. 148.

62. E. Glover, *Psychoanalysis* (London: John Bale Medical Publications, 1939).

63. Ch. Brenner, *An Elementary Textbook of Psychoanalysis* (New York: International Universities Press, 1963).

64. Freud, *Repression*, p. 91.

65. Sigmund Freud, *The Passing of the Oedipus Complex*, (London and New York: The Hogarth Press and the Institute of Psychoanalysis, 1933) vol. 2, p. 54.

66. Ibid.

67. Ibid.

Chapter III

1. Freud, *The Interpretation of Dreams*, p. 542.

2. Ibid., p. 543.

3. Ibid., p. 544.

4. Ibid., p. 545.

5. Ibid., p. 547.

6. Freud, *Three Essays on the Theory of Sexuality*, p. 95.

7. Sigmond Freud, *The Predisposition to Obsessional Neurosis* (New York and London: Hogarth Press and the Institute of Psychoanalysis, 1933) p. 130.

8. Freud, *Repression*, p. 95.

9. Freud, *The Interpretation of Dreams*, p. 548.

10. Freud, *The Predisposition to Obsessional Neurosis*, p. 138.

11. Freud, *The History of the Psychoanalytic Movement*, p. 293.

12. Freud, *Three Essays on the Theory of Sexuality*, p. 95.

13. Freud, *The Unconscious*, p. 128.

14. Freud, *Mourning and Melancholia*, p. 158.

15. Ibid., p. 159.

16. Sigmund Freud, *The Ego and the Id* (New York and London: Hogarth Press and the Institute of Psychoanalysis, 1935).

17. Ibid., p. 36.

18. Ibid., p. 37.

19. Freud, *Inhibitions, Symptoms, and Anxiety*.

20. Freud, *The Unconscious*, p. 62.

21. Freud, *Inhibitions, Symptoms, and Anxiety*, p. 63.

22. Freud, *Mourning and Melancholia*, p. 162.

23. Freud, *Inhibitions, Symptoms, and Anxiety*, p. 63.

24. Ibid.

25. Freud, *Mourning and Melancholia*, p. 160.

26. Ibid., p. 159.

27. Freud, *The Ego and the Id*, p. 36.

28. Sigmund Freud, *From the History of the Infantile Neurosis* (New York and London: Hogarth Press and the Institute of Psychoanalysis, 1913), Vol. III, Collected Papers, p. 588.

29. Freud, *Inhibitions, Symptoms, and Anxiety*, p. 52.

30. Ibid., p. 89.

31. Freud, *The Origin of Psychoanalysis*, p. 149.

32. Ibid.

33. Freud, *Further Remarks on the Defence Neuro-psychoses*, p. 162.

34. Freud, *The Interpretation of Dreams*, p. 162.

35. Freud, *Inhibitions, Symptoms, and Anxiety*, p. 62.

36. Freud, *The Origin of Psychoanalysis*.

37. Freud, *Further Remarks on the Defence Neuro-psychoses*.
38. Freud, *Repression*, p. 95.
39. Freud, *Mourning and Melancholia,* p. 158
40. Freud, *Inhibitions, Symptoms, and Anxiety*, p. 64.
41. Ibid., p. 66.
42. Freud, *New Introductory Lectures*, p. 92.
43. Brenner, *The Nature and Development of the Concept of Repression in Freud's Writings*.

Chapter IV

1. Freud, *Three Essays on the Theory of Sexuality*, p. 94.
2. Ibid., p. 95.
3. Freud, *Beyond the Pleasure Principle*, p. 65.
4. Freud, *The Ego and the Id*, p. 65.
5. Freud, *An Outline of Psychoanalysis*, p. 23.
6. Freud, *Three Essays on the Theory of Sexuality*, p. 94.
7. Freud, *The Unconscious*, p. 130.
8. Ibid., p. 159.
9. Freud, *Mourning and Melancholia*, p. 160.
10. Ibid.
11. Freud, *The Ego and the Id*, p. 36.
12. Fenichel, *The Psychoanalytic Theory of the Neuroses*.
13. Freud, *The Ego and the Id*, p. 37.
14. Ibid., p. 65.
15. Ibid., p. 61.
16. Ibid., p. 62.
17. Ibid., p. 63.
18. E. Pumpian-Mindlin, "The Systematic Restatement of the Libido Theory," *Annals of the New York Academy of Sciences*, 76 (January 23, 1963).
19. Freud, *The Ego and the Id*, p. 65.
20. Ibid., p. 64.
21. Freud, *Beyond the Pleasure Principle*, p. 66.
22. Ibid., p. 52.
23. Ibid., p. 53.
24. Freud, *The Ego and the Id*, p. 37.

PART TWO

Chapter I

1. Freud, *Three Essays on the History of Sexuality*, p. 59.
2. Freud, *The Predisposition to Obsessional Neurosis*, p. 129.
3. Sigmund Freud, *An Autobiographical Study* (New York: W. W. Norton, 1952), p. 72.
4. Freud, *An Outline of Psychoanalysis*, p. 26.
5. Ibid.
6. Freud, *The Defence Neuro-Psychosis*, p. 62.
7. Sigmund Freud, *Heredity and the Etiology of the Neuroses* (New York and Vienna: International Psychoanalytic Press, 1924), p. 145.
8. Freud, *The Justification for Detaching from Neurasthenia a Particular Syndrome: The Anxiety Neurosis*.

9. Sigmund Freud, *The Etiology of Hysteria* (New York, London, and Vienna: International Psychoanalytic Press, 1924), p. 193.

10. Ibid.

11. Ibid.

12. Freud, *The History of the Psychoanalytic Movement*, p. 294.

13. Ibid.

14. Ibid., p. 295.

15. Ibid., p. 296.

16. J. Breuer and Sigmund Freud, *Studies on Hysteria* (New York: Basic Books Inc., 1957), p. 48.

17. Ibid., p. 125.

18. Ibid., p. 135.

19. Freud, *The History of the Psychoanalytic Movement*, p. 294.

20. Ibid., p. 294.

21. Breuer and Freud, *Studies on Hysteria*, p. 246.

22. Freud, *The Origin of Psychoanalysis*, p. 215.

23. Freud, *My Views on the Part Played by Sexuality in the Etiology of the Neuroses*, p. 276.

24. Freud, *The History of the Psychoanalytic Movement*, p. 299.

25. Freud, *The Origin of Psychoanalysis*, p. 300.

26. Ibid., p. 204.

27. Ibid., p. 216.

28. Ibid., p. 217.

29. Freud, *Sexuality in the Theory of the Neuroses*.

30. W. Riese, "The Pre-Freudian Origin of Psychoanalysis."

Chapter II

1. Freud, *The Interpretation of Dreams*, p. 97.

2. Ibid., p. 99

3. Ibid., p. 102.

4. Ibid., p. 104.

5. Ibid., p. 122.

6. Ibid., pp. 153–54.

7. Ibid., p. 160.

8. Ibid., p. 162.

9. Ibid., p. 160.

10. Ibid., p. 350.

11. Ibid., p. 351.

12. Ibid., p. 353.

13. Ibid., p. 353.

14. Ibid., pp. 354–57.

15. Ibid., p. 359.

16. Ibid., p. 104.

17. Ibid., p. 360.

18. Ibid., p. 396.

19. Ibid., p. 397.

20. Ibid., p. 398.

21. Freud, *The Predisposition to Obsessional Neurosis*, p. 129.

22. Freud, *New Introductory Lectures*, p. 103.

Chapter III

1. Freud, *Three Essays on the Theory of Sexuality*, p. 13.

2. Ibid., p. 46.

3. Ibid., p. 47.

4. Ibid., p. 62.

5. Ibid., p. 47.

6. Ibid., p. 62.

7. Ibid., p. 46.

8. Sigmund Freud, *The Instincts and Their Vicissitudes* (New York and London: Hogarth Press and The Institute of Psychoanalysis, 1934), Vol. IV, Collected Papers.

9. Freud, *An Autobiographical Study*, p. 72.

10. Freud, *An Outline of Psychoanalysis*, p. 26.

11. Freud, *Three Essays on the Theory of Sexuality*, p. 97.

12. Freud, *The Interpretation of Dreams*, p. 116.

13. Freud, *Three Essays on the Theory of Sexuality*, p. 93.

14. Ibid., p. 82.

15. Sigmund Freud, *On Narcissism: An Introduction* (New York and London: Hogarth Press and The Institute of Psychoanalysis, 1934), Vol. IV, Collected Papers.

16. Freud, *Three Essays on the Theory of Sexuality*, p. 82.

17. Ibid.

18. Ibid., p. 41.

19. Ibid., p. 48.

20. Freud, *The Predisposition to Obsessional Neurosis*, p. 129.

21. Freud, *Three Essays on the Theory of Sexuality*, p. 94.

22. Freud, *The Instincts and Their Vicissitudes*, p. 64.

23. Freud, *An Outline of Psychoanalysis*, p. 19.

24. Freud, *New Introductory Lectures*, p. 98.

25. Freud, *Three Essays on the Theory of Sexuality*, p. 88.

26. Th. Szasz, "A Critical Analysis of Some Aspects of the Libido Theory," *Annals of the New York Academy of Sciences* 76 (1959).

Chapter IV

1. Freud, *The Instincts and Their Vicissitudes*, p. 64.

2. Freud, *Three Essays on the Theory of Sexuality*, p. 59.

3. Ibid.

4. Ibid., p. 48.

5. A discussion of the hedonistic theories will be found in J. Watson, *Hedonistic Theories* (London and New York: James Maclehose and Sons and Macmillan Co., 1895).

6. Freud, *Three Essays on the Theory of Sexuality*, p. 60.

7. Sigmund Freud, *The Infantile Genital Organization of the Libido* (London and New York: Hogarth Press and the Institute of Psychoanalysis, 1933), p. 245.

8. Freud, *The Origin of Psychoanalysis*, p. 224.

9. Ch. Brenner, *An Elementary Textbook of Psychoanalysis*, p. 121.

10. Freud, *Three Essays on the Theory of Sexuality*, p. 104.

11. Freud, *The Origin of Psychoanalysis*, p. 229.

12. C. S. Ford and F. A. Beach, *Patterns of Sexual Behavior* (New York: P. Hoeber Inc., 1949).

13. Kardiner, Karush, and Ovesey, "A Methodological Study of Freudian Theory," p. 500.

14. Freud, *Three Essays on the Theory of Sexuality*, p. 100.

15. Freud, *The Instincts and Their Vicissitudes*, p. 81.

16. Sigmund Freud, *The Passing of the Oedipus Complex* (London and New York: Hogarth Press and the Institute of Psychoanalysis, 1933).

17. Freud, *Three Essays on the Theory of Sexuality*, p. 104.

18. Ibid., p. 78.

19. Freud, *An Autobiographical Study*, p. 70.

20. Freud, *The Instincts and Their Vicissitudes*, p. 81.
21. Freud, *Three Essays on the Theory of Sexuality*, p. 115.
22. Freud, *The Ego and the Id*, p. 62.
23. Ibid., p. 63.
24. Ibid., p. 62.
25. Freud, *The Interpretation of Dreams*, p. 611.

Chapter V

1. Freud, *Three Essays on the Theory of Sexuality*, p. 12.
2. Freud, *Beyond the Pleasure Principle*, p. 45.
3. Ibid., p. 47.
4. Ibid., p. 50.
5. Ibid.
6. Ibid., p. 51.
7. Ibid., p. 58.
8. Ibid., p. 68.
9. Ibid., p. 74.
10. Ibid., p. 74.
11. Ibid., p. 44.
12. Ibid., p. 75.
13. Ibid., p. 79.
14. Freud, *The Predisposition to Obsessional Neurosis*, p. 129.

Addenda

15. Plato, "The Symposium," *Great Books of the Western World* (Chicago: Encyclopaedia Britannica, 1952), p. 153.
16. Ibid., p. 154.
17. Ibid., p. 156.
18. Ibid., p. 160.
19. Ibid., p. 163.
20. Ibid.

Part Three

Chapter I

1. Freud, *The Origin of Psychoanalysis,* pp. 174–75.
2. Ibid., p. 142.
3. Freud, *The Interpretation of Dreams*, p. 538.
4. Freud, *The Origin of Psychoanalysis*, p. 262.
5. Freud, *The Interpretation of Dreams*, p. 615.
6. Ibid., p. 616.
7. Freud, *An Outline of Psychoanalysis*, p. 109.
8. Freud, *The Interpretation of Dreams*, p. 617.
9. Freud, *The Origin of Psychoanalysis*, p. 417.
10. Freud, *The Interpretation of Dreams*, p. 616.
11. Ibid., p. 593.
12. Ibid., p. 541.
13. Sigmund Freud, *Metapsychological Supplement to the Theory of Dreams* (New York and London: Hogarth Press and the Institute of Psychoanalysis, 1934), p. 147.

14. Freud, *The Interpretation of Dreams*, p. 541.

15. Freud, *The Ego and the Id*, p. 10.

16. Freud, *New Introductory Lectures*.

17. Freud, *An Outline of Psychoanalysis*, p. 41.

18. Ibid., p. 109.

19. Freud, *The Interpretation of Dreams*, p. 610.

20. Sigmund Freud, *A Note Upon the Mystic Writing Pad* (London and New York: Hogarth Press and the Institute of Psychoanalysis, 1950), p. 179.

Chapter II

1. Freud, *Beyond the Pleasure Principle*, p. 47.

2. Freud, *The Origin of Psychoanalysis*, p. 142.

3. W. R. Hess, *The Functional Organization of the Diencephalon*. ed. J. R. Hughes (New York: Grune and Stratton, 1957).

4. F. Bremer, "L'activité Cérébrale au Cours du Sommeil et de la Narcose," *Bull. Acad. Royale Med. Belgique* 2 (1937): 68–86.

5. P. Bard, "A diencephalic Mechanism for the Expression of Rage," *American Journal of Physiology* 84 (1928): 490–515.

6. S. W. Ranson, "Some Functions of the Hypothalmus," *Bull. New York Academy of Medicine* 13 (1937): 241–271.

7. G. Moruzzi and H. W. Magoun, "Brain Stem Reticular Formation and Activation of the E.E.G." *E.E.G. Clinical Neurophysiology* 1 (1949): 455–473.

8. H. W. Magoun, "The Ascending Reticular Activating System," *Res. Publ. Assoc. Nerv. and Ment. Disorders* 30 (1952): 480–92.

9. H. Jasper, C. Aimone-Marsan, and J. Stoll, "Corticofugal Projection to the Brain Stem," *Archives of Neurol. and Psych.* 67 (1952): 155–66.

10. F. Bremer and C. Terzuolo, "Interaction de L'écorce Cerebrale et de la Formation Reticulée du Tronc Cerebral dans le Mechanism de L'eveil et du maintien de L'activité vigile," *J. of Physiology (Paris)* 45 (1953): 56–57.

11. J. D. French, "Brain Lesions Associated with Prolonged Unconscious," *Archives of Neurol and Psych.* 68 (1952): 727–40.

12. J. D. French, R. Hernandez-Peon, and R. B. Livingston, "Projections from Cortex to Cephalic Brain Stem (Reticular Formation) in Monkeys," *Journal of Neurophysiology* 18 (1955): 74–95.

13. J. P. Arana-Iniquez Segundo and J. D. French, "Behavioral Arousal by Stimulation of Brain in Monkey," *Journal of Neurophysiology* 9 (1946): 165–71.

14. H. W. Magoun and R. Rhines, "An Inhibitory Mechanism in the Bulbar Reticular Formation," *Journal of Neurophysiology* 9 (1946): 165–71.

15. K. E. Hagbarth and D. B. Kerr, "Central Influences on Spinal Afferent Connections," *Journal of Neurophysiology* 17 (1954): 295–307.

16. J. C. Eccles, P. Fatt, and S. Landgren, "Central Pathway For Direct Inhibitory Action of Impulses in Largest Afferent Nerve Fibers," *Journal of Neurophysiology* 19 (1956): 75–98.

17. J. D. Green, M. Mancia, and R. van Baumgarten, "Effects of Antidromic Stimulation of the Lateral Olfactory Tract," *Journal of Physiology* 25 (1962): 467.

18. R. Hernandez-Peon, H. Scherrer, and M. Jouvet, "Modification of Electrical Activity in Cochlear Nucleus during Attention in Unanesthetized Cats," *Science* 123 (1956): 331–32.

19. M. Jouvet, "Analyse Electroencephalographique de quelques Aspects du Conditionement chez le Chat," *Acta Neurologica Latina-America* 2 (1936): 107–115.

20. H. Gastaud, "The Neurological Basis of Conditioned Reflexes and Behavior," *Ciba Symposium* (London) 1957.

21. J. H. Masserman, *Behavior and Neuroses* (Chicago: University of Chicago Press, 1943).

22. J. M. Delgado, H. Roswald, and E. Looney, "Evoking Conditional Fear by Electrical Stimulation of Subcortical Structures in the Monkey Brain," *Journal of Comparative Physiology and Psychology*.

23. Association for Research in Nervous and Mental Diseases, *The Interrelationship of Mind and Body* (Baltimore: Williams and Wilkins Co., 1939).

24. Josiah Macy Jr. Foundation, Conferences on the "Problem of Consciousness" (1950–54).

25. Hixon Symposium, *Cerebral Mechanisms in Behavior* (New York: John Wiley and Sons Inc., 1951).

26. First Int. Congress of Neurological Sciences," Les Etats de Conscience en Neurologie," (1957) Brussels.

27. Josiah Macy Jr. Foundation, *Conferences on Central Nervous System and Behavior*.

28. "Evolution of the Nervous System," American Association for the Advancement of Science.

29. Kaiser Symposium, *The Physiology of Emotions* (Springfield, Illinois: Charles C. Thomas Publ., 1961).

30. Oxford Symposium, *The Cerebral Mechanisms and Learning* (1961).

31. Brain Institute of Research of California: First Conference (1961).

32. International Congress on "States of Consciousness," (Genoa 1963).

33. Princeton Symposium on Learning, Remembering, and Forgetting (1963).

34. N. Kleitman, "The Role of the Cerebral Cortex in the Development and Maintenance of Consciousness," Fifth Conference of Josiah Macy Jr. Foundation (New York 1954).

35. E. von Hartman, *The Philosophy of the Unconscious* (New York: Harcourt Brace & Co., 1931).

36. H. Rothmann, "Zusammenfassender Bericht uber Rothmannschen Grosshirnlosen Hund," *Zeits. f. Gesamt Neurol. u. Psych.* 87 (1923).

37. J. Zeliony, quoted by A. Ferraro, "Etude Anatomique du Systeme Nerveux d'un Chien dont le Pallium a ete enleve" *Imprimerie Zuidam Utrecht Holland* 1924.

38. B. Brouwer, "Etude Anatomique du Systeme Nerveux Central des deux Chats par Dusser de Barenne," *Archives Neerlandaises de Physiologie* (1920).

39. Additional References to the activities of decorticated animals can be found in Bard Ph: "Central Nervous Mechanisms for Emotional Behavior Patterns in Animals in Interrelationship of Mind and Body," *Proceedings of the Association for Research in Nervous and Mental Diseases* Vol. XIX 1939.

40. K. De Snoo, "Das Trinkenden Kind im Uterus," *Monatschr. F. Geburt. u. Gyneko,* 105 (1937): 88.

41. J. Piaget, "The Problem of Consciousness in Child Psychology" Fourth Conference Josiah Macy Jr. Foundation on Problems of Consciousness (New York 1953).

42. P. Weiss, "Discussion of Lashley's Paper in *The Cerebral Organization and Human Behavior* (Baltimore: Williams and Wilkins Co., 1958).

43. R.R. Grinker, "Problems of Consciousness," Fourth Conference of the Josiah Macy Jr. Foundation (1954).

44. Th. Alajouanine, "Les Alterations des Etats de Conscience," *Transactions of First International Congress of Neurological Sciences* (Brussels 1957).

45. W. Penfield, "Consciousness and Centrencephalic Organization," Transactions of First International Congress of Neurological Sciences (Brussels 1957).

46. P. Weiss, "Discussion of Lashley's Paper."

47. Ibid.

48. Ibid., p. 140.

49. Ibid., p. 73.

50. Ibid., p. 134.

51. R. C. Bickford, *Changes in Memory Function Produced by Electrical Stimulation of the Temporal Cortex in the Brain and the Human Behavior* (Baltimore, Williams & Wilkins, 1958).

52. H. Hyden, "Activation of Nuclear RNA of Neurons and Glia in Learning in the Anatomy of Memory," *Science and Behavior Books, Inc.* (1965).

urones and Neuroses in "Physiology of Emotions." *Third Kaiser Symposium* (Springfield: Thomas Charles Publ.).

54. J. C. Eccles, "Possible Ways in Which Synaptic Mechanisms Participate in Learning, Remembering, and Forgetting." Princeton Symposium 1963 and *The Anatomy of Memory* (Palo Alto: Science and Behavior Books, 1965).

55. Ibid.

56. R. W. Sperry, *Summation of Eccles Presentation*.

Chapter III

1. Freud, *The Origin of Psychoanalysis*, p. 174.
2. Freud, *The Interpretation of Dreams*, p. 611.
3. Freud, *The Origin of Psychoanalysis*, p. 261.
4. Ibid., p. 262.
5. Freud, *The Interpretation of Dreams*, p. 613.
6. Ibid., p. 615.
7. Sigmund Freud, *The Unconscious in Psychoanalysis (London: Hogarth Press and the Institute of Psychoanalysis, 1924), p. 25.*
8. *Freud, The Unconscious,* p. 104.
9. Ibid., p. 105.
10. Ibid., p. 106.
11. Freud, *The Interpretation of Dreams*, p. 615.
12. Freud, *The Unconscious*, p. 106.
13. Ibid., p. 111.
14. Holt, "The Concept of Psychic Energy."
15. Freud, *An Outline of Psychoanalysis*.
16. Freud, *The Unconscious*, p. 128.
17. Ibid., p. 129.
18. Freud, *The Ego and the Id*, p. 16.
19. Freud, *The Unconscious*, p. 127.
20. Ibid., p. 119.
21. Freud, *The Interpretation of Dreams*, p. 280.
22. Ibid.
23. Ibid., p. 284.
24. Ibid., pp. 306–08.
25. Ibid., p. 611.
26. Freud, *The Unconscious*, p. 119.
27. Freud, *The Ego and the Id*, p. 30.
28. Freud, *New Introductory Lectures*, p. 74.
29. Ibid., p. 105.
30. Freud, *An Outline of Psychoanalysis*, p. 53.
31. von Hartmann, *The Philosophy of the Unconscious*.
32. Freud, *The Unconscious*, p. 107.
33. Ibid., p. 112.

Chapter IV

1. Most of the data on the structural development of the nervous system were taken from the textbook of N. R. F. Maier and T. C. Schneirla, *Principles of Animal Psychology* (New York and London: McGraw Hill, 1935).

2. G. H. Parker, *The Elementary Nervous System* (Philadelphia: Lippincott, 1919).

3. J. Brachet, "Le Role et la Localization des Acides Nucleiques au Cours du Development Embryonaire." *Comptes Rendus de la Societé de Biology Paris* 142 (1949): 1241.

4. M. C. Niu, "Current Evidences Concerning Chemical Inducers in Evolution of Nervous Control," ed. A. Bass. *American Association for the Advancement of Sciences* (1959).

5. Henry Ey, *Etudes Psychiatriques* (Paris: Desckee de Brouwer and Co., 1948–53).

6. Freud, *An Outline of Psychianalysis*, p. 19.

7. Ibid., p. 34.

8. Freud, *The Interpretation of Dreams*.

9. Freud, *Beyond the Pleasure Principle*, p. 47.

10. G. E. Coghill, "The Biological Basis of Conflict," *Behavior Psychoanalytic Review* 20 (1933).

11. Wheeler, *Essays on Biological Philosophy* (1939).

12. H. Bergson, *Creative Evolution* (New York: Henry Holt and Co., 1911).

13. E. W. Sinnot, "A Common Basis for Development and Behavior in Evolution of the Nervous System," *American Association for the Advancement of Science* (1959).

14. L. Day and M. Bentley, "A Note on Learning in Paramecium," *Journal of Animal Behavior* 1 (1911): 67–73.

15. L. K. Losina-Losinsky, "Zur Enahrungsphysiologie der Infusorien," *Arch, Protozoa* 74 (1931): 18–120.

16. J. Loeb, "Die Bedeutung der *Tropismen* fur die Psychologie," *Sixth Congress Intern. of Psychology* (Geneve 1900) and *La Question des Tropismes* (Paris: Press Univeritaire, 1930).

17. M. D. Rose, *L'Instinct dans le Comportement des Animaux et de L'homme.* (Paris: Masson et Cie, 1956).

18. *G. Viaud, Taxies et Tropismes dans le Comportement Instinctif in: L'Instinct dans le Comportement des Animaux et le L'homme* (Paris: Masson et Cie, 1956).

19. Gastaud, *The Neurophysiological Basis of Conditioned Reflexes and Behavior.*

20. Alajouanine, "Les Alterations des Etats de Conscience."

21. V. G. Dethier, "Microscopic Brains," *Science* 143 (1964): 1138–45.

22. Ibid.

23. A. Binet, *Alterations of Personality* (New York, Appleton and Co., 1896).

24. V. Urbantschitsch, *Subjective Optical Imagery* (Vienna: Deuticke Ed., 1907).

25. J. G. Miller, "Discrimination Without Awareness," *American Journal of Psychiatry* (1939); "Unconscious Processes and Perceptions," *An Approach to Personality*, ed. R. R. Blake and G. V. Ramsey (New York: Ronald Press).

26. R. Thompson and J. W. McConnell, "Learning in Flatworm," *Journal Comp. Physiology and Psychology* 48 (1955); Smith-Klein and French. *Laboratories Report on the Flatworm Phenomenal Memory, Report #6.* (Jan.–Feb. 1963).

27. J. W. McConnell, A. I. Jacobson, and D. P. Kimble, "Memory Transfer through Cannibalism in Planaria," *Journal of Neuropsychiatry* 3 Supp. 1 (Aug. 1962).

Summary

1. Freud, *Three Essays on the Theory of Sexuality*, p. 95.

2. Ibid., p. 96.

3. Freud, *The Interpretation of Dreams*, p. 61.

4. Breuer and Freud, *Studies in Hysteria*, p. 48.

5. Ibid., p. 135.

Bibliography

Alajouanine, Th. "Les Altérations des Etats de Conscience."
Transactions of First Intern. Congress of Neurological Sciences (Brussels 1957).

American Association for the Advancement of Science.
The Evolution of the Nervous System (1959).

Ariens Kappers, C. V. Anatomie Comparée du Systeme Nerveux.
Paris: Masson and Co., 1947.

Association for Research in Nervous and Mental Diseases.
The Inter-relationship of Mind and Body. Baltimore: Williams and Wilkins Co., 1939.

Bard, P. "A Diencephalic Mechanism for the Expression of Rage."
Amer. Journ. of Physiology 84 (1928): 490–515.

Beres, D. "Concept of Psychic Energy," The Journal of the American Psychoanalytic Assoc. vol. 11 no. 3 (July 1963).

Bergson, H. Creative Evolution. New York: Henry Holt and Co. 1911.

Bertanlaffy, V. L. The Systematic Restatement of the 'Libido theory.'
Annals of the New York Academy of Sciences Vol. 76 (January 23, 1959).

Bickford, R. C. et al: "Changes in Memory Function Produced by Electrical Stimulation of the Temporal Cortex in the Brain and the Human Behavior."
Baltimore: Williams and Wilkins Co. 1958.

Binet, A. Alterations of Personality.
New York: Appleton and Co., 1896.

Brachet, J. "Le Role et la Localization des Acides Nucleiques au Cours du Development Embryonaire."
Comptes Rendus de la Société de Biology Paris: 142 (1949): 1241.

Brain Institute of Research of California "First Conference." (1961).

Bremer, F., and Terzuolo, C. "Interaction de L'écorce Cerebrale et de la Formation Reticulée du Tronc Cerebral dans le Mechanism de L'eveil et du maintien de L'activite vigile."
J. of Physiology (Paris) 45 (1953): 56–57.

Bremer, F. "L'activité Cérébrale au Cours du Sommeil et de la Narcose."
Bull. Acad. Royale Med. Belgique 2 (1937): 68–86.

Brenner, Ch. An Elementary Textbook of Psychoanalysis.
New York: International Universities Press, 1963.

Brenner, Ch. *The Nature and Development of the Concept of Repression in Freud's writings. The Psychoanalytic Study of the Child* 12 (1957).
Breuer, J. & Freud, Sigmund *Studies on Hysteria.*
New York: Basic Books Inc. Publishers, 1957.
Brouwer, B. "Etude Anatomique du Systeme Nerveux Central de deux Chats opérés par Dusser de Barenne."
Archives Neerlandaises de Physiologie (1920).
Buscaino, V. M. "Fondements Neurologiques des Phenomenes de Conscience."
Transactions of the First Intern. Congress of Neurological Sciences. (Brussels, 1957).
Coghill, G. E. "The Biological Basis of Conflict in Behavior."
Psychoanalytic Review. 20 (1933).
Day, L., and Bentley, M. A note on Learning in Paramecium.
Journ. Animal Behavior 1 (1911): 67–73.
Delgado, J. M.; Roswold H.; and Looney, E. "Evoking Conditional Fear by Electrical Stimulation of Subcortical Structures in the Monkey Brain."
J. of Comparative Physiol. and Psychol.
De Snoo, K. "Das Trinkenden Kind im Uterus."
Monatschr. f. Geburt. u. Gyneko. 105 (1937): 88.
Dethier, V. G. "Microscopic Brains," *Science* vol. 143 (1964): 1138–1145.
Eccles, J. C. "Possible Ways in which Synaptic Mechanisms Participate in Learning, Remembering and Forgetting."
Princeton Symposium 1963, and *The Anatomy of Memory,* Palo Alto, Calif.: Science and Behavior Books 1965.
Eccles, J. C.; Fatt, P.; and Landgren, S. "Central Pathway for Direct Inhibitory Action of Impulses in Largest Afferent Nerve Fibers."
Journ. of Neurophysiology 19 (1956): 75–98.
Ey, H. *Etudes Psychiatriques.* 3 volumes.
Paris: Desckee de Brouwer and Co., 1948–1953.
Fenichel, O. *The Psychoanalytic Theory of the Neuroses.*
New York: W. W. Norton & Co., Inc., 1946.
Ford, C. S. & Beach, F. A. *Patterns of Sexual Behavior.*
New York: P. Hoeber, Inc. Publishers, 1949.
French, J. D. "Brain Lesions Associated with Prolonged Unconsciousness."
Archives of Neurol. and Psych. 68 (1952): 727–740.
French, J. D.; Hernandez-Peon, R.; & Livingston, R. B. "Projections from Cortex to Cephalic Brain Stem (Reticular Formation) in Monkeys."
Journ. of Neurophysiology 18 (1955): 74–95.
Freud, Anna *The Ego and the Mechanisms of Defence.*
New York–London: Hogarth Press and the Institute of Psychoanalysis, 1937.
Freud, Sigmund. *An Autobiographical Study.*
New York: W. W. Norton & Co. Inc., 1952.
Freud, Sigmund. *Beyond the Pleasure Principle.*
London: The Hogarth Press and the Institute of Psychoanalysis, 1948.
Freud, Sigmund. *A Case of Paranoia (Dementia Paranoidea).*
New York–London: Hogarth Press and the Institute of Psychoanalysis, 1933. Vol. 3 of Collected Papers.
Freud, Sigmund. *Comments on Jensen's Novel "Gradiva."*

Freud, Sigmund. *The Defence Neuro-Psychoses*.
New York–London: The International Psychoanalytic Press, 1924. Vol. 1 of Collected Papers.
Freud, Sigmund. *A Disturbance of Memory on the Acropolis*.
New York–London: The Hogarth Press and the Institute of Psychoanalysis, 1950. Vol. 5 of Collected Papers.
Freud, Sigmund. *The Ego and the Id*.
New York–London: The Hogarth Press and the Institute of Psychoanalysis, 1935.
Freud, Sigmund. *The Etiology of Hysteria*.
New York–London–Vienna: The International Psychoanalytic Press, 1924. Vol. 1 of Collected Papers.
Freud, Sigmund. *From the History of the Infantile Neurosis* (1918).
New York–London: The Hogarth Press and the Institute of Psychoanalysis, 1913. Vol. 2 of Collected Papers.
Freud, Sigmund. *Further Remarks on the Defence Neuro-psychoses*.
New York–London: The International Psychoanalytic Press, 1924, vol. 1 of Collected Papers.
Freud, Sigmund. *Heredity and Etiology of the Neuroses*.
New York–Vienna: The International Psychoanalytic Press, 1924. Vol. 1 of Collected Papers.
Freud, Sigmund. *The History of the Psychoanalytic Movement*.
New York–London–Vienna: The International Psychoanalytic Press, 1924. Vol. 1 of Collected Papers.
Freud, Sigmund. *The Infantile Genital Organization of the Libido*.
London–New York: The Hogarth Press and the Institute of Psychoanalysis, 1933. Vol. 2 of Collected Papers.
Freud, Sigmund. *Inhibitions, Symptoms, and Anxiety*.
London–New York: The Hogarth Press and the Institute of Psychoanalysis, 1936.
Freud, Sigmund. *The Instincts and their Vicissitudes*.
New York–London: The Hogarth Press and the Institute of Psychoanalysis, 1934. Vol. 4 of Collected Papers.
Freud, Sigmund. *The Interpretation of Dreams*.
New York: English Translation by J. Strachey Basic Books, Inc., 1955.
Freud, Sigmund. *The Justification for Detaching from Neurasthenia a Particular Syndrome: The Anxiety Neurosis*.
London–New York: The International Psychoanalytic Press, 1924. Vol. 1 of Collected Papers.
Freud, Sigmund. *Metapsychological Supplement to the Theory of Dreams*.
New York–London: Hogarth Press and the Institute of Psychoanalysis, 1934. Vol. 4 of Collected Papers.
Freud, Sigmund. *Mourning and Melancholia*.
New York–London: The Hogarth Press and the Institute of Psychoanalysis, 1934. Vol. 4 of Collected Papers.
Freud, Sigmund. *My Views on the Part Played by Sexuality in the Etiology of the Neuroses*.
New York–London–Vienna: The International Psychoanalytic Press, 1924. Vol. 1 of Collected Papers.
Freud, Sigmund. *New Introductory Lectures*.

New York: W. W. Norton & Co., Trans. J. H. Spratt 1933.

Freud, Sigmund. *A Note upon the Mystic Writing Pad*.
London–New York: The Hogarth Press and the Institute of Psychoanalysis, 1950. Vol. 5 of Collected Papers.

Freud, Sigmund. *On Narcissism. An Introduction*.
New York–London: The Hogarth Press and the Institute of Psychoanalysis, 1934. Vol. 4 of Collected Papers.

Freud, Sigmund, & Breuer, J. *On the Psychical Mechanisms of Hysterial Phenomena*.
New York–London–Vienna: The International Psychoanalytic Press, 1924. Vol. 1 of Collected Papers.

Freud, Sigmund. *The Origin of Psychoanalysis. Letters to Wilhelm Fliess*.
New York: Basic Books, Inc., 1954.

Freud, Sigmund. *An Outline of Psychoanalysis*.
New York: W. W. Norton & Co., Inc., 1949.

Freud, Sigmund. *The Passing of the Oedipus Complex*. London–New York: The Hogarth Press and the Institute of Psychoanalysis, 1933. Vol. 2 of Collected Papers.

Freud, Sigmund. *The Predisposition to Obsessional Neurosis*.
New York–London: The Hogarth Press and the Institute of Psychoanalysis, 1933. Vol. 2 of Collected Papers.

Freud, Sigmund. *Repression*.
London: Hogarth Press and the Institute of Psychoanalysis, 1934. Vol. 4 of Collected Papers.

Freud, Sigmund. *Sexuality in the Theory of the Neuroses*.
New York–London–Vienna: The International Psychoanalytic Press, 1924. Vol. 1 of Collected Papers.

Freud, Sigmund. *Three Essays on the Theory of Sexuality*.
London: Imago Publishing Co. Ltd., 1949. First English Edition.

Freud, Sigmund. *The Unconscious*.
New York–London: The Hogarth Press and the Institute of Psychoanalysis, 1934. Vol. 4 of Collected Papers.

Freud, Sigmund. *The Unconscious in Psychoanalysis*.
London: The Hogarth Press and the Institute of Psychoanalysis, 1924. Vol. 1 of Collected Papers.

Gastaud. H. "The Neurophysiological Basis of Conditioned Reflexes and Behavior."
London: *Ciba Symposium*, 1957.

Gerard, R. W. Discussion on Learning and Remembering at the Princeton Symposium. (1963)

Gerard, R. W. Neurones and Neuroses in "Physiology of Emotions."
Third Kaiser Symposium. Springfield: Thomas Charles Publ.

Glover, E. *Psychoanalysis*.
London: John Bale Medical Publications, 1939.

Green, J. D.; Mancia, M.; and van Baumgarten, R. "Effects of Antidromic Stimulation of the Lateral Olfactory Tract."
Journal of Physiology 25 (1962): 467.

Grinker, R. R. Discussion in "Problems of Consciousness.
Fourth Conference of the Josiah Macy Jr. Foundation (1954).

Hagbarth, K. E., and Kerr, D. B. "Central Influences on Spinal Afferent Connections."

Journ. of Neurophysiology 17 (1954): 295–307.
Hartman von, E. *The Philosophy of the Unconscious.*
New Edition in one volume. New York: Harcourt, Brace & Co., 1931.
Hernandez-Peon, R.; Scherrer, H.; and Jouvet, M. "Modification of Electrical Activity in Cochlear Nucleus during Attention in Unanesthetized Cats."
Science 123 (1956): 331–332.
Hess, W. R. *The Functional Organization of the Diencephalon.*
New York: Grune & Stratton, 1957. Ed. J. R. Hughes.
The Hixon Symposium. *Cerebral Mechanisms in Behavior.*
New York: John Wiley & Sons, Inc., 1951.
Holt, R. "The Concept of Psychic Energy."
The Journal of the American Psychoanalytic Assoc. Vol. 11 No. 3 (July 1963).
Hyden, H. "Activation of Nuclear RNA of Neurons and Glia in Learning in The Anatomy of Memory."
Science and Behavior Books, Inc., 1965.
International Congress on "States of Consciousness."
Genoa, Italy. (April, 1963).
Jackson, J. Hughlings. *Remarks on Evolution and Dissolution of the Nervous System.*
Journ. of Mental Sciences (1888).
Jasper, H.; and Aimone-Marsan, C.; & Stoll, J. "Corticofugal Projection to the Brain Stem."
Archives of Neurol. and Psych. 67 (1952): 155–166.
Jasper, H., and Rheinberger, M. "The Electrical Activity of the Cerebral Cortex in Unanesthetized Cat."
Amer. Journ. of Physiology 119 (1937): 186–196.
Josiah Macy, Jr. Foundation. "Conferences on Central Nervous System and Behavior." (1958–60).
Josiah Macy, Jr. Foundation. "Conferences on the Problem of Consciousness." (1950–1954).
Jouvet, M. "Analyse electroencephalographique de quelques aspects du conditionement chez le chat."
Acta Neurological Latina-Americana 2 (1936): 107–115.
Kaiser Symposium. *The Physiology of Emotions.*
Springfield, Ill.: Charles C. Thomas Publ., 1961.
Kardiner, A., Karush, A., and Ovesey, L. "A Methodological Study of Freudian Theory."
International Journal of Psychiatry Vol. 2, No. 5 (September 1966).
Kleitman, N. "The Role of the Cerebral Cortex in the Development and Maintenance of Consciousness."
Fifth Conference Josiah Macy Jr. Foundation (New York: 1954).
Kubie, L. "The Concept of Psychic Energy."
The Journal of the American Psychoanalytic Assoc. Vol. 11 No. 3 (July 1963).
"Les Etats de Conscience en Neurologie."
First Int. Congress of Neurological Sciences. Brussels: 1957.
Loeb. "Die Bedeutung der Tropismen für die Psychologie."
VI Cong. Intern. of Psychology Geneve 1900. Also in *"La Question des Tropismes."* Paris: Presse Universitaire, 1930.

Losina-Losinsky, L. K. Zur Ernahrungsphysiologie der Infusorien
    Arch. Protozoa 74 (1931): 18–120.
Magoun, H. W. "The Ascending Reticular Activating System."
    Res. Publ. Assoc. Nerv. and Ment. Disorders 30 (1952): 480–492.
Magoun, H. W. *The Waking Brain.*
    Springfield: Charles Thomas Publ. 1958.
Magoun, H. W., and Rhines, R. "An Inhibitory Mechanism in the Bulbar Reticular Formation."
    Journ. of Neurophysiology 9 (1946): 165–171.
Maier, N. R. F., and Schneirla, T. C. *Principles of Animal Psychology.*
    New York: McGraw-Hill Book, Inc., 1935.
Massermann, J. H. *Behavior and Neuroses.*
    Chicago: The University of Chicago Press, 1943.
McConnell, J. W.; and Jacobson, A. I.; and Kimble, D. P. Reported by McConnell, J. W. in "Memory Transfer through Cannibalism in Planaria."
    Journal of Neuropsychiatry. Vol. 3. Suppl. 1 (August 1962).
McCullough, W. S. "The Systematic Restatement of the Libido Theory."
    Annals of the New York Academy of Sciences. Vol. 76 (January 23, 1959).
Miller, J. G. "Discrimination without Awareness."
    Amer. Journ. of Psychiatry (1939).
Miller, J. G. "Unconscious Processes and Perceptions" in *An Approach to Personality.*
    Ed. Blake, R. R. and Ramsay, G. V. New York: The Ronald Press.
Modell, H. A. "The Concept of Psychic Energy."
    The Journal of the American Psychoanalytic Association Vol. 11, No. 3 (July 1963).
Morison, R. S. and Dempsey, E. W. "A Study of Thalamo-cortical Relations."
    Amer. Journ. of Psychology 135 (1942).
Moruzzi, G., and Magoun, H. W. "Brain Stem Reticular Formation and Activation of the E.E.G."
    E.E.G. Clinical Neurophysiology 1 (1949): 455–473.
Niu, M. C. "Current Evidences Concerning Chemical Inducers in Evolution of Nervous Control."
    Ed. A. Bass. *American Assoc. for the Advancement of Sciences* (Washington, D.C. 1959).
Ostow, M. "Attempt at the Systematic Restatement of the Libido Theory."
    Annals of the New York Academy of Sciences Vol. 76. (January 1959): 1038–1065.
Ostow, M. "The Concept of Psychic Energy."
    The Journal of the American Psychoanalytic Assoc. Vol 11, No. 3 (July 1963).
Oxford Symposium. *The Cerebral Mechanisms and Learning.* (1961)
Parker, G. H. *The Elementary Nervous System.*
    Philadelphia: Lippincott, 1919.
Penfield, W. "Consciousness and Centrencephalic Organization," in *Transactions of the First Intern. Congress of Neurol. Sciences* (Brussels, 1957).
Piaget, J. "The Problem of Consciousness in Child Psychology."
    Fourth Conference on Problems of Consciousness The Josiah Macy Jr. Foundation (New York: 1953).

Plato. "The Symposium."
    Great Books of the Western World. Chicago: University of Chicago. By Encyclopedia Brittanica, Inc., 1952.
Princeton Symposium on: *"Learning, Remembering and Forgetting."* (1963).
Pumpian-Mindlin, E. "The Systematic Restatement of the Libido Theory."
    Annals of the New York Academy of Sciences. Vol. 76 (January 23, 1959).
Ranson, S. W. "Some Functions of the Hypothalamus."
    (Harvey Lecture) *Bull. New York Acad. of Medicine* 13 (1937): 241–271.
Riese, W. "The Pre-Freudian Origin of Psychoanalysis."
    Science and Psychoanalysis. New York: Grune and Stratton, 1958.
Rose, M. D. "Discussion of Tropisms."
    L'Instinct dans le Comportement des Animaux et de L'homme. Paris: Mason et Cie, 1956.
Rothman, H. "Zusammenfassender Bericht über Rothmannschen Grosshirnlosen Hund."
    Zeits. f. Gesamte Neurol. u. Psych 87 (1923).
Sanford, N. "The Systematic Restatement of the Libido Theory."
    Annals of the New York Academy of Sciences Vol. 76 (January 23, 1959).
Scheibel, M., and Scheibel, A. *Reticular Formation of the Brain*.
    Ed. Jaspers, et al. Boston and Toronto: Little Brown & Co., 1958.
Segundo, J. P.; Arana-Iniquez; and French, J. D. "Behavioral Arousal by Stimulation of Brain in Monkey."
    Jour. of Neurophysiology 9 (1946): 165–171.
Sinnot, E. W. "A Common Basis for Development and Behavior in Evolution of the Nervous System."
    Public. 52 of 1959. *American Assoc. for Advancement of Science*. Washington.
Sperry, R. W. Summation of Eccles Presentation. (see 24).
Szasz, Th. "A Critical Analysis of some Aspects of the Libido Theory."
    Annals of the New York Academy of Sciences Vol. 76 (1959).
Thompson, R., and McConnell, J. W. Learning in Flatworm.
    Journ. Comp. Physiology and Psychology 48 (1955). Also in "Smith-Klein and French Laboratories Report on the Flatworm Phenomenal Memory." Report no. 6 (Jan.–Feb. 1963).
Urbantschitsch, V. *Subjective Optical Imagery*.
    Vienna: Deuticke Ed. 1907.
Viaud, G. *Taxies et Tropismes dans le Comportement Instinctif in 'L'Instinct dans le Comportement des Animaux et de L'homme*.
    Paris: Masson et Cie, 1956.
Waelder, R. W. "The Concept of Psychic Energy."
    The Journal of the American Psychoanalytic Assoc. Vol. 11, no. 3 (July, 1963).
Watson, J. *Hedonistic Theories*.
    London–New York: James MacLehose & Sons and Macmillan Co. 1895.
Weiss, P. Discussion of Lashley's paper in *The Cerebral Organization and Human Behavior*.
    Baltimore: Williams and Wilkins Co., 1958.
Wheeler, E. *Essays on Biological Philosophy*. 1939

337

Zeliony, I. Quoted by A. Ferraro in: "Etude Anatomique du Systeme Nerveux d'un Chien dont le Pallium à été enlevé."
Imprimerie Zuidam Utrecht Holland (1924).